The Play of Language

The Play of Language

LEONARD F. DEAN

New York University

WALKER GIBSON

University of Massachusetts

KENNETH G. WILSON

University of Connecticut

NEW YORK

OXFORD UNIVERSITY PRESS

LONDON 1971 TORONTO

Contents

Introduction

Our language is immediately interesting because it is human. It is as fascinating and complicated as people. Talk about language naturally becomes personal or moral or social or political. The first section, Openers, illustrates this. Learning "correct" English, an apparently simple matter of linguistic habit formation, was an agonizingly emotional part of Alfred Kazin's early life, and there are obviously deep personal feelings and moral convictions beneath Kurt Vonnegut's seemingly flat account of speaking and acting "correctly" or "politely." Other illustrations are on all sides. An editorial in a recent *New York Times* (May 4, 1970) carries a linguistic headline, "Webster's New American Dictionary," but the purpose or subject of the editorial is more than simple linguistic definition, as a single sample will show: "Credibility: maintenance of the belief that the United States is a superpower that angers easily and will use its military force suddenly, without notice or consultation."

The third selection is an attempt to reduce feeling by taking a long view of linguistic change—although neutrality may in fact simply bring in a different set of feelings. At any rate, Albert Marckwardt was trying to persuade people who feel personally threatened by changes in English usage to stand back from their anxieties and feel change as part of a very long historical pattern. This detachment not only helps to reduce anxiety, but it also transforms language into a more nearly impersonal subject suitable for objective observation. Section II, Changes, is a series of such observations—on language in general, on the English language, on Colonial American English, on grammar, shifting meanings, and related topics.

It is hoped that the information and detachment gained from the objective observations in Section II will enable the reader to keep his feet and his cool in the warm discussion of Standards in Section III. The discussion is warm because it is involved with a deep question: On what terms should the established community let in the young and the new-comers? When you are young and outside, English seems to mean chiefly being tested and sorted. You are always being asked to spell, to recite, to write your theme, to step up and say your piece. When you do it right often enough, the elders beam and let you in with them, but it is often hard to know what doing it right means. The situation at the beginning of *King Lear* is familiar. Three girls are tested by being asked to make speeches saying how much they love their father. The two older daughters are quite contemptuous of their father and his egotistical idea of a community, but they are on the make and so they comply cynically by mouth-ing flowery speeches. The youngest daughter is revolted by the situation, and so she becomes stubbornly idealistic and refuses to say anything at all. She is disinherited and expelled, and the result is violence and dis-order.

But when things are right, it is wonderful, as Shakespeare went on to show in *The Winter's Tale*. The girl being tested is Perdita, a shep-herd's daughter. Her assignment is to act as hostess of a big picnic for the whole community and to say the right thing to everybody, young and old, high and low. Her father wants her to do it just the way her mother did, and he remembers with pride and affection how hard his wife worked and what a wonderful hostess she had been in the old days:

> SHEPHERD. Fie, daughter! When my old wife lived, upon   55
>   This day, she was both pantler, butler, cook;
>   Both dame and servant; welcomed all, served all;
>   Would sing her song, and dance her turn; now here
>   At upper end o' th' table, now i' th' middle;
>   On his shoulder, and his; her face o' fire   60
>   With labor and the thing she took to quench it,
>   She would to each one sip. You are retired,
>   As if you were a feasted one, and not
>   The hostess of the meeting. Pray you bid
>   These unknown friends to 's welcome, for it is   65
>   A way to make us better friends, more known.
>   Come, quench your blushes, and present yourself
>   That which you are, mistress o' th' feast. Come on,
>   And bid us welcome to your sheep-shearing,
>   As your good flock shall prosper.   (IV, iv)

Perdita performs this assignment, but in her own way. She repeats the past, and yet at the same time she redefines and refreshes it. One of her tests along the way is a trick question about the meaning of the word *corpse*. She knows the standard meaning, but she insists that in her new dictionary it means the boy she loves alive in her arms. She is talking with the boy, Florizel, who is really a prince dressed as a shepherd, while she passes out flowers to the guests:

> Daffodils,
> That come before the swallow dares, and take
> The winds of March with beauty; violets, dim,   120
> But sweeter than the lids of Juno's eyes,
> Or Cytherea's breath; pale primroses,
> That die unmarried ere they can behold
> Bright Phoebus in his strength (a malady
> Most incident to maids); bold oxlips, and   125
> The crown imperial; lilies of all kinds,
> The flower-de-luce being one. O, these I lack
> To make you garlands of, and my sweet friend,
> To strew him o'er and o'er!
> FLORIZEL.   What, like a corse?
> PERDITA. No, like a bank for Love to lie and play on;   130
> Not like a corse; or if, not to be buried,
> But quick and in mine arms.

Florizel agrees that her English, the way she speaks and acts, is naturally correct, even better than the past:

> FLORIZEL.   What you do   135
> Still betters what is done. When you speak, sweet,
> I'd have you do it ever; when you sing,
> I'd have you buy and sell so; so give alms,
> Pray so; and for the ord'ring your affairs,
> To sing them too. When you do dance, I wish you   140
> A wave o' th' sea, that you might ever do
> Nothing but that—move still, still so,
> And own no other function. Each your doing,
> So singular in each particular,
> Crowns what you are doing in the present deeds,   145
> That all your acts are queens.

Everyone finally recognizes that Perdita is really a princess, and at the happy ending her definition of *corpse* is accepted, the harsh distinctions between young and old, high and low dissolve, and it is even possible to joke about social levels of English usage. The shepherd and his son realize that "we must be gentle, now we are gentlemen." In fact they can swear now: "Not swear it, now I am a gentleman? Let boors and franklins say it, I'll swear it."

The reality of the happy ending is the theme of the last section, Language as Metaphor and Play. It is part of an old dream or question: Can you have fun and still be good? Can you play around and still make sense? The dream hints that the best way to be good and make sense linguistically is to take a chance on the language. It is something like open admissions, or falling in love with a stranger. It can lead to trouble and it looks foolish, but it is a persistent dream even though it is not the Roman thing to do, as Shakespeare pointed out. There is nothing dreamy about the Rome that Antony returns to after his tour of duty in the East. Of course it is perfectly all right to have an affair with Cleopatra —it comes with the tour; it is a normal part of the big, brassy, sexy show that the desk-bound Roman colonels are so eager to hear about. But in Rome things are arranged more sensibly: you marry Caesar's sister, the thoroughly respectable Octavia, for the good of the party and the partnership. And then Enobarbus, who has been regaling the Roman colonels, is caught up in a version of the dream:

> Age cannot wither her, nor custom stale
> Her infinite variety: other women cloy
> The appetites they feed, but she makes hungry
> Where most she satisfies; for vilest things
> Become themselves in her, that the holy priests
> Bless her when she is riggish.

Riggish is an old and interesting word, with meanings like loose, lascivious, immoral, tricky, mischievous, prankish, tomboyish, playful, all fancied up. It is not the kind of thing that priests ordinarily bless. Bishop Hall in 1634 sounded more like the conventional churchman: "The wanton gesticulations of a virgin in a wild assembly of gallants warmed with wine, could be no other than riggish and unmaidenly." In fact Enobarbus's whole speech is a series of foolish contradictions—or oxymorons as they are known technically from the two Greek words meaning "pointedly foolish." But this kind of language does permit Enobarbus or Shakespeare to play into a kind of truth that "Roman" language cannot express or contain. His foolish metaphors, like Perdita's assertion that a corpse should be the boy she loves alive in her arms, redefine reality and point to its endlessly fresh possibilities.

Openers

The first three authors in Section I are concerned with the same distinction between two kinds of language. The distinction is one between "standard," "correct" English, the language of the establishment, on the one hand, and "non-standard," "uncultured" English, the language of the streets, on the other hand. Thus Kazin knew he would be penalized by the Wasp world for speaking "broken" or "foreign" English. Vonnegut argues that school kids have adopted a pattern of non-standard English calculated to "show hatred" toward the older establishment. And Marckwardt, looking at these two kinds of language from a scholar's point of view, believes that English teachers must be aware of those lapses from "propriety" that do in fact penalize people in the practical business of life.

How did we get into this box of having two languages, one "superior" to the other, with all the unfortunate consequences of anxiety, snobbery, and failure? The explanation is one that most Americans are reluctant to mention. It is a question of social and economic *class,* and the "inferior" languages of our non-establishment classes are *symptoms* of socio-economic inferiority, not causes of it. People speak a ghetto dialect because they are forced to live in ghettoes; the reverse is simply not true. It is of course possible to "upgrade" one's sub-standard dialect in order to improve oneself in the social-economic competition. Kazin himself is a noteworthy example. But for the society as a whole, a more sensible way of going about the problem, if certainly a more difficult one, is to remove the causes of class differences. There would be no slum children if there were no slums.

No book on language, however playful, can ignore the socio-economic origins of dialectal differences. And the most conspicuous group of Americans suffering the consequences of dialectal differences are the blacks. Recently it has become fashionable among educators to preach a policy of "bi-dialectalism" in the teaching of blacks—that is, to introduce an establishment dialect for job-seeking, and to encourage retention of the original black dialect for home use. This view has appealed to many concerned teachers; Marckwardt suggests some of its details. But what if this too is a cover-up for continued segregation? The author of the last piece in the section, addressing English teachers, argues that bi-dialectalism is just more white supremacy. He is not persuaded that the key to salvation is to enforce on everyone the language of middle-class white businessmen. What do you think? As you read James Sledd's radical argument, consider the almost overwhelming consequences of those socio-economic differences that our first three authors have illustrated.

ALFRED KAZIN

Brownsville School Days

I worked on a hairline between triumph and catastrophe. Why the odds should always have felt so narrow I understood only when I realized how little my parents thought of their own lives. It was not for myself alone that I was expected to shine, but for them—to redeem the constant anxiety of their existence. I was the first American child, their offering to the strange new God; I was to be the monument of their liberation from the shame of being—what they were. And that there was shame in this was a fact that everyone seemed to believe as a matter of course. It was in the gleeful discounting of themselves—what do we know?—with which our parents greeted every fresh victory in our savage competition for "high averages," for prizes, for a few condescending words of official praise from the principal at assembly. It was in the sickening invocation of "Americanism"—the word itself accusing us of everything we apparently were not. Our families and teachers seemed tacitly agreed that we were somehow to be a little ashamed of what we were. Yet it was always hard to say why this should be so. It was certainly not—in Brownsville!—because we were Jews, or simply because we spoke another language at home, or were absent on our holy days. It was rather that a "refined," "correct," "nice" English was required of us at school that we did not naturally speak, and that our teachers could never be quite sure we would keep. This English was peculiarly the ladder of advancement. Every future young lawyer was known by it. Even the Communists and Socialists on Pitkin Avenue spoke it. It was bright and clean and polished. We were expected to show it off like a new pair of shoes. When the teacher sharply called a question out, then your name, you were expected to leap up, face the class, and eject those new words fluently off the tongue.

There was my secret ordeal: I could never say anything except in the most roundabout way; I was a stammerer. Although I knew all those new words from my private reading—I read walking in the street, to and from the Children's Library on Stone Avenue; on the fire escape and the roof; at every meal when they would let me; read even when I dressed in the morning, propping my book up against the drawers of the bureau as I pulled on my long black stockings—I could never seem to get the easiest words out with the right dispatch, and would often miserably signal from my desk that I did not know the answer rather than get up to stumble and fall and crash on every word. If, angry at always being put down as lazy or stupid, I did get up to speak, the black wooden floor would roll away under my feet, the teacher would frown at me in amazement, and in unbearable loneliness I would hear behind me the groans and laughter: *tuh-tuh-tuh-tuh.*

The word was my agony. The word that for others was so effortless and so neutral, so unburdened, so simple, so exact, I had first to meditate in advance, to see if I could make it, like a plumber fitting together odd lengths and shapes of pipe. I was always preparing words I could speak, storing them away, choosing between them. And often, when the word did come from my mouth in its great and terrible birth, quailing and bleeding as if forced through a thornbush, I would not be able to look the others in the face, and would walk out in the silence, the infinitely echoing silence behind my back, to say it all cleanly back to myself as I walked in the streets. Only when I was alone in the open air, pacing the roof with pebbles in my mouth, as I had read Demosthenes had done to cure himself of stammering; or in the street, where all words seemed to flow from the length of my stride and the color of the houses as I remembered the perfect tranquillity of a phrase in Beethoven's *Romance in F* I could sing back to myself as I walked—only then was it possible for me to speak without the infinite premeditations and strangled silences I toiled through whenever I got up at school to respond with the expected, the exact answer.

It troubled me that I could speak in the fullness of my own voice only when I was alone on the streets, walking about. There was something unnatural about it; unbearably isolated. I was not like the others! I was not like the others! At midday, every freshly shocking Monday noon, they sent me away to a speech clinic in a school in East New York, where I sat in a circle of lispers and cleft palates and foreign accents holding a mirror before my lips and rolling difficult sounds over and over. To be sent there in the full light of the opening week, when everyone else was at school or going about his business, made me feel as if I had been expelled from the great normal body of humanity. I would gobble down my lunch on my way to the speech clinic and rush back to the school in time to make up for the classes I had lost. One day, one unforgettable dread day, I stopped to catch my breath on a corner of Sutter Avenue, near the wholesale fruit markets, where an old drugstore rose up over a great flight of steps. In the window were dusty urns of colored water floating off iron chains; cardboard placards advertising hairnets, Ex-Lax; a great illustrated medical chart headed The Human Factory, which showed the exact course a mouthful of food follows as it falls from chamber to chamber of the body. I hadn't meant to stop there at all, only to catch my breath; but I so hated the speech clinic that I thought I would delay my arrival for a few minutes by eating my lunch on the steps. When I took the sandwich out of my bag, two bitterly hard pieces of hard salami slipped out of my hand and fell through a grate onto a hill of dust below the steps. I remember how sickeningly vivid an odd thread of hair looked on the salami, as if my lunch were turning stiff with death. The factory whistles called their short, sharp blasts stark through the middle of noon, beating at me where I sat outside the city's magnetic circle. I had never known, I knew instantly I would never in my heart again submit to, such wild passive despair as I felt at that moment, sitting on the steps before The Human Factory, where little robots gathered and shoveled the food from chamber to chamber of the body. They had put me out into the streets, I thought to myself; with their mirrors and their everlasting pulling at me to imitate their effortless bright speech and their stupefaction that a boy could stammer and stumble on every other English word he carried in his head, they had put me out into the streets, had left me high and dry on the steps of that drugstore staring at the remains of my lunch turning black and grimy in the dust.

KURT VONNEGUT, JR.

Topics: Good Missiles, Good Manners, Good Night

I went to high school in Indianapolis with a nice girl named Barbara Masters. Her father was an eye doctor in our town. She is now the wife of our Secretary of Defense.

I was having lunch in Indianapolis recently with another man who had known her in school. He had an upper-class Hoosier accent, which sounds like a bandsaw cutting galvanized tin. He said this: "When you get to be our age, you all of a sudden realize that you are being ruled by people you went to high school with."

He was uncomfortably silent for a moment, then he said: "You all of a sudden catch on that life is nothing but high school. You make a fool of yourself in high school, then you go to college and learn how you should have acted in high school, and then you get out into real life, and that turns out to be high school all over again—class officers, cheer leaders, and all.

"Richard M. Nixon," he went on. There was another silence. We had no trouble imagining that we had gone to school with Mr. Nixon, too.

"So optimistic, so blooming with mental health," I said.

I live on Cape Cod now, and, on my way home from Indianapolis, I read an article by Dr. Ernest J. Sternglass in the September *Esquire*. Dr. Sternglass, a professor of radiation physics at the University of Pittsburgh, promised that, if Mr. Laird's and Mr. Nixon's Safeguard anti-missile system was ever used, all children born after that (anywhere) would die of birth defects before they could grow up and reproduce.

So I marveled again at the cheerfulness of our leaders, guys my age. They were calling for nothing less than the construction of a doomsday machine, but they went on smiling. Everything was O.K.

Humans and Bombers

Mr. and Mrs. Laird and I graduated from high school in 1940, incidentally. That was when we got to see the first obituaries of ourselves—in our year books.

At a party a few months ago, a Hoosier friend told me that Mrs. Laird read my books and liked them. She had supposedly said that I was to get in touch with her, if I was ever in Washington, D.C. That seemed wild to me. I was a pacifist. I thought most American weapons were cruelly ridiculous. My newest book was about utterly pitiful things that happened to unarmed human beings on the ground when our bombers went about their technical duties in the sky.

Pentagon Pacifism?

But then I remembered high school, where all of us learned to respect each other's opinions—no matter what the opinions were. We learned how to be unfailingly friendly—to smile. So, maybe, the Secretary of Defense would be friendly about my pacifism and all that, and I would be expected to be friendly about the end of the world and all that.

As it happened, I found myself in Washington last June, so I left a friendly message for Mrs. Laird at her husband's office in the Pentagon. "I will be at the Sheraton Park for three days," I said. There was no reply. Maybe Mrs. Laird's supposed enthusiasm for my work was a hoax.

Word of honor—if I had been invited into the Laird home, I would have smiled and smiled. I would have understood that the defense establishment was only doing what it had to do, no matter how suicidally. I would have agreed, hearing the other fellow's side of the story, that even for planets there are worse things than death. Upon leaving, I would have thanked the Lairds for a nice time. I would have said, "I only regret that my wife couldn't have been here, too. She would have loved it."

I would have thanked God, too, that no members of the younger generation were along. Kids don't learn nice manners in high schools any more. If they met a person who was in favor of building a device which would cripple and finally kill all children everywhere, they wouldn't smile. They would show hatred.

ALBERT H. MARCKWARDT

The English Language:
A Long View

About Christmastime last year some of us received a message from one of our Nassau Club *Korpsbrüder,* viewing with alarm what he characterized as a communications crisis, a shocking decline in the use of the native tongue. Not only the present generation of students but those of the past twelve to fifteen years as well were charged with a total incapacity to employ the English language with accuracy and force, both in speech and in writing. "It's not merely the abandonment of sentence and paragraph structure that threatens our capacity to make ourselves understood; it's also the use of words without even a dim notion of their meaning," the author told us, and he then went on to place a good share of the responsibility upon "the advocates of full permissiveness in the structure of sentences and the meanings of words." "The language is a living thing," they say. "Let it grow; let it go in any direction it will."

This sketchy summary does much less than justice to the closely knit and well-reasoned presentation, which ran to some six pages, but it does raise two fundamental issues which have concerned a good many of us at one time or another. Is the English language really going to pot? If so, has it been the result of a laissez-faire attitude on the part of a significant sector of the linguistic and educational professions? These are questions which merit thoughtful consideration and as honest an answer as the circumstances will permit.

For the record, it must be pointed out that a feeling of despair about the present state of the language and the incapacity of those who use it is a hardy perennial, which extends of course to other forms of socially

A paper read in 1968 to the Nassau Club of Princeton and printed here with the permission of the author.

conditioned behavior. We slip easily into the lament "O Tempora! O Mores!" and language, possibly because it is so intensely personal, becomes an easy target for our suspicion.

"And certaynly our langage now used varyeth ferre from that which was used and spoken when I was born," wrote William Caxton in 1490. "For we Englisshe men ben borne under the domynacion of the mone which is never stedfaste but ever waverynge, wexynge one season and waneth and dyscreseth another season. And that comyn Englysshe that is spoken in one shyre varyeth from another." The specific incident which set off this cry of dismay was some uncertainty about the proper plural of *egg*. A certain merchant had asked a country wife if she had any eggs, and her response was that she knew no French. One of the merchant's companions explained that *eyren* was what the man wanted, and of course he got them at once. "Lo, what sholde a man in thyse days now write, eggs or eyren," Caxton went on to complain. "Certaynly it is hard to playse every man bycause of dyversitie and change of langage," and at this point he begins to sound strikingly like our contemporary Christmas letter: "For in these dayes every man that is in ony reputacyen in his contre will utter his commynycacyon and maters in such terms that few men shall understonde them."

Not much more than half a century later, Roger Ascham, writing in the *Toxophilus* (1545), copiously included in a condemnation of the current state of language not only English but Italian, Spanish, French, Dutch—by which he presumably meant German—and even Latin, except for Cicero and one or two other authors. "They be all patched clouts and rags in comparison with fair woven broadcloths," he charges. "And truly, if there be any good in them, it is either learned, borrowed, or stolen from some one of those worthy wits of Athens." This last must be understood as a professional plug, of course. Ascham was a teacher of Greek.

Skipping a few centuries, let us listen now to Thomas Sheridan, father of Richard Brinsley Sheridan, the playwright, writing in 1780. "Yet so little regard has been paid to [the English language] that out of our numerous array of authors, very few can be selected who write with accuracy. Nay, it has lately been proved by a learned Prelate in an essay upon our grammars, that some of our most celebrated writers, and such as have hitherto passed for our English classics, have been guilty of great solecisms, inaccuracies, and even grammatical improprieties, in many places of their most finished works." If Sheridan believed this about the language of the most finished writers, what must he have thought about undergraduate English, or even worse, the language of the man in the street?

Just a century later the story was still the same. For the first time, now, we have a reflection of the attitude in the United States, in a quotation from Edward S. Gould, in his book *Good English or Popular Errors in Language:* "For example, the English language, within the last quarter of a century, through the agency of good writers, critics, and lexicographers, has in many respects been greatly improved; but through the heedlessness of those who should be its conservators and the recklessness of those who have been, and are, its corrupters, it has deteriorated in other respects in a greater proportion."

The year 1941 gives us a dialogue between Brigadier General Edwin P. Parker, then commanding general at Fort Bragg, and T. H. Fielding, now the author of a series of travel guides. It went as follows, at least according to the *New Yorker:*

> "Fielding? That's your name, isn't it?"
> "Yes, sir."
> "Fielding, this is the biggest Goddamned Field Artillery Replacement Training Center in the country."
> "Yes, sir."
> "We've got five hundred and fifty new buildings right in this area, and there was nothing but scrub pine and sand five months ago. No one knows how to get to the PX. Everyone asks a thousand jerkwater questions. We need to write out the answers. What we need is a guidebook, but no one can write it. There have been four tries, all terrible. The chaplain tried and *his* book was the worst. Now it's your turn."

I am happy to report that Fielding's attempt was successful, and it was this experience that really started him on his career writing guidebooks.

It is all very well, of course, to recite a catalogue of these prophecies of doom, even somewhat amusing, but they do not constitute a wholly satisfactory answer to the issue that has been posed. Suppose that the cry of "Wolf!" is really genuine at long last. How do we know that the language really isn't coming apart at the seams? At this juncture I believe we must look at the situation from a demographic point of view, especially in the light of our educational aims.

Let us begin with a consideration of the number of native speakers of the language. There are undoubtedly something like 275,000,000, more than a fiftyfold increase over the numbers who spoke it at the time of Shakespeare. Even so, we are greatly outnumbered by the Chinese, possibly by the speakers of Hindi-Urdu, and we may well be equalled by the Russians. The uniqueness of English, however, lies in its geographical spread. It is spoken as a first or native language on four continents of the globe, a distribution that is unparalleled in any of the other languages of wider communication.

It is well known that no two speakers of a language ever use it in identical fashion. Certainly, they have not precisely the same vocabulary. There are at least minor differences in pronunciation; indeed the same individual will not pronounce his vowels and consonants in identical fashion every time he utters them. Everyone possesses in addition certain individual traits of grammatical form and syntactical order, constituting that peculiar and personal quality of language which we call style, all of which is implicit in the familiar statement, "Style is the man." No two men are identical; no two styles are the same. If this be true of but two persons, the potential of difference resident in a language spoken by more than a quarter of a billion with a geographical spread extending over virtually the entire globe truly staggers the imagination.

Historically this situation has resulted in the development of not one but several prestige-bearing dialects, which is another way of saying standard forms of the language. In England, the one that is best known is called Received Pronunciation, often identified in the public mind with BBC English, although there has been a recent change in BBC policy in this respect. Even so, certain types of regional pronunciation are firmly established in the North, and no matter how uniform cultivated British speech may sound to us, the British themselves commonly recognize three types of Received Pronunciation: the *conservative* RP forms used by the older generation, and traditionally by certain professions and social groups; the *general* RP forms, most commonly in use and typified by the pronunciation used exclusively by the BBC until recently; and the *advanced* RP forms, used mainly by young people of exclusive social groups—mostly of the upper classes, but also, for prestige value, in certain professional circles.

In the United States the range of acceptability is even wider, if we consider the pronunciation patterns of several recent occupants of the presidential chair: Messrs. Eisenhower, Kennedy, and Johnson. Each of them, in his own time, seemed to part of his constituency to be speaking a rather unusual regional form of the language and to the rest of it perfectly normal English. The truth of the remark of a little old lady in Texas, to the effect that it was so nice to have someone in the White House who didn't speak a dialect, was brought home to me forcefully last summer, when I addressed a group of English teachers in Kentucky about regional differences in American English. Part of the discussion which followed dealt with emotional reactions to different varieties of speech, how many of us are prone to translate dialect differences into judgments about character. Virtually every person in the room commented that when they heard a coastal New England dialect, they immediately associated it with a sense of superiority on the part of the speaker, coldness, and even snippiness. If there were any reactions there against what someone has referred to as the corn-pone overtones of former President Johnson, they were not mentioned, and I suspect that there were none. Kentucky and Texas English, though by no means identical, have too much in common.

What I have been saying about ranges in the standard pronunciation of English in England and the United States could be applied with equal facility to the English of Canada, to that of South Africa, to Australia, and indeed to Ireland. Not only do the countries differ among themselves, but there is patently more than a single acceptable form within each country. There is what might be called a fairly broad area of permissibility, understandable in the light of the numbers and geographic spread to which I have already referred, a characteristic typical of a more or less open society. This is in direct contrast, for example, with the situation prevailing in a much more stratified and circumscribed social order, such as that of Spain, where the term *Castellano* (Castillian) is used synonymously with *Español* to mean the standard language.

I realize that for the past several paragraphs I have been writing principally about pronunciation, where the concern of those who are troubled over the present state of the language is with other features of it, principally the grammatical structure, and I shall come back to this in good time. My present purpose is to establish the premise of alternatively acceptable forms in any aspect of the language, and obviously we generally make this concession not only with pronunciation but with large areas of the vocabulary as well. Scarcely any of us would insist upon asking for a spool of thread in a London shop, if he knew that to get what he wanted he would have to call it a reel of cotton, nor would he consider the Briton coming to these shores anything but pigheaded if he insisted upon using his term in Woolworth's on Main Street. But we shall deal with the grammatical factor after we look at the changing situation in our schools, for this is where we often place the blame for the supposed decline in the ability to use the language.

In order to place the current school situation in proper focus, it will be helpful to compare what goes on now, our current language program so to speak, with what prevailed at an earlier period. The beginning of the century, 1900, is convenient for our purpose, since most of the present-day critics would feel that the schools were discharging their function reasonably well at that time. Let us ask them, what were we doing with English and how were we doing it?

It was a time when the total enrollment in all the colleges and universities in the United States amounted to very little more than 250,000 and constituted only 4 per cent of the population with ages ranging from eighteen to twenty-one. There were 630,000 students in the secondary schools, both public and private, representing no more than 10 per cent of those in the appropriate age group. In short, one youth out of ten was attending high school; one person out of twenty-five was in college.

Although among this restricted population there were undoubtedly some instances of the children of share-croppers, factory workers, and recent immigrants pulling themselves up socially and economically by their bootstraps, the vast majority of the students must have come from homes where Standard English was the normal vehicle of communication. The problem of superimposing the prestige dialect of the language upon that which represented the linguistic heritage of the lower middle or working class was minor, if indeed it existed at all.

What, then, went on in the high-school and college English classrooms? Chiefly the reading and discussion of literature and the periodic writing of essays. The essays, moreover, were written according to models which made up the bulk of the textbooks of rhetoric of the time. Such popular texts as Genung's *Practical Elements of Rhetoric,* Hart's *Manual of Composition and Rhetoric,* and Hill's *Beginnings of Rhetoric and Composition,* devoted relatively little space either to a formal presentation of grammar or to specific items of usage. These matters were the reponsibility of the elementary schools, which already included a fairly high percentage of the eligible school children of the country.

As time went on, this relatively simple pedagogical situation changed considerably. By 1930 over 50 per cent of the children in the age group from fourteen to seventeen were in the secondary schools, five times the percentage for 1900. More and more students were going to college, possibly one in ten by 1930, compared to one in twenty-five at the turn of the century. An inevitable consequence of this was a shift in responsibility for what came to be called "the decencies" in language from the elementary to the secondary schools. No longer could the high-school teacher depend upon the home environment to establish and reinforce competence in the use of Standard English. The high-school classrooms now included children from both sides of the tracks, and English-teaching necessarily had to assume a remedial function. These changes were reflected in the colleges as well, especially those which for one reason or another were unable or unwilling to establish rigorous standards for admission. These same tendencies have, of course, gone on at an accelerated pace, so that we now have virtually the entire youth population in the secondary schools, and about 40 per cent enrolled in higher education.

As a consequence of this shift in school population, the textbooks of rhetoric, which had been the staple of the high-school and college courses, were replaced by handbooks of usage. These reflected a shift in emphasis from rhetorical nicety to linguistic propriety, and they were soon accompanied by auxiliary workbooks which permitted but one approved response to any of the linguistic quandaries they propounded, no matter how ambivalent the language might be. Thus, over a period of as little as twenty-five years, it had become necessary for the secondary schools and even the colleges to assume a large share of responsibility for the development of native-language competence.

For a number of reasons, the teachers of English, especially those in the secondary schools, were not at all well prepared to cope with this new situation. For one thing, their professional training included little or no work in the structure or history of the language. For many of them, teaching was a step upward on the social scale; they lacked sophistication about linguistic matters, and even confidence in their own ability to handle the language. They were scarcely equipped to go about their tasks in any way other than attempting to resort to a shotgun corrective technique, inevitably doomed to ineffectiveness by virtue of creating two forms of the language, one reserved for the English classroom, and the other one, employed by most students on the occasions where actual communication was involved.

Nothing has occurred since 1930 except, as I have already pointed out, the continued influx of an ever-increasing proportion of our youth population. Thus, the situation has not been altered in any material way. Even so, we have not yet examined the total implication of our native-language teaching program in the schools. What is it that we are driving at? What command or degree of command of the native language do we aim to produce?

Our answer to the question, rightly or wrongly, is usually phrased in terms such as these: We are an open society and a prosperous one, characterized by constant social movement from the bottom toward the top. Therefore, in order to fulfill our obligation to the students in our schools, we must provide them with a command of their native language which will enable them to function effectively in any position or situation which their abilities may call or entitle them to. This follows naturally, from our general commitment to education in the United States, but from the point of view of training in the English language it is not merely a large order; it is colossal. No other nation has ever attempted anything like it. Britain, with about 5 per cent of her youth population in higher education, and having recently deferred the raising of the compulsory school-attendance age from fifteen to sixteen, has not undertaken an obligation that even remotely approaches ours, and she is typical of a fair number of western European countries. From the point of view of the upward social mobility that I have mentioned, and the increasing pressures upon the schools for admitting more and more students to secondary and higher education, the countries of western Europe are just beginning to face a situation which we have been confronting for some three or four decades. My only concern in pointing this out is to re-emphasize the fact that we have set ourselves a formidable linguistic task—namely, superimposing the prestige dialect (I use the term in the broadest possible sense) of the language upon that which literally millions of our students speak natively, and that which they continue to hear and use in their home, the local playground, and other places away from school.

In the interest of clarity, I should like to restate the three principal points which have been advanced thus far. First, the feeling that the language is deteriorating, both in terms of its total expressive capability and the capacity of the individual to employ it, is one of several centuries' standing, though this does not necessarily militate against its accuracy at this particular moment in time. Second, that the large number of speakers of English and the broad areas over which they are spread are likely to result in a broader range of acceptability than has been the case up to the present. Third, that owing to a change in the nature and extent of our school population and the existence of certain attitudes relative to the function of education, we have accepted a linguistic responsibility far more extensive than other educational system has ever undertaken.

Nevertheless, I can hear the skeptical ask, "What's so hard about teaching youngsters to speak and write properly? Why not tell them what's right and what's wrong and hold them to it?" This is a fair question, but it needs to be considered from two points of view, one pertaining to the nature of language and language learning, and the second having to do with the current state of grammar and how it is, or has been, taught. It is better, I believe, to deal first with the matter of grammar.

First of all, we must distinguish between grammar as a mode of describing the structure or behavior of a language on the one hand and a set of socially approved usages as opposed to those which bear some degree of stigma on the other. The statement that the object of the verb in an active sentence becomes the subject of the verb in a passive construction, and that the subject must be governed by the preposition *by* is a valid grammatical observation, but it is doubtful that it, in itself, has any great utility in teaching most native speakers to employ the language. It is no more than an explicit statement of a pattern of language behavior which most of us had mastered before we entered kindergarten.

On the other hand, such socially approved forms as *see-saw-seen* or *know-knew-known* have little or no rationale behind them. For those who grow up in an atmosphere where Standard English is spoken, they are absorbed with little or no effort. For those who come from a non-Standard milieu, they simply have to be learned by brute force in order to become a matter of automatic response. True enough, certain generalizations about the structure of the language do bear directly upon errors and infelicities which occur with some frequency: for example, the observation that verbs and their subjects agree in number, that one says "The boy goes" and "The boys go."

It was this latter point which was directly responsible, some fifty years ago, for the development in the schools of what was called functional grammar—namely, a concentration upon those particular rules or observations about the language which had this kind of direct connection with the most frequent departures from Standard English in the speech and writing of the students. Persuasive as the notion may have seemed, it was no more effective than anything that had been done previously. There were several reasons for its failure.

In the first place, it assumed that in speaking or writing, the individual operates in an essentially deductive fashion, proceeding from general principle to specific performance. This seems not to be true, either with one's native language or in acquiring a foreign tongue. Second, by virtue of this concentration upon a relatively small number of items and the grammatical principles behind them, the student, and all too often the teacher, lost sight of the structural system of the entire language and indeed the concept that language is a series of interlocking systems; the bits and patches that he was given seemed fairly meaningless. Third, there was a failure to recognize the important difference between the structures of the written and the spoken language, particularly that the written language, lacking the resources of intonation, stress, pause, and the possibility of self-interruption and restatement, had necessarily to resort to a tighter organization and to establish certain restrictions in the ordering of sentence elements. Finally, there was a noticeable lag between the day-by-day usage even of socially acceptable speakers and the canons of usage as set forth in the school grammars.

Any one of these factors could have created serious difficulties for the language program in the schools. The four of them together have constituted a real hindrance to effective operation. My reason for mentioning them, however, is not so much to emphasize a failure as to suggest the complexity of what it is we are trying to do, to point out that it is more than a "Do this!"–"Don't do that!" type of situation.

Where, then, do we stand in terms of the concern which was expressed at the outset of this discussion? Has the language gone to the dogs? Are we on the verge of a communications breakdown?

As we know, this is by no means the first time that this fear has been expressed, and recently we in the United States have searched our souls more anxiously for answers than have our compatriots in the other English-speaking countries. As with the prophecies on the disintegration of English, the answers over the past two centuries have sounded much the same. They generally run as follows: there is in this country little evidence of numbers of persons attaining to a distinguished and highly expert command of the language. On the other hand, there is more uniformity here than in other English-speaking countries, and more people employ the language with what might be called a fairly tolerable degree of capability than is the case elsewhere.

There is evidence of this in the assessment of Noah Webster in the late eighteenth century, in the comments of Tocqueville in the nineteenth. As late as 1944 Sir Denis Brogan wrote, "The creation of a common literacy and a common spoken and written tongue, intelligible everywhere except possibly in the deep South, is an achievement as remarkable as the creation of Mandarin Chinese or Low Latin or Hellenistic Greek, and this tongue is certain to be the new *lingua franca* of the world." In short, the use of the language here, as well as other aspects of human behavior, seems to reflect the leveling process characteristic of a democratic social order.

I am quite aware that this modest claim of achievement may not be enough to satisfy those who view the language situation with alarm but, considered in a sanguine spirit, it does seem to give us something to build on. So now the questions become: Where do we go from here? How do we get the results that we would like?

To arrive at an answer, we must go back to the present state of English, which I took pains to describe earlier, and also to an awareness of the language-learning process. In view of the number of speakers and the spread of English throughout the world, we shall have to accustom ourselves to accepting a larger number of linguistic alternatives than has been the case in the past, especially those to which no deep social stigma has been attached. This will not be easy. Our conditioning to linguistic behavior, as to any other, has been almost entirely in the direction of approving a single type and rejecting alternatives. The term *cultural bound* can be as appropriately applied to our reactions to native-language behavior as to the customs of other countries. Fortunately, we have much better information about the actual state of English usage than we had a generation ago, even if this has not always found its way into the school textbooks.

Second, we must learn to discriminate between those departures from earlier canons of linguistic propriety which bear a social stigma and those which do not. *Lay* for *lie* is unquestionably a class marker; *real* for *very* will raise a few hackles; whereas *someone else's* for *someone's else,* a point of contention one or two generations back, will no longer turn a hair. We must give up the assumption that if the pupil's language is challenged on every conceivable ground, he will be left with a residual correctness which is generally satisfactory. What he most often acquires is a strange assortment of linguistic taboos and a lack of confidence that he will ever use the language well.

The time that is thus saved can be given over to continued practice, positive suggestion, stress upon organization and clarity of experience, and the relation of these qualities to a viable grammar and rhetoric. Let us remember that by the time the student enters school, he has already accomplished one amazing feat. He has learned the essential structure of a language, his native language, something that those of us in our adult years do with a second language only with immense effort, and indifferent success. He controls the sound system, the regular inflectional patterns, and the basic elements of the word order.

The first task of the schools is to teach him how to master the writing system both receptively and productively: to teach him to read and to express himself in writing. At the beginning of the fourth grade, or thereabouts, his mastery of the writing system has progressed to a point where it is capable of serving as an extension of his linguistic experiences. From this point on well into adolescence, as he develops in maturity, there is a corresponding growth in his command of the language and in his linguistic capability. Our task is to gear the language-teaching program in the schools to this natural growth, so that he is able to give concise and forceful expression to his developing ideas. As I have already suggested, he must be made aware of the particular demands that the writing system imposes upon linguistic expression. Those who do not speak the standard language, and there will be many, must be given a special regimen aimed at the specific points of contrast between Standard English and their native dialect, but this must be a carefully planned and executed program.

There is nothing radical in these suggestions, unless a language program with pin-point planning and a realistic concept of outcome is so considered. Because of our improved linguistic resources, both with respect to factual data about the standard language and our knowledge of the language-learning process, we are in a better position to undertake such a program than we have ever been before. The problem is more complex, but the tools have improved. I must remind you, however, that any thoroughgoing educational change has been estimated to take at least a quarter of a century to put into effect. In the light of this, I can only suggest that we reconvene in March 1993 and take another inventory.

JAMES SLEDD

Bi-Dialectalism: The Linguistics of White Supremacy

Because people who rarely talk together will talk differently, differences in speech tell what groups a man belongs to. He uses them to claim and proclaim his identity, and society uses them to keep him under control. The person who talks right, as we do, is one of us. The person who talks wrong is an outsider, strange and suspicious, and we must make him feel inferior if we can. That is one purpose of education. In a school system run like ours by white businessmen, instruction in the mother tongue includes formal initiation into the linguistic prejudices of the middle class.

Making children who talk wrong get right with the world has traditionally been the work of English teachers, and more recently of teachers of that strange conglomerate subject which we call speech. The English teacher in the role of linguistic censor was once a kind of folk heroine (or anti-heroine), the Miss Fidditch of the linguists' diatribes. Miss Fidditch believed in taking a strong stand. It never occurred to her that her main job was making the lower classes feel so low that they would try to climb higher. Instead, Miss Fidditch taught generations of schoolchildren, including future linguists, to avoid *ain't* and double negatives and *used to could* and *hadn't ought,* not because *ain't* would keep them from getting ahead in the world, but because *ain't* was wrong, no matter who used it, and deserved no encouragement from decent people who valued the English language. She did her job all the better for thinking that she was doing something else.

Miss Fidditch is not popular any longer among educators. Though

From the *English Journal,* December 1969. Reprinted by permission of the National Council of Teachers of English and James Sledd.

the world at large is still inclined to agree with her, the vulgarizers of linguistics drove her out of the academic fashion years ago, when they replaced her misguided idealism with open-eyed hypocrisy. To the popular linguists, one kind of English is as good as another, and judgments to the contrary are only folklore; but since the object of life in the U.S.A. is for everybody to get ahead of everybody else, and since linguistic prejudice can keep a man from moving up to Schlitz, the linguists still teach that people who want to be decision-makers had better talk and write like the people who make decisions. The schools must therefore continue to cultivate the linguistic insecurity which is already a national characteristic but must teach the youngsters to manipulate that as they manipulate everything else; for neither Miss Fidditch's dream of a language intrinsically good, nor a humbler ideal of realizing the various potentialities of the existing language in its responsible use, can get in the way of the citizenry in its upward anguish through the pecking order. The linguists think that people who do knowingly what Miss Fidditch did in her innocence, will do it more efficiently, as if eating the apple made a skilled worker out of Eve.

As long as most people agreed that up is toward Schlitz and another TV set, and as long as they could pretend that every American eaglet can soar to those great heights, Fidditch McFidditch the dialectologist could enforce the speech-taboos of the great white middle class without complaint: either the child learned the taboos and observed them, or he was systematically penalized. But the damage done to the Wasps' nest by World War II made difficulties. People who talked all wrong, and especially black people, began to ask for their share of the loot in a world that had given them an argument by calling itself free, while a minority of the people who talked right began to bad-mouth respectability and joined the blacks in arguing that it was time for a real change. Some black people burned up the black parts of town, and some students made study impossible at the universities, and in general there was a Crisis. Optimists even talked of a revolution.

The predictable response of the frightened white businessman's society was to go right on doing what it had done before—which had caused the crisis—but to do it harder and to spend more money at it. Education was no exception. Government and the foundations began to spray money over the academic landscape like liquid fertilizer, and the professional societies began to bray and paw at the rich new grass. In that proud hour, any teacher who could dream up an expensive scheme for keeping things as they were while pretending to make a change was sure of becoming the director of a project or a center and of flying first-class to Washington twice a month. The white businessman strengthened his control of the educational system while giving the impression of vast humanitarian activity.

Black English provided the most lucrative new industry for white linguists, who found the mother lode when they discovered the interesting locutions which the less protected employ to the detriment of their chances for upward mobility. In the annals of free enterprise, the early sixties will be memorable for the invention of functional bi-dialectalism, a scheme best described by an elderly and unregenerate Southern dame as "turning black trash into white trash." Despite some signs of wear, this cloak for white supremacy has kept its shape for almost a decade now, and it is best described in the inimitable words of those who made it. Otherwise the description might be dismissed as a malicious caricature.

The basic assumption of bi-dialectalism is that the prejudices of middle-class whites cannot be changed but must be accepted and indeed enforced on lesser breeds. Upward mobility, it is assumed, is the end of education, but white power will deny upward mobility to speakers of black English, who must therefore be made to talk white English in their contacts with the white world.

An adequate florilegium may be assembled from a volume entitled *Social Dialects and Language Learning* (NCTE, 1964), the proceedings of a conference of bi-dialectalists which was held in 1964. William A. Stewart of the Center for Applied Linguistics begins the chorus (p. 13) by observing among our educators "a commendable desire to emphasize the potential of the Negro to be identical to white Americans"—a desire which is apparently not overwhelming, however, among the Black Muslims or among the young men who have enjoyed pot-shooting policemen for the past few summers. Editor Roger W. Shuy next speaks up (p. 53) for social climbing by our American Indians, who have been notably reluctant, throughout their unfortunate association with their conquerors, to adopt our conquering ways. Our linguistic studies, Shuy remarks in the purest accents of fidditchery, "should reveal those elements, both in speech and writing, which prevent Indians from attaining the social status which, with socially acceptable language, they might otherwise attain." A similar desire to be at peace with status-holders is suggested (p. 66) by Ruth I. Golden, who opines that "a human being wants most of all to be recognized as an individual, to be accepted, and to be approved." Since Southern speech brings "negative reactions when heard by employers in Detroit," where Dr. Golden labors in the schools, she devotes herself to stamping out /i/ for /e/ in *penny* and to restoring /l/ in *help* (p. 63 f.).

An admirable scholar from New York, William Labov, then agrees (p. 88) that "recognition of an external standard of correctness is an inevitable accompaniment of upward social aspirations and upward social mobility," and advises that people who (like Jesus) prefer not to take excessive thought for the morrow can probably be made to. In Labov's own words, "since the homes of many lower-class and working people do not provide the pressures toward upward social mobility that middle-class homes provide," and since adults in those lower reaches are sometimes resistant to middle-class values, we must "build into the community a tolerance for style shifting which is helpful in educational and occupational advancement," and we must build into the children, "starting from a level not much above the nursery school and going on through high school, a tolerance for practice in second role playing" (pp. 94–97, 104).

Presumably Labov sees nothing wrong in thus initiating children into the world of hypercorrection, insecurity, and "linguistic self-hatred" which marks, as he has said elsewhere, "the average New Yorker" (*The Social Stratification of English in New York City,* Center for Applied Linguistics, 1966, Chapter XIII); and Charles Ferguson, the eminent ex-director of the Center for Applied Linguistics, is equally confident of *his* right and duty to remake his fellow men in his directorial image. Talking about the Negroes in our Northern cities, Ferguson says that "we have to face a rather difficult decision as to whether we want to make these people bi-dialectal . . . [please to remark Ferguson's choice of verbs] or whether we want . . . to impose some kind of standard English on these people and to eradicate the kind of substandard English they speak" (p. 116). To cite another NCTE volume (*Language Programs for the Disadvantaged* [NCTE, 1965], p. 222), if the black children of the ghetto "do not learn a second kind of dialect, they will be forever prevented from access to economic opportunity and social acceptance." Middle-class white prejudice will rule eternally.

The bi-dialectalists, of course, would not be so popular with government and the foundations if they spoke openly of the supremacy of white prejudice; but they make it perfectly clear that what they are dealing with deserves no better name. No dialect, they keep repeating, is better than any other—yet poor and ignorant children must change theirs unless they want to stay poor and ignorant. When an NCTE "Task Force" set out to devise *Language Programs for the Disadvantaged* (NCTE, 1965), it laid down a perfect smoke screen of such hypocrisy, as one would expect from persons who felt called upon to inform the world that "without the experience of literature, the individual is denied the very dignity that makes him human" (p. v) but that not "all disadvantaged children are apathetic or dull" (pp. 24 f.).

"In this report" (p. 117), "teachers are asked to begin by accepting the dialect of their students for what it is, one form of oral communication. . . ." Teachers are warned particularly that they "need to accept the language which Negro children bring to school, to recognize that it is a perfectly appropriate vehicle for communicating ideas in the Negro home and subculture" (p. 215), that it is "essentially respectable and good" (p. 227). But though teachers must not attack "the dialect which children associate with their homes and their identity as Negroes" (p. 215), they must still use all the adult authority of the school to "teach standard informal English as a second dialect" (p. 137), because the youngster who cannot speak standard informal English "will not be able to get certain kinds of jobs" (p. 228).

The most common result of such teaching will be that white middle-class Midwestern speech will be imposed as mandatory for all those situations which middle-class white businessmen think it worth their while to regulate. In the words of Chicago's Professors Austin and McDavid (p. 245), "future educational programs should be developed in terms of substituting for the grammatical system of lower-class Southern speech [read: black Chicago speech] that of middle-class Chicago white speech—at least for those economic and social situations where grammatical norms are important." Labov goes so far as to ask (*Social Dialects and Language Learning,* p. 102) whether Northern schools should tolerate Southern speech at all—whether they should not also correct the "cultivated Southern speech" of privileged children who move North. . . .

The immorality of that effort is the chief reason why enforced bi-dialectalism should not be tolerated even if it were possible. Predators can and do use dialect differences to exploit and oppress, because ordinary people can be made to doubt their own value and to accept subservience if they can be made to despise the speech of their fathers. Obligatory bi-dialectalism for minorities is only another mode of exploitation, another way of making blacks behave as whites would like them to. It is unnecessary for communication, since the ability to understand other dialects is easily attained, as the black child shows when she translates her teacher's prissy white model *"his* hat" into *"he* hat." Its psychological consequences are likely to be nervous affectation, self-distrust, dislike for everyone not equally afflicted with the itch to get ahead, and eventual frustration by the discovery that the reward for so much suffering is intolerably small. At best the altered student will get a somewhat better job and will move up a few places in the rat-race of the underlings. At worst he will be cut off from other blacks, still not accepted among whites, and economically no better off than he was before.

White teachers should hope, then, that their black students will be recalcitrant, so that bi-dialectalism as a unilateral condition for employment can be forgotten. It would make better sense, if pedagogues insist on living in a fantasy world, to require whites to speak black English in their dealings with blacks, since the whites have more advantages than the blacks and consider themselves more intelligent; or perhaps we should be hard-headedly consistent in our brutalities and try to eradicate the vices which really do enrage employers—like intellectual questioning, or the suspicion that ours is not the best of possible worlds.

Indeed, the educationists' faith in education would be touching if it were not their way of keeping up their wages. Nothing the schools can do about black English or white English either will do much for racial peace and social justice as long as the black and white worlds are separate and hostile. The measure of our educational absurdity is the necessity of saying once again that regimented bi-dialectalism is no substitute for sweeping social change—*necessity* being defined by the alternative of dropping out and waiting quietly for destruction if the white businessman continues to have his way.

The reply that the educational system should not be politicized is impossible for bi-dialectalists, since bi-dialectalism is itself a political instrument. They may purge themselves of inconsistency, and do what little good is possible for English teachers as political reformers, if instead of teaching standard English as a second dialect they teach getting out of Vietnam, getting out of the missile race, and stopping the deadly pollution of the one world we have, as horribly exemplified by the current vandalism in Alaska.

One use for a small fraction of the resources that would thus be saved would be to improve the teaching of the English language. Bi-dialectalism would never have been invented if our society were not divided into the dominant white majority and the exploited minorities. Children should be taught that. They should be taught the relations between group differences and speech differences, and the good and bad uses of speech differences by groups and by individuals. The teaching would require a more serious study of grammar, lexicography, dialectology, and linguistic history than our educational system now provides— require it at least of prospective English teachers.

In the immediate present, the time and money now wasted on bi-dialectalism should be spent on teaching the children of the minorities to read. Already some of the universal experts among the linguists have boarded this new bandwagon, and the next round of government grants may very well be for programs in reading and writing in black English. That might be a good thing, particularly if we could somehow get rid of the tired little clique of operators who have run the professional societies of English teachers for so long. Anyway, the direct attack on minority language, the attempt to compel bi-dialectalism, should be abandoned for an attempt to open the minds and enhance the lives of the poor and ignorant. At the same time, every attempt should be made to teach the majority to understand the life and language of the oppressed. Linguistic change is the effect and not the cause of social change. If the majority can rid itself of its prejudices, and if the minorities can get or be given an education, differences between dialects are unlikely to hurt anybody much.

(The phoniest objections to this proposal will be those that talk about social realism, about the necessity for doing something even—or should one say particularly?—if it's wrong. That kind of talk makes real change impossible, but makes money for bi-dialectalists.)

SECTION II

Change

Language is shifty, tricky, quicksilver stuff: that much is clear. It does *change,* and it keeps on changing, but it is hard to catch and exhibit linguistic change happening. What is living has to be turned into specimens. There is both loss and gain, as in any objective study. A dead trout is easier to see and examine, but he is not quite the trout he was. He may even give the impression that trout can be tamed and managed.

Section II reminds us of the many sorts of change we can find in our language. Gleason describes the general aspects of language and the kinds of change to which each is subject. Wilson sketches a short history of English which points up obvious major changes in vocabulary, in sounds and pronunciation, in inflections, and in the way we string our words together. Marckwardt then focusses on the English of one time and place, to illustrate the forces of change that left their marks on our colonial English. It is a "before" picture, for which we supply the "after."

Others—Fries and Roberts and Hall and Hubbell—show us that it is not just the vocabulary that changes. Bryant looks closely at one of a thousand thousand items, just to see how change has operated on the syntax of the split infinitive. Robertson and Cassidy discuss the fascinating ways words change their meanings, even when we don't want them to. And they show us, too, how words become "good" or "bad," just from the way we use them. In the last essays, Wilson and Ohmann talk about change in the very fiber of the grammar itself.

Linguistic change cannot be stopped, not while we use the language. We receive it (we say) in pretty good shape when we are young, parts of it a little tattered, perhaps, and some of it a bit dated, but on the whole serviceable, and with some of the recent repairs and additions looking quite new and shiny and solid. And when years later we pass it on, we find we have left our marks on it, whether we knew it or wanted it to happen or not. Finally, these or other metaphors are a way of trying to talk about language as though it were both process and artifact.

27

H. A. GLEASON, JR.

Language

As you listen to an unfamiliar language you get the impression of a torrent of disorganized noises carrying no sense whatever. To the native speaker it is quite otherwise. He pays little attention to the sounds, but concerns himself instead with some situation which lies behind the act of speech and is, for him, somehow reflected in it. Both you and he have failed to grasp the nature of the phenomenon. Neither the casual observer nor the usual native speaker can give any real information about a language. To be sure, some people, Americans perhaps more than most others, have decided notions about language. But the ideas held and discussed come far short of giving a complete picture of the language and sometimes have very little relationship to the facts. Even people with considerable education are often wholly unable to answer certain quite simple questions about their language. For most people language is primarily a tool to be used, rather than a subject for close and critical attention.

It is probably well that it is so. Yet there are important human problems into which language enters intimately and on which it exerts such a profound influence that an understanding of its mechanism would contribute materially to their solutions. Moreover, every phase of human activity is worthy of study. Thus, for practical reasons, as well as to satisfy man's innate curiosity, language deserves careful and intelligent study.

Language has so many interrelationships with various aspects of human life that it can be studied from numerous points of view. All are valid and useful, as well as interesting in themselves. Linguistics is the science which attempts to understand language from the point of view of its internal structure. It is not, of course, isolated and wholly autonomous, but it does have a clearly and sharply delimited field of inquiry, and has developed its own highly effective and quite characteristic method. It must draw upon such sciences as physical acoustics, communications theory, human physiology, psychology, and anthropology for certain basic concepts and necessary data. In return, linguistics makes its own essential contributions to these disciplines. But however closely it may be related to other sciences, it is clearly separate by reason of its own primary concern with the structure of language.

What then is this structure? Language operates with two kinds of material. One of these is sound. Almost any sort of noise that the human vocal apparatus can produce is used in some way in some language. The other is ideas, social situations, meanings—English lacks any really acceptable term to cover the whole range—the facts or fantasies about man's existence, the things man reacts to and tries to convey to his fellows. These two, insofar as they concern linguists, may conveniently be labeled *expression* and *content*.

The foreigner who hears merely a jumble of sounds has not really heard the language, not even the part of it which we have called *expression*. All that he has heard is sounds, the material which language uses to carry its message. This is not the domain of the linguist, but that of the physicist. The latter can analyze the stream of speech as sound and learn many things about it. His findings have both theoretical and practical importance; the designs of telephones, radios, and much other electronic equipment depends in an essential way upon such findings. They also contribute basic data to linguistics, and to numerous other sciences, including psychology and physiology, as well as to physics itself.

The linguist is concerned with sound as the medium by which information is conveyed. To serve in this way, speech must be something quite different from the jumble of sound apparent to the foreigner. It is, in fact, an organized system or structure, and it is this structure that lies within the subject field of linguistics. The linguist analyzes speech as an orderly sequence of specific kinds of sounds and of sequences of sounds. It is orderly in terms of a very complex set of patterns which repeatedly recur and which are at least partially predictable. These patterns form the structure of *expression,* one major component of language in the sense that the linguist uses the term.

The native speaker has his attention focused on something else, the subject of the discourse. This may be a situation which is being described, some ideas which are being presented, or some social formula which is being repeated. None of these things are language, any more than are the sounds which convey speech. The subject of the discourse stands on the opposite side and in much the same relationship to speech as do the sounds. The speaker comprehends what he is talking about in terms of an organizing structure. This structure causes him to select certain features for description and determines the ways in which he will interrelate them. It also cuts the situation up into portions in a characteristic way. These selected features, like the sounds mentioned above, also form patterns which recur, and which are at least partially predictable. These recurrent patterns are the structure of *content,* a second major component of language as the linguist treats it.

Finally, these two structures are intimately related and interacting, Parts of the structure of expression are associated in definite ways with parts of the structure of content. The relations between these two complex structures are themselves quite complex. In every language they are different from what is found in every other language. The differences may be profound and extensive, or they may be relatively slight. But in every instance, the two structures are intricate and their relationships quite characteristic.

The native speaker uses this complex apparatus easily and without conscious thought of the process. It seems to him simple and natural. But to a speaker of another of the world's three thousand languages it may present quite a different picture. It may give an impression of being cumbersome, illogical, or even ridiculous. Actually, of course, the strange language is merely different. A true picture of language can only be had by seeing languages more objectively. Such a view will emphasize the immense complexity, the arbitrariness, and the high degree of adequacy for their purposes—features which are shared by all languages in spite of their divergencies.

The dual structure of language can best be made clear by an example. . . .

Consider a rainbow or a spectrum from a prism. There is a continuous gradation of color from one end to the other. That is, at any point there is only a small difference in the colors immediately adjacent at either side. Yet an American describing it will list the hues as *red, orange, yellow, green, blue, purple,* or something of the kind. The continuous gradation of color which exists in nature is represented in language by a series of discrete categories. This is an instance of structuring of content. There is nothing inherent either in the spectrum or the human perception of it which would compel its division in this way. The specific method of division is part of the structure of English.

By contrast, speakers of other languages classify colors in much different ways. In the accompanying diagram, a rough indication is given of the way in which the spectral colors are divided by speakers of English, Shona (a language of Rhodesia), and Bassa (a language of Liberia).

The Shona speaker divides the spectrum into three major portions. *Cips^wuka* occurs twice, but only because the red and purple ends, which he classifies as similar, are separated in the diagram. Interestingly enough, *citema* also includes black, and *cicena* white. In addition to these three terms there are, of course, a large number of terms for more specific colors. These terms are comparable to English *crimson, scarlet, vermilion,* which are all varieties of *red.* The convention of dividing the spectrum into three parts instead of into six does not indicate any difference in visual ability to perceive colors, but only a difference in the way they are classified or structured by the language.

The Bassa speaker divides the spectrum in a radically different way:

ENGLISH	purple	blue	green	yel-low	orange	red

SHONA	cips^wuka	citema	cicena	cips^wuka

BASSA	hui	zīza

into only two major categories. In Bassa there are numerous terms for specific colors, but only these two for general classes of colors. It is easy for an American to conclude that the English division into six major colors is superior. For some purposes it probably is. But for others it may present real difficulties. Botanists have discovered that it does not allow sufficient generalization for discussion of flower colors. Yellows, oranges, and many reds are found to constitute one series. Blues, purples, and purplish reds constitute another. These two exhibit fundamental differences that must be treated as basic to any botanical description. In order to state the facts succinctly it has been necessary to coin two new and more general color terms, *xanthic* and *cyanic,* for these two groups. A Bassa-speaking botanist would be under no such necessity. He would find *zīza* and *hui* quite adequate for the purpose, since they happen to divide the spectrum in approximately the way necessary for this purpose.

Now for a simple statement of structure in the expression pa[
language: The sounds used by English are grouped into consonants and
vowels (and some other categories). These are organized into syllables
in a quite definite and systematic way. Each syllable must have one
and only one vowel sound. It may have one or more consonants before
the vowel, and one or more after the vowel. There are quite intricate
restrictions on the sequences that may occur. Of all the mathematically
possible combinations of English sounds, only a small portion are admitted as complying with the patterns of English structure. Not all of
these are actually used, though the unused ones stand ready in case
they should ever be needed. Perhaps some day a word like *ving* may
appear in response to a new need. *Shmoo* was drawn out of this stock
of unused possibilities only a few years ago. But *ngvi* would be most
unlikely: it simply is not available as a potential English word, though
it contains only English sounds.

Six of these permissible sequences of sounds are somehow associated
with the six portions into which English language-habits structure the
spectrum. These are the familiar *red, orange, yellow, green, blue, purple.*
This association of expression and content is merely conventional. There
is no reason why six others could not be used, or why these six could
not be associated with different parts of the spectrum. No reason, that is,
except that this is the English-language way of doing it, and these are
conventions to which we must adhere reasonably closely if we are to be
understood. Sometime in the past history of the language, these conventions became established and have persisted with only gradual
changes since. In their ultimate origins, all such conventions are the
results of more or less accidental choices. It is largely fortuitous that the
spectrum came to be so divided, that the specific words were attached
to the colors so distinguished, or, indeed, that the sounds from which
they were formed were so organized that these words were possible.
These irrational facts, with many others like them, constitute the English language. Each language is a similarly arbitrary system.

The three major components of language, as far as language lies
within the scope of linguistics, are the structure of expression, the
structure of content, and vocabulary. The latter comprises all the specific
relations between expression and content—in the familiar terminology,
words and their meanings.

Vocabulary comes and goes. It is the least stable and even the least
characteristic of the three components of language. That portion of the
vocabulary which changes most freely is sometimes referred to as "slang."
But even staid and dignified words are constantly being created and
continually passing out of active use, to be preserved only in literature

which is dated by their very presence. While certain types of words are more transient than others, none are absolutely immortal. Even the most familiar and commonly used words, which might be expected to be most stable, have a mortality rate of about twenty percent in a thousand years.

Moreover, in the life history of an individual speaker the birth and death of words is very much more frequent than in the language community as a whole. Every normal person probably learns at least three words every day, over a thousand a year, and forgets old ones at an appreciable but lower rate. This figure must be a minimum, because most people have total vocabularies which could only be reached through even more rapid acquisition of vocabulary during at least part of their life.

We have no comparable method by which the rate of change of content structure can be estimated. The learning of new vocabulary, particularly technical terms associated with the learning of new concepts, does of course imply certain minor changes. But it is quite evident that change rarely touches the most basic features in any given language. With regard to the structure of expression the facts are clearer. Few, unless they learn a second language, will add, subtract, or change any of their basic sound patterns after they reach adolescence. Grammatical constructions may increase, but at a rate much slower than the increase of vocabulary. Vocabulary is indeed the transient feature of language.

In learning a second language, you will find that vocabulary is comparatively easy, in spite of the fact that it is vocabulary that students fear most. The harder part is mastering new structures in both content and expression. You may have to free yourself from the bondage of thinking of everything as either singular or plural. Perhaps the new language will organize content into singular, dual, and plural (here meaning "three or more"). Or perhaps the new language will not give routine consideration to the matter. English speakers can never make a statement without saying something about the number of every object mentioned. This is compulsory, whether it is relevant or not. In Chinese, objects are noted as singular or plural only when the speaker judges the information to be relevant. The Chinese experience suggests that it actually seldom is, for that language operates with only occasional references to number.

You will have to make similar changes in habits of thought and of description of situations in many other instances. You may, for example, have to learn to think of every action as either completed or incomplete, and to disregard the time of the action unless it has special relevance. The reorganization of thinking and perception may extend much deeper than such changes. In some languages, situations are not analyzed, as they are in English, in terms of an actor and an action. Instead the fundamental cleavage runs in a different direction and cannot be easily stated in English. Some of these divergences between languages have been described by Benjamin L. Whorf. His formulation has been widely debated and perhaps is not at present susceptible to rigorous testing. Yet the papers are very suggestive and can be read with profit by every student of linguistics or languages.

You will also have to reorganize your habits of making and hearing sounds. You will have to discriminate between sounds that you have learned to consider the same. You will find that others, in clear contrast in English, function as one, and you will have to learn to respond to them as to one sound. Patterns which seem impossible will have to become facile, and you will have to learn to avoid some English patterns that seem to be second nature.

The most difficult thing of all, however, is that these profound changes will have to become completely automatic. You will have to learn to use them without effort or conscious attention. In this learning process constant disciplined practice is essential. Special ability may be helpful, but probably much less so than is popularly supposed. An understanding of the basic principles of language structure—that is, the results of modern linguistic research—while not indispensable, can contribute in many ways.

As we listen to a person speaking our native language we hear not only what is said, but also certain things about the speaker. If he is an acquaintance, we recognize him. If not, we identify him as male or female and perhaps obtain some idea of his age, his education, and his social background. A person's voice serves at least two functions in communication. One is linguistic, in that it serves as the vehicle of the expression system of language. The other is non-linguistic, in that it carries information of a quite different sort about the speaker.

This distinction is made, at least roughly, even by the unsophisticated. If we are told to REPEAT exactly what another says, we will duplicate (provided our memory serves us adequately) every feature which is included in the language expression system. We can do that, if it is our own language, even without understanding the content. In repeating we will make no effort to reproduce anything beyond the linguistically pertinent features. If, however, we are asked to MIMIC another, we attempt to reproduce not only the linguistic features, but every discernible characteristic. Few can mimic with any degree of success, whereas every normal native speaker can, perhaps with a little practice, repeat exactly up to the limit imposed by his memory span.

The most basic elements in the expression system are the *phonemes*. These are the sound features which are common to all speakers of a given speech form and which are exactly reproduced in repetition. In any language, there is a definite and usually small number of phonemes. In English there are forty-six. Out of this limited inventory of units, the whole expression system is built up. In many respects the phonemes are analogous to the elements of chemistry, ninety-odd in number, out of which all substances are constructed.

The phoneme is one of those basic concepts, such as may be found in all sciences, which defy exact definition. Yet some sort of working characterization is necessary before we go on. The following is hardly adequate beyond a first introduction to the subject, but will make it possible to proceed with the analysis and enumeration of the phonemes of English. . . .

With this in mind, we may define a *phoneme* as a minimum feature of the expression system of a spoken language by which one thing that may be said is distinguished from any other thing which might have been said. Thus, if two utterances are different in such a way that they suggest to the hearer different contents, it must be because there are differences in the expression. The difference may be small or extensive. The smallest difference which can differentiate utterances with different contents is a difference of a single phoneme. This description is best illustrated by a full-scale application in the presentation of the phonemic system of a language. . . .

There are two things about phonemes that must be explicitly pointed out in anticipation of any such presentation:

Phonemes are part of the system of one specific language. The phonemes of different languages are different, frequently incommensurable. It is for this reason that a foreigner hears only a jumble which he cannot repeat. The sounds of the unfamiliar language do not fit into his phonemic system, and so he can comprehend no order in a simple utterance. If anything which is said about the phonemes of one language happens to apply to those of another, we must regard it as fortuitous.

Phonemes are features of the spoken language. Written language has it own basic unit, the grapheme. Something will be said about this later. If, of necessity, written words are cited as illustrations, it must be constantly borne in mind that the written form is not, and cannot be, an illustration of a phoneme. Instead, it is the spoken form which the written form is expected to elicit which illustrates the phoneme under discussion. This inevitably introduces a major difficulty into the presentation. The illustrative words have been selected with the intention that they should be as generally as possible pronounced by all Americans in the same way. Undoubtedly this principle of selection fails in some instances because of dialect and individual peculiarities of the writer and the reader. Such instances will not vitiate the argument. For some Americans other examples might be needed, but examples can be found which will lead to the same results.

The thinking that most Americans do about language is almost exclusively concerned with written English. A written language is, of course, a valid and important object of linguistic investigation. It can, however, easily mislead the unwary. Most of the misunderstandings which Americans have about language arise from a failure to keep clearly in mind the nature and limitations of a written language.

A written language is typically a reflection, independent in only limited ways, of spoken language. As a picture of actual speech, it is inevitably imperfect and incomplete. To understand the structure of a written language one must constantly resort either to comparison with the spoken language or to conjecture. Unfortunately, recourse has been too largely to the latter. Moreover, conjecture has been based not so much upon an intimate knowledge of the ways of languages in general (the results of descriptive linguistics) as to a priori considerations of supposed logic, to metaphysics, and a simple prejudice. While logic and metaphysics are important disciplines and can make significant contributions to an understanding of language, the customary manner of applying them has redounded neither to their credit nor to the elucidation of language structure. Linguistics must start with thorough investigation of spoken language before it proceeds to study written language. This is true of languages with long histories of written literature, such as English, no less than those of isolated tribes which have never known of the possibility of writing.

The second basic unit in the expression system is the *morpheme*. This again cannot be exactly defined. . . . For the present, however, let us characterize a *morpheme* as follows: It is the unit on the expression side of language which enters into relationship with the content side. A morpheme is typically composed of one to several phonemes. The morpheme differs fundamentally from the phoneme, which has no such relationship with content. That is, phonemes have no meanings; morphemes have meanings.

The simpler words of English are morphemes. Other words consist of two or more morphemes. Like the phonemes, the morphemes enter into combinations in accordance with definite and intricate patterns.

The expression structure is merely the sum of the patterns of arrangement of these two basic units.

Using the phoneme and the morpheme as their basic units, linguists have been able to build a comprehensive theory of the expression side of language, and to make detailed and comprehensive statements about the expression systems of specific languages. This is what is ordinarily called *descriptive linguistics*. It is the basic branch of linguistic science. Others are *historical linguistics,* dealing with the changes of languages in time, and *comparative linguistics,* dealing with the relationships between languages of common origin. Descriptive linguistics is conventionally divided into two parts. *Phonology* deals with the phonemes and sequences of phonemes. *Grammar* deals with the morphemes and their combinations.

In some respects linguistics has developed more precise and rigorous methods and attained more definitive results than any other science dealing with human behavior. Linguists have been favored with the most obviously structured material with which to work, so this attainment is by no means due to any scientific superiority of linguists over other social scientists. It is also the direct result of the discovery of the phoneme, a discovery which allows the data to be described in terms of a small set of discrete units. Within a given language, a given sound is either a certain phoneme or it is not; there can be no intergradation. This fact eliminates from linguistics a large measure of the vagueness and lack of precision characteristic of most studies of human behavior. It would be presumptuous to claim that this advantage has been thoroughly exploited by linguists, but it is certainly fair to say that in some places, linguistics has achieved an appreciable measure of scientific rigor and has the foundations for further development in this regard.

The chief evidence for the high order of development of linguistics as a science lies in the reproducibility of its results. If two linguists work independently on the same language, they will come out with very similar statements. There may be differences. Some of these differences will be predictable. Very seldom will any of the differences be deep-seated. Usually it will be quite possible to harmonize the two statements and show that by simple restatements one result can be converted into the other. That is, the two results will have differed largely in inconsequential ways, often only in external form.

The content side of linguistics has developed much less rapidly and to a very much less impressive extent than the study of expression. Indeed, it cannot as yet justifiably be called a science. Undoubtedly this has been a source of frustration in linguistics as a whole. One of the greatest short-comings of descriptive work with the expression aspect of language has been a lack of understanding of the relationships between expression and content, and the inability to use the analysis of content in attacking related problems in expression. Here is the great frontier in linguistic knowledge on which we may look for progress in the next decades.

There have been three reasons for this neglect of the content side. First, linguists have been late in comprehending the real significance of the two-sided nature of language. Their attention has been diverted from this basic problem by the great advances being made within the analysis of expression.

Second, there has been no way to gain access to the content structure except through the expression structure. This requires an inferential method which has not appealed to linguists busy with building a highly rigorous method for the handling of more directly observed data. Content has therefore had an inferior status in the eyes of linguists.

Third, the content, apart from its structure, has not been amenable to any unified study. The substance of content is, of course, the whole of human experience. Thousands of scientists have labored, each in some one of numerous disciplines, in elucidating this mass of material. But there is no one approach which can comprehend the whole and so serve as a starting point for comparison of the different structures which can be imposed upon it. Only isolated portions of the content system can as yet be studied as structure imposed on a measurable continuum of experience. The examples of structuring of color concepts discussed above suggest the possibilities and make the lack of further opportunities for comparison the more tantalizing.

In contrast, the expression plane starts with much simpler materials. The sounds producible by the human voice can be studied comprehensively by several approaches. Two of these have reached the degree of precision which makes them useful to linguistics: *articulatory phonetics,* a branch of human physiology, and *acoustic phonetics,* a branch of physics. . . . It is hard to imagine the scientific study of the expression aspect of speech attaining anywhere near the present degree of development without the aid of phonetics. The structure can be systematically described only because the underlying sounds can be accurately described and measured.

KENNETH G. WILSON

The History of
the English Language

The English language is usually said to have begun in the sixth and seventh centuries, when the Germanic Angles, Saxons, and Jutes invaded and settled the Celtic island of Britain.[1] With the techniques of historical linguistics and philology, in spite of the lack of written records, we have been able to reconstruct the older forms, sounds, and vocabularies of the invaders' language in remarkable detail, working mainly from later written sources and from our knowledge of linguistic change. The Celtic language, together with most of the Roman linguistic remains, disappeared from England, except for a few place names. The history of English had begun.

The Ancestral History

The shift into a new territory of a large number of speakers of a language, isolated from the homeland and in contact with a new language and culture, sets in motion its own rates and kinds of change, so that although the home language may continue strong and pursue its own life, the two strains—here two strains of a West Germanic language—will develop independently and will eventually become different enough from each other as to be no longer mutually intelligible. As a result there will be two separate languages.

The continental origins are important: there the Germanic languages were already fully formed; they belonged to a family of languages,

From the *Sixty-ninth Yearbook*, Part II, of the National Society for the Study of Education. © 1970 by the National Society for the Study of Education. Reprinted by permission of the publisher.

Indo-European, which was already important in the history of the world, both in influence and in numbers of speakers.

Although we have never heard or seen it, scholars have managed to reconstruct much of Indo-European; from the study of many related languages they have been able to re-create the sounds, the grammar, and the vocabulary of this ur-language from which so many of the modern western and some of the eastern languages have come. The reconstruction itself is a fascinating story, but here we can say only that somewhere in the period 3500 to 2000 B.C., there was a people living probably in northeastern Europe who spoke a language we now call Indo-European. Centuries of migrations, conquests, divisions, and expansions splintered this language (which had itself probably splintered off from another, earlier language) into new languages, some of which in turn spawned still more languages, not regularly or predictably in time, but gradually or spasmodically, as the vagaries of human society drove the people apart. Today we find descendants of the Indo-European language family stretched over almost the entire globe, and we recognize the ancient history of the family in its name. Indo-European languages are native to a wide swath from northern Europe across the eastern Mediterranean into India, and more recently they have been planted in North America, Africa, and Australia.

Through historical linguistic techniques, English can be traced to its origins. It belongs to the Germanic subdivision of a major subgroup of Indo-European. Sound shifts—systematic evolutions in what happened to certain sounds of the Germanic languages only—plus certain grammatical characteristics, such as the loss of nearly all inflectional signs of tense and aspect except the distinction between the present and the preterit, distinguish the Germanic languages. And similar differences distinguish the West Germanic languages from those of the East and North. Thus English traces its history from the West Germanic group to an Anglo-Frisian group and finally to English itself.

The History of the Speakers of English

In the eighth and ninth centuries we begin to find texts in English written by Englishmen; it is then that we begin the documented history of the language. We have some convenient names: Old English or Anglo-Saxon is the language of the early Middle Ages, roughly from the beginnings to 1000 or 1100. Middle English is the language from 1100 or so to the Renaissance, to about 1500 or 1550. Early Modern English is Renaissance English, lasting perhaps until 1700, and Modern English is the language from the beginning of the eighteenth century until today. These "periods" are arbitrary; more often they measure the social history of its speakers rather than characteristic differences in the language itself, although the differences are there: the English of Alfred, of Chaucer, and of Shakespeare differed markedly, just as our own differs from Shakespeare's. Conventional histories of English examine and try to account for the gross differences in the language at each of these periods.

But the history of *what* is the history of English? Certainly the history of its vocabulary, of its words and their meanings, would be a major consideration. But there are other important aspects too.

In some ways, the history of the speakers themselves is the most important part of the history of a language. Who were the people, how did they live, what did they speak about, whom did they meet, and what happened to them? Social history will be reflected above all in the vocabulary, since a people will invent and adapt words and their meanings to fit its daily requirements; as these change, so will the vocabulary change.

To the student of language history, however, there are other kinds of historical study which are equally important: the history of the sounds of the language, and the development of its grammar—the forms of the words, their inflections and the grammatical meanings they contain, and the constantly evolving rules of the syntax—these too can be historically traced. In this brief account we can only offer reminders of the social history and of the military, economic, political, and religious activities of the English people which affected the history of their language.

We must study the effects of the Scandinavian invasion, wherein a similar Germanic people came into close (and eventually submerged) relationship with the English. The Norman invasion and the several centuries of Norman and French domination of government and upper-class life left their marks, as did the migrations of people from the Low Countries into London in the later Middle Ages. The Renaissance, that time of expansion and invention, inquiry and experiment—political, geographical, social, military, scientific, and religious—affected the quality of English life and left its marks on the language. The development of the Empire in the eighteenth and nineteenth centuries is important: Englishmen began to know the whole world, and the scientific and commercial prowess of the industrial revolution made England the great mercantile and naval power we now think of as Victorian. And then came the great wars of the modern era, with the tremendous social, economic, and political upheaval they left in their wake: all these forces and events have left their marks on the English language.

The American Speakers of English

We need more than a simple footnote, too, to pick up the American version of this social history, which from the seventeenth century on began to run a separate course.[2] Important are the very facts of the arrival of the English on this continent. For example, both the New England and Virginia settlements spoke dialects from the English Home Counties—from the area around London—but different social class dialects; hence the language in these two locations, though essentially Elizabethan at the outset, differed markedly.

And the English encountered other Europeans when they came: in the Great Lakes and Mississippi areas they found the French had been there first, naming the places and animals and tribes, and pronouncing the Indian words in a French that the English could only anglicize. In lower New York, the Dutch had left their mark on the social and topographical order, and in Florida and the Southwest, the Spanish had long since named the geographical parts. And everywhere there were the Indians, not many people in all but speaking many dialects and languages. All these facts of social and political history have left their signs on the American varieties of English, just as they have left them on American life itself.

Later history is important too. A nation of immigrants, we owe something to the kinds of people who settled the various sections of the country: to the Germans in Pennsylvania and the lower Ohio Valley, to the Scotch in the lower Midwest and the uplands of the Border States, to the Scandinavians in the upper Midwest, and to the Irish in Boston and the Italians in New York, just to name a few. As the country assumed the role of inspiration to the downtrodden, thousands of the economically and politically "out" came from the countries of central and southern Europe. And the Negro deserves our attention: he made little mark on the language at first, so low was his social status; but in recent years his words, his dialects, and his special meanings have made a solid impact—on the life of Americans and the American version of English.

All these contacts had their effects—some major, some trivial. But there is much more. We began by being a rural country, with a frontier which stayed open until the First World War. But now we are a great industrial power, an urban society, and these changes have changed the language too.

Hence one vital part of the history of the language is the history of its speakers—who they were, whom they met, how they lived, and what they did and thought and strove for; these things shape speakers' words and the way they say them and even the way they string them together.

The History of the English Vocabulary

When we study the history of the vocabulary, we can see the importance of social history; vocabulary changes most quickly of all the aspects of language. English in the seventh century displays a predominantly Germanic vocabulary. There are a few Roman words dating from continental encounters with the Romans, and there are a few others picked up from the Roman remains the English found in Britain. But the words are mostly Germanic.

Since the English drove out the British Celts, the latter added almost no Celtic words to the language—a few place names and little more. Missionary culture from Britain's conversion to Christianity added Latin names for religious things. But when the Vikings came and settled down, the two Germanic strains borrowed freely from each other. Actually, many of their words were similar, and sometimes the two similar words were both kept, a shift being made in the meaning of one or the other: *shirt* and *skirt* were originally the same Germanic word; both versions were kept, with different meanings (2: 113). Occasionally, the Scandinavian word displaced the English one: *egg* replaced the English *ey*, first in the Northern dialect and then in all English.

With Norman and later massive French influences in the Middle Ages, the English vocabulary changed markedly. It borrowed wholesale from French. With Christianity it had accepted Latin words; now it often borrowed the same words again, this time in their French forms and with their French meanings. It borrowed the names of all sorts of French ideas: words for government, law, dress, food, manners, and the like. Chaucer's fourteenth-century vocabulary looks very different from King Alfred's ninth-century one, mainly because so many of Chaucer's words were borrowed from French.

The renaissance brought a different sort of change: [3] scholars and writers deliberately added words or made them up from Latin and Greek, and travelers brought back Italian names for exotic things (2: 113). As English explorers, businessmen, and soldiers went farther and farther afield, even some eastern Mediterranean and New World words began to appear in the language.

In this country, immigration had an effect on the vocabulary, though not in proportion to the numbers of immigrants. The Germans were the most numerous of the non-English-speaking immigrants, yet they have left us only many words for food and drink, a few words for educational matters, and surprisingly little else. The Italians illustrate the whole pattern nicely. When in the seventeenth and eighteenth centuries, the English milords began to take the grand tour, Italian words for music and painting and other aspects of art and cultivation were added to English; we cannot discuss music and painting without using borrowed Italian terms. But when the poor Italians came to New York in the early twentieth century, they had little interest for us except as laborers. We did not ape their language except in jest; they hurried instead to learn ours. As a result, American English added the names of a few Italian dishes to its vocabulary from this contact, and little more.

The point is important: when two cultures come into contact, everything seems to depend upon who is master, or at least upon who feels inferior. Hence English borrowed massively from French during the Middle Ages, when French power and culture seemed demonstrably superior. But in the past two centuries, English has borrowed from French only the terms for hairstyles and women's dress and the like, while terms of technology and the names of soft drinks the French have borrowed from us.

The History of the Sounds of English: Phonology

We can also study the history of the *sounds* of English. Using written records from the Middle Ages and the early Renaissance, we can tell from the unfixed spelling a good deal about how the words were pronounced. The histories of English sounds have been elaborately worked out, and the changes are regular, according to generalizable patterns. It is possible to reconstruct these changes, so that we can make reasonable guesses at what Shakespeare's language (or Chaucer's or Alfred's) actually sounded like.

Once the spelling became fixed, we lost a good bit of the information previously provided when each man spelled the way he spoke, but in literature—Hardy's Wessex novels, for example—we find evidence in the author's attempt to suggest or imitate the sounds of the spoken language by unconventional spelling. Mark Twain did this sort of thing well in *Huckleberry Finn*.

With nineteenth- and twentieth-century skills in phonetic notation, and most recently with the development of the phonograph and wire and tape recorders, scholars have learned to record permanently the sound of the language. The history of English sounds before modern times was often a matter of scholarly deduction; henceforth it will be able to rely on accurate recordings.

The History of English Word-Forms: Morphology

We are on even more elaborately detailed ground when we turn to the history of English forms and inflections. Old English was a highly inflected language, as were its Germanic progenitors. It still carried distinctive endings (*a*) for four forms of the verb, (*b*) for number in several parts of speech, (*c*) for case in nouns and adjectives (including both weak and strong declensions in adjectives), and (*d*) for person, number, and case in pronouns. It inflected its demonstratives.

There are useful generalizations we can make about the history of English morphology: we can say first of all that the general trend has been for inflections to disappear and be "replaced" by other means of giving the needed grammatical information. Nouns illustrate the pattern: Alfred's nouns had four cases—nominative, genitive, dative, and accusative. But the case distinctions began to drop off, perhaps partly because the heavy forward stress characteristic of Old English (words tended to be stressed on the first or root syllable) began to make it hard to distinguish among unstressed endings like *–an, –en, –em, –am,* and the like, and partly because other devices began to serve the same purpose. Word order was becoming fixed, so that one looked for nominative case nouns toward the beginning of sentences, and therefore soon one did not require the reassurance of a case ending to know one had a subject before a verb. By Chaucer's time, of case in nouns, only an all-purpose nominative form, a genitive form, and a few relic dative-accusatives were left. Today, although we still have both the "nominative" all-purpose form and the genitive, the datives and accusatives are gone; there are now only two cases in nouns, and for the genitive there is an alternative: a periphrastic construction with *of* which permits us to say *the road's surface* without the genitive inflection, as *the surface of the road.*

Pronouns also show the disappearance of some case inflections since Old English. Middle English still distinguished some of the datives and accusatives: *hine* was accusative, *him,* dative. Now we have coalesced these two into *him,* a form we might logically call a dual-purpose objective case form.

The pattern of deteriorating inflections is felt everywhere: case has disappeared from adjective, and even some of the signs of tense in verbs are coalescing. Only the third person singular still maintains a distinctive inflection in the present tense: *he swims,* but *I, you, we, you,* and *they* merely *swim.*

Old English had two very different schemes for signalling the past tense and the past participle. The strong verb system had eight distinctive classes of vowel change to signal tense; we see one class pattern reflected in the forms of the Modern English verb *drink, drank, drunk* (OE *drincan, dronc, druncon, druncen*). The strong verb system was very large in Old English; but the weak system, which ended both preterit and past participle with a dental suffix, also included large numbers of verbs, and in the end it has come to dominate. Hundreds of our formerly strong verbs have taken on the weak pattern: *grip, gripped, gripped; gleam, gleamed, gleamed,* and so on. The increasing dominance of the weak pattern is clear in the child's language: he usually says *swimmed* at first, until he learns the older strong form which we now retain as a kind of exception to the trend. And when we make new verbs—*televise,* for example—we make them on the weak system model; the preterit is *televised,* with the dental suffix.

Changes of this sort, reflecting the general replacement of much of the inflectional system by other grammatical devices, might lead us to attempt too hasty a generalization. It is true that inflections have been disappearing, and that distinctive forms like those of the subjunctive have been diminishing in use. But there is another tendency to be considered too: the smaller the number of inflections left, and the higher the frequency of their occurrence in our speech and writing, the more likely we are to retain them. Hence the pronouns retain more of case than do the nouns, and most of those that remain seem fairly strongly entrenched. And while much of the subjunctive is weakening (one seldom hears "If he arrive early" any more), other parts of it seem as strong as ever ("If I were you" and "I asked that he come tomorrow" seem firmly entrenched).

Hence we can see that the history of English morphology does permit generalizations; but it is also clear that students of the language need to realize the importance of looking at individual words and individual grammatical devices in great detail if they would have an accurate appreciation of this aspect of linguistic history.

The History of English Word Order: Syntax

An oversimplified statement of a thousand years of syntactic change might go something like this: Word order and function words (prepositions and conjunctions and the like) were already grammatical devices in Old English, but fewer in number and apparently simpler and less forceful in operation than they are today; by the Middle English period, these devices were beginning to be more powerful and more numerous, and the closer we get to the Modern English period, the more these devices take on the force of overriding signals of grammatical meaning, capable in many instances of canceling out the significance of the inflections that remain.

Case is no longer so important as is the *word order* component of syntax: "Him hit John" is not really ambiguous today; we ignore the small boy's error of case, and we know unquestionably who hit whom. But in Old English, had *John* carried a nominative inflection, the roles of striker and struck would clearly have been reversed.

English syntax has, then, an increasingly complex history; nor are we always entirely sure of the degree of complexity or the true force of word order and function words in Old English. There are many open questions here. But we do know that the subject-verb-object and subject-verb-complement patterns have become very powerful. Positions for modifiers too have developed distinctive patterns, since we must rely on position to tell us which adjective goes with which noun, now that inflections are no longer doing the job.

Our question patterns involve either (*a*) reversal of subject and verb, a pattern more common in Early Modern English and before than it is today (*Rides he to the wars?*), or (*b*) the use of auxiliaries in the reversed position with the verb itself tagging along later (*Can I come too? Does he ever ride?*). We also have a list of question-asking function words which fall into normal subject position, often with a reversal of subject and verb, to make questions: *Whom is he calling? Where are you going? What happened?*

Major patterns of syntax then have developed over the past thousand years of English; they are laws which govern the way we string our words together. When case is gone, we pick out the indirect object in one of two syntactic ways: word order (John gave *his brother* the book) or function word (John gave the book *to his brother*) where the prepositional phrase replaces the indirect object construction.

The history of English syntax illustrates the trend toward fixed patterns in English; it also illustrates two important principles for any language study: (*a*) we must always examine particulars and test the accuracy of generalizations; and (*b*) it helps to understand the English of today or any other day if we can see how the pattern under study evolved over the centuries.

The History of English Grammars [4]

Prior to the eighteenth century there were no full-dress attempts to describe the structure of English. Since then, grammarians and laymen both have struggled with each other in attempting to understand its structure and to "improve" it. Many of the misunderstandings have arisen from the term *grammar* itself: English grammar is first of all the system of patterns and rules which enables us to use the language. Whether we can describe and state these patterns and rules or not, they do exist: even little children and the mentally defective can speak English; they "know" English grammar even if they cannot tell us what it is they know. But *an* English grammar is also any specific attempt to *describe* the structural system of English. And finally, to confuse the situation further, English grammar in the schools and to the layman has also come to refer simply to points of difficulty and variation, to the choices on which we have placed strong values—in short, to usage. Here we shall concern ourselves solely with the second of these uses of the term *grammar:* the history of attempts to describe the structure of English.

Universal Grammar

Systematic study of the structure of English had to await both the "coming of age of English," when it had gained respectability, and the eighteenth-century zeal for order, regularity, and the power of generalization. Universal grammar was a logical beginning, based as it was on ideas of the similarities (and the classical authority) of Latin and Greek. If English seemed to lack something to be found in this universal grammar, it must be a flaw, and it must be corrected.

Pioneer grammarians like Robert Lowth and Joseph Priestly leaned heavily on universal grammar: Lowth's extremely influential *A Short Introduction to English Grammar* (1762) reported variations between English and Latin constructions, and cited English authorial practices to illustrate the rules for English structure. Everywhere Lowth (like Dr. Johnson in his *Dictionary*, 1755) assumed that universal grammar should be the guide to English grammarians; he sought usually to bring English into line (10: 68–70).

Modern linguistic scholarship had until a recent reawakening of interest, very largely disproved the old universal grammar. Part of the problem was that of the blind men and the elephant: comparative grammarians had arrived at their conclusions about universal grammar from an examination of many languages—ancient and modern—but as luck would have it, nearly all were Indo-European. Hence, they found so many similarities that principles seemed obvious. But as anthropologists began to describe the languages they encountered in Asia, Africa, and the Pacific, as well as the Indian and Eskimo languages of the Western Hemisphere, almost all the principles of universal grammar turned out to be unsound.

School Grammars

Despite the fact that the most influential of the old school grammars was written in England, school grammars are a peculiarly American phenomenon, fostered by the American zeal for popular education. Lindley Murray's *English Grammar Adapted to the Different Classes of Learners* (1795) was the most widely used and widely imitated of the school grammars. An American who moved to Britain after the Revolution, Murray composed a grammar which was oversimple, dogmatic, and logical at the expense of accurate observation. It laid out "the rules" of English grammar, treating syntax, parts of speech, rules for parsing, spelling, and a number of other topics. It was clear, forceful, and incredibly successful. Gleason remarks:

> Murray frankly appeals to expediency in determining his rules. He recognizes that there are only two case forms in the noun, but considers it easier to teach three, since there are three in the pronoun. His grammar deals almost entirely with words—their classification and forms comprising etymology, and their uses constituting syntax. . . . Almost nothing is said about the order of words (10:71–72).

Within the tradition of school grammars, others began to try to show graphically the structure of the English sentence. Alonzo Reed and Brainerd Kellogg perfected a scheme for diagraming which combined the analytical features of parsing with earlier and clumsier attempts at graphic display of sentence structure. It too caught on (10: 73–74).

The chief problems with school grammars were that they oversimplified and that they stressed logic at the expense of accuracy. They were teachable grammars, and in the schools they were—and are—used prescriptively. In the effort to be clear and firm, they often obscured complexities and falsified the facts of English structure in the effort to be orderly and "complete."

Traditional Grammars

In continental Europe, the nineteenth and early twentieth centuries provided a fine group of scholarly English grammars. Not textbooks, these were fresh, exhaustively detailed examinations of the structure of English. Conservative and careful, the traditional grammarians closely examined the language, especially the written language, classifying meticulously, never glossing over difficulties, always reporting the details that did not seem to fit.

These grammars were traditional in that they were organized around the conventional classifications of parts of speech, elements of the sentence, and types of sentence. Whatever their descriptions lack in power (that is, in strength of generalization) is made up in detail of description. The classics are Poutsma's *A Grammar of Late Modern English*, Kruisinga's *A Handbook of Present-Day English,* and Jespersen's *A Modern English Grammar on Historical Principles.* Jespersen's seven-volume work is both typical and innovative: he was a thoroughly trained historical linguist, and he had the fine ability of the small boy in *The Emperor's Clothes;* he could observe accurately and though he worked within a tradition, he was seldom bound by it (10: 77–78).

The great European reference grammars have flaws. But their quality has never really ceased to be admired, and they have more recently been given new praise by the transformational-generative grammarians, who see in their attention to detail and in their insistence on dealing with total meaning a kindred spirit of investigation into English structure.[5]

Structural Grammars

Structural grammars depend on the work of descriptive linguists, particularly in that they work wholly from real samples of English. The key document is Charles Carpenter Fries' *The Structure of English,* which begins by reclassifying the parts of speech into four form-classes and fifteen groups of function words. Fries makes some good distinctions: for example, he finds that auxiliaries clearly are not like traditionally classified verbs because they neither display the full formal patterns of verb morphology nor do they distribute themselves as traditional verbs do. He concludes that they are function words.

His attempts at more rigorous adherence to schemes of classification based first on form and then on position or function, rather than on all three intermixed, were a major contribution, since they permitted grammars to deal more powerfully with the details observed.

This reassessment of the parts of speech caused much of the furor which Fries' book stirred up, particularly among teachers, but the main thrust of the book was its attempt to deal with syntax, especially with the patterns of English word order (10: 79–80).

Much pedagogy has been developed from combining Fries' close look at real samples of language and his efforts at generalizations about syntax with the strong emphasis on the spoken language which stems from the linguists, especially from the work of Trager and Smith (21). This combination has led to solid attempts at fairly full structural grammars, such as W. Nelson Francis' *The Structure of American English* (8), the most widely used text for the training of English teachers in grammar during the past decade.

The Contributions of American Linguists

Beginning with Leonard Bloomfield, American anthropologically oriented linguists began to apply to the English language the descriptive methods they used in dealing with exotic languages among Pacific islanders, Eskimos, and Indians. What followed was a series of studies, among them the Smith-Trager *An Outline of English Structure* (1951) (21). It was the first full treatment of English sound structure—including stress, pitch, and juncture—together with a brief but perceptive account of morphology; it did not go far into syntax (10: 82–84). The spoken language was the key; hence the linguists of the forties and fifties attacked the traditional grammarians for their reliance upon the written language and for dealing with meaning as a whole.

Intonation patterns were seen as components of grammar, and this led to what some linguists call "phonological syntax," the elaboration of the grammar of the spoken language. Archibald Hill's *Introduction to Linguistic Structures* (1958) developed this line of descriptions further, although, like much structural analysis, it was not always well received (12).

Eugene Nida, *A Synopsis of English Syntax* (16), concentrated exclusively on syntax; the scheme of immediate constituent analysis which he employed has been widely modified and developed. Gleason says:

> Each construction was described as consisting of two parts (very rarely three or more) of specific types and in a definable relation. Long sentences are described in terms of many layers of such simple constructions, one within another (10:85).

In the end we find people like Francis developing fairly comprehensive descriptions, in which the immediate constituent technique is elaborately worked out, and in which four kinds of structure are described: predication, complementation, modification, and coordination (8:291ff). Francis and others have polished these approaches for use in teaching, but they have by no means resolved all the problems of describing English structure, particularly syntax.

Transformation-Generative Grammars

Beginning with assumptions by Noam Chomsky and others, a whole series of new schemes for describing the manufacture of English sentences has begun to appear recently. None has actually presented a full grammar as yet, and all differ in detail, in completeness, and in some of their assumptions, but they also have some assumptions in common:

1. That there are some universal principles describing what it is that people know when they know (i.e., use unconsciously) any natural language.

2. That the structure of the language itself can be stated in a detailed hierarchy of rules for making sentences.

3. That such a set of rules will generate *all* English sentences, not just those already available for analysis, but others yet unspoken and unwritten.

Most of the attempts at writing such generative grammars begin from Noam Chomsky's idea that the structure of a language has three parts: (*a*) a small "kernel" of sentence types, or short distinctive formulas involving subjects, verbs, and complements; (*b*) a large number of rules for transforming these types by substitution, reordering, and combining their parts; and a list of morphophonemic rules which will enable us to turn into actual sentences the "structured strings" of terms which result from the application of transformational rules to one or more of the kernel types (4).

The structures revealed by this kind of grammatical description are exceedingly complex, as are the systems of rules, and thus far no complete grammar has been written, although a number of broadly successful efforts have been made at describing the gross patterns and at working out some of the details of specific parts such as the structures involving English nominals, or those which generate English questions.

Conclusion

The history of the attempts to describe English structure has been relatively short but incredibly active in recent years. Since the development of transformational-generative theories, we have seen many revisions, not only of the details but of basic assumptions. Not all grammarians accept the tripartite scheme described above.

Furthermore, the attention given to total meaning by this kind of grammar, in great contrast to the bell-jar atmosphere which structural grammarians try to create in separating grammatical meaning from total meaning, has led to a number of elaborate new schemes of description which are still in the hands of the theorists: *stratificational grammar*, for example, separates "deep structure," or meaning, from "surface structure" or the actual final syntax of the sentence.

What some students of language conclude from this lively recent series of developments is that although we are not yet "home free," we are eventually going to be able to write a full grammar of this language from a transformational-generative point of view. Others disagree, although they admit that in the attempt we will continue to learn much more about how people "know" languages and what the psycholinguistic facts truly are.

Meantime it is clear that teachers of English must know at least three broad schemes of structural analysis—the scholarly traditional, the structural, and the transformational-generative. All give useful information about the structure of English, and all offer methodological advice to those whose job it is to teach English.

THE HISTORY OF ENGLISH LEXICOGRAPHY

The Beginnings

Lexicography, the art of dictionary-making, has always had a very practical purpose, right from the very beginning.[6] From the very first wordbooks to the wide diversity to be found in the many kinds of modern dictionaries, all have been made primarily as practical tools. The dictionary is not a particularly old idea, moreover; and an examination of some of the practical purposes and of the books that have resulted shows us several threads:

1. Medieval scholars constantly sought to compile treatises which would incorporate all that was known about everything: these encyclopedias grew into alphabetical lists of the names of things, of natural phenomena, and of man's institutions; they often resembled dictionaries, and their development into the modern encyclopedia has at several points intertwined with that of the dictionary.

2. A more direct ancestor of the dictionary is the word-list, the gloss of "hard" or foreign words assembled to help the medieval reader with a difficult text. In Latin manuscripts of important works, English monks wrote marginal glosses in Latin and English, explaining the meanings of unfamiliar Latin terms. In the fourteenth and fifteenth centuries, collections of these glosses were separately compiled, to help students read

important books, and to help the English scholar discover the proper Latin term for an English idea. Hence the *glossarium* was a first in the lineage of modern English dictionaries.

3. During the sixteenth and seventeenth centuries, Englishmen were traveling, exploring, studying, and doing business all over Europe, the Near East, and even the New World, and to help them make their way, experienced people began to put together English–foreign-language phrase books and dictionaries. Some of the earliest and best were for English-French, English-Spanish, and English-Italian.

4. Still another practical book resulted from Renaissance interest in the English vocabulary. Many scholars, irked by the seeming inelegance and imprecision of English, began consciously to manufacture English words on Latin, Greek, Italian, and French models. They borrowed especially from the classical languages: words like *contiguate, splendente, adjuvate,* and *panion* were coined or borrowed in great numbers, and the reader soon needed help. While many of these coinages soon disappeared, others remained in the language, so that today we find it difficult to imagine how strange such words as *relinquish, antique,* and *illustrate* must have looked to sixteenth-century readers. The dictionary of "hard words" was created to help.

5. The wholesale manufacture of new words also contributed to the development of dictionaries indirectly: men of letters were split into two camps during the Renaissance—those who favored and those who hated these coinages. This quarrel over "inkhorn terms" focused attention on the vocabulary and gave impetus to the production of lists and essays from both attackers and defenders. More groundwork was being laid for the production of the modern dictionary.

6. Finally, the rise of the middle class, and later, the industrial revolution produced still other markets for dictionaries—the same practical markets which letter-writers and books of etiquette were serving; somehow they were all to help the new bourgeoisie acquire the gentle patina.

The First Great Modern Dictionaries

We have space here to mention only four of the great dictionaries which first wove together the several threads described above; two were English, two American; all four have shaped the art of lexicography as we know it today.

1. Nathaniel Bailey's *Universal Etymological Dictionary of the English Language* (1721) was the first. It was "the first to pay attention to current usage, the first to feature etymology, the first to syllabify, the first

to give illustrative quotations, the first to include illustrations, and the first to indicate pronounciation." [7]

2. Samuel Johnson used Bailey's work and many others when he wrote his own great *Dictionary* (1755). He began his enormous task in the hope of recording, repairing and fixing once and for all the vocabulary of English. When he had finished, he ruefully concluded that change was inexorable; he came to a view of the lexicographer's task which is still one of the most accurate—and poignant. He tried to fix orthography, and he used English authors of reputation for his illustrative citations. His work is often idiosyncratic and sometimes erratic, especially in the etymologies. But above all, he made a truly comprehensive dictionary, and he wrote good definitions, avoiding circularity and seeking precision and clarity. His book was the first great "authority," and in its many subsequent editions and imitations, both in Britain and the United States, it came to play the very role of arbiter that Johnson had originally intended but had despaired, in the end, of achieving.

3. In 1828, leaning heavily on Johnson and Bailey, Noah Webster published the first of his "big" dictionaries, *An American Dictionary of the English Language*. In his early dictionaries, Webster too had a program: he sought to distinguish American spelling, pronunciation, and meaning from those of British English. Like Johnson, Webster greatly improved the style of definition-writing, seeking succinct, accurate statements and using American illustrations wherever he could. His later editions were more conservative, and he gave up his spelling reforms, but like his famous spelling book, Webster's later dictionaries became household words, particularly after the Merriam family began to publish them. His name, more than any other, is still synonymous with *dictionary*.

4. One of the main reasons American lexicography pushed forward so rapidly in the nineteenth century was the great commercial rivalry which grew between Webster and Joseph Worcester, whose *Comprehensive Pronouncing Dictionary of the English Language* appeared in 1830. It leaned heavily on Webster's 1828 edition, but, as Harold Whitehall points out, it "was characterized by the additions of new words, a more conservative spelling, brief, well-phrased definitions, full indication of pronunciation by means of diacritics, use of stress marks to divide syllables, and lists of synonyms (26:xxxiii)." From the 1840's on, the Webster and Worcester dictionaries, first edited by the famous men themselves and later by their successors in their names, multiplied and grew in fame. In the end, Webster's successors won out, but not before both dictionaries were placed throughout this westward-marching nation. The frontier brought with it the first popular movements in education, and with the Bible and Webster's "Blue Back Speller" as both the tools and the sym-

bols of this zeal for universal literacy, reliance on "the dictionary" as the arbiter of taste, the judge of meaning, and the authority on spelling and pronunciation was permanently fastened on the American character.

Lexicography Today

English today offers its users the most complete and varied array of dictionaries in the world. We can give here only the briefest account of the variety, but what is most significant is the ready availability of continually updated dictionaries of the very highest quality, and at relatively low cost. We lean heavily on our dictionaries, and competition keeps them good.

We have fine *historical dictionaries;* the *Oxford English Dictionary* [8] is the greatest of these. This ten-volume work prints long entries with dated citations in context for every word in the vocabularly. A work of enormous scholarship, its qualities have become the model for all historical considerations of the vocabulary of English. No lexicographer can work without the *Oxford* at his elbow. Its work on pronunciation is British and minimal and its supplement is dated 1933; but for history it is unmatched. Other historical dictionaries use it as a point of departure: for American English differences from British English, we have the four-volume *A Dictionary of American English on Historical Principles* (5), and Mathews' two-volume *Dictionary of Americanisms* (15). Historical dictionaries of Middle English, Early Modern English, and Scottish are all either being published or prepared. For accurate, detailed, complete information about the history of an English word, these are the works to consult.

Our commercial *unabridged dictionaries* are a unique type. The most famous currently is the Merriam-Webster Third Edition of the *New International* (24). At their best, the great commercial unabridged dictionaries offer incredibly complete information about spellings, pronuncitations, meanings, usage, synonyms, and brief etymologies. Some are encyclopedic, like the old *Century* (3) of 1889 and 1909; though badly out of date now, the *Century* is remembered as displaying the highest standard for the quality of its definitions. Most of the commercial houses which make unabridged dictionaries maintain files and revise regularly; almost all produce smaller, abridged dictionaries, based on the big book.

Desk and *collegiate* dictionaries are also uniquely American, one-volume books which are the most widely used of all. Their virtues are their currency and their compactness. Competition keeps their editors revising regularly, and they are noted for excellent definitions, up-to-the-

minute information on spelling, pronunciation, and usage, and a surprising amount of encyclopedic information. The current best * are
probably Merriam-Webster's *Seventh New Collegiate* (22), Funk and
Wagnalls' *Standard College Dictionary* (9), the *American College Dictionary* (1), and the college editions of *Webster's New World Dictionary
of the American Language* (23) and the Random House dictionary (19).
Each has its peculiar virtues and defects, but competition keeps each trying to outdo the others. Sold on the strength of the American need for
reassurance, they are a remarkable kind of lexicography.

There are also dozens of other kinds of dictionaries, each for a
special purpose: graded school dictionaries abound, many of them of
good quality; the dictionaries of usage, which (like the old "hard word"
books) deal only with problems which they discuss in little illustrated
essays, have multiplied; there are special-vocabulary dictionaries, covering the technical vocabulary of special fields; and there are dictionaries
of synonyms, to name only a few.

Conclusion

Not just the usual problems plague the lexicographer today—the
selection of entries, the documentation of his findings, the wording of
definitions, and the like; he also faces a very basic decision when he sets
out to make a dictionary. On the one hand, modern linguistic science
has given him clear evidence that the best dictionary is the one which
records the language as it is, warts and all. Where the pattern of usage is
unclear or divided, he must let his readers know that this is so. On the
other hand, however, the layman insists that there must be right answers
to his questions about language, and he expects the dictionary to give
him these. The lexicographer expects to *describe* standards; the layman
wants him to *set* them, and he uses his dictionary as though it were a
law book, not a report of current custom. The quarrel over *Webster III*
illustrates this quandary all too clearly: the scholar of language wants
full information, wants shade and nuance clearly delineated—not just
in meanings, but in every aspect of every entry. He wants as many minority reports as possible. The layman (and many other professional users
of language too) insists that the dictionary ought to set a standard to
which everyone may adhere.

The lexicographer is not a scientist; he is a writer, an editor, an
artist. He must draw conclusions, and even as he tries to distinguish two

---

* Since this essay was written, another good desk dictionary has appeared: *The American
Heritage Dictionary of the English Language,* edited by William Morris (New York:
American Heritage Publishing Co. and Houghton Mifflin Company, 1969).

shades of meaning in a definition, he is creating, not just reporting. Yet he must be careful not to display his personal crotchets about the language he wishes English were, to the detriment of his description of the English we actually have.

To use his dictionaries, therefore, teacher and student alike need full awareness (*a*) of how he works, (*b*) of the information he has to work with, and (*c*) of the problems of choice posed him by limitations of taste, space, and time. Once he has that, any user of dictionaries can use them intelligently, both as a guide to what the world expects of his English, and as a clear picture of how others actually use theirs. Among other things, he will realize that, depending on his purpose, not one, but many dictionaries can help him.

Teaching Language History in the Schools Today

We are having a kind of Renaissance in interest in language history today. As suggested at many points in the discussions above, there are many kinds of history of language and language-related matters, and nearly all can be made interesting to the student.

Two things are happening: first, through the teacher-training programs, summer linguistic institutes, and in-service programs, the English teachers themselves are studying the history of the language, filling themselves with lore. And such study stresses everywhere the need both for information and for generalization; it lays emphasis both on trends and on the importance of specific investigations.

Second, the teachers in turn are changing the curriculum. Materials are being developed, texts being written, and lessons being created to introduce pupils at all levels to the various aspects of the history of their language. The curriculum centers in several states are publishing materials to aid the teacher. School libraries are acquiring the dictionaries and reference works. And teachers themselves have come to see what enormous curiosity nearly everyone, properly stimulated, has.

In its own right, and for the kind of social perceptivity we seek to foster in school children, the study is both fascinating and good. And it also directs attention at a major problem of the schools: to manipulate his language well—a major goal of education—the student seems likely to profit a great deal from learning how his language came to be.

NOTES

1. The first section of this chapter relies heavily on three good histories of English: Baugh (2); Robertson and Cassidy (20); and Pyles (18).
2. The best account is by Marckwardt (14).
3. The best account is by Baugh (2:240–305).
4. In this section, I have relied heavily on Gleason (10:67–87).
5. Gleason cites three modern works in this tradition: Zandvoort (27); Jespersen (13); and Curme (7, 6).
6. A useful summary is found on pages 4–9 of Guralnik (11).
7. Guralnik (11) as reprinted in *Harbrace Guide to Dictionaries* (26:4).
8. This dictionary (17), sometimes called the *New English Dictionary*, was published in ten volumes between 1884 and 1927; a corrected reissue with a one-volume supplement was published in 1933.

BIBLIOGRAPHY

1. *The American College Dictionary*. New York: Random House, 1947 and later printings.
2. Baugh, Albert C. *A History of English Language*. 2d ed. New York: Appleton-Century-Crofts, 1957.
3. *The Century Dictionary*. New York: Century Co., 1889.
4. Chomsky, Noam A. *Syntactic Structures*. Janua Lingurum, Series Minor, No. 4, The Hague: Mouton & Co., 1957.
5. Craigie, Sir William, and Hulbert, James R. (eds.). *A Dictionary of American English on Historical Principles*. Chicago: University of Chicago Press, 1938.
6. Curme, G. O. *Parts of Speech and Accidence: A Grammar of the English Language*. Vol. 2. Boston: D. C. Heath & Co., 1953.
7. ———. *Syntax: A Grammar of English Usage*. Vol. 3. Boston: D. C. Heath & Co., 1931.
8. Francis, W. Nelson. *The Structure of American English*. New York: Ronald Press, 1958.
9. *Funk and Wagnalls' Standard College Dictionary*, Text ed. New York: Harcourt, Brace & World, 1963 and later printings.
10. Gleason, H. A., Jr. "English Grammars" in his *Linguistics and English Grammar*, pp. 67–87. New York: Holt, Rinehart & Winston, 1965.
11. Guralnik, David B. *The Making of a New Dictionary*. Cleveland: World Publishing Co., 1953.
12. Hill, Archibald. *Introduction to Linguistic Structures: From Sound to Sentence in English*. New York: Harcourt, Brace & World, 1958.
13. Jespersen, J. O. H. *Essentials of English Grammar*. New York: Henry Holt & Co., 1933.
14. Marckwardt, Albert H. *American English*. New York: Oxford University Press, 1958.
15. Mathews, Mitford M. (ed.). *Dictionary of Americanisms on Historical Principles*. Chicago: University of Chicago Press, 1951.

16. Nida, Eugene. *A Synopsis of English Syntax*. Norman, Okla.: Summer Institute of Linguistics, 1960.
17. *Oxford English Dictionary*. 10 vols. Oxford: Clarendon Press, 1884–1927 (one-volume supplement published in 1933).
18. Pyles, Thomas. *The Origins and Development of the English Language*. New York: Harcourt, Brace & World, 1964.
19. *The Random House Dictionary of the English Language*. New York: Random House, 1966.
20. Robertson, Stuart, and Cassidy, Frederic G. *The Development of Modern English*. 2d ed. New York: Prentice-Hall, 1954.
21. Trager, George L., and Smith, Henry Lee, Jr. *An Outline of English Structure*. Studies in Linguistics, Occasional Papers, No. 3, reprinted. Washington: American Council of Learned Societies, 1957.
22. *Webster's Seventh New Collegiate Dictionary*. Text ed. Springfield, Mass.: G. & C. Merriam Co., 1963 and later printings.
23. *Webster's New World Dictionary of the American Language*. College ed. Cleveland: World Publishing Co., 1953 and later printings.
24. *Webster's Third New International Dictionary of the English Language*. Springfield, Mass.: G. & C. Merriam Co., 1961.
25. Whitehall, Harold. "Introduction," *Webster's New World Dictionary of the American Language*. College ed. Cleveland: World Publishing Co., 1960.
26. Wilson, Kenneth G., Hendrickson, R. H., and Taylor, Peter Alan. *Harbrace Guide to Dictionaries*. New York: Harcourt, Brace & World, 1963.
27. Zandvoort, R. W. *A Handbook of English Grammar*. London: Longmans, 1957.

ALBERT H. MARCKWARDT

The Language of the Colonists

In considering the history and development of American English we must remember that the courageous bands who ventured westward into the unknown with Captain John Smith or on board the *Mayflower,* as well as those who followed them later in the seventeenth century, were speaking and writing the English language as it was currently employed in England. Consequently, whatever linguistic processes operated to produce the differences between American and British English which exist today must either have taken place in American English after the colonists settled on this continent or have occurred in British English after the emigrants left their homeland. Or, as a third possibility, there may have been changes in both divisions of the language after the period of settlement. We cannot, however, escape the conclusion of original identity and subsequent change.

Our first concern, therefore, is with the kind of English spoken by Smith's Virginians, Calvert's Marylanders, the Plymouth Fathers, the Bostonians of the Massachusetts Bay Colony, Roger Williams' Rhode Islanders, and Penn's Quakers. What was the state of the language at the time they left the shores of their native England?

The answer to this entails making a comparison between the memorable dates of our early colonial history with those pertinent to the English literary scene throughout the seventeenth century. It shows, for example, that Jonson was at the height of his career and that Shakespeare was still writing when Jamestown was settled. Plymouth Colony was founded before the publication of Shakespeare's First Folio and less than a decade after the completion of the Authorized Version of the Bible.

Dryden, who is often called the father of modern prose, was not born until after the settlement of the second colony in New England. His

From *American English.* © 1958 by Oxford University Press, Inc. Reprinted by permission of the publisher.

Essay of Dramatic Poesy was not written until the capture of New York by the English, nor were the essays of Cowley, equally modern in style and temper. The publication date of *Paradise Lost* is somewhat later, and that of *Pilgrim's Progress* actually follows King Philip's War in point of time. I mention these in particular because we often think of these last two works as indicative of the same kind of dissent against the Anglican Church as that which is reflected in the colonial settlement, particularly in the north. Yet Massachusetts, Connecticut, and Rhode Island were all established and flourishing by the time these books appeared. Even such late prose representative of Elizabethan exuberance, complication, involution, and to some extent lack of discipline as Burton's *Anatomy of Melancholy* and Browne's *Religio Medici* postdate the establishment of the early New England settlements.

The émigrés who accompanied Smith and Bradford had learned their native language long before the years 1607 and 1620 respectively. Many of them were mature; some were old. Even a man of forty on the Jamestown expedition would presumably have learned to speak English about 1570; John Rolfe, the future husband of Pocahontas, acquired his native tongue probably in 1587. A young man of twenty-one, John Alden for example, in the Mayflower company must have learned English at the height of Shakespeare's career; Miles Standish, when Shakespeare was beginning to write. In short, the earliest English colonists in the New World were speaking Elizabethan English, the language of Shakespeare, Lyly, Marlowe, Lodge, and Green, when they came to America—not the measurably different English of Dryden, Defoe, and Bunyan. This is important and necessary for our understanding of some of the distinctive features which American English was to develop later on.

Next, what was the general state of Elizabethan English? How many people spoke it? The population of England, excluding Ireland and Scotland, in Shakespeare's time has been estimated at 4,460,000. This is a little more than the present population of Massachusetts, somewhat less than that of Michigan. Of these, probably 200,000 lived in London in 1600; the population in 1605 is given as 224,275. This is approximately the population of Syracuse, New York, or Oklahoma City. These people and possibly 25,000 more in the immediate vicinity spoke London English, the regional variety which was in the process of becoming a standard for the English-speaking world as a whole.

Naturally the language sounded somewhat different from its twentieth-century counterpart. Certain though not all of these differences provide us with a partial explanation of the current variations in pronunciation between British and American English. For one thing, many words which are now pronounced with the vowel of *meat* had, at the time of the earliest settlements in America, the quality of present-day English *mate*. In fact, Londoners were accustomed to hear both the *ee* and the *ay* sounds in such words as *meat, teach, sea, tea, lean,* and *beard.* The conservative *ay* pronunciation continued in the language as late as the time of Pope. On occasion Shakespeare was capable of rhyming *please* with *knees* and at other times with *grace.* Without this double pronunciation a speech such as that by Dromio, "Marry sir, she's the Kitchin wench, & al *grease (grace)*" would have lost its punning effect.

It is quite possible that words which today have the vowel of *mate* were also pronounced at times with the vowel of *sand.* In addition to the play on the words *grease* and *grace* cited in the foregoing paragraph, there is in *All's Well* another punning passage involving a common or highly similar pronunciation of *grace* and *grass:*

> CLOWN: Indeed sir she was the sweete margerom of the sallet or rather the hearbe of grace.
> LAFEW: They are not hearbes you knave, they are nose-hearbes.
> CLOWN: I am no great Nebuchadnezar sir, I have not much skill in grace.

A rhyme such as the following from *Venus and Adonis* suggests the same conclusion:

> Even so poor birds, deceived with painted grapes . . .
> Even so she languisheth in her mishaps.

There was undoubtedly quite as much fluctuation in words which are generally spelled with *oo;* those of the *food, good,* and *flood* classes respectively. It is only recently that the pronunciation of many of these words has become standardized. All three of these words constitute one of Shakespeare's rhymes, and a half-century later Dryden rhymed *flood* with *mood* and *good.* Even today certain words of this class (*roof, room, root, hoof, coop, soot,* etc.) are pronounced variously in different parts of the United States.

At the time of which we are writing, the vowel of *cut* had but recently developed in London speech and was not yet a feature of all the English dialects. Combinations of *ir, er,* and *ur* in words like *bird, learn,* and *turn* had not long before coalesced into a vowel which was more like the sound to be heard over most of the United States today than that which is characteristic of southern British English. Contemporary pronunciation was far from settled in words like *clerk,* which seemed to be classed part of the time with the sound of *dark* and at other times with the vowel of *jerk.* Moreover, this variation affected many more words than it does now. Shakespeare rhymed *convert* with *art, serve* with *carve, heard* with *regard.*

In addition, the language at that time had no sound like the stressed vowel of present-day *father* or *calm.* The diphthongs characteristic of such words as *house* and *loud* had, instead of the *ah* first element commonly employed today, a sound something like the final vowel of *Cuba.* The whole diphthong was pronounced in a manner quite similar to that which may be heard at the present time in tidewater Virginia or in the Toronto area. The diphthong in words like *bite* and *bide* began with this same neutral element. The so-called short *o* sound of *cot* and *fog* was always pronounced with the lips somewhat rounded, as in Modern English *fall.*

Nor were the stress patterns of Shakespeare's English absolutely identical with those of the modern period. A line such as "The light will show, character'd in my brow," indicates clearly that in such a trisyllabic word as *character'd,* the stress had not yet shifted to the first syllable. A good many two-syllable words which now stress the first, at that time had the accent on the second. Note, "And there I'll rest, as after much *turmoil.*" Many derivatives in *-able* had a distinct stress, at least secondary in value, on the suffix. A line such as "What *acceptable* audit canst thou leave?" can scarcely be read in any other fashion.

Many words show a double stress pattern: *sincere* with stress at times on the first and at times on the second syllable; *confiscate* on occasion has initial stress, and elsewhere on the second syllable. It is probably fair to say that just as with vowel quality, the language during the Elizabethan period permitted somewhat more latitude than it does today.

It must be kept in mind, moreover, that the pronunciations which have just been discussed reflect only the language practices of the inhabitants of London and its environs, constituting approximately 5 per cent of the five million who spoke English at that time. The remaining 95 per cent spoke the regional or provincial dialects. Those who live in the United States find it hard to conceive of the extent to which regional dialects may differ even today within an area no larger than one of our moderate-size states.

At the present time, to select just a single instance, a word such as *about* will be pronounced with the stressed vowel of *bite* in Devon, with the vowel of *boot* along the Scottish border, with the vowel of *father* and a final consonant more like *d* than *t* in London Cockney, and with a pronunciation something like *abaeut* in Norfolk.

To anyone who has grown up in a tradition of relative linguistic uniformity over a territory virtually three million square miles in area, such differences in speech present in a country only one-sixtieth as large are startling, to say the least. But in the England of today, regional dialects are confined to a relatively small portion of the population as compared with three centuries ago. There can be little question about the wide prevalence of dialect and the general lack of uniformity of speech among the vast majority of the settlers of the seventeenth century.

Seventeenth-century English differed from its modern counterpart in other aspects of speech as well. Although the language had in general developed most of the inflections which are used in present-day English—the noun plurals, the object form *them* in the plural pronoun, the past tense and past participle forms of the weak verb—a few interesting earlier features still remained. Among these were the double forms of the pronoun of address: *thou* and *ye* or *you*. Because the distribution of these was governed partly by considerations of social rank and in part on the basis of emotional overtones, their very presence in the language made for a subtlety which today must be achieved through quite different means. Note, for example, in the following well-known passage from the first part of *Henry IV*, how the choice of pronouns reflects Hotspur's shift of mood from jesting concealment to stern warning, concluding with a gentler and more intimate tone:

> Come, wilt *thou* see me ride?
> And when I am o'horseback, I will swear
> I love *thee* infinitely. But hark *you*, Kate;
> I must not have *you* henceforth question me
> Whither I go, nor reason whereabout.
> Whither I must, I must; and, to conclude,
> This evening must I leave *you*, gentle Kate.
> I know *you* wise; but yet no farther wise
> Than Harry Percy's wife. Constant *you* are,
> But yet a woman; and for secrecy,
> No lady closer; for I well believe
> *Thou* wilt not utter what *thou* dost not know;
> And so far will I trust *thee*, gentle Kate.

And again in Kate's preceding speech but one, her change from exaggeration to gentle entreaty is indicated in precisely the same manner.

> Come, come, *you* paraquito, answer me
> Directly unto this question that I ask.
> In faith, I'll break *thy* little finger, Harry,
> And if *thou* wilt not tell me all things true.

Actually, at one point slightly later than Shakespeare's time, this matter of the second personal pronoun became a politico-religious issue.

The Quakers, committed to a belief in the innate equality of all men, interpreted the duality of the pronoun of address as a negation of that equality and argued, quite intemperately at times, for a return to an older state of the language where the two forms were differentiated solely on the basis of number. In the following passage, George Fox, the founder and leader of the sect, set forth his views in no uncertain terms.

> Do not they speak false English, false Latine, false Greek . . . and false to the other Tongues, . . . that doth not speak *thou* to *one,* what ever he be, Father, Mother, King, or Judge; is he not a Novice and Unmannerly, and an Ideot and a Fool, that speaks *You* to *one,* which is not to be spoken to a *singular,* but to many? O Vulgar Professors and Teachers, that speaks Plural when they should Singular. . . . Come you Priests and Professors, have you not learnt your Accidence?

It is worth noting that the English language did eventually go along with Fox's democratic notions by giving up the pronoun differentiation based upon social status, but in so doing, ironically selected the form which he considered inappropriate for the task.

This double supply of pronouns also carried with it an accompanying difference in verb structure, for *thou* as subject regularly demanded a verb ending in *-est.* *Ye* or *you* as subjects were accompanied merely by the simple or root form of the verb. Thus we would have had at this time *thou teachest* but *ye* or *you teach, thou knowest* but *you know.* After the *thou* forms fell into disfavor, so too did the verb inflections in *-est,* leaving the second person singular of the verb identical with the first person and with all forms of the plural.

In addition Elizabethan English represents a period of change from an earlier *-eth* inflection for the third person singular of the verb to the *-s* forms characteristic of the language today. There is an interesting difference here between the practice of Shakespeare and that of the contemporary King James Version of the Bible. The latter regularly uses *-eth:* "He maketh me to lie down in green pastures." In his ordinary dramatic prose, Shakespeare employs *-s* regularly for all verbs except *have* and *do,* which retain the archaic *hath* and *doth* (the latter only occasionally) presumably because these were learned as individual forms early in life by the average speaker instead of as part of an over-all pattern.

Even here, however, one must exercise due caution in interpreting the *-eth* spellings. In the middle of the seventeenth century one Richard Hodges wrote *A Special Help to Orthographie,* which consisted chiefly in listing words "alike in sound but unlike both in their signification and writing." Among the homophonic pairs which appear in this treatise are *roweth* and *rose, wrights,* and *righteth,* Mr. *Knox* and *knocketh.* He goes on to say in explanation:

Therefore, whensoever *eth* cometh in the end of any word, wee may pronounce it sometimes as *s,* and sometimes like *z,* as in these words, namely,
in *bolteth it,* and *boldeth it,* which are commonly pronounc't, as if they
were written thus, *bolts* it, and *bolds* it: save onely in such words, where
either *c, s, sh, ch, g,* or *x* went before it: as in *graceth, pleaseth, washeth,*
matcheth, rageth, taxeth: for these must still remaine as two syllables. How-
beit, if men did take notice, how they use to speak, in their ordinary
speech to one another, they might plainly perceive, that in stead of
graceth, they say *graces,* and so they pronounce al other words of this
kinde, accordingly.

Unquestionably the best way to acquire a feeling for many of the
differences between the language of today and that of the age of Eliza-
beth is to observe with some care a selection of one of the earliest examples of what might be called American English. The following selection
from William Bradford's *History of Plimoth Plantation* will serve the
purpose:

In these hard and difficulte beginnings they found some discontents and
murmurings arise amongst some, and mutinous speeches and carriages in
other; but they were soone quelled and overcome by the wisdome, patience, and just and equall carrage of things by the Gov[erno]r and better
part, which cleave faithfully togeather in the maine. But that which was
most sadd and lamentable was, that in 2 or 3 moneths time halfe of their
company dyed, espetialy in Jan: and February, being the depth of winter,
and wanting houses and other comforts; being infected with the scurvie and
other diseases, which this long voiage and their inacomodate condition has
brought upon them; so as ther dyed some times 2 or 3 of a day, in the
aforesaid time; that of 100 and odd persons, scarce 50 remained. And of
these in the time of most distres, ther was but 6 or 7 sound persons, who,
to their great comendations be it spoken, spared no pains, night nor day,
but with abundance of toil and hazard of their owne health, fetched them
woode, made them fires, drest them meat, made their beads, washed their
lothsome cloaths, cloathed and uncloathed them; in a word, did all the
homly and necessarye offices for them which dainty and quesie stomacks
cannot endure to hear named; and all this willingly and cherfully, without any grudging in the least, shewing herin their true love unto their
freinds and bretheren. A rare example and worthy to be remembered.
Tow of these 7 were Mr. William Brewster, ther reverend Elder, and
Myles Standish, ther Captain and Military comander, unto whom my selfe,
and many others, were much beholden in our low and sicke condition. And
yet the Lord so upheld these persons, as in this generall calamity they were
not at all infected either with sickness, or lamnes. And what I have said
of these, I may say of many others who dyed in this generall visitation,
and others yet living, that whilst they had health, yea, or any strength con-

tinuing, they were not wanting to any that had need of them. And I doute not but their recompence is with the Lord.

But I may not hear pass by an other remarkable passage not to be forgotten. As this calamitie fell among the passengers that were to be left here to plant, and were hasted a shore and made to drinke water, that the sea-men might have the more bear, and one in his sickness desiring but a small can of beere, it was answered, that if he were their owne father he should have none; the disease begane to fall amongst them also, so as allmost halfe of their company dyed before they went away, and many of their officers and lustyest men, as the boatson, gunner, 3 quarter-maisters, the cooke, and others. At which the m[aste]r was something strucken and sent to the sick a shore and tould the Gov[erno]r he should send for beer for them that had need of it, though he drunke water homward bound.

Most noticeable, perhaps, in the passage just quoted are a number of words no longer current in the language. Among them are *inacomodate* and *hasted. Yea, unto,* and *beholden* are rarely employed except in certain set phrases and at times in religious connections. Other words have come to be used in contexts quite unlike those in which they appear in this passage. For instance, *carriages* no longer signifies behavior in the abstract sense; *clothed,* here meaning the specific act of dressing, has become more general in its use. *Offices* is used here in the sense of services; *lustiest* to mean healthiest. Though by no means inclusive, these examples suggest the changes which have taken place in the English vocabulary during the last three centuries, both with respect to the words it comprises and the meanings of these words.

Likewise, certain changes in the forms of words have taken place. Almost at the beginning of the passage, *other* was used as a plural pronoun, although the modern form *others* appeared later on. *Scarce,* in an adverbial use, indicates that the fetish of the *-ly* ending was somewhat less strong at that time than it is at present. As might be expected, the most pronounced differences are in the verb forms, where *clave* and *drunke* appear as past tenses and *strucken* as a past participle.

Differences in syntax are even more numerous. The plural form of the abstractions *discontents* and *murmurings* would be unlikely to appear in present-day usage, as would *commendations.* Closely connected with this same problem of number is the lack of agreement between subject and verb in, "There was but 6 or 7 sound persons." The word *as* in constructions like, "so as ther dyed," and "as in this generall calamity," would today be replaced by *that.* At the same time, certain pronominal uses of *that* in this selection would unquestionably call for *who* in the language of today.

Even more striking than any of these features is the sentence structure. In general the sentences lack unity and are replete with dangling phrases and clauses. The first sentence in the selection contains fifty-three words, the second eighty-three, and the third attains a total of one hundred and six. These are all long according to modern standards. Ironically enough, the third sentence is followed by an eight word fragment that does not fit the modern pattern of the conventional sentence at all. In the second sentence the parallelism of the phrases introduced by *being* and *wanting* is faulty. The majority of the sentences are without coherence and direction in the present sense of these terms.

The proper conclusion, however, is not that Bradford was a bad writer—in fact he was not—but that there were differences between seventeenth-century prose and our own. Some of these differences are purely a matter of historical development. The roots of our modern forms and practices were already in the language. It is even more important to recognize this as a period prior to a certain codification, settlement, one might almost say a jelling, of English written prose. A man's spelling was still his own concern, as is clearly evident, and so too, to some extent, were his sentences. If this codification or jelling took place after the two speech areas, England and America, were already separated, it is more than possible that the settling processes might not work out in the same way in both places.

Consequently, since the earliest American settlers employed Elizabethan English, it is the highly variable and complex character of that medium that provides us with an explanation of the beginning of the divergence in the two great streams of our language. It remains to be seen how, and through what means, this divergence developed throughout the course of the intervening centuries.

CHARLES C. FRIES

A Classification of Grammatical Phenomena

In the attempt to gather, analyze, and record the significant facts from any such mass of material as the specimens here examined, one cannot depend upon general impressions and note only the special forms that attract attention. If he does, the unusual forms and constructions or those that differ from his own practice will inevitably impress him as bulking much larger in the total than they really are. Those forms and constructions that are in harmony with the great mass of English usage will escape his notice. This seems to me to be a fundamental difficulty with the earlier editions of Mencken's *The American Language* and accounts in part for the difference between his representations of "The Common Speech" and the results given here. Mencken, for example, prints in the 1924 edition of his book the "Declaration of Independence in American," as one of his "Specimens of the American Vulgate" or, as he says, "translated into the language they use every day." [1]

> When things get so balled up that the people of a country have to cut loose from some other country, and go it on their own hook, without asking no permission from nobody, excepting maybe God Almighty, then they ought to let everybody know why they done it, so that everybody can see they are on the level, and not trying to put nothing over on nobody.
>
> All we got to say on this proposition is this: first, you and me is as good as anybody else, and maybe a damn sight better; second, nobody ain't got no right to take away none of our rights; every man has got a right

to live, to come and go as he pleases, and to have a good time however he likes, so long as he don't interfere with nobody else. That any government that don't give a man these rights ain't worth a damn; also, people ought to choose the kind of government they want themselves, and nobody else ought to have no say in the matter.

In the 176 words here quoted there are, for example, five uses of the multiple negative. Every negative statement except one has two or three negative particles. This excessive use of the multiple negative construction cannot be found in any actual specimens of Vulgar English. Even in Old English, where the use of the double negative was normal, less than 35 per cent of the total negative statements occur with multiple negative particles. Such a complete use of the multiple negative construction as Mencken displays will only be heard from those who consciously attempt to caricature Vulgar English. Most of the comic writers produce their language effects in similar fashion by seizing upon a few such especially noticeable or spectacular forms and expressions of Vulgar English and then working them excessively. Such representations of Vulgar English become grossly inaccurate both because the amount of deviation from the standard forms is greatly exaggerated and also because many of the forms characteristic of Vulgar English that are not sufficiently picturesque to be funny are completely ignored.[2]

In order to avoid errors of this kind we have in the study of this material tried first to record *all* the facts in each category examined. For example, every preterit and past participle form was copied on a separate slip of paper in order that we might determine not only the kind of variety that existed in actual usage but also something of the relative amounts of that variation. In similar fashion all instances with forms expressing number in verbs and in demonstratives used attributively as well as in substantives were gathered to form the basis of the summaries we offer concerning concord in number. We do not assume that the absolute frequency of occurrence of particular forms in the limited material here examined is in itself significant; we have simply tried to make sure of the *relative* frequency of the language usages appearing here in order to give proportion to our picture of actual practice and to prevent a false emphasis upon unusual or picturesquely interesting items.

This approach to the gathering and analysis of the language facts to be observed in our material made necessary some system of classification by which those facts of essentially similar nature should be inevitably brought together. We were seeking to record as completely as possible the methods used by the English language to express grammatical ideas and to discover the precise differences in these methods as employed by the various social dialects. The outlines of our grouping quite naturally settled themselves. The facts gathered in an early preliminary study of our material all fitted into a classification made up of three general types of devices to express grammatical ideas.

First of all there were the *forms* of words. The way in which the word *tables* differs from the word *table* indicates one grammatical idea; the way in which *roasted* differs from *roast,* or *grew* from *grow* expresses another; and the way in which *harder* differs from *hard* shows another. These examples illustrate the expression of grammatical ideas by the *forms* of words. Other ideas, however, are also shown by word forms as *truth* differing from *true,* or *kindness* from *kind,* or *rapidly* from *rapid,* or *stigmatize* from *stigma,* or *national* from *nation,* or *writer* from *write.* These latter derivational forms will not be included here although it is difficult to draw an exact line between them and the grammatical forms with which we are especially concerned. It is enough for our purpose to point out that most of these derivational forms are, in Present-day English, chiefly vocabulary or word-formation matters rather than inflectional matters and that we have limited our study to grammatical structure and have excluded vocabulary. But these "forms of words" as we shall use them are interpreted broadly to include even entirely different words as *we* or *me* or *us* in relation to *I, went* in relation to *go,* and *worse* in relation to *bad.*[3]

Second, there were the uses of *function* words. These words frequently have very little meaning apart from the grammatical relationship they express. Examples are *of* in "A house *of* stone," or *with* in "He struck the animal *with* a rod," or *more* in "A *more* important battle," or *have* in "They *have* had their reward," or *going* in "He is *going* to go to New York." Many of the grammatical ideas formerly expressed by the *forms* of words are now expressed by such function words.

Third, there were the uses of *word order.* Word order is often an important item of the idiom of a language, but it is not always a grammatical device as it is in English. In Latin, for example, the periodic structure with the verb at the end occurs very frequently, but the word order in such a sentence as "Nero hominem interfecit" has nothing whatever to do with indicating the so-called "subject" and "object." The basic meaning of the Latin sentence remains unchanged with every possible order of these three words. In English, however, "Nero killed the man" and "The man killed Nero" express very different ideas and that difference comes to us solely through the order in which the words are placed. Some of the grammatical ideas formerly expressed in English by the forms of words are now expressed by *word order.*

All the language facts gathered from the letters here examined were classified in one of these three groups—the uses of the forms of words, the uses of function words, or the uses of word order—and there studied. In respect to each group the description will first set forth the practice of Group I or "standard" English and then indicate the deviations from that practice, characteristic of Group III, or of Group II and Group III combined. Some of the significance of these language facts will, however, be best revealed by showing them in relation to similar situations as they appeared in older stages of the English language, for even complete statistics of the relative frequency of two alternative forms in any single period of language history can never give us a guide as to the relative importance of those forms or the direction of change. For such purposes the statistics must be viewed in relation to the situation in a previous or in a later period. For example, if we were living at the close of the first quarter of the fifteenth century, the bare fact that the alternative pronoun forms *them* and *hem* were used with a relative frequency of approximately 20 per cent of *them* to 80 per cent of *hem* would tell us little without the knowledge that *hem* was the form that was being superseded and that the tendency to use *them* in its place had already progressed one fifth of the way along which the forms *they* and *their* had already gone much farther. In the effort therefore to make clear the significance of the records of contemporary English which formed the basis of this study it will frequently be necessary to picture the present usage against the background of the practice in older stages of the language. We shall try always to deal with the patterns of the language to which particular forms belong and to show the path along which these patterns have developed.

It will be clearly evident as we proceed that the three general types of grammatical processes in accord with which our language material has been classified are not now and have not been in the history of the English language thoroughly coordinate or of equal value. As a matter of fact any one of the three could have served quite adequately all necessary grammatical needs. Instead, they overlap in the expression of grammatical ideas and in some respects may be said to compete for the expression of the same ideas. The function-word method and the word-order method of expressing dative and accusative relationships have, for example, almost entirely displaced the inflectional method. In the early stages of the language there is no doubt that the use of the forms of words as a grammatical process was much more important than the grammatical uses of either word order or of function words. Some of the problems of usage in Present-day English arise where there is such a so-called conflict between two types of grammatical processes for the expression of a single grammatical idea. While, therefore, we shall classify and describe our language details in accord with the demands of each of the three types of grammatical processes indicated above, it will be necessary to discuss them in relation to the historical patterns with which they are connected and sometimes to refer to the use of a competing type of grammatical process for the expression of the same idea. . . .

NOTES

1. H. L. Mencken, *The American Language* (New York, Alfred A. Knopf, 3rd ed., 1924), p. 398. See, however, the following quotation from the 4th edition, 1936, Preface, p. vii: "I have also omitted a few illustrative oddities appearing in that edition [the 3rd edition]—for example, specimens of vulgar American by Ring W. Lardner and John V. A. Weaver and my own translations of the Declaration of Independence and Lincoln's Gettysburg Address. The latter two, I am sorry to say, were mistaken by a number of outraged English critics for examples of Standard American, or of what I proposed that Standard American should be. Omitting them will get rid of that misapprehension. . . ."

2. See also Professor Robert J. Menner's comments in his article "The Verbs of the Vulgate," *American Speech,* January, 1926, pp. 230–231. Concerning *The American Language* he says, "but Mencken seems to have gathered his forms from all kinds of sources, oral and written; it is impossible to distinguish those he has observed personally from those he has found in contemporary writers of comic stories. Furthermore, he gives the impression of preferring to record as characteristic of the common speech whatever is furthest removed from the language of litera ture. . . ."

Part of Professor Menner's remarks concerning the accuracy of the writers of comic stories follows: "Ring Lardner . . . employs only forms of the verb which are familiar, or at least conceivable, in colloquial speech. But he besprinkles the conversation of his characters with barbarisms much more plentifully and consistently than they occur in actual life. This is the inevitable exaggeration of comic art. 'He win 10 bucks,' is funnier than 'He won 10 bucks,' and Mr. Lardner now uses the preterite *win* almost consistently, though, according to my observation of oral practice, it is used, even in class D, only once out of ten times."

3. For a thorough analysis of the problem involved here see Leonard Bloomfield, *Language* (New York, Henry Holt and Co., 1933), pp. 207–246. On pages 222 and 223 occur the following statements: ". . . The structure of a complex word reveals first, as to the more immediate constituents, an outer layer of *inflectional* constructions, and then an inner layer of constructions of *word-formation*. In our last example [the word *actresses*], the outer, inflectional layer is represented by the construction of actress with [= ez] and the inner word formational layer by the remaining constructions, of *actor* with *-ess* and of *act* with [-r]. . . . Another peculiarity of inflection, in contrast with word-formation, is the rigid parallelism of underlying and resultant forms. Thus, nearly all English singular nouns underlie a derived plural noun, and, vice versa, nearly all English plural nouns are derived from a singular noun. Accordingly, English nouns occur, for the most

part, in parallel *sets of two;* a singular noun (*hat*) and a plural noun derived from the former (*hats*). Each such set of forms is called a *paradigmatic* set or *paradigm,* and each form in the set is called an *inflected form* or *inflection.* . . . It is this parallelism, also, which leads us to view entirely different phonetic forms, like *go: went,* as morphologically related (by suppletion): *go* as an infinitive (parallel, say, with *show*) and *went* as a past-tense form (parallel, then, with *showed*)."

PAUL ROBERTS

Phonemes

Definition of a Phoneme

English has a total of forty-five sound units called *phonemes*. A phoneme is not exactly a single sound. It is rather a collection of similar sounds which are likely to sound identical to the speaker of the language. For example, English has a phoneme /p/, which occurs in the words *pin, nip, spin, appear, upper.* All these "p" sounds are different. /p/ is not the same at the beginning of a word as at the end, not the same before a stressed syllable as after one, and so on. Yet these differences are not significant for English, and we who speak English have learned to ignore them.

In some languages these differences *are* significant. A speaker of Hindi or Korean, for example, would feel that the "p" in *pin* and the "p" in *spin* are not the same sound at all, for in these languages these sounds belong to separate phonemes. Such a person learning English would have to train himself to overlook this difference. On the other hand, we, if we were to learn Hindi or Korean, would have to train ourselves to recognize the difference and to react to it.

Languages differ widely in the number of phonemes they have. English, as we have said, has forty-five. Other languages have as few as eighteen or twenty or as many as seventy or eighty.

Vowels and Consonants

Of our forty-five English phonemes, twelve are intonation phonemes —units of stress, pitch, and juncture. . . . The other thirty-three are vowels and consonants—twenty-four consonants and nine vowels. This is for the language as a whole. Many individual speakers, however, have only seven or eight vowels.

We shall not try here to describe the mechanism by which the sounds are produced but shall instead focus our attention on the result. The key given below relates principally to the author's California speech. This key will serve well enough to indicate the consonants occurring the country over; in the vowels there is more variation, and some readers will probably use quite different vowels in some of the words given.

Here, then, is the key. Note that when we write phonemes, we put them in diagonal lines to distinguish them from letters of the ordinary alphabet.

/p/ The first sound in *pin*, second in *spin*, last in *nip*.

/t/ The first sound in *tick*, second in *stick*, last in *kit*.

/k/ The first sound in *cat*, second in *scat*, last (ck) in *tack*.

/b/ The first sound in *ban*, last in *nab*.

/d/ The first and last sounds in *dad*.

/g/ The first and last sounds in *gag*.

/c/ The first sound (ch) in *chin*, last (tch) in *watch*.

/j/ The first sound in *Jim* or *gin*, last (dge) in *fudge*.

/f/ The first sound in *fall*, last (gh) in *laugh*.

/θ/ The first sound (th) in *thick*, last (th) in *breath*.

/s/ The first sound in *sin*, last in *hiss*.

/š/ The first sound (sh) in *shake*, last (sh) in *smash*.

/v/ The first sound in *vine*, last (ve) in *give*.

/ð/ The first sound (th) in *then*, last (the) in *breathe*.

/z/ The first sound in *zeal*, last in *his*.

/ž/ The last sound (ge) in *rouge*, as most people say it; the middle consonant in *vision* or *measure*.

/m/ The first and last sounds in *mum*.

/n/ The first and last sounds in *Nan*.

/ŋ/ The last sound (ng) in *sing, hang, tongue*.

/l/ The first sound in *law*, last (ll) in *fall*.

/r/ The first and last sounds in *roar*. (But many speakers do not pronounce a final /r/ in *roar*.)

/y/ The first sound in *you*.

/w/ The first sound in *woo*.

/h/ The first sound in *his, hike, who*.

/i/ The vowel sound in *pit, bin, ship, tick, knit, fill, sing, pish, his, hiss*.

/e/ The vowel sound in *hep, beck, dead, beg, breath, flesh, strength*.

/æ/ The vowel sound in *nap, sack, bag, last, razz, rang, pal*.

/ɨ/ For many speakers the first vowel in *sugar* or *children*. Some speakers do not have this vowel except in syllables with weak stress, where it is very common, or before /r/, as in *sir, girl, fur*.

/ə/ The vowel sound in *but, dug, flood, tough, tongue*.

/a/ For the author, the vowel sound in *hot, cot, bomb, balm, rob, shock.* Many speakers have /ɔ/ in some of these words.

/u/ The vowel sound in *put, could, foot, pull, rook, stood.*

/o/ This does not occur except as part of a diphthong in most American speech. Some New Englanders have it in *home* or *whole.*

/ɔ/ For the author, the vowel sound in *law, wash, fought, caught, hog.* Some speakers have /a/ in some of these words.

Diphthongs

In addition to these simple sounds, English has a variety of diphthongs, consisting of one of the simple vowels plus a gliding sound. We represent the glide with /y/ or /w/, depending on what sort of glide it is. Here are some common diphthongs:

/iy/ The vowel sound in *he, heat, field, beam, beat, sneak, queen, clean.*

/ey/ The vowel sound in *way, rain, Spain, plain, blame, stay, scale, steak, snare.*

/ay/ The vowel sound in *my, sky, write, kind, style, mice.*

/ɔy/ The vowel sound in *boy, boil, coin, Troy, point.*

/aw/ The vowel sound in *out, bout, round, mouse, cow.*

/ow/ The vowel sound in *go, snow, rode, moan, drove.*

/uw/ The vowel sound in *who, moo, rude, tomb, cool, few.*

Many other diphthongs occur in the various dialects of English. You may have others in addition to or in place of these.

Now here are examples of words written in phonemic transcription. Some people might pronounce some of them differently. The pronunciations given are common, though not universal, in the Central and Western United States.

pick	/pik/	train	/treyn/	rough	/rəf/
rib	/rib/	laugh	/læf/	cuff	/kəf/
drive	/drayv/	dream	/driym/	bent	/bent/
hung	/həŋ/	pink	/piŋk/	scream	/skriym/
out	/awt/	toes	/towz/	boil	/bɔyl/
food	/fuwd/	sir	/sɨr/	quick	/kwik/
should	/šud/	suds	/sədz/	talked	/tɔkt/
gross	/grows/	full	/ful/	sticks	/stiks/
grows	/growz/	zone	/zown/	bags	/bægz/
maimed	/meymd/	veiled	/veyld/	hopes	/howps/
rouge	/ruwž/	judged	/jəjd/	chips	/cips/
nudge	/nəj/	youth	/yuwθ/	these	/ðyz/
vines	/vaynz/	thick	/θik/	then	/ðen/
wants	/wants/	thin	/θin/	crashed	/kræšt/

In words of more than one syllable, syllables with weak stress are likely to have the vowel /ɨ/. The vowel /ə/ often occurs under weak stress at the beginning and end of words. Other possibilities are:

father	/fáðɨr/	chicken	/cíkɨn/	measure	/méžɨr/
woman	/wúmin/	about	/əbáwt/	ended	/éndɨd/
women	/wímɨn/	event	/əvént/	whether	/hwéðɨr/
vision	/vížɨn/	sugar	/šúgɨr/	pretty	/prítiy/
meager	/míygɨr/	shambles	/šǽmbɨlz/	drowning	/dráwniŋ/
singing	/síŋiŋ/	reproach	/rɨprówc/	sofa	/sówfə/

ROBERT A. HALL, JR.

Analogy

Internal borrowing, or *analogy*, is the kind of change that takes place when a child says *foots* instead of *feet*, *oxes* instead of *oxen*, *sticked* instead of *stuck*, or *breaked* instead of *broke*. We usually call such forms as *foots, oxes, sticked, breaked* "mistakes" and all of us—even the most illiterate users of sub-standard English—train our children to say *feet*, not *foots*, and so on. Yet what lies at the root of these "mistakes" is an extremely widespread process, which we call *analogical replacement*. What has happened when the child has said *foots* or *sticked*? Simply this: he has heard and learned a whole host of "regular" formations—plural formations such as *root—roots, hat—hats, book—books, map—maps, box—boxes*, and past formations like *kick—kicked, lick—licked, trick—tricked, rake—raked*, in the hundreds and thousands. He has simply made his new formation of a plural for *foot* or *ox* by abstracting (unconsciously, for the most part) the "regular" ending *-s, -es* and adding it to *foot* or *ox*. Likewise, he has taken the "regular" past ending *-ed* or *breaked* "on the analogy" of other pasts like *kicked, raked*, and so on. He is making what we often call an *analogical new-formation*, by borrowing an element of linguistic form or construction (here the noun-plural suffix *-s -es* or the verb past suffix *-ed*) from one part of our linguistic structure (here the "regular" formations) and adding it to another (here the "irregular" forms). This is a kind of borrowing, just like external borrowing; but the source of borrowing is not somewhere outside but within the language itself, and so we call it internal borrowing.

Analogical changes of this kind are often presented in the shape of proportional formulas, with x standing for the new-formation, thus

hat : hats = foot : ("*hat* is to *hats* as *foot* is to *x*")
box : boxes = ox : x

$$kick : kicked = stick : x$$
$$rake : raked = break : x$$

Sometimes, objections are made to our statement of analogical replacements in a proportional formula, such as those we have just given; critics say that naive speakers would not be capable of exact enough reasoning to make up a formula of this sort and carry it out. There are two answers to this objection: (1) that what we are giving here is a description of what takes place, not a statement of reasoning that we might necessarily expect from a naive speaker, who speaks normally without abstract analysis and who habitually does perfectly many things he could not possibly describe; and (2) that even naive speakers from time to time are perfectly conscious of the basis for their analogical formations. The great Danish linguistician Otto Jespersen tells the story of a Danish child who should, according to normal Danish usage, have said *nikkede* "nodded" as the past of *nikker* "nod," but said *nak* instead on the analogy of *stak* "stuck," whose present is *stikker*. When the child was corrected, he immediately retorted *"Stikker —stak, nikker—nak,"* showing that he knew perfectly well on what analogy he had made the new past tense form, and stating it in the form of a proportion.

From the point of view of the present language, analogical new-formations like *oxes* or *taked* are "mistakes," forms that would be uttered only by children or others learning the language, or by adults when tired or flustered (that is, as "slips of the tongue"), and that would not be accepted by any native speaker at present. But there are always some forms with regard to which our usage is not fully settled, even that of normal adult native speakers of the language, and for which we may use first one and then another alternative. We have, for instance, the "irregular" plural formation *hoof—hooves,* and the "strong" past tenses *wake—woke, dive—dove;* yet we often hear and make regularized forms for these words: *hoofs, waked, dived.* That is to say, in some respects our usage is *fluctuating;* and in the course of time, we will gradually come to favor one competing form over the other (say, *dived* over *dove*), until at last one is triumphant and drives out the other completely in normal everyday usage.

What we often fail to realize, however, is that some forms which seem fully fixed in our present language were, in earlier times, analogical new-formations, and went through a period of newness, and then of fluctuation, before displacing older forms entirely. Our plurals *days* and *cows* are both analogical replacements of earlier forms which would have sounded quite different if they had developed normally into Modern English. Old English had the singular *dag* "day," plural *dagas,* and *cū* "cow," plural *cȳ* (in which the letter *y* stands for a vowel like that spelled *u* in French or *ü* in German); the Old English plurals, had they developed normally, would have given *dawes* and *kye* (rhyming with *high*) in present-day English. But we do not say *day—dawes* or *cow—kye*; we use the regularized plurals *days* and *cows* instead. This is because around the year 1200, our linguistic ancestors made an analogical new-formation, borrowing the stem *day* from the singular to replace the stem *dawe-* in the plural before the ending *-s*. In the plural of *cow*, there were two successive analogical formations. Around the year 1300, people started to use the plural *kyn*, with the analogical plural ending *-n* (which was then very frequent, but survives now only in *oxen, children, brethren*). The form *kyn* survives at present as an archaism, *kine*; in its turn, it was replaced around 1600 by the plural *cows*, in which the plural ending *-s* was borrowed from the majority of nouns and added to the singular *cow*. There must have been a time when *days* seemed as much of a "mistake" as *foots* does now, and—slightly later—a period when *days* and *dawes* were in competition just as *hoofs* and *hooves* are now. If we extend our time-perspective far enough back, we can see that we use relatively few plural formations which are direct continuations of those in use four or five thousand years ago.

These considerations are of importance when it comes to judging forms like *hisn, hern,* and so forth, or *he done*. When an "ignorant" person borrows the ending *-n* from the possessive pronoun *mine* and adds it to the adjectives *his, her, our, your* and *their,* to make the distinctive possessive pronouns *hisn, hern, ourn, yourn, theirn,* this procedure on his part is not due to ignorance or stupidity. It is due to exactly the same process of analogizing, or regularizing the forms of the language, that we saw in the instances of *cows* or *days*, and that has gone on in producing a great many other forms we now use. The analogy in this instance is, of course:

my : mine = his : x

and so forth. Likewise, such a past tense as *he done* is traceable to some such analogy as this:

he has kicked : he kicked = he has done : x

That such forms as *hisn* or *he done* are not accepted as part of the standard language is not due to any defect in the forms themselves—they are prefectly respectable analogical forms, with as much right to existence as *cows* and *days;* the thing that makes them unacceptable is simply the connotation of social disfavor which has been attached to them.

Very often, internal borrowing (analogy) comes into play when lin-

guistic forms become irregular and grammatical relationships are obscured as a result of changes in phonemes. This is what happened in the
case of English *day—dawes;* it has happened in recent centuries in such
instances as those of the old plurals *eye—eyen, shoe—shoon, brother—
brethren,* which have now been replaced by the more transparent and
easily understandable formations *eyes, shoes, brothers* respectively; or
in such past tense of verbs as *help—holp, work—wrought,* now regularized by analogy in the new-formations *helped, worked.* In English noun
plurals and verb pasts and past participles, the trend of development is
slowly but surely toward analogical leveling of irregularities; even
though forms like *gooses, mouses* or *drinked, writed* are simply "errors" or
"blunders" now, they may perhaps be perfectly normal by two or three
hundred years from now. Today's analogical "mistakes" are often tomorrow's competing forms, and day-after-tomorrow's "correct" forms.

ALLAN F. HUBBELL

Multiple Negation

"I couldn't find nobody there." This sentence, as anyone who will read this probably knows, contains a double negative, a construction with a fascinating history. Today in all parts of the English-speaking world, its use or avoidance is one of the clearest marks of differentiation between different social groups. Among those who have had comparatively little formal schooling and whose social and occupational status is relatively low, the construction is extremely common. Among the well-educated and more "privileged," it is rare almost to the point of non-existence. In many circles, in fact, a double negative uttered by a presumably educated person would cause the same embarrassed silence as a loud belch in church.

The avoidance of this usage by the more cultivated members of the English speech-community is roughly about three hundred years old. In earlier English, the doubling, tripling, or even quadrupling of negatives was frequent even in the most formal literary styles. King Alfred, for example, in a translation made late in the ninth century, writes a sentence which in modern form would read: "No man had never yet heard of no ship-army." A little later, in the oldest English version of the Gospels, we read: "The five foolish maidens took lamps, but didn't take no oil with them." In the fourteenth century, Chaucer writes of his "gentle knight" that "in all his life he hasn't never yet said nothing discourteous to no sort of person" (four negatives!). As late as Shakespeare's time, the construction was still possible in Standard English, particularly in speech. Thus, in *Romeo and Juliet,* when Mercutio is confronted by Tybalt, he cries out, "I will not budge for no man's pleasure."

In the course of the seventeenth century, however, the multiple negative began to go out of educated use. Undoubtedly the chief cause of its

From *Inside the ACD,* October 1957. © 1957 by Random House, Inc. Reprinted by permission of the publisher.

gradual disappearance was the influence of classical literary Latin, then considered the most nearly perfect language. The fact that Cicero and Caesar did not multiply negatives even in the most emphatic statements of negation weighed heavily with those who aspired to write well. In the latter half of the century, furthermore, there developed a growing distaste for the extravagance and exuberance of Elizabethan English. The piling up of negatives was presumably felt to be one of the extravagances to be shunned.

After 1700 it is rather difficult to find examples of the multiple negative in educated written English. We of course know less about the spoken usage of the eighteenth century and it may be that for a time many avoided doubling negatives in writing but not in speech. But speech too in time conformed and since then Standard English has been quite uniform in this avoidance.

Our school grammars commonly tell us that the double negative is improper because "two negatives make an affirmative," that is, because "I couldn't find nobody there" really means "I could find somebody there." This curious notion appears to have been first set afloat by an eighteenth-century grammarian, Lowth, and it quickly came to be repeated on every side. It rests primarily on an analogy with algebra, where two negative signs cancel one another in certain operations. But ordinary language is not the language of algebra and utterances containing a double negative are regularly interpreted in the sense intended by the speaker and never in an opposite sense. Furthermore, if the reasoning were sound, a triple negative like King Alfred's or like "I won't give you no bubble gum for nothing" would be quite acceptable in modern Standard English. Of course it is not.

Nonstandard English, in this respect as in some others, is intensely conservative and tenacious of past practice. For two hundred years now, school children have had it dinned (and sometimes beaten) into them that they must not double or triple their negatives. For some of them the instruction is quite superfluous, for they have already learned Standard English at their mothers' knees. The usage of some others comes to be altered. There are those who determine quite early in life that they are going to move up the social ladder and who sense that their inherited speechways will be a bar to advancement. But the usage of a very considerable number is almost unaffected by the school instruction they receive. They leave high school continuing to use a nonstandard variety of the language and, among other things, still multiplying negatives in a fourteenth-century profusion.

Observing this "perverse" adherence to inherited patterns, teachers sometimes think despairingly that there must be some really fundamental fault in their methods. There must be, they feel, some pedagogical device not yet hit upon which could produce much greater results. But to think in this fashion is to misconceive the situation. An individual's linguistic usage is among other things the outward sign of his most deepseated group loyaties. If the usage of the group or groups with which he identifies himself is not that of Standard English, the schools are not likely to have much effect on his practice. For the blunt fact is that only if his loyalties shift will his grammar change. In a democratic society, the schools have an obligation to make a knowledge of the standard language available to everyone. And teachers have an obligation to make this instruction as interesting and meaningful as possible. They should not be surprised, however, if the nonstandard forms of English continue to flourish. They are hardy growths and will be with us for a long time to come.

MARGARET M. BRYANT

Split Infinitive

The split infinitive *("to* openly *examine," "to* fully *express")* occurs more commonly in standard informal writing than in formal writing. Whether to avoid or to use this construction is a matter of style. A split infinitive may eliminate awkwardness or ambiguity or add emphasis or clarity. On the other hand, it is advisable not to place too many words between *to* and the infinitive as in "I planned *to,* after consulting my friend, *buy* one." The result is awkwardness.

An infinitive is said to be split if an adverb or an adverbial construction comes between the word *to* and the infinitive *"to* accurately *count"; "to* in some manner *compensate"; "to* either *write* or forget." This construction has occurred in the works of the best of writers since the beginning of the fourteenth century and has continued to the present time. Those who consider this construction to be nonstandard might consider Willa Cather's "I've heard enough *to* about *do* for me" or Booth Tarkington's "The truth is I have come *to* rather *dislike* him." More recent examples are: ". . . fresh approaches created in order *to* effectively *reach* the multi-billion dollar . . . market" *(New York World-Telegram and Sun,* Dec. 2, 1957, 14); ". . . it took until about 1910 for the phonograph *to* entirely *supersede* the music box" *(Hobbies,* Aug., 1957, 80); ". . . where it takes a password *to* even *gain* entrance" *(ibid.,* Dec., 1957, 39).

Since the Old English period, the relative frequency of the infinitive with *to* has increased over that of the simple infinitive. In the material examined for his *American English Grammar,* Fries found simple infinitives used only 18% of the time. With the increasing use of this infinitive combination has come the placing of other words between the *to* and the infinitive, so that the so-called "split infinitive" has become rather common in modern writing.

A contributing influence to the rising practice is, undoubtedly, the use of *to* with two infinitives, the second of which has an adverb directly before it, as in "He has the ability *to understand and* fully *sympathize* with others" and "All that you have to do is *to write and* patiently *wait* for an answer." Here *fully* and *patiently,* placed before the second infinitive in each instance, come after the *to.*

A second contributing factor may be found in word order. In Modern English, modifiers are usually placed directly before the words they modify, as in "She *successfully* finished the book" or "She delighted in *successfully* finishing the book." As a result, there is pressure to put the adverbial modifier of an infinitive immediately before the infinitive and after the *to.*

Then there are other split expressions which have not gained the publicity of the split infinitive. In a sentence such as "He is as clever in his writing as his sister," one observes a split comparison. Often one sees a split subject and predicate, as in "He, instead of writing me, called in person." Furthermore, the split finite verb phrase is constantly used, as in "I have never heard him"; "If the desired result is ever reached . . ."; "He will be highly recommended." So by analogy one finds words placed between the *to* and the infinitive.

The split infinitive is used to avoid ambiguity, to gain emphasis or the desired shade of meaning, or to attain the most natural and effective word order. In "If Mr. Smith will find time *to completely examine* the papers, he will discover what the facts are," placing *completely* before the infinitive will give the awkward *time completely to examine,* as well as what is called "a squinting modifier," one that may be interpreted in two ways (modify *find* or *examine*). Putting it after *examine* separates *examine* from its object and produces the clumsy *examine completely the papers.* In another sentence, such as "I desire *to* actually *learn* to read Arabic," if the intent is to have *actually* modify the infinitive *learn* and to avoid a split infinitive one may write: "I desire actually to learn to read Arabic," where *actually* may be considered as modifying *desire* rather than *learn,* or one may write: "I desire to learn actually to read Arabic," where it may be considered as modifying *read.* In either statement the author has a squinting modifier, for each may be interpreted in two ways. This is particularly true when another verbal construction precedes an infinitive. On the other hand, the sentence is clear if the infinitive is split. There is no ambiguity whatever.

In some sentences a split infinitive is hard to avoid unless the idea is completely rearranged or rewritten. Take Theodore Roosevelt's "His fortune having been jeopardized, he hoped *to* more than *retrieve* it by going into speculations in the Western Lands" (*The Winning of the West,* Vol.

1, Ch. II). The word order of this sentence cannot be changed without modifying the author's meaning. Consider also. "The men in the district are declared *to* strongly *favor* a strike."

In one comparative study based on the reading of a daily newspaper (Kovitz), the split infinitive occurred 21.7% of the time. In another based on miscellaneous reading (Hotchner), it occurred 17.9% of the time. The average of the two shows the split infinitive occurring 19.8% of the time. Three additional studies (Lindsay, Nass, M. Richardson) encountered the split infinitive twenty times, giving a total in the five studies of thirty-nine instances.

Other Evidence

Bryant, *CE*, 8 (Oct., 1946), 39–40; Curme, *MLN*, 29 (Feb., 1914), 41–45; *Syntax*, 1931, 458 *ff.;* Fowler, *MEU*, 558–60; Fries, *AEG*, 130–33; Jespersen, *MEG*, Pt. V, *Syntax*, IV, 330; Pooley, *TEU*, 100–6; Rice, *EJ*, XXV (Mar., 1937), 238–40; Roberts, *UG*, 204–6.

STUART ROBERTSON

AND FREDERIC G. CASSIDY

Changing Meanings and Values

of Words

Even though it is generally recognized that meanings change, many people still cling, curiously enough, to the quite contradictory notion that words all have "true" meanings, that changes somehow take us away from the "true" meaning, and that the way to find out what a word "really means" is to find out what it once meant. This is particularly true in respect to borrowed words in English, the belief evidently being that the meaning of the word in contemporary English and the meaning of the Latin or Greek word from which the English word is derived must be one and the same. A little reflection should show that an appeal to etymology in order to establish the present meaning of the word is as untrustworthy as an appeal to spelling in order to establish its present pronunciation. And for a reason that is almost exactly parallel: change of *meaning* is likely to have altered the etymological sense, which is thereby rendered archaic or obsolete, just as change of *sound* is likely to be unrecorded in the "antiquarian" spelling that so frequently characterizes Modern English. The study of etymology has great value and interest—a point to which we shall later return—but its usefulness in settling the question of what a word means is subject to considerable qualification.

Let us see what results when one ignores the idea that a word may change its meaning, and appeals to its etymology in order to determine its present meaning. A handbook of only twenty-odd years ago on "correct English" [1] sets forth the following dictum: *"Dilapidated . . .* Said of a building or other structure. But the word is from the Latin *lapis,* a stone,

From *The Development of Modern English,* 2nd ed. © 1954 by Prentice-Hall, Inc. Reprinted by permission of the publisher.

and cannot properly be used of any but a stone structure." One might just as reasonably argue that because *candidate* is related to the Latin *candidus* (white), it cannot properly be used of an aspirant for political office unless he is clothed in a suit of white material. More clearly even, one might protest that *holiday* properly describes Christmas or Easter, but should never be used of Independence Day or Labor Day; or that *bonfire* should not be applied except where the combustible material is bone. These arguments are not much more grotesque than some that have been seriously maintained in defense of an etymological crotchet, while ignoring the fact of change of meaning. Indeed, one who argues on this basis is a victim of the "etymological fallacy."

The fact is that what a word once meant is not necessarily what it now means; the etymological meaning has often died out, and a quite new development is the living descendant. This is particularly true of words in common or popular use. Words, after all, are for the most part purely conventional symbols. They mean only what those who are using them agree to make them mean. Exactly the same principles apply to "learned" words, but because their traditional users have generally known the language from which they were borrowed, or of whose elements they were composed, they have tended to preserve the etymological meaning —indeed, it is conventional to use such words with an eye to their source; thus they are less prone to alterations of meaning than are popular words. It is in this way, incidentally, that a cultural tradition holds in check, to some extent, the constant tendency of language to change.[2]

Change of meaning, however, though usually unpredictable, is not utterly arbitrary; as we shall see in a moment, it often proceeds along familiar paths. Furthermore, though it takes place in all languages, it does not proceed at the same rate even in related ones. If we look at cognate words in English and German, for example, which might have been expected to have the same meaning, we often find them widely different, and the difference is most commonly the result of some radical change of sense in the English word. Opposite instances can be found, admittedly, in which the English word has stood still and the German one changed; yet it is usually the latter which is conservative. Examples of this characteristic English shift in meaning are the following: *Schlagen* and *slay* are originally the same word, but the German word retains the general meaning of "smite" or "strike" while the English word has become narrowed to mean "strike with fatal consequences" or "kill."[3] *Knabe* is the cognate in German of Old English *cnapa* or *cnafa*, and has the same meaning, "boy"; but Modern English *knave* has a radically different one; the German *Tier* means any kind of animal, as did the cognate Old English *deor*, but in Modern English *deer* means one particular kind of animal.

Generalization and Specialization

One very common type of change is that in which the "area" of the meaning is changed. When a word that has referred broadly or inclusively begins instead to refer narrowly or exclusively, this is an example of "specialization" of meaning; the contrary is called "generalization." Interestingly enough, the same word may undergo both processes at different stages of the development of its meaning. *Go,* for example, is a verb of motion that seems as general as possible in meaning, and presumably this is also the basic meaning; early in its history in English, however, it must have specialized, for Old English *gān* sometimes means "walk," and in Middle English *ryde or gon* (ride or walk) is a familiar formula. Although the present meaning is the generalized one, the specialization "walk" was still possible in the late seventeenth century, as we see in these phrases from Bunyan: "I am resolved to run when I can, to go when I cannot run, and to creep when I cannot go." [4]

Borrowed words are quite as likely as native ones to undergo such transformations in meaning. *Virtue* [5] is connected with Latin *vir* (man). Thus, *virtue* first meant "manliness" in general; but its meaning later specialized to stand for the manly quality most in demand in the military state, namely "fortitude" or "warlike prowess"—the meaning familiar in Caesar's *Commentaries*. But a still later Latin meaning is more comprehensive, and it was this very general meaning that was attached to *virtue* when it was borrowed in English through French. One possible specialization was "power," as in "Virtue had gone out of him," or even "magical power," as in "the virtue of the spell" or Milton's "virtuous ring and glass." More commonly, however, the word in English retained a general sense of "noble quality"—though more and more with reference to moral rather than to mental or physical characteristics. But another specialization limits its application to women; for example, "All the sons were brave, and all the daughters virtuous," where *virtuous* is equivalent to "chaste." "A woman's virtue" will today be interpreted in only the last sense. A curious evolution, indeed, when one recalls that the etymological meaning is "manliness."

The foregoing are particularly striking examples, but hundreds of others could be cited. We find generalization in such everyday words as *picture,* once restricted, as the etymology would suggest (compare: the *Picts*, "painted ones"), to a *painted* representation of something seen, but now applicable to photograph, crayon drawing, and so forth; *butcher,* who once slew one animal only, the goat (French *bouc*); the verb *sail,* which has been transferred to *steam* navigation, just as *drive* has been transferred to self-propelled vehicles; *injury,* which once was limited to "injustice"; *zest,* which meant "bit of lemon-peel"; *chest,* which usually meant "coffin"—"He is now deed and nayled in his cheste"; [6] *pen,* which meant "feather," but which is now much more likely to mean a writing implement tipped with metal than a quill; *quarantine,* from which the original meaning of a "forty" days' isolation has quite disappeared; and *companion,* which has likewise lost the etymological sense of "one who (shares) bread with" another.

But generalization of meaning does not always stay within bounds; under some conditions the meaning becomes so broad that, in extreme cases, there is hardly any meaning left. We have a whole set of words, used conversationally when we either do not know, or cannot remember, or perhaps will not take the trouble to search for a more precise term: the *what-you-may-call-it* kind of work—*thingumabob, doohickie, jigger,* and so on.[7] Not so long ago *gadget* was imported into the U. S. from England, and has found a very hearty welcome into this company.

Another type, in which generalization goes even farther, has aroused strong opposition from guardians of literary style, who realize that emptiness and "jargon" result from the indiscriminate use of "words that mean little or nothing, but may stand for almost anything":[8] such words are *thing, business, concern, condition, matter, article, circumstance.* As we all recognize at once, these are words that have a fairly exact sense, but which also have acquired the ability to fit into a wide variety of everyday contexts, in which their meaning becomes extremely vague—in fact, almost wholly dependent on the context. The word *deal* is the current American favorite in this group, its gamut of meaning running all the way from perfectly favorable ("Your job sounds like a pretty fine deal") to thoroughly unfavorable ("I won't take part in any of his deals"). This word serves the purpose, and is going through the same general sort of development, that *proposition* did a generation ago.

Even more frequent than generalization, and even more readily illustrated in numberless familiar instances, is the opposite process of specialization. *Steorfan* is an Old English word, cognate with the German *sterben,* which meant "die"; but the standard Modern English meaning ("starve") is a specialized one, namely "die from hunger." Another specialization, "die from cold," is found in certain Modern English dialects: "[he] . . . bid her come . . . sit close by the fire: he was sure she was starved" is from the Yorkshire dialect of *Wuthering Heights* (Chapter XXX). The older meaning of *meat* was "food" in general, as one might suspect from the archaic phrase *meat and drink* and from the compound *sweetmeat*. For the meaning "meat," the older term was *flesh* or *flesh meat*. It is interesting to observe, incidentally, that the German cognate for *flesh, Fleisch*, suggests first of all the specialized sense of "meat"; this is the present meaning, too, of French *viande*, while the English *viands* retains the general sense of "food." *Coast* is a borrowing, through French, from a Latin word for "side" or "rib" (compare Modern English *inter-costal*), and once meant "border" or "frontier"—the "coast of Bohemia" was not always an absurdity. But *coast* in present use not only has the usual specialization "seashore"; as employed in the eastern United States, it means specifically "Pacific coast." *Shore*, on the other hand, means, in parts of the east at any rate, "Atlantic shore." [9] In some of the same localities, however, "eastern shore" means what elsewhere would have to be expanded into "eastern shore of the Chesapeake in Maryland," just as in part of New England "the cape" means definitely "Cape Cod." *Token* formerly had the broad meaning "sign," but was long ago special-ized to mean a physical thing that is a sign (of something)—as in *love token*, or the metal tokens used on streetcars or buses.

An *undertaker* once could undertake to do anything; nowadays he only undertakes to manage funerals. So, to people in general, *doctor* stands only for *doctor of medicine*. *Liquor*, which once was synonymous with *liquid*, is now definitely specialized. *Reek*, like the German *rauchen*, once had the broad meaning "smoke," as it still has in the Scotch dialect; but the standard Modern English use limits it quite definitely to unpleas-ant exhalations. *Disease* meant "discomfort"—"lack of ease" in general. *Girl* meant "young person (of either sex)." The limitation of *corpse* to *"dead* body" made it necessary to re-borrow the word in its Modern French form *corps* for another possible meaning of "body," and to make occasional use of the original Latin, *corpus*, for still another sense, "com-plete collection of writings." *Corn*, in general American use, will be im-mediately understood as "Indian corn" or "maize." But the word itself once meant simply "grain," and so, in other parts of the English-speaking world, it is differently specialized [10]—in Scotland, to mean "oats," and in England "wheat." Keats's allusion to "Ruth amid the alien corn" prob-ably calls up, to many American readers, a very different picture from what the poet had in mind.

What are the factors that account for specialization of meaning? One is, of course, that localities and groups of people have their own special-ized associations for words that otherwise may convey a broader meaning. It has been well remarked that "every man is his own specializer." [11] *Pipe*, for example, calls up different ideas in the mind of the smoker, the plumber, and the organist. *Ring* may be thought of in connection with jewelry, opera, politics, or pugilism—even though, in the last connection, the "squared circle" has long since superseded the original truly circular shape. Quite apart from particular or local specializations, however, there are a great many words whose meaning has become specialized for nearly everybody. A second factor that helps to account for both generalization and specialization is the fading of the etymological significance of the word. Thus, to illustrate the one point, *arrive* [< Lat. *ad* (to) + *ripa* (shore)] originally applied to the end of a voyage only, and was used without the preposition, since this was included in the word. Milton's "ere he arrive the happy isle" illustrates a use that is in strict accord with the etymology of the word. When, however, consciousness of the Latin parts that made up the word was weakened, it was no longer used transitively, but in the phrase "arrive at," and with the more generalized application to the end of any journey.

Yet another factor is the competition among synonymous words. The borrowing of the Latin *animal* and the French *beast* meant that, with the native *deer*, English would have possessed three exactly synonymous terms for one idea; it is obviously in the interests of economy that *deer* should have specialized to mean one particular species of animal rather than "animal" in general, and that *beast* should have acquired connotations that limit its sphere. *Bird* and *fowl*, *dog* and *hound*, *boy* and *knave*, *chair* and *stool* are further instances of words that were once synonyms but that have been differentiated in meaning here by the specialization of the second term of each pair.

A further remark about generalization and specialization is suggested by some of the words just alluded to. The degree of specialization which a language exhibits seems to depend on cultural need. In a culture in which the coconut is essential—as in Polynesia—an extremely complex vocabulary is said to have grown up, with different terms for many stages or ripeness of the fruit. So also, the Eskimos have different terms for falling snow, snow on the ground, snow packed hard like ice, slushy snow, wind-driven flying snow, and other kinds.[12] Many similar examples could be cited, for the languages of peoples of undeveloped culture appear to be particularly rich in specialized terms. At one time in the course of the English language it must have seemed desirable to speakers to make verbal distinctions in connection with groups of animals—mostly those of interest to farmers and hunters. An elaborate set of what are called "company terms" was accordingly developed, some (but by no means all) of which survive today. The better known ones include a *herd* or a *drove* of cattle, but a *flock* of sheep (or birds), a *school* of fish, a *pack* of wolves (or hounds), a *covey* of partridges, and a *swarm* of bees. But there are others far more esoteric,[13] such as *nye* of pheasants, *cete* of badgers, *sord* of mallards, *wisp* of snipe, *doylt* of tame swine, *gaggle* of geese, *harras* of horses, and *kennel* of raches. There is a similar profusion of names for the same animal (*cow, heifer, bull, calf, steer*, and *ox*), the young of various animals (*puppy, kitten, kid, calf, colt, lamb*, and so forth), and the male and female of the same species (*gander* and *goose, drake* and *duck, horse* and *mare, cock* and *hen, dog* and *bitch*).[14] The need for a generic term is of course particularly felt here, and it is supplied, not quite satisfactorily, by the convention of making either the name of the male (*horse* and *dog*) or of the female (*cow, duck*, and *goose*), or even that of the young of the species (*chicken* and *pig*), perform a larger duty.

Elevation and Degradation

If generalization and specialization may be said to involve a change in the "area" of meaning, elevation and degradation [15] involve the rising or falling of meaning in a scale of values. Thus a word which once denominated something bad (or at least neutral) but comes to refer to something good, has undergone *elevation* of meaning; the reverse of this process, obviously, represents a *degradation* of meaning.

And here a word of warning: we must not confuse the linguistic signal with the thing it stands for, though that error is too often made. It is not the word as such which is bad or good, or which becomes elevated or degraded, but only the meaning which society chooses to put upon it. As we shall see, society often reverses itself in the course of time, and words which were once disapproved may become "respectable," while others that had social favor may lose it. This would not be possible if the value were inherent in the word. With this in mind, then, let us illustrate degradation of meaning.

Many terms that are now descriptive of moral depravity were once quite without this suggestion. *Lust*, for example, meant simply "pleasure," as in German; *wanton* was "untaught"; *lewd* was merely "ignorant," "lerned and lewed" being a phrase commonly standing for "clergy and laity"; *immoral* was "not customary"; *vice* "flaw"; *hussy*, "housewife"; *wench*, "young girl"; and *harlot*, "fellow" (of either sex). In a similar way, words that impute rascality have often been thoroughly innocent labels: *villain*, for example, was "farm laborer"; *counterfeiter*, "imitator" or "copyist"; *pirate* (at least in its earlier Greek sense), "one who adventures or tries"; *buccaneer*, "one who smokes meat"; *ringleader*, simply "leader" (in a good or a neutral sense); *varlet, knave*, and *imp* meant merely "boy"; and *sly, crafty*, and *cunning* all implied the compliment "skilful." A perennial form of humor—the city man's ridicule of the countryman—is witnessed in the degradation of such nouns as *peasant*, *boor* (compare German *Bauer* and Dutch *Boer*), and *churl,* and in the frequent implication of such adjectives as *bucolic, rural, rustic,* and *provincial.*

When a word may be applied in two possible ways, one favorable or complimentary and the other reverse, it is extremely likely that it will specialize in the less desirable sense. Thus, *suggestive* is likely to mean only "evilly suggestive," though it *may* still mean "informative" or "illuminating," and though the noun *suggestion* has escaped any such specialization—just as the verb *to harbor* is limited to unworthy or illegal concealment (as in "harboring a criminal" or "harboring thoughts of revenge"), while the noun *harbor* retains the old broad and literal meaning of "haven." *Asylum,* through association with the idea of "refuge for the insane," has followed a course like that of the verb *harbor.* A *libel,* in Middle English and early Modern English, was simply a "brief bit of writing" (from Lat. *libellum,* little book); now it is definitely limited to something malicious or defamatory. *Doom* once meant "judgment"; now it means only "condemnation." *Reek,* as we have seen, can now stand only for unpleasant distillations; *stink* and *stench* have specialized in the same way from a formerly neutral meaning, and *smell* and even *odor* seem likely to follow their lead. A *smirk* was once merely a smile, without the suggestion of affectation. One could formerly *resent* benefits as well as injuries, and *retaliate* for favors as well as slights; compare with the present meanings of these words the ordinary implications of the phrase "get even with" or "get square with."

On the other hand, instances of words that have traveled an opposite path, from the humble to the exalted, or from the base to the refined, are not far to seek. The institution of chivalry brought about the elevation of *knight* (youth) and *squire* (shield-bearer); and *chivalry* itself was invested by the Romantic Revival with a glamor that the word (as we see from its source, Fr. *cheval,* horse) did not originally possess. "Romantic" ideas in the late eighteenth and early nineteenth centuries were similarly responsible for the gain in dignity of such words as *bard,* once a term of contempt like *vagabond; minstrel,* once applicable to juggler and buffoon as well as musician; and *enthusiasm,* in the earlier eighteenth century akin to *fanaticism.* Like *knight,* other terms for rank or position have had the good fortune to take on added prestige when the offices for which they stood changed their character, and when their own etymological meanings were forgotten. Such is the history of *marshal* (originally, "horse-servant"), *chamberlain* (room-attendant), *minister* (servant), *constable* (stable-attendant), *governor* (pilot), and *steward* (sty-guardian). It is true that in a number of these words the extent of the elevation fluctuates: *marshal* is a less dignified title when it is applied to the lone policeman of an American village then when it is applied to the highest ranking officers of the English or the French army; there is a similar variation between the American and the British connotations for *constable,* just as *steward* may suggest a club attendant as well as the Lord High Steward of England, or even the royal dynasty of the *Stewarts* (or Stuarts); [16] likewise, *governor* may mean the warden of an English prison or the chief administrative officer of one of our American states. On the whole, however, the fact that any present implication of these words represents a gain in dignity over the etymological one is patent enough. So too it is with a number of political and religious labels: *Tory, Whig, Puritan, Quaker,* and *Methodist* are well-known examples of names that were originally applied in contempt but that have taken on dignified associations (though, to some, *Puritan* and perhaps *Tory* still convey a derisive significance). Archbishop Trench long ago pointed out that the influence of Christianity elevated *angel* from merely "messenger," *martyr* from "witness," and *paradise* from "park," through the Biblican application to the abode of our first parents (as in *Paradise Lost* and *"earthly paradise"*) to the "blisful waiting-place of faithful departed spirits." [17] Miscellaneous further illustrations of elevation are *pretty* from an early meaning "sly," through "clever," to something approaching "beautiful"; *nice* from an etymological meaning "ignorant," through its earliest English sense "foolish," and later ones like "particular," to its present broad and vague colloquial meaning of "pleasant" or "acceptable"; and *fond* from "foolish" to "affectionate."

The usual view of degradation and elevation has been that the downward path is far the more common. Despite McKnight's protest to the effect that elevation has been less noticed simply because it is less dramatic,[18] there seems to be every reason to agree with the general verdict. Examples of elevation, after all, are far less easy to find than examples of degradation, which indeed meet us at every turn. Besides, most of the words that have been cited as undergoing elevation fall into a few obvious categories, while the types of degradation are extremely various. The truth of the matter would appear to be that degradation has been more noticed not because it is more spectacular but simply because it is omnipresent, as elevation is not. Why should this be so, and why should the use of words be made difficult by a lurking leer, a hint of unpleasant connotation that makes a word that appears to be absolutely right in denotation impossible for a given occasion? It is hard to escape the conclusion that there is a disagreeable commentary on human nature here. How difficult it is for superlatives to retain their superlative force—because the general tendency is to apply them on light occasion and hence to weaken their meaning! So *fair* comes to mean "passable," and indeed is often equivalent to "not good"; and *quite* has passed, in its usual American application at least, from "entirely" or "completely" to "moderately." The tendency to procrastinate finds illustration in a whole series of words or phrases—*by and by, presently, anon, immediately, directly,* and *soon* itself—that have "slowed up," changing their meaning from "now" or "at once" to "soon" or "after a time." It is scarcely a far-fetched interpretation to see in the narrowing of *demure* to apply to *mock* modesty, of *genteel* to *spurious* gentility, of *sophistication* to *worldly* wisdom, of *egregious* to notoriety rather than fame, of *sanctimonious* to *pretended* holiness, and of *grandiose* to *tinsel* (itself an example of degradation) grandeur—to see in all these, and dozens of others that might be mentioned, the workings of human motives like suspicion, contempt, and general pessimism.

NOTES

1. *Write It Right,* by Ambrose Bierce, New York (Neale), 1928. The work is well worth investigating as a striking demonstration of what pedantry, combined with ignorance of linguistic processes, will do for one. To much of it, a witty definition of Bierce's own is curiously applicable: *"positive*—mistaken at the top of one's voice."

2. Some of this holding in check is unconscious, some conscious; we shall have to postpone to a later chapter the question of the values and judgments upon which conscious attempts to control language are based.

3. The Latin word *caedere,* though unrelated to English *slay,* has undergone exactly the same specialization of meaning.

4. Quoted by Bradley, *The Making of English,* p. 182.

5. This history is given in greater detail in Greenough and Kittredge, *Words and Their Ways in English Speech,* pp. 241–242.

6. Chaucer's clerk, speaking of Petrarch (*Clerk's Prologue,* line 30).

7. Louise Pound has collected more than 100 such terms now current in popular speech: "American Indefinite Names," *American Speech,* Vol. VI, No. 4 (April 1931), pp. 257–259.

8. Greenough and Kittredge, *op. cit.,* p. 235.

9. In Philadelphia it is often used in a still more specific sense, "southern New Jersey shore"; it sometimes bears a yet more localized signification: "Atlantic City," which occurs repeatedly in the headlines of Philadelphia newspapers.

10. In other Germanic languages, the cognate word has still different specializations in various places: "barley" in Sweden, "rye" in north Germany, and "spelt" in south Germany. (Jespersen, *Mankind, Nation, and Individual,* p. 212.)

11. Quoted by Greenough and Kittredge, *op. cit.,* p. 251.

12. See B. L. Whorf, "Science and Linguistics," *The Technology Review,* Vol. XLII, No. 6 (April 1940), reprinted in *Four Articles on Metalinguistics,* Washington, D.C. (Foreign Service Institute), 1950, p. 6. For further examples see Jespersen, *Language,* pp. 429–431.

13. These, and many others, are mentioned in an editorial comment in *The New York Times* for November 20, 1930. All but *doylt* are recorded in the *Oxford Dictionary.*

14. McKnight, *English Words and Their Background*, p. 239, calls attention in greater detail to the lack of generalizing terms in the animal kingdom, and suggests further that the variety of names for sea craft (*sloop, schooner, brig, ship, boat, dinghy, bark,* and so on) is a similar survival of primitive habits of thought.

15. Elevation is also called *aggradation* or *amelioration,* and degradation is also called *degeneration* or *pejoration.*

16. Greenough and Kittredge, *op. cit.,* p. 296.

17. Archbishop Richard Chevenix Trench, *On the Study of Words,* New York (Armstrong), 20th ed. (no date), p. 114.

18. *English Words and Their Background,* p. 292; cf. also Janet Aiken, *English Present and Past,* p. 112, and G. A. Van Dongen, *Amelioratives in English.*

KENNETH G. WILSON

English Grammars and
the Grammar of English

The word "grammar," used loosely, can refer to nearly everything about a language from its sounds and spelling to syntax and semantics. We often use it to mean usage in speech or writing compared with current standards of correctness: "Her grammar was awful." Or a grammar can be a book, usually a textbook, on any of these aspects of a language. Modern students of the language, however, also understand two narrower meanings, which are our particular concern in this essay:

1. *The* grammar of a language is the system of devices which carry the structural "meanings" of that language in speech and writing. This system specifies the way words in a given language are related to each other, so that we may extract meaning beyond the relatively simple lexical or dictionary meanings of the words themselves.

2. *A* grammar is a description of *the* grammar of a language. That is, any full description of the patterned system of signals employed by a language is a grammar of that language. Although the system itself (*the* grammar) may remain relatively constant, our grammars—our descriptions of the system—may improve. We may come to write more accurate, more efficient descriptions.

This distinction between *the* grammar as the system itself and *a* grammar as any description of the system is the source of much confusion when linguists address laymen, and often when grammarians address each other. A few statements about the grammar of English will help to clarify the problem.

The grammar of a language changes in time, but the rate of change

From *Standard College Dictionary*, text edition. © 1963 by Funk & Wagnalls Company, Inc., New York: Harcourt, Brace & World, Inc.

102

is relatively slow when compared with that of words and meanings. Since the grammatical system is not fixed while the language is in use, we can expect to have to re-describe it periodically in order to keep abreast of the changes. For example, the grammar of English during the Renaissance included a question pattern which reversed the subject and verb: *Feels the king sick?* We still retain that pattern with *be* and *have* (*Is the king sick?*), but we rarely use it with other verbs. Instead, we have a relatively new pattern with the word *do: Does the king feel sick?* Since changes like this come very slowly, however, *a* grammar of *the* grammar will, if accurate, be useful on most counts for many years, though not for centuries.

The English grammatical system is peculiar to English. No other language has a grammar quite like it, though closely related languages such as Norwegian and Dutch show many points of grammatical similarity, and other Indo-European languages such as Latin and French display at least a few. But descriptions of none of these languages will fit the English grammatical system, any more than descriptions of English will fit theirs. There may be some grammatical devices which every known language shares with every other, but so far we do not know what they are. For example, German and Finnish have case, and so does English, but there are languages which lack case entirely. Comparing the grammars of various languages is instructive, but each grammar is unique; each belongs only to its own language.

The system of English grammar, then, is the object for study—the same system that little children usually master with no formal instruction by the age of four or five. By imitating the speech they hear, and by trial and error, they learn to use the language; they come to "know" English grammar. They cannot talk *about* it, perhaps, but they know it at least to the extent of being able to use it unconsciously and with great precision.

That the system exists and that every native user responds to it are perhaps most quickly illustrated by a nonsense sentence: *These foser glipses have volbicly merfed the wheeple their preebs.* Although we do not know what most of the words mean (except for the "empty" words, *These, have, the,* and *their*), we "know" the grammar of the sentence. We can identify every part of speech; we can assert that *glipses* is a plural noun and a subject, that *volbicly* is an adverb modifying the verb phrase *have merfed,* and that *wheeple* is probably an indirect object. We know this, even though we do not know the "full," lexically meaningful words. The words we do recognize contain very little lexical meaning (try to define *the*), but give us considerable grammatical "meaning."

We have learned objectively a great deal about this grammatical system, about the features which signal the grammatical meanings to which we respond. In what follows, we shall examine three different grammars of English, three different methods of describing the grammar of contemporary English: traditional grammars, structural grammars, and generative grammars. We can learn a good deal about our language from each, because each has certain advantages over the others, just as each has certain flaws. But examination of all three should lead us closer to the ultimate goal, a clear view of the system itself.

Underlying each of these three kinds of grammar is the single purpose of describing in rules and generalizations the contemporary system of signaling grammatical meaning in English. The best of these grammars, obviously, will be the one that is most accurate and most efficient. It will need to be accurate because of course we want our description to be right, no matter how complicated this may make it. Ideally, we would like the description to be efficient, too, because we want our grammar to be teachable. We want to be able to teach English to foreigners, and we want to be able to help the native user of the language make better choices among the possible alternative grammatical structures English affords. To do this, we will need to be able to give him rigorously accurate information about where these choices lie, and we will also need a description efficient enough to permit him to learn quickly what he needs to know.

Finally, however, there is an even more important reason for seeking the best description of the English grammatical system. Language is perhaps the most distinctive and most basic of all human activities; it sets us apart from all other animals. As a humane study, as an end in itself, therefore, language merits our every effort to understand what it is and how it works. The liberally educated man will find all his attempts at following the Socratic injunction, "Know thyself," leading him sooner or later to the study of the language he uses. This means, among other things, studying its grammar.

Traditional Grammars of English

It is not our purpose here to write a history of English grammars, but we will nevertheless begin with the oldest and most respected of grammatical descriptions, the traditional grammars of English. The word *traditional* suggests that these grammars are old, and that they have had that kind of approval which stems from custom and long use. In fact, traditional grammars were first devised during the Renaissance, and they were based primarily on the grammars of classical Latin then current, since Latin seemed to the English grammarians of that era the most nearly perfect language the world afforded. At the outset, these English grammars were neither very accurate nor very efficient; they were usually attempts to find in English the equivalents of forms and constructions which could be found in Latin, or, failing that, to insist that such forms be developed and that English grammar be corrected and improved to meet that standard. This side of traditional grammars—their reforming zeal in the effort to make English grammar conform to the system of Latin grammar—we usually call prescriptive, because these grammarians attempted to prescribe what English should be, rather than to describe what it currently was.

In recent years the quarrel between prescriptive and descriptive grammarians has been confused and unfortunate, since in the process some excellent traditional grammars, which were in many ways descriptive, have been wrongly accused of the same prescriptivism which had at so many points been typical of earlier traditional grammars. The real quarrel is not between description and prescription, but between describing and failing to describe.

In the beginning, many of the traditional grammars were poor things, inaccurate and inefficient. But by the nineteenth century there existed some really excellent traditional grammars, highly detailed and impressively accurate, which, given the limitations of their assumptions, were as descriptive as many modern grammars of English. It is that sort of traditional grammar which sheds real light on the grammar of English, and that is the sort we will examine here.

The distinguishing fact about traditional grammars is that they are notional: they are based on meaning rather than form or syntax. The chief weaknesses of the traditional grammars stem from that notional point of departure. These grammars are circular in their reasoning: they can describe the English sentence only by first understanding the total meaning of that sentence. Knowing that a sentence is a question or a statement, they can begin to describe the way it is put together. They can then name and describe the parts of the sentence and discuss their relationships in great detail. But the primary assumptions all depend on the total meaning of the sentence. This practice results in both strengths and weaknesses.

No brief discussion of traditional grammars will fully demonstrate the strengths of those grammars, primarily because the main strength of traditional grammars lies in their meticulously recorded details. Indeed, they *require* an almost endless listing of details because they are obliged to work from outside the language, from specific sentences; they cannot penetrate to the principles which will organize sentences yet unuttered or unwritten. Therefore their bulk is enormous and they are inefficient. (Because of that inefficiency they have been terribly watered down in textbook versions so as to be almost worthless.) Their main characteristics, then, are great inefficiency, great accuracy, and great length—there are no really good short ones. Here, therefore, we will merely illustrate methods.

Traditional grammars usually begin with the definition of a sentence: Curme's [1] is a good one: "A sentence is an expression of a thought or feeling by means of a word or words used in such form and manner as to convey the meaning intended." [2] Kinds of sentences then follow, with distinctions based on the meaning we see in them: exclamatory, declarative, and interrogative, or command, statement, and question. This kind of grammar classifies the sentences it encounters by grasping their intention, their meaning. Then it turns to a discussion of the parts and their internal arrangements.

The chief point of interest here is that from meaning-based points of departure our traditional grammar has now begun to define and classify according to function in the sentence. That it begins in meaning and ends in function is an illustration of its circular reasoning. Consider the sentence *John gave Mary the book*. It is a sentence because it expresses a complete thought, a meaning. It is a statement because it asserts. This is notional reasoning. But next we shift the ground. *John* is the subject of the sentence because it expresses the actor, the doer of the action expressed by the verb; *gave* is the simple predicate because it expresses the action the actor did; *Mary* is the indirect object because it is the receiver of the action specified in subject and predicate; and *book* is the direct object because it is the thing acted upon. This is a bald statement of the traditional grammatical reasoning, but it illustrates fairly well: we identify the parts functionally only by knowing first what the sentence means. In effect, the chief weakness is this circularity. For this reason syntax is not a strong point of traditional grammars.

Overlapping categories also cause awkwardness. When we classify a group of objects we must use the same criteria for all of them: if we class some birds according to color and some according to size, we will not have a coherent set of observations. Our categories must be discrete, and we must apply them uniformly to all the materials under study.

Once past the primary assumptions, however, traditional grammars go on to describe a wealth of syntactic detail. They make a distinction between phrases and clauses, the latter containing subjects and predicates, the former not, and they observe how these fit into the simple sentence or connect to it as modifiers, compounds, or dependencies of various sorts. All these parts and their functions are named, and we end with a very detailed account of the kinds of constructions in English sentences and how they function, usually elaborately illustrated with real examples.

A second line of development in traditional grammars is the examination of the smaller units, the parts of speech. Some traditional grammars begin here; all of them eventually define the parts of speech. Again, these classifications are based on either meaning or function or both. And some classifications, like the pronoun, may also be based partly on form, although this is usually only a peripheral consideration.

The main fact is this: meaning is the basis for defining the two most important of the traditional parts of speech, the noun and the verb. A noun, for example, is defined in traditional grammars as "the name of a person, place, or thing," or as "a word used as the name of a thing, quality, or action." We can identify and classify nouns, then, only by knowing their referents, the concepts or things for which they stand. In these traditional, notional grammars the noun as a part of speech is defined notionally.

Traditional grammars usually identify eight parts of speech: noun, verb, adjective, adverb, preposition, conjunction, pronoun, and interjection. The nouns—sometimes called substantives—are name-words. They can be further subdivided into proper and common nouns, proper nouns being the names of particular people, places, events, organizations, etc., which English usually distinguishes formally only by capitalization in writing. All other nouns, usually not capitalized, are common nouns. (Other groupings of nouns are also notional: categories such as collective nouns and abstract nouns are defined in traditional grammars on the basis of their meaning or on the basis of logic: *committee,* a collective noun, is described as being either singular or plural, depending on the unanimity of the membership, on whether it is thought of as a unit or a collection of individuals. This is a notional distinction.) Traditional grammars lean rather heavily on the written language, as the distinction between common and proper nouns shows. (A further circularity is often added to the layman's view of language as he decides that proper nouns are proper nouns *because* we capitalize them!) The notions behind the distinction are usually clear in speech too, although if context is missing we can think of isolated examples—*the city* and *the City,* for example— which are distinctive only in writing.

Once the traditional grammar has identified nouns by their meanings, it turns almost at once to examine the function of nouns; it becomes clear that words we have classed as nouns serve regularly as subjects, objects of various kinds, and predicate complements. And then we discover some of these same nouns used apparently as adjectives, as in "The *chocolate* cake was made of dark *chocolate*." The functions became extremely complex and require elaborate illustration and classification. Again, accuracy leads away from efficiency.

Adjective definitions in traditional grammars are partly notional too, but mainly they are functional; they are notional only in that they depend on our ability to identify nouns notionally so that we can then identify adjectives and pronouns by means of their functional relationships to nouns.

In traditional grammars, an adjective is a word "that modifies a noun or a pronoun." Curme's definition [3] continues, "i.e., a word that is used with a noun or pronoun to describe or point out the living being or lifeless thing designated by the noun or pronoun: a *little* boy, *that* boy, *this* boy, a *little* house." This is a functional definition. Further classes are both notional and functional. Adjectives are either descriptive or limiting: "*little* boy" is descriptive, "*this* boy" is limiting. This is a notional distinction. Adjectives are also either attributive (placed before or in immediate contact with the noun) or predicative (following a verb like *be*). This is a functional distinction. And the whole class depends on the prior, notional identification of the noun.

The pronoun is even more complex and is also classed by form—formally. The base definition in a traditional grammar usually goes something like the one from this dictionary: a pronoun is "a word that may be used instead of a noun or noun phrase (personal, relative, demonstrative, indefinite, and reflexive pronouns), or as an adjective (adjective pronoun), or to introduce a question (interrogative pronoun)." In each of these categories our identification depends ultimately on our identification of nouns. It is notional first, and then functional.

But this then raises an interesting point: how do we tell nouns from pronouns if functionally they do the same work? The answer is "partly from meaning, partly from form." Pronouns take most of their meaning (except for the grammatical matter of case) from the nouns they replace. They have no other referents, as can be seen from the definitions of the various pronouns in this dictionary. But their forms are distinctive, since they are a small, finite list of words. The personal pronouns, for example, show many distinctive formal characteristics: case (*I, my, mine,* and *me*), number (*I* and *we*), person (*I, you,* and *he*), and gender (*he, she,* and *it*). But the personal pronouns are a finite list, and we are not likely to add new ones as readily—or at least as speedily—as we add other words to the vocabulary. Pronominal changes occur of course, but only very slowly. (Note how long it is taking to lose completely the *thou, thy, thine, thee,* and *ye* forms, which have been disappearing for hundreds of years.) Thus the pronoun illustrates an even greater circularity of reasoning in traditional grammars, since form, function, and meaning all are used as bases for identifying and classifying pronouns.

The definition of the verb in traditional grammars is also notional, perhaps with an overtone of functionalism. Curme says, "The verb is that part of speech that predicates, assists in predications, asks a question, or expresses a command: 'The wind *blows.*' 'He *is* blind.' '*Did* he *do* it?' '*Hurry!*' "[4] This is a notional definition. Verbs are further classed as transitive or intransitive (verbs that require or do not require an object), linking or auxiliary. These are functional classifications.

The other parts of speech—adverb, preposition, conjunction, and interjection—are similar mixtures of notional and functional distinctions. The chief flaw is the circularity of reasoning which stems from the notional point of departure. The chief virtue of these traditional grammars when they are well done is that they are so fully detailed. The terminology developed for classrooms has been a hindrance to later grammars in some ways, but ultimately it has served as a useful standard: no modern grammar can be said to be accurate, however high its apparent efficiency, if it cannot account for all the varieties of construction so fully delineated in the best traditional grammars. The traditional terminology is still useful.

Two other problems of traditional grammars are worth noting here. The first is the question of functionalism and the special variety of traditional grammar which grew up during the thirties and forties of this century under the name *functional grammars.*

At their best, functional grammars were written by traditional grammarians who were trying to avoid some of the circular reasoning and overlapping categories of meaning-based descriptions. By describing subjects, objects, and other functional categories and then classing words and constructions solely on the basis of their use in these functions or positions in the sentence, these grammarians felt they could write a more rational grammatical description of English. They did succeed in increasing efficiency somewhat, but ultimately at the cost of losing much detail which was the strength of the traditional grammars.

At their worst, functional grammars became a worthless watering-down of the detail of the good traditional grammars. *Functional* became a synonym for practical or useful; the teaching of English in the schools had come around to an almost exclusive interest in the most common mistakes in usage made by students, and since functional grammar seemed to be simpler to teach than the more elaborate traditional descriptions, it was the work of only a decade to destroy almost completely the effectiveness of full traditional grammars and replace them with truncated, diluted imitations which were called "functional."

A second problem with traditional grammar was its orientation almost exclusively to the written language. Spelling, punctuation, and the written versions of grammatical constructions were the material for analysis, and as a result many people came to feel that the written language was the standard from which the spoken language was a sloppy falling-away. This had awkward consequences for the writing of grammars: it meant that many constructions regularly heard in the language were simply not described because they were not encountered in the written language. It meant too that the system of grammar—*the* grammar of English—began to be viewed as a consciously learned thing, a subject composed of the terminology—the names of parts and functions—which the grammarians had invented originally to describe the grammar. The means became—and in many minds has remained—confused with the end.

We have much to thank traditional grammars for; they have managed to examine the details of written English and to describe and classify them with splendid accuracy and thoroughness. They have supplied us with useful terminology for the discussion of many aspects of grammar. And many of their particular observations remain, circular reasoning or no, the clearest and best accounts we have of some of the small but vexing problems we encounter when we try to describe the grammar of English. No student of the language can sensibly ignore traditional grammars of English.

But in the end, traditional grammars have not solved the problem. Mainly because they work from outside the language, because they can only classify and describe the endless numbers of existing sentences, they lead us to parsing and naming of parts. But they do not help us very much in our effort to describe the system of patterns the child "knows," and they do not give us the kinds of generalizations we need for efficiency. Above all, they do not give us knowledge of the rules of the English grammar so that we can see precisely how sentences yet unuttered and unwritten will inevitably be formed. They do not tell us how or why.

Structural Grammars of English

The term *structural grammars* is arbitrary, used here to designate those attempts at describing the grammar of English which are based on the methods of modern descriptive linguistics. These grammars have several marked advantages over most traditional grammars.

1. They begin with the spoken language.

2. They begin with forms and work back to meaning, irrespective of whether the form is an inflectional suffix, an intonation marker, or a slot in a set pattern.

3. They try to work exclusively with grammatical meaning rather than with total meaning.

4. Since they consciously attempt to generalize, they are often very efficient.

The writing of structural grammars goes back more than thirty years. The descriptive linguistic work of men like Leonard Bloomfield and Edward Sapir marks the beginning in this country of the kind of careful analysis of all aspects of language which led to the writing of structural grammars.

Structural English grammars are extremely accurate on phonology and morphology; they are perhaps less successful in describing syntax, especially the larger units. Good structural grammars tend to be more candid about their weaknesses, however, than those traditional grammars which with their pedagogical aims often sought to present a logically coherent grammar of English sometimes even at the expense of accuracy.

Structural grammars of English describe four major kinds of grammatical signal. These are the patterned devices which give us, usually with considerable redundancy, the grammatical meanings of our utterances:

1. Signals from the *forms* of words.
2. Signals from the *function words*.
3. Signals from the *order* of words and word groups.
4. Signals from the *intonation* of words or word groups.

These signals can be investigated in several reasonable orders, but the distinguishing characteristic of structural grammars is their interest in describing the spoken language; this interest makes sound the most helpful starting point.

Structural grammars, therefore, generally begin with the phonemes, which while not grammatical signals in themselves, since they have no meaning, are nonetheless the important basic concept. A phoneme is one of the distinctive classes of sounds in a language. Of all the hundreds of speech noises the human voice can make, only a relative few are distinctive or significant in any given language. In English there are twenty-four consonant phonemes, three of which are often called semi-vowels (/h/, /w/, and /y/). These consonant sounds are distinctive in English; one can neither speak nor understand English unless he can make and identify these sounds. In fact, any native English-speaking listener will constantly try to class all speech sounds he hears into one of the phonemes of English. He cannot help himself.

But the phoneme is only a category, not a finite sound. The difference between *phonetics* (the study of speech sounds) and *phonemics* (the study of the significant speech sound classes in a given language) illustrates this distinction: a *phonetic* description of an utterance reports exactly the nature and qualities of the sounds, whether they are significant in the language or not. It gets every detail. A *phonemic* transcription is much more gross. Because /t/ and /d/ are phonemic (i.e., significantly distinctive) in English, this kind of transcription will note when each one occurs, but it will not be interested in the many variations of these two sounds (as in a more or less sharply exploded [t] which a phonetic transcription would record). Phonemics needs only to tell the /t/ from the /d/ and from all other phonemes of English, so that it can distinguish *matter* /mætər/ from *madder* /mædər/. Note that *phonemic* transcriptions are enclosed between virgules; *phonetic* transcriptions, between brackets. The following list shows the special phonemic symbols used in this essay and their equvivalents in the pronunciation key of the *Standard College Dictionary: Text Edition;* all other phonemic characters are identical with the key:

/æ/ = a; /ey/ = ā; /iy/ = ē; /č/ = ch; /ay/ = ī; /ǰ/ = j; /ŋ/ = ng; /ow/ = ō; /ɔ/ = ô; /aw/ = ou; /uw/ = ōō; /ə/ = u; /š/ = sh; /ð/ = th; /ž/ = zh.

In addition to the twenty-four consonant phonemes in English there are nine vowel phonemes. There are also at least seven diphthongs (vowel plus semi-vowel) common to most dialects, and other diphthongs peculiar to one or two dialects.

These vowel and consonant phonemes—the segmental phonemes— are not the only significant sounds in English. Stress too is phonemic, and so are pitch and clause terminals. The four stresses, four pitches, and three clause terminals comprise the suprasegmental phonemes, the phonemes which make the intonation contour of English. Another phoneme, open juncture, is considered segmental by some, suprasegmental by others. The intonation curve or contour (sometimes called *prosody*) contains important grammatical signals in the spoken language.

English has four levels of stress, labeled (from heaviest to lightest) primary / ́ /, secondary / ̂ /, tertiary / ̀ /, and weak or unstressed / ̆ /. A one-syllable word spoken alone has a primary stress: /yés/. Two-syllable words have a primary and one other stress when they are spoken in isolation: /névər/ /spíydbòwt/. Most of the time, in utterances of three or more syllables, we make our distinctions among three of these levels: primary, either secondary or tertiary, and weak, or primary, secondary, and either tertiary or weak. Occasionally, however, English grammatical meanings depend on our distinguishing all four levels. We can hear all four in the phrase *the red greenhouse* /ðə̆ rêd gríynhàws/. *Green house* and *greenhouse* /grîyn háws/ and /gríynhàws/ are distinguished from each other mainly by difference in stress pattern; the stresses help us tell an adjective plus noun from a compound. These four levels of stress are phonemic in English.

Pitch is also phonemic in English. There are four levels, usually numbered from lowest to highest, all relative rather than absolute. Every speaker and every listener distinguishes the four. /gôw hów m/ illustrates levels 2, 3, and 1. /gôw hówm/, a question, is distinguished from the command partly by the fact that pitch remains on third level instead of falling to first. "Go home!" he screamed illustrates the fourth level of pitch: /gôw hów m híy skriymd/. These four levels of pitch are phonemic in English.

Finally, open juncture and clause terminals are phonemic in English. Close juncture is the relationship which exists between segmental phonemes in sequence, as within most words. Open juncture /+/ helps us distinguish *sly twitch* from *slight witch* /slây + twǐ č̌/ from /slâyt +| wǐ č̌/. Open juncture is sometimes described as a slight pause, sometimes as a modification of the phonemes on either side of the juncture, but in any case it is clearly a thing we listen for: *I scream* /ây+ skríy m/ and *ice cream* /âys+ kríy m/ can be distinguished from each other only because of the difference in placement of the open juncture, which so often separates our words for us.

Clause terminals require a definition of *clause* different from that used in traditional grammars. In structural grammars a clause is a string of segmental phonemes under a single pitch contour containing one primary stress and marked at both ends either by silence or a terminal. There are three clause terminals, described in structural grammars as level, rising, or falling, since they appear to be modifications of pitch within one of the numbered levels of pitch.

Falling clause terminals occur at the ends of many utterances (we use either /↘/ or /#/ to transcribe this phoneme, and we sometimes call it a double cross juncture): *I'm going home.* /âym+gòwiŋ+| hów m↘/.

When the utterance ends, the voice trails off and down from the first level of pitch.

Rising clause terminals occur most frequently between larger syntactic units in the utterance and at the ends of some questions: *Fred, who came late, missed his dinner.* /fré\d↗huw+kêym+⌐léy\t↗mǐstiz +⌐dín\ər↘/. Rising clause terminals are transcribed either/↗/ or /|||/, and are sometimes called double bar junctures.

Level clause terminals /→/, or single bar junctures /||/, are the least noticeable of the terminal breaks in a sequence of phonemes, just slightly stronger than an open juncture: *Their best outfielder hit a home run.*

/ðèr+bêst+⌐âwt\fíyldər→hît+ə+hòwm+⌐rə\n↘/.

These four stresses, four pitches, open juncture, and three clause terminals are phonemic in English. This means that like the segmental phonemes, these suprasegmental phonemes are significant English sounds. Individually they have no meaning. A third level pitch at the end of a segment or clause does not mean *question* by itself, any more than a rising clause terminal in that position does. The two together, however, at the end of a full intonation contour, *e.g.*, /₂³′³↗/, do mean question, provided, of course, that no stronger signal interferes. Usually intonation, the grammatical meaning attached to an intonation curve, is strong enough to counteract or modify the effects of other grammatical signals—for example: *He's a sailor.* /hîyz+ə̆+⌐séyl\ər↘/. In this utterance we have a /₂³′₁↘/ curve, which in conjunction with other signals, can signify a statement. A /₂³′³↗/ pattern for the same segment will mean question, despite other signals signifying a statement: /hîyz+ə̆+⌐séylər↗/ (incredulous). A /₂³′₂↗/contour will signify an included or incomplete utterance: /hîyz+ə̆+⌐séyl\ər↗/ *He's a sailor, but.* . . .

A morpheme is hard to define, since it too is merely a category perhaps it will suffice in a general discussion such as this to say that a morpheme—which is composed of one or more phonemes—is the smallest meaningful unit in a language. Sometimes the meaning is lexical, as in {kæt} and many affixes; sometimes it is grammatical. In the paragraph above we have examples of intonation contours which are morphemic;

that is, they can carry meaning—in this instance, grammatical meaning. These morphemes are grammatical signals in the spoken language. In the written language, we replace them with punctuation, capitalization, and italics as far as is possible and necessary. The relationship between intonation and punctuation is not exact, just as that between the segmental phonemes and the conventional spelling of English is not exact, but in both instances the system is roughly efficient. When we read, we normally throw primary stresses toward the end of each segment: *Give me the ball*. This sentence has its primary stress on *ball*. If we want to stress *me*, as opposed to someone else, we have to write the sentence "Give *me* the

ball" or "Give ME the ball" /gĭv+ | mĭy+ \ ðə+bɔ́l ↘/.

The suprasegmental phonemes of stress, pitch, and clause terminals, then, are necessary to structural grammars of English because in contours these phonemes become morphemic; they contain grammatical meaning. The segmental phonemes are necessary because in clusters they too contain meaning, both lexical and grammatical. We can describe these segmental forms more accurately by seeing them in their phonemic transcriptions than by seeing them conventionally spelled.

Let us turn next to the segmental morphemes of English which contain grammatical meaning. First, those morphemes which are the grammatical "endings" or *inflections:*

1. *Plurals of nouns*. The main morphemic pattern is usually called the *-s* plural inflection. It turns out to have three forms when we examine it phonemically: The plural of *ship* is *ships* /šips/; we add /s/. The plural of *dog* is *dogs* /dɔgz/; we add /z/. The plural of *dish* is *dishes* /dišɨz/; we add /ɨz/. If we make new words we form their plurals on this major pattern, accommodating the form of the inflection to the final sounds of the singular.

There are several minor patterns too. They fall mainly into two groups, those from older English patterns such as *man: men, woman: women, foot: feet,* and *ox: oxen* (which make their plurals either by changing a vowel or adding an *-en* inflection), plus *sheep* and *deer* (which add no inflection for the plural); and those patterns which came from other languages along with words we borrowed: *alumnus: alumni, genus: genera, criterion: criteria,* etc. There are a good many of these minor patterns, some exhibited in only a word or two, and others, especially those from Latin, in a good many. But the list of patterns is finite.

The dominant pattern is the so-called *s*-plural pattern, the {-Z₁} morpheme. We can see the force of that pattern by watching two factors— the word's history and the frequency of its use—work to make borrowed words conform to the dominant pattern. *Stadium,* for example, while it retains the Latin form *stadia* in some uses, has even more commonly developed the standard {-Z_1} form *stadiums* for its plural. The older English forms, such as *man: men,* apparently are retained primarily because of frequency of use; we are used to hearing them with the older forms. Children, however, always learn the dominant pattern first, and will often be heard experimenting with *man: mans* until they observe the difference in practice around them.

2. *Genitives of nouns.* A second morphemic pattern which signals grammatical meaning is the genitive inflection for nouns, often called the {-Z_2} inflection. It has exactly the same form as the {-Z_1} inflection's major pattern — /s/ after voiceless consonants except for /s/, /š/, and /č/; /z/ after voiced consonants and vowels, except for /z/, /ž/, and /ǰ/; and /ɨz/ after the six exceptions.

Genitives are formally recognizable, then, in the spoken form. When a word already carrying the plural inflection turns genitive, we usually do not add the genitive inflection, so the distinction is lost in speech. In writing we move the apostrophe: *boss: boss's* (singular), *bosses: bosses'* (plural). If the singular already ends in /s/, /z/, or /ɨz/, we have two possible courses for making a genitive: add nothing, as in *Keats* /kiyts/: *Keats'* /kiyts/, or add the relevant genitive inflection anyway: *Keats* /kiyts/: *Keats's* /kiytsɨz/. .

3. *Past tense (preterit) and past participles of verbs.* The major pattern, often called the dental suffix, is the so-called weak verb pattern used in the majority of English verbs. To form the past tense and past participle, this pattern adds /t/, /d/, or /ɨd/, according to the sound at the end of the infinitive. *Fish* adds /t/ to become /fišt/; *rig* adds /d/ to become /rigd/; *bat* adds /ɨd/ to become /bætɨd/.

The strong verb patterns, such as that of *swim, swam, swum,* are a second morphemic series for signaling tense. The Old English Class III pattern of *swim* has the largest number of verbs left in it, but there are examples of all seven classes still in use: *drive-drove-driven* (I), *freeze-froze-frozen* (II), *spring-sprang-sprung* (III), *steal-stole-stolen* (IV), *speak-spoke-spoken* (V), *shake-shook-shaken* (VI), and *grow-grew-grown* (VII). Charles C. Fries counted sixty-six of these strong verbs still displaying these older patterns, twenty-four of them reduced, however, to two forms, such as *shine, shone, shone* and *swing, swung, swung.*[5] If we add new verbs to the vocabulary, we make them conform to the weak or dental suffix pattern: the past tense of *garf* is /garft/. We can find a few verbs, like *dive* and *prove,* which maintain two sets of forms for preterit and past participles, apparently because they have begun but not completed the switch to the weak pattern. There are also a few other patterns for a handful of verbs like *be, have, go,* and *do,* but the entire list of patterns for verbs is not very long.

4. *Third person singular present-tense verb inflection.* This inflection is also morphemically distinctive. It is usually called the {-Z₃} inflection, because it is formed exactly like the major pattern for plurals of nouns and genitives of nouns: *I go* /gow/: *he goes* /gowz/; *I please* /pliyz/: *he pleases* /pliyzɨz/; *I sleep* /sliyp/: *he sleeps* /sliyps/.

5. *Present participles of verbs.* The *ing* /-iŋ/ form for present participles in English is also a morpheme.

6. *Verb subjunctives.* There are still some morphemic signals for the subjunctive mood in English, although we have dropped a good many of the older forms and, where we do retain the concept, often signal it by means of function words such as *should.* The inflections show up chiefly in the verbs *be, have,* and *do,* in object clauses after verbs such as *ask, command,* and *request,* and in conditional clauses, especially those with the function word *if.* Other verbs also show a subjunctive occasionally, but since it is much reduced in use, and since it shows up only in the third person singular of the present tense of most verbs ("If he *arrive* in time, we'll be safe"), examples are not often encountered except in the most formal discourse or after verbs like *ask* or *request.* Mainly the subjunctive appears with *be* and *have,* both as full verbs and as auxiliaries (function words): "If I *be* in time," "if you *be* given a chance," "if he *have* a place for me." Since *be* also has the distinctive *was* form in the past indicative first and third person singular, the subjunctive *were* is distinctive there too: "if I *were* you," "if he *were* here."

7. *Adjectives.* In adjectives there are morphemic patterns of inflection for the comparative and superlative degrees. /ər/ and /ɨst/ are added to nearly all one-syllable adjectives (*big* /bigər/ /bigɨst/) and to two-syllable adjectives of relatively high frequency (*happy* /hæpiyər/ /hæpiyɨst/), but to almost no three-or-more-syllable adjectives. The comparative and superlative functions are accomplished by the function words *more, most, less,* and *least* where the inflections do not occur (*beautiful, more beautiful, most beautiful*).

8. *Pronouns.* The pronouns have distinctive forms. In addition to the personal pronouns, which have distinctive forms for case, number, person, and—in third person singular—gender, *who* and *whom* are distinguished for case, *this* and *these* and *that* and *those* for number, and *who* and *which* for one aspect of gender.

9. *Other morphemic indicators.* Finally, grammatical information is given us morphemically by a long series of word-forming affixes (both pre-

fixes and suffixes), by vowel changes which occur medially, and by shifts in stress, all of which make functional change in English possible. Here are a few sample pairs:

arrive, v.	arrival, n.	súbject, n.	subjéct, v.
defend, v.	defense, n.	big, a.	bigness, n.
true, a.	truth, n.	friend, n.	befriend, v.
way, n.	away, adv.	broad, a.	abroad, adv.[6]

These nine categories of morphemic signals comprise the main grammatical information given in English by morphology. To them we must add the description of the intonation morphemes described earlier. Modern grammars of English find these descriptions, based on the spoken language, to be accurate and efficient generalizations of part of the English grammatical system. Further generalizations, such as those we have mentioned in connection with spelling and punctuation above, are needed to adapt them to the written language.

We turn next to the grammatical information that comes from function words, but here it is useful to pause first to consider what structural grammars do with parts of speech. Two distinct approaches, plus an adaptation of these, are apparent:

1. Some structural linguists use morphology alone to define the parts of speech, and simply exclude from the parts of speech those words which do not fit strict morphological categories. Nouns are words which can be inflected for the plural and for the genitive, verbs are words which can be inflected for the past tense, past participle, etc., and adjectives are words which can be inflected for the comparative and superlative. These parts of speech can also be identified by the contrastive morphemic affixes mentioned above.

2. Other structural linguists use function or position in the sentence as the exclusive criterion for classing parts of speech. Nouns or Class I words (mainly but not exclusively nouns formally defined) are words which can fit in the positions of subject and objects in a sentence such as "*John* gave *Mary* the *book*," or in positions after prepositions in patterns such as "in the *night*" and "on the *table*."

Verbs in this system are words which fit in the position of *goes, given,* and *was* in the following sentences: "John *goes* to school." "John has *given* the book to Mary." "John *was* sick."

Adjectives are then words which fit either after verbs in patterns such as "John was *sick*" (or exclusively there) or before nouns in patterns such as "the *sick* boy."

Adverbs have more positions: before or after verbs, as in "John went *willingly"* and "John *willingly* went," at the beginnings or ends of sentences, as in *"Willingly,* John went home" and "John went home *willingly,"* or before adjectives, as in *"pleasingly* plump" (although this last position is not accepted by a good many grammarians, who prefer to classify words which appear in this position as function words).

This positional classification of parts of speech turns up two kinds of lists of words: huge, open-ended lists of nouns, verbs, adjectives, and adverbs, and finite lists, often very short, of auxiliaries, prepositions, pronouns, articles, and the like. In other words, most of these positional classifications describe four parts of speech plus several finite lists of function words.

3. Finally, there are reconciliations of formal and positional bases of classification in modern grammars. For example, we can, as James Sledd does,[7] describe adjectives as words which inflect for the comparative and superlative, and then, after noting the positions in which these adjectives will function, we can classify as adjectivals all other words and word groups which, while they will not inflect for comparison, will function in the same structural positions as do these formally distinctive adjectives. Similarly, we can distinguish between nouns (a formal category) and nominals (a positional category which includes and is typical of nouns, but which contains other words and word groups), verbs and verbals, etc.

In any event, a rigorously formal or rigorously positional description of parts of speech—or a combined method—leads us to the third of the main kinds of grammatical signals distinguished by structural English grammars: function words.

We may designate function words either by labeling them with arbitrary symbols (type A, type B, etc.) or with descriptive labels, often ones borrowed for convenience from traditional grammars. The number of categories varies with the assumptions of the grammarian, but generally we will find at least these groups, all of which are finite lists of words which, while they may contain full lexical meanings, are usually "empty" or partly "empty" words, whose main meaning is grammatical.

1. Auxiliaries are words such as *may, shall, be,* and *have* that combine in various ways with verbs. *Do,* for example, lives a separate life both as verb and as auxiliary; some list it also as a special question-asking function word: *"Did* he *do* it?" In speech *have* and *has* distinguish the full verb from the function word in the present tense: *I have two books* /hæv/, and *I have to go home* /hæf/. These function words signal *verb* or *predication,* and when we use them, they rather than the verb itself take the inflections for number and tense which make for agreement of subject and verb and for logical sequence of tenses.

2. Prepositions are a finite list of function words which signal a

special structure of modification: "the man *in* the street." These structures always have noun (or nominal) objects, and they can fit as units anywhere that nominals, adjectivals, or adverbials can fit.

3. Determiners are a longer but still finite list of words which mark constructions headed by nouns or nominals. *The, a, an, this, that,* etc., are determiners: *"these* boys," *"the* big house."

4. Conjunctions are a short finite list of function words which relate words or larger structures to each other. There are two parts to the list: one, fairly small, is composed of words such as *and* and *but,* which are used to join words or constructions in parallel: "John *and* I came *and* sat here *and* there early *and* often, *and* we liked the atmosphere." The other, larger part contains conjunctions which relate subordinate or dependent structures, mainly those with verbs in them, to the main part of the sentence. *"Since* he came, we've been busy." "I like her *because* she's gay."

5. Pronouns are often not classed in structural grammars as function words but as a special group of nominals. Since they have limited and mainly grammatical meanings, however, and since they comprise short, finite lists of forms, they can fit the broad definition of function words. They can also be broken up into lists which classify largely under other function-word and part-of-speech classes.

6. Interrogatives are a finite list of function words used as the first element in questions, especially with *be* and the function word *do. "When* is he coming?" *"Who* does he think he is?" Obviously some of these overlap with pronouns.

7. Intensives are a group of function words which fit before adjectives or adjectivals in modification patterns. *Very* in "It's a *very* large order," and "He felt *very* sick," is the most common word of the class.

8. Finally, various modern grammars add function word classes for a handful of words almost empty of other than grammatical meaning. *Not,* for example, and its contracted form *n't,* mean *negative. There,* as in "There *there* is a place" (the first *there* is an adverb, the second the function word), means a transposed sentence pattern wherein the subject follows the verb.

After function words we come finally to the description of syntax as structural grammars treat it. Syntax deals with the kinds of grammatical meaning signaled by the order of words in an utterance and with the order of smaller units within various contained structures.

In the first place, most structural grammars use a different sort of definition of the sentence, a definition based on the spoken language, although of course it is adaptable to the written language as well. These definitions vary according to the grammarian's assumptions, but at any rate they are never notional. Here are two typical definitions:

1. A sentence is an utterance, either from silence to silence, or from $/_2{}^{3/3}\nearrow/$ or any falling clause terminal to silence, to $/_2{}^{3/3}\nearrow/$, or to any falling clause terminal.

2. A sentence is an utterance which elicits certain responses. In this definition, statements elicit nods or other tacit or verbal signs of agreement or comprehension, questions elicit answers, and commands elicit action responses.

Classification of sentences on this second ground leads us to generalizations about what Charles C. Fries calls "situation utterances" and "response utterances," [8] two classes which differ or can differ grammatically mainly in that response utterances can be fragmentary, without predication. "On Tuesday" is a response utterance, an answer to a question.

Most structural grammars treat syntactic relationships by means of description of immediate constituents; hence structural grammars are often called immediate-constituent grammars. Briefly, immediate-constituent analysis consists in discovering how sentences are put together by taking them apart according to hierarchies of grammatical relationships. Unlike the parsing of traditional grammars, however, IC analysis uses an order dictated by the several structures themselves, which W. Nelson Francis calls [9] modification, predication, complementation, and coordination. "All larger structures," says Francis, "are simply combinations of these. . . ."

1. *Modification.* There are various forms of this, depending on what part of speech or positional substitute functions as the head of the structure. If a noun or nominal is head, we get a structure such as: *a sunny day*, with *day* as head. *A day with sun, a day having sun,* and *a day which is sunny* are all structures of modification. IC analysis takes the syntactic relationships apart in hierarchical layers which we can describe graphically in various ways:

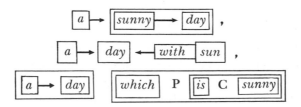

etc. (P means *predication;* C means *complementation.*) This process can be continued as each structure is broken up, until we have reached the ultimate constituents, the individual words and their morphemic components.

2. *Predication.* This is the relationship keyed to subject and verb, but of course it can be much more complex:

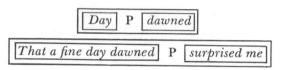

are the immediate constituents of two sentences. The parts of the second sentence can then be analyzed into their immediate constituents.

3. *Complementation.* These are the structures that include the developments of full predicates. To complete the IC analysis of the last example above, we break down the IC's,

. These structures account for all sorts of object complements and subject complements and their modifiers.

4. *Coordination.* These structures are usually parallel constructions joined by a coordinator—usually a function word, a conjunction:

| Horses | and | dogs | | He wrote her | but | she didn't answer. |

(Some modern grammarians prefer to do without this structural class, arguing that there are more consistent explanations. For example, most instances of subordinate clause structure would be classified under "modification" in this scheme.)

IC analysis may look a bit like the diagraming traditional grammar often uses in teaching, in order to make parsing and naming of parts more graphic, but there is a vital difference in purpose and assumptions. In IC analysis we are concerned with identifying and discovering the function of layers of grammatical structures. We seek grammatical meaning only. We want to show how English sentences work—the main goal of all structural English grammars.

Generative Grammars of English

The newest of grammatical theories are embodied in attempts, so far not fully worked out in all details, but clearly very promising, to write what are called generative grammars of English. In many ways generative grammars are merely a special development of structural grammars, rather than a completely new departure: the phrase analysis, the structured strings of morphemes, and the materials which make possible the statement of morphophonemic rules in generative grammars all stem directly from modern descriptive linguistic investigation. All owe a good deal to structural grammars. But generative grammars differ from structural grammars in certain primary assumptions: generative grammars are predicated on a slightly different definition of the grammar of English than that used by most structural grammars. For one thing, it is a definition which tries to predict the possible grammatical forms sentences may take, rather than simply to describe after the fact the forms that sentences already written or uttered have taken. This definition says that the grammar of English is a set of laws or rules which we "know," which enables us to utter English sentences and only English sentences. Generative grammars try to state those rules which "generate" all possible English sentences and only English sentences. These grammars rest on several important observations from mathematics and communication theory. Paul Roberts' computer analogy is probably as descriptive as any general statement.[10] It assumes that we, like computers, have certain built-in laws and the information to use with those laws. We unconsciously abstract the laws from our trial and error imitation as children, and we soon reach the point where we do not have to imitate sentences we have heard. We come to "know" rules which let us form completely new sentences that meet the criteria of English grammar.

An objective knowledge of English grammar is of course the generative grammarians' goal. And, building in large part upon the details—such as those of morphology and phrase structure—worked out by linguists whose descriptions of English provided us with our descriptive grammars, such men as Noam Chomsky, Robert B. Lees, and others have begun to state the rules of that grammar.

The main lines of their investigations are these: we begin with the description of kernel sentences—a list of simple, declarative, active sentences with no complex elements, no complex developments of verb or noun phrases. From these we can derive all other sentences by means of rules for transformations—rules which change or develop a kernel sentence by developing one or more of its phrase structures into different but still grammatical parts of a different but still grammatical English sentence. We work with structured strings of morphemes—those same morphemes the modern grammarians uncovered for us. Then finally we can arrive at any particular sentence by applying the morphophonemic rules —the third part of a generative grammar—which will enable us to convert any properly structured string of morphemes, transformed or not, into either a written or spoken English sentence.

This newest grammatical description promises to tell us still more about how the language works, and it promises especially to help us grasp syntax as descriptive grammars have not always been completely successful in doing.

For example, it describes the kernel sentences "lions growl" and "John raises flowers." Regular transformations give us "the growling of lions" and "the raising of flowers," but as transformations from two different kernel sentences.

We can then see a reasonable explanation for the ambiguity of "the shooting of the hunters": the relation of *shoot* to *hunters* is different in the two kernels from which the ambiguous structure can be derived ("hunters shoot" and "John shoots hunters"), since ". . . neither 'they growl lions' nor 'flowers raise' are grammatical kernel sentences." [11]

Above all, generative grammars promise to be able to help us toward the solution of one of the hardest problems grammars have had to deal with: how to state the rules that make the grammar of our sentences predictable, instead of our being obliged by our grammatical descriptions only to analyze sentences we have already written or spoken. Full generative or transformational grammars remain to be written, but in their present state they already have told us a great deal, and their future looks very bright.

Conclusion

The grammar of modern American English has been described by many grammars—traditional, structural, and now generative. We now know that grammar is best studied apart from semantics, that the system itself can be better delineated if we avoid the notional naming of parts.

We know too that the signals of English grammar can be described, that we can get grammatical information from morphemes (intonational, inflectional, and word-forming morphemes), from function words (which are morphemes too), and from syntactic patterns of strings of morphemes. We know also that much of the terminology of the traditional grammars, under different definition, is useful to us in our descriptions, as is the full notional system of traditional grammars in reminding us of what we need to know about the relation of grammar to total meaning. We know further that close attention to the spoken language and its sounds has enabled us to see more precisely what it is that is being patterned in English grammar; structural grammars have taught us that, as they have also shown us something about the hierarchies of constituent analysis. We know too that the grammar of English is peculiar to English, an analytic language which is precisely like no other language on earth.

In short, we know a great deal—although by no means all—about the grammar of English, and it is clear that at present the study of all three grammars of English is necessary for the man who wishes fully and consciously to understand his language, how he uses it, and how it uses him.

Notes

1. George O. Curme, *Syntax* (New York, 1931) and *Parts of Speech and Accidence* (New York, 1935).
2. Curme, *Syntax*, p. 1.
3. *Parts of Speech and Accidence*, p. 42.
4. *Ibid.*, p. 63.
5. *American English Grammar* (New York, 1940), p. 61.
6. A nearly complete list appears in Charles C. Fries, *The Structure of English* (New York, 1952), pp. 110–41.
7. *A Short Introduction to English Grammar* (New York, 1959), pp. 79 ff.
8. *The Structure of English*, pp. 37 ff.
9. *The Structure of American English* (New York, 1958), pp. 292 ff.
10. *English Sentences* (New York, 1962), p. 1.
11. These examples and the quotation are from Noam Chomsky, *Syntactic Structures* (The Hague, 1957), p. 89.

RICHARD OHMANN

Grammar and Meaning

A grammar can set out to do any of a number of things. It can assert the propriety of certain forms of language, and urge them upon all speakers and writers; such, in intent, are many of the older school grammars. Or it can attempt a neutral description of the way members of a speech community actually talk; this is the aim of much grammatical scholarship in this century. Again, a descriptive grammar can look at the speech or writing of a specified group within the society—educated people, say, or professional writers. In short, the same conflicts in purpose that have troubled dictionary editors and their publics beset grammarians as well.

In the past two decades, a still different perspective on grammars and their use has developed, through the work of the linguist Noam Chomsky and many others. They refer to the grammars they build as *generative*. The rules of such a grammar must account for—or, to put it another way, must be capable of generating—every conceivable sentence of a language that is felt by native speakers of that language to be grammatical or, as it is usually put, well-formed. But in addition to describing the facts of language, a generative grammar tries to explain them; in this it differs from grammars of other kinds. To explain the facts of language is to link a description of them to what we know about human mental capacities. So a generative grammar is actually a theory of a particular language—more precisely, a theory of the knowledge that any fluent speaker has of that language. Herein is another sharp difference between generative and other grammars: what a generative grammar describes and explains is not merely the linguistic "output" of speakers, but their *understanding* of language. In brief, a grammar of this sort attempts to describe part of human mentality. In the view of generative grammarians, grammar is a part of human psychology.

From *The American Heritage Dictionary of the English Language,* edited by William Morris. © 1969, 1970 by American Heritage Publishing Co., Inc. Reprinted by permission of the publisher.

Language, like the body, is so comfortable and familiar that we hardly notice its presence or its complexity. Yet once examined closely, the accomplishment of any ordinary speaker is rather astonishing. He can produce and understand an indefinite number of new sentences—sentences he has never encountered previously. Put before 25 speakers a fairly simple drawing, ask them to describe in a sentence the situation it portrays, and they will easily come up with such examples as:

> A bear is occupying a telephone booth, while a tourist impatiently waits in line.
> A man who was driving along the road has stopped and is waiting impatiently for a grizzly bear to finish using the public phone.
> A traveler waits impatiently as a bear chatters gaily in a highway phone booth.

Almost certainly, each of the 25 sentences will be different from all the others, yet each will adequately describe the drawing. Speech is creative; it is in no rigid way determined by given circumstances. Moreover, as the bear-and-telephone examples show, the ability to come up with a suitable sentence does not depend on having associated the sentence with the situation before: it is obviously unlikely that any speaker who produced one of these particular sentences had ever before encountered it, much less the situation it describes. The same is true of a speaker's ability to understand new sentences produced by other people. Probably all the sentences in this essay are new to the reader, yet if they are grammatical, he should have no trouble perceiving their structure and understanding them.

The number of possible sentences in English is enormous—for all practical purposes infinite. Using the vocabulary and structures supplied in any 25 typical sentences, and permuting them in all possible ways (so long as the resulting sentences are grammatical), one could usually construct billions of sentences. An analysis by computer shows that the 25 sentences about the bear in the phone booth yield the materials for 19.8 billion sentences, all describing just one situation. When one reflects that the number of seconds in a century is only 3.2 billion, it is clear that no speaker has heard, read, or spoken more than a tiny fraction of the sentences he *could* speak or understand, and that no one learns English by learning any particular sentences of English. What speakers *have* learned is a grammar. And the examples show one requirement we must make of a grammar: that it be capable of generating an infinite number of grammatical sentences. But the grammar itself must be finite, since the finite human brain must "contain" it.

A closely related ability, common to speakers of English, which our grammar must account for, is that of telling sentences from nonsentences —that is, of distinguishing the grammatical from the ungrammatical. Anyone to whom English is native can do this, not only in blatant cases ("Leave me" versus "Me leave"), but also in subtler pairings:

> Got he a chance?
> Has he a chance?
> The accident was seen by thousands.
> The accident was looked by thousands.

In each pair, the two members differ only slightly in their make-up, yet one is clearly an English sentence and one is not. We must, apparently, posit a "grammatical intuition" of some intricacy that allows such discriminations, without the speaker's consciously knowing how he makes them.

One may want to attribute this capacity to something other than a grammatical intuition, but no other explanation seems adequate. Speakers do not need to learn to create sentences, understand new sentences, and distinguish between English and non-English through formal instruction; preschool children, illiterates, and feeble-minded adults are capable of these acts. Nor is the grammatical sense based entirely on meaning. The meaning of many ungrammatical sentences can be grasped as, for instance, that of "Got he a chance?" and "The accident was looked by thousands." Conversely, meaningless (or at least mystifying) sentences may be grammatical, as is the case with:

> Fragile hippos cheat lucidly.
> The flat mountains multiply backwards.

Note that even these "nonsense" sentences can be paired with closely related nonsentences:

> Fragile hippos seem lucidly.
> Multiply backwards mountains flat the.

"Meaningful" is not identical with "grammatical." Speakers have a special grammatical knowledge, and that knowledge is what a grammar must explicate.

Here are a few more abilities that speakers of English have:

1. They can perceive more than one grammatical structure in the same sequence of words. Thus, "I had three books stolen" has at least three meanings, depending on which way its words are related to one another. This is evident if we expand the sentence three ways:

I had three books stolen from me.
I had three books stolen for me.
I had three books stolen, when something interrupted my burglarizing.

2. Speakers can notice differences in structure among sentences that look alike:

The cow was found by a stream.
The cow was found by a farmer.

3. They can see likenesses in basic structure (and meaning) among sentences that look quite different:

The cow was found by a farmer.
A farmer found the cow.
Was the cow found by a farmer?
The farmer's finding the cow pleased everyone.

These three abilities suggest another requirement we must make of an English grammar: that it abstract considerably from the physical signals of speech, including word order, since often the way speakers understand sentences is related in no direct way to these overt characteristics.

Perhaps this brief discussion is enough to hint at the difficulty of explaining what speakers of English know. It is time to make an even more abbreviated sketch of a theory that could handle the task.

For purposes of illustration, let us pretend that we are dealing with an "English language" that includes only four known words, namely: *the, guard, saw,* and *someone.* What is required to start with is a set of analytical rules that will show how sentences are generated, or constructed, in this very limited language. Such rules we will call *phrase-structure* rules, meaning by "phrase structure" either a single word or two or more words that serve a particular grammatical function. By studying the way in which the four words in this "English language" are used, we can derive a fundamental phrase-structure rule: A sentence may consist of a noun phrase followed by a predicate. In a generative grammar, as compared with older-style grammars, it is found to be useful to express such rules in a more abstract, symbolic form than that used in traditional parsing, so that we get:

Sentence $\longrightarrow$ Noun Phrase $+$ Predicate

(The arrow means "may consist of.") Now let us add more rules:

Predicate ⟶ Verb + Noun Phrase
Noun Phrase ⟶ Article + Noun
Noun Phrase ⟶ Pronoun
Article ⟶ *the*
Noun ⟶ *guard*
Verb ⟶ *saw*
Pronoun ⟶ *someone*

This group of rules actually constitutes a very simple grammar, which is capable of generating four sentences:

The guard saw $\begin{cases} \text{the guard.} \\ \text{someone.} \end{cases}$

Someone saw $\begin{cases} \text{someone.} \\ \text{the guard.} \end{cases}$

But since English actually has infinitely more sentences than this, the grammar must be enlarged if it is to perform its task. We might try adding a word and expanding one rule accordingly:

Article ⟶ $\begin{cases} the \\ a \end{cases}$

This adds several sentences to the grammar's output. Here's another rule that might be expanded:

Noun ⟶ $\begin{cases} guard \\ light \end{cases}$

This adds sentences such as:

Someone saw the light.
The guard saw a light.

But it also introduces sequences like "The light saw a guard," which is not grammatical. Thus the rules will have to be modified in some way. For instance, we might try marking nouns as "animate" and "inanimate," and verbs as taking animate or inanimate subjects. This we could suggest by a simple notation like:

Verb ⟶ _____ *saw*
          (animate)

and by assigning "features" to the nouns: "guard" would have the feature +animate, while "light" would have the feature −animate. Thus, the grammar would allow only "guard" to appear as subject of "saw."

There are clearly implications here for semantics—the science of meanings. Although the features +animate and −animate are purely syntactic—that is, based on syntactic compatibility—they evidently have their semantic analogues. That is to say, words like *someone, guard,* and *cow* have an element of meaning in common, just as they behave in some ways alike syntactically. Native speakers of English, like those of any language, must in some sense have words unconsciously "indexed" by syntactic and semantic features, so that they can capitalize on whatever is systematic about the English lexicon. A time may come when some dictionaries, too, will arrange words in such a way—thus, for instance, allowing the semantic information in a dictionary to be stored in and easily retrieved from a computer in many ways other than the alphabetical one which necessarily prevails today.

In any case, phrase-structure rules account for the basic structures of English, and for the main grammatical relationships such as subject-verb and verb-direct object. For a while, grammarians thought that a complete grammar of English might be composed of phrase-structure rules, but it now seems clear that such a grammar would be quite inadequate. Among other faults, it would have far too many separate rules and structures. The 19 billion sentences about the bear in the phone booth would require many thousands of phrase-structure rules to account for the different patterns of word arrangement used. This is far too much apparatus, it would seem, to explain the speaker's accomplishment. Just as clearly, phrase-structure rules cannot explain the ambiguity of a sentence like "I had three books stolen," whose words can have any of three different structures. Again, a grammar constructed out of phrase-structure rules alone will have nothing to say about relationships such as that between:

A farmer found the cow.

and

The cow was found by a farmer.

Yet it would obviously be grammatically economical, as well as psychologically right, to explain such relationships.

For these and other reasons, it is necessary to add a second kind of rule to the grammar: the *transformation.* Transformations apply not to single units, but to whole structures; they may add to or subtract from those structures, or change the order of elements, or substitute one element for another. For example, a transformation changes the structure:

Noun Phrase[1] + Past Tense + Verb + Noun Phrase[2]

to

Noun Phrase[2] + Past Tense + *be* + *by* + Noun Phrase[1]

This (in crudely simplified form) is the *passive* transformation, the rule that accounts for the relationship between:

A farmer found the cow.

and

The cow was found by a farmer.

In addition to representing a similarity that every speaker of English is aware of, the passive transformation has the great advantage of economy. Rather than having passive forms generated by a whole separate set of phrase-structure rules, just one rule converts any active form (with a transitive verb and a direct object) into the corresponding passive. Savings like this begin to make the grammar manageable, just as, presumably, they make it possible for a speaker of English to understand without difficulty a large number of sentences he has never heard before.

Other transformations combine two or more structures to create complex ones. For instance, a sentence like "The farmer's finding the cow pleased everyone" would not be generated by phrase-structure rules alone. Rather, these rules would separately generate the structures:

The farmer + find + the cow

and

(Something) + please + everyone

Then a transformation would convert the first of these into:

The farmer's finding the cow

and another would substitute this structure for *something*. Other combining transformations generate relative clauses, adverbial clauses, complement structures, and the like, and so build the more complex sentences of English.

There is one important thing to notice at this point. The basic grammatical relationships that are indicated in the simple sentences by word order often have a different representation in the complex sentences built up by transformation. Thus, in the simple structure:

The farmer + find + the cow

farmer is subject of the verb *find,* whereas in:

The farmer's finding the cow pleased everyone

farmer appears as an adjectival modifier and *find* as a noun. Yet any speaker knows that the "real" relationship between "farmer" and "find" is the one revealed in the simple structure, not in the final sentence. Otherwise he would not understand what the sentence said—would not notice that there was a subject-verb connection between "farmer" and "find" or, to put it another way, that the farmer indeed found the cow.

One way to interpret the native speaker's insight into more complicated sentences is to say that each sentence has a *deep structure,* built up by the application of phrase-structure rules; and this deep structure expresses all the basic content, or meaning, of a sentence. Another implication of such findings for semantics is that many words that are transformationally derived need not be separately defined. For example, the word *dismissal* often occurs in sentences such as:

His dismissal of the undersecretary caused alarm.

This has as part of its deep structure:

He + dismiss + the undersecretary

No meaning is added by the transformation; hence *dismissal* really need not be thought of as a separate word with the meaning "act of dismissing." All the necessary information is provided by a definition of *dismiss,* along with the relationship between *he* and *dismiss.* Notice that we also have sentences such as:

His dismissal by the undersecretary caused alarm.

Here the deep structure reveals a different relationship:

The undersecretary + dismiss + him

In other words, the phrase *his dismissal* is in itself ambiguous. However, the ambiguity results not from multiple meanings of the word *dismissal*, but rather from the possibility of tying *his dismissal* to either of the two deep structures cited. If dictionaries did not have to serve people other than native speakers, there would be no more point in having a second definition of *dismissal* ("condition of being dismissed") than in having the first. Both are unnecessary to a speaker who knows the word *dismiss* and the two transformations that can produce *his dismissal*. To generalize, there is a great deal of syntax concealed in complex words, and to capitalize on that fact would be to bring out many regularities in the lexicon.

To return to the main theme: the part of a grammar that deals with syntax has two kinds of rules, which collaborate to produce deep structures and surface structures. Deep structures represent basic meaning, and surface structures are wholly responsible for the sound of a sentence —such features as stress, intonation, and the quality of the vowels.

Hence, a generative grammar with transformational rules mediates between sound and sense, and so provides a model of part of what every native speaker knows. Although there are many unsolved problems in grammar—indeed, many areas of confusion and open controversy—at least the assumptions outlined here have been and continue to be fruitful.

That being so, it may be well to add a few words of speculation on the implications of such a grammar for the study of mind. No grammar of a language, to repeat, is adequate unless it is compatible with the facts of language learning—for instance, the fact that the child hears an irregular scattering of sentences and nonsentences, and from that sample somehow builds an adequate theory of the language being spoken around him. How could he ever do that if his language has roughly the form described here? In the past, the standard answer has been "induction": The child generalizes from his sensory experience, groups sounds together, associates them with meanings.

But if what the child must learn is a grammar with deep structures— as seems quite certain—then this picture of language learning is impossible. There simply are no physical signs, no sensory representations, of many critical features of meaning which the child has to extract from the stream of speech—namely, most of the features represented in deep structure. Hence a child approaching the task of acquiring the language spoken around him would be utterly incapable of doing so if he were equipped only with a *tabula rasa*. He must have some initial presuppositions about what he is to find in the stream of speech; that is so say, he must have some innate mental structure that is peculiarly adapted to the creative and rapid learning of language.

Furthermore, since a child will learn with equal ease whatever language he is first exposed to, his innate assumptions must pertain equally well to all languages. It follows that all languages have some structure in common. If it has seemed implausible, for a long time, that this could be so—that there could be a universal grammar—perhaps that is because surface structures do vary widely among the thousands of languages of the world. It may nonetheless be true that deep structures of all languages are much alike and are closely related to universal categories of human thought and perception. This exciting possibility today beckons on the horizon of generative-transformational grammar.

Aids to Study and Topics for Writing

Aids to Study

1. What is the difference between *expression* and *content* in language?
2. From your knowledge of a foreign language, find a good example of difference in content between that language and English. Are differences in idioms, such as those between French and English versions of "I'm hungry" and "He's eighteen years old," illustrations of differences in content?
3. Vocabulary is arbitrary. Write the word *pain* on a slip of paper. If it were found by a Frenchman, what would it mean? What other words can you think of which illustrate the same point?
4. Vocabulary "is the least stable and even the least characteristic of the three components of language." Explain why this should be so.
5. In learning a second language, says Professor Gleason, vocabulary is the easiest matter, yet students fear it most. Read (or perhaps your instructor will read to you) Mark Twain's essay, "The Wonderful German Language." Does the American humorist agree with the fearful students or with the linguists about what offers the greatest difficulty in learning a language?
6. What is a phoneme? What is a morpheme? What is the significant difference between them?
7. Get good definitions for *phonology, morphology, syntax,* and *rhetoric.* What's the difference between *syntax* and *rhetoric?* Between *grammar* and *syntax?* Between *grammar* and *rhetoric?*
8. What are the semantic problems you encounter in dealing with terms like *rhetoric, syntax,* and *grammar?*
9. What would a science be if it were *autonomous?*

136

Topics for Writing

1. Explain in an essay what it is about language that linguists are interested in.
2. Make up some nonsense words, and explain why they take the form they do. *Can* you really make up words with absolute freedom as to the sounds you employ?
3. Obviously, Professor Gleason's way of looking at language is different from the view that most of us have as laymen. Write an essay in which you list some of the things you or your parents and friends always thought were true about language, but which linguistics seem to controvert.

WILSON, THE HISTORY OF THE ENGLISH LANGUAGE

Aids to Study

1. Which of the several kinds of language history Wilson lists (pp. 42–44) seems to you most interesting, most familiar, and most useful for your own purposes? (Why? Were you aware that the others might exist? If not, why not?) Explain.
2. How should our having changed from a rural to an industrial-urban nation have affected our language? List some of the things that are different and try to discover some linguistic evidence of the change.
3. Wilson says that the weak verb system—the one which forms the past tense and the past participle by adding a dental suffix—is now dominant. Coin some new verbs and test this generalization.
4. *Whom* as an objective or accusative form is often said to be disappearing from Standard English. Is *whom* disappearing from your own speech and writing? Does it make any difference whether you are speaking or writing? Does the place in the sentence or the kind of construction seem to make a difference in your practice?
5. What signs of the different kinds of grammars Wilson discusses do you find in reviewing your own formal schoolwork in grammar? Was it school-grammar, descriptive, generative? A combination? None of these? Cite some examples of the things you studied and see where they fit in Wilson's scheme.

Topics for Writing

1. Look up in as many English-foreign language dictionaries as are available the word for *father, hound, foot, mother,* and *hundred.* Then write an essay explaining the similarities and differences you find.
2. "When two cultures come into contact, everything seems to depend upon

who is master, or at least upon who feels inferior" (p. 45). What evidence of this sort of contest can you see in your own language practices as you moved from home and high school to college? Illustrate your discussion with as many examples as possible.

MARCKWARDT: THE LANGUAGE OF THE COLONISTS

Aids to Study

1. What dates do most historians use to include the American Colonial period? How much of the country was settled, how much even explored by the end of that period? Was your own state settled by then?
2. Where, in England, did the main groups of colonists come from? Which groups probably spoke a London dialect?
3. How do puns and rimes from Shakespeare's plays help us discover the sounds of his language?
4. Make a list of the vowels in Shakespeare's English which are different from our modern ones.
5. What differences in stress does Professor Marckwardt describe in comparing Elizabethan and modern American English?
6. What was Shakespeare's practice with second person pronouns? How did it differ from ours?
7. What's an *"inacomodate* condition" (p. 68)?
8. Where did the expression "to dress meat" come from? Do we still use it?
9. *Queasy*—What's its history?
10. How did Bradford pronounce *boatswain?* Look into the history of the word and its pronunciation.

Topics for Writing

1. Rewrite in good modern English the passage from William Bradford's *History* (pp. 68–69). Then write an essay in which you discuss the differences, besides those Professor Marckwardt cites, between your version and Bradford's. How many of these can you give reasons for?
2. Look locally—in place names, names of animals, trees, and the like—for evidence of the first settlers' arrival. Were English-speaking settlers the first Europeans to arrive? If not, what signs can you see that others were there first? Write an essay in which you report some of your findings.
3. What signs of Indian influence on English do you find in your state or local area? Write an essay in which you describe and explain these linguistic relics.

FRIES: A CLASSIFICATION OF GRAMMATICAL PHENOMENA

Aids to Study

1. In the quotation (pp. 71–72) from Mencken's "Vulgate" version of the opening lines of the Declaration of Independence, what grammatical problems
do you see besides the double negatives? List these, and with the aid of a
dictionary, account for the odd forms and the substandard syntax.

2. What about the vocabulary in the passage Mencken rewrote? How much of
it is still slang? How much of it is not in your desk dictionary at all? Can
you account for the omissions? Would you change any of these labels to
conform to more nearly current standards?

3. What is the difference between the *dative* and *accusative* cases in Latin?
Does English preserve formal distinctions between them? Are there inflections to distinguish them in nouns? In pronouns? How did the term *objective case* arise in English?

4. Look closely at the dialogue in the comic strips in your daily newspaper.
What substandard or Vulgar English do you find there? Do Professor Fries's
remarks about comic writers' use of such language seem to be borne out?

5. What are the three types of device English uses to express grammatical
ideas? Find new examples of each.

6. What is *vulgate?* What has it in common with the *Vulgate Bible?*

7. What is a *preterit?* Is this a better term to use than *past tense?*

8. What are *demonstratives* (p. 72), and how would you use them *attributively?* Compose some examples.

9. *Concord*—Does your desk dictionary record Fries's specialized meaning for
this word (p. 72)?

10. Write a "dictionary definition" of *function word,* and then compare yours
with your desk dictionary's definition.

11. Does your desk dictionary record a special grammatical or linguistic meaning for the term *frequency?* Should it? Why?

12. Is there any difference between *word order* and *syntax?* Explain.

Topics for Writing

1. Mencken's "Vulgate" version of lines from the Declaration of Independence
sounds dated. Rewrite them using more nearly current vulgate language.
Now, without consulting the original, rewrite them in the best expository
prose you can muster. Then, compare both versions with the original document's wording, and discuss the differences. What kinds of things did you

change in your two versions, and what are the chief differences between your "good" version and the historical original?

2. What advantages can you see to stripping away semantics and concentrating on "grammatical" meaning when you're examining grammar? Write an essay in which you explore the problem.

3. Of all the material you previously considered part of the study of grammar, what does Fries seem to include, and what does he seem to exclude?

ROBERTS: PHONEMES

Aids to Study

1. Go carefully through Roberts's list of phonemes on pages 78 and 79. Pronounce all the words, especially in context: that is, put them in sentences, sometimes at the beginning, sometimes in the middle, sometimes at the end. Do the same with the examples on pp. 79–80. Then make a list of phonemes—and of sample words in which they occur—wherein your speech seems to differ from Roberts's California speech.

2. Compare your lists with those of others in your class who were born and raised in the same town or county or state as you. Do you find consistent dialectal differences in phonemes?

3. Now practice transcribing these words exactly as you normally pronounce them. Be sure to put them in sentences so that you can hear them as you normally say them.

a.	king	g.	often
b.	rather	h.	surprised
c.	possible	i.	Tuesday
d.	follow	j.	Wednesday
e.	Canadian	k.	February
f.	something	l.	absorb

4. Practice making a few simple phonetic transcriptions, being certain that you record the actual sounds you usually make. Transcribe your full name, the way you would say it in response to a question. Transcribe these words: *clothes, interesting, machinery, roof, psychology, execute, executive, screams.* Transcribe this sentence, exactly as you would normally say it: "How do you get to the bookstore from here?"

5. Check your pronunciations—as you've transcribed them—with those in your desk dictionary. Any disagreements?

6. Transcribe these words the way you normally say them:

a. tenth	f. debt	k. few	p. balm
b. length	g. doubt	l. blue	q. bomb
c. strength	h. pneumatic	m. cot	r. Mary
d. finger	i. graph	n. caught	s. merry
e. singer	j. news	o. cat	t. marry

7. How many of the vowels and diphthongs Roberts describes do you actually have? Which ones are you missing? Do you know anyone—a speaker of a different dialect—who has these sounds?

Topics for Writing

1. Write an essay in which you consider some of the advantages and disadvantages in a system of spelling reform for English which might propose to use some or all of the phonemic alphabet in place of our conventional one.
2. If you are currently studying a foreign language, write an essay in which you describe and discuss the phonemic differences between that language and English. Why are such phonemes—like the French *r* and *u*—hard for you to learn?

HALL: ANALOGY

Aids to Study

1. Think of some more examples of "mistakes" resulting from *internal borrowing* or *analogy*. For example, what is the past tense of the verb *sneak?*
2. What are the reasons that some analogical forms are respectable while others are unacceptable?
3. What are the plurals of *mongoose, moose, stadium?* Why should you hesitate over some of these? What about *data* and *agenda?* Write down the singular and plural forms *you* would use, and then see what your desk dictionary records for all these words.
4. Look up *analogy* in your desk dictionary, and compare the meanings marked *Philology* or *Linguistics* with the one labeled *Logic.* How does this distinction bear on problems of grammar and usage?
5. Consult a historical dictionary for the curious analogical development of the verb *ring.*
6. Words like *beautifuler* and *bestest* are formed on analogy. With what, and how?
7. What archaic plurals like *kine* can you think of? Have all of them been replaced by a regular plural? Check your desk dictionary to see.
8. What principal parts do you use for the verb *dream?* What does your desk

dictionary say about the problem? How has the process of analogy worked here?

9. How do you account for the humorous noun *invite* (instead of *invitation*)? How does analogy figure in its existence?

10. What are the current plurals for these words: *curriculum, status,* and *stimulus?* Is analogy at work on any of them?

Topics for Writing

1. Analogy has forced many of our former strong verbs into the weak verb pattern. Besides *dive* and *dream* and the others Hall cites, what ones can you think of that are currently under some strain? Which ones do adults most often form on the weak pattern? Write an essay in which you survey the subject.

2. What, in logic, is a *false analogy?* Does the same thing exist in linguistic change? Explore this question in an essay.

HUBBELL: MULTIPLE NEGATION

Aids to Study

1. When did the multiple negative cease to be acceptable in good English?
2. What arguments does Hubbell use against the "logical" prohibition of multiple negatives?
3. Why does Hubbell think the double negative continues to be a problem, despite all the teaching aimed against it?
4. How *can* we teach Standard English, according to the author? Does he agree with the views on this subject expressed by Fries?
5. Is the use of the double negative a problem of cultural level or geographical dialect or something else? What is the evidence to support your view?
6. Is *can't hardly* a double negative? How will you decide?
7. *Not infrequent, not unlikely,* and *not uncommon* have two negative elements each. How do they differ from what we usually call double negatives?
8. *Can't help but* and *couldn't help but* are sometimes cited as double negatives. Is that what they are? What labels would you give them?

Topics for Writing

1. In his final paragraph, Hubbell concludes that "group loyalties" are the only really effective forces in making people change their language habits. Is there evidence to support this statement in changes in your own language practices since you entered college? Document your answer in an essay.

2. Write an essay in which you explore the usage situations and appropriate labels if any for this expression: *We haven't but one hour left.*

BRYANT: SPLIT INFINITIVE

Aids to Study

1. This is one of those accounts of usage which anger purists and other laymen by giving variant information, rather than a simplistic rule. Would it be better (truer? more helpful?) to simply proscribe the split infinitive? Or would you rather have the whole truth, even if it is complicated? (By the way, did you notice the split infinitive in the second sentence, before it was pointed out? Now that you've seen it, would you prefer "simply to proscribe," or doesn't it matter? How many of your classmates noticed it? Does that information help you to decide your own usage?)

Topics for Writing

1. Some people hate to hear or see *contact* used as a verb. How do you feel about it? Now consult some dictionaries and usage guides. How did the problem arise, and what seems to be a sensible attitude for today? Write an informal report.
2. Many people feel that use of the superlative (*smallest, largest, fattest*) in comparing only two things is bad English. Try some examples in your own speech and writing. Describe your own practice and make whatever observations you can about it. Then consult the usage guides and dictionaries and try your hand at writing an entry for your own usage guide on this point. Model it on the Bryant piece.
3. Select another problem of divided usage and consult the dictionaries and usage guides on its history and present distribution. Then take your own survey of current usage, and write a full report. What should our attitude toward it be? Does its history—the reason that it became a problem—affect our attitude?

ROBERTSON AND CASSIDY: CHANGING MEANINGS AND VALUES OF WORDS

Aids to Study

1. What further examples of the "etymological fallacy" can you think of? Check them in an unabridged dictionary to see what happened to their meanings.
2. Consult the *OED* for the following words: *affair, awful, minister, gentle,*

shade, sergeant, shears, scissors, cad, boor, gossip, hussy. What processes of semantic change does each illustrate?

3. Here is the *OED* entry for *frock*. What seems to have caused each of the changes it shows in historical development?

Frock (frǫk), *sb.* Forms: 4–5 frokke, 5 frogge, 4–6 frok(e, *Sc.* or *north.* frog, 6–7 frocke, 6– frock. [a. F. *froc* (recorded from 12th c.); of uncertain origin.

Cf. Pr. *floc* frock, med. L. *froccus, floccus*. Some scholars regard the *fl*-forms as the original, and identify the word with L. *floccus*, OF. *floc* FLOCK *sb.*[2] Others regard *froc* as adopted from a Teut. word, OHG. *hroch* (once), OS. *hroc* (once), OFris. *hrokk* (rare); but in these forms it is believed by many Germanists that the *hr*- is a misspelling without phonetic significance, the usual forms being OHG. *roch* (mod. Ger. *rock*), OFris. *rokk*, OE. *rocc*.]

1. A long habit with large open sleeves; the outer and characteristic dress of a monk. *Rarely,* a cassock (of an Anglican clergyman). Hence, the priestly office which it indicates. Cf. UNFROCK *v.*

1350 *Durh. MS. Cha. Roll,* In xj pannis..præter ij frokkes. **1362** LANGL. *P. Pl.* A. v. 64 Of a freris frokke were the foresleuys. *c* **1440** *Promp. Parv.* 179/2 Froke, monkes habyte..*cuculla.* **1466** *Paston Lett.* No. 549 II. 270 For a cope called a frogge of worsted for the Prior of Bromholm xxvi *s.* viii *d.* **1548** UDALL *Erasm. Par. Luke* xix 3–4 An other poynteth to some one of the pharisaical sort, clad in a blacke frocke or cope. **1683** TEMPLE *Mem. Wks.* 1731 I. 465 A French Monk, who some time since had left his Frock for a Petticoat. **1762** H. WALPOLE *Vertue's Anecd. Paint.* I. iii. 51 As the frock of no religious order ever was green, this cannot be meant for a friar. **1810** SCOTT *Lady of L.* III. iv, The Hermit by it stood, Barefooted, in his frock and hood. **1887** W. GLADDEN *Parish Problems* 333 It was the utterance of such words as these that cost the great Carmelite preacher [Father Hyacinthe] his frock.

2. An upper garment worn chiefly by men; a long coat, tunic, or mantle.

13.. *E. E. Allit. P.* B. 1742 þe kyng comaunded anon to clepe þat wyse, In frokkes of fyn cloþ. **1375** BARBOUR *Bruce* x. 375 With blak froggis all helit thai The Armouris at thai on thame had. *c* **1425** WYNTOUN *Cron.* VIII. xxxviii. 57 Ilkane a gud Burdowne in hand, And royd Frogis on þare Armyng. *c* **1460** *Towneley Myst.* (Surtees) 241, I wold be fayn of this frog [Christ's coat] myght it fall vnto me. **1500–20** DUNBAR *Poems* li. 3 To giff a doublett he als doure, As it war off ane futt syd frog. **1527** *Lanc. Wills* I. 6 And also that he geiff to Richard Fene a jakett called my frocke. **1611** BIBLE *Ecclus.* xl. 4 From him that weareth purple and a crown, vnto him that is clothed with a linnen frocke. **1649** G. DANIEL *Trinarch., Hen. V,* clxxix, Another girds his Frock, wᵗʰ a sure Thonge. **1700** DRYDEN *Sigism. & Guisc.* 144 Yet (for the wood perplexed with thorns he knew) A frock of leather o'er his limbs he drew. **1848** W. H. KELLY tr. *L. Blanc's Hist. Ten Years* II. 559 Kings at arms covered with long frocks of cloth of gold.

fig. **1604** SHAKS. *Ham.* III. iv. 164 (Qo. 2) That monster custome..to the vse of actions faire and good..giues a frock or Liuery That aptly is put on to refraine night.

b. *Frock of mail:* a defensive garment, armour. Cf. *coat of mail.*

1671 MILTON *Samson* 133 Samson..Made arms ridiculous, useless the.. frock of mail Adamantean proof. **1835** BROWNING *Paracelsus* III. 715, I have addressed a frock of heavy mail, Yet may not join the troop of sacred knights.

fig. **1841–4** EMERSON *Ess., Politics* Wks. (Bohn) I. 244 The gladiators in the lists of power feel, through all their frocks of force and simulation the presence of worth.

3. A loose outer garment worn by peasants and workmen; an overall; more fully *smock-frock.*

a **1668** DAVENANT *News from Plymouth* IV. i, *Cable.* Come your affair, Squire of the Frock! Briefly Dispatch! Where is this courteous Damsel? *Porter.* At my House, Sir. **1698** FRYER *Acc. E. India & P.* 95 Flesh-coloured Vests, somewhat like our Brickmakers Frocks. **1724** DE FOE *Mem. Cavalier* (1840) 237, I had pistols under my grey frock. **1777** WATSON *Philip II* (1839) 525 Three officers..disguised like the peasants of that country with long frocks. **1840** R. H. DANA *Bef. Mast* xxxvi. 136 The duck frocks for tarring down rigging. **1883** C. WALFORD *Fairs* 153 Dealers in haubergs, or waggoners' frocks.

b. A wearer of a smock-frock; a poor person.

1612 W. Parkes *Curtaine-Dr.* (1876) 25 The rich and the poore, euen from the furd gown to the sweating frock. **1625** B. Jonson *Staple of N.* v. ii, *Porter.* Sir, I did give it him. *P. sen.* What..A frock spend sixpence!

c. A woollen 'guernsey' or 'jersey' worn by sailors; *esp.* in *Guernsey* or *Jersey frock.*

1811 W. Thom *Hist. Aberd.* vi. 150 Besides stockings, they make frocks, mitts, and all sorts of hosiery. **1825** Jamieson, Frock, a sort of worsted netting worn by sailors, often in lieu of a shirt. **1856** Emerson *Eng. Traits, Voy. Eng. Wks.* (Bohn) II. 13 The sailors have dressed him in [a] Guernsey frock. **1867** Smyth *Sailor's Word-bk.*, Frog, an old term for a seaman's coat or frock. *Ibid.*, *Jersey frocks,* woollen frocks supplied to seamen.

4. The outer garment, for indoor wear, of women and children, consisting of a bodice and skirt; a gown, dress.

The word is now applied chiefly to the garment worn by children and young girls, cf. *short frock;* that worn by women is commonly called a *dress; gown* is also current, though (exc. in the U.S.) less generally. (But in the language of fashionable society the use of *frock* for 'dress' has within the last few years been revived.)

1537 *Bury Wills* (Camden) 134, I wyll my goddowter and seruant, shall haue my wosted kyrtell..and my froke. **1550** Crowley *Way to Wealth* 325 Let youre wiues therefore put of theire fine frockes and Frenche hoodes. **1613** Drayton *Poly-olb.* xviii. 284 And on her loynes a frock with many a swelling pleate. **1705** *Lond. Gaz.* No. 4117/4 Cloathed with a red Damask Coat, with blue Flowers, and over it a white Holland Frock. *Ibid.* No. 4149/4 James Smith, upwards of 4 years of Age, in a hanging Sleeve Coat, and a painted Frock..is missing. **1755** Johnson s. v. *Frock,* A kind of gown for children. **1818** *La Belle Assemblée* XVII. No. 108. 87/2 The newest ball-dress is composed of a frock of tulle, over a rose-coloured slip of satin. **1833** Ht. Martineau *Three Ages* iii. 108 Striving to patch up once more the girl's frock and the boy's coat. **1867** Trollope *Chron. Barset* II. xlv. 9, I don't think I've ever been in London since I wore short frocks. **1882** Miss Braddon *Mt. Royal* II. vii. 143 Fishky..looked lovely in her white satin frock and orange-blossoms. **1884** *Girl's Own Paper* 28 June 618/3, I think 'frock' seems to be applied to the morning costume, and 'dress' to that of evening only. **1889** Barrie *Window in Thrums* 172 There could never be more than a Sabbath frock and an everyday gown for her.

5. A coat with long skirts. In mod. quots. = Frock-coat.

1719 De Foe *Crusoe* ii. vi, A light coat like a frock. **1748** Smollett *Rod. Rand.* (1812) I. 387 A gentleman dressed in a green frock came in. **1770** Richardson *Anecd. Russian Emp.* 325 A light blue frock with silver frogs. **1839-40** W. Irving *Wolfert's R.* (1855) 162, I observed the Duke of Wellington..He was alone, simply attired in a blue frock. **1855** Thackeray *Newcomes* I. 128 Dine in your frock..if your dress-coat is in the country. **1876** Besant & Rice *Gold. Butterfly* III. 194 The coat..a comfortable easy old frock, a little baggy at the elbows.

b. A coat of a similar 'cut' used as a military uniform; *spec.* see quot. 1881.

1753 Hanway *Trav.* (1762) I. vii. xcii. 422 He..appears..always in his regimentals, which are a blue cloth frock with silver brandenburgs. **1881** Wilhelm *Milit. Dict.*, Frock, in the British service, the undress regimental coat of the guards, artillery, and royal marines. **1890** *19th Cent.* Nov. 842 The stable jacket will retain its freshness, as its owner drills in his 'service frock'.

6. *attrib.* and *Comb.*, *frock-body; frock-like* adj.; † *frock-clothes, dress* (*rare*), dress of which a frock-coat is a part: so *frock-suit;* † *frock-man* = 3 b; *frock-uniform,* undress uniform (see 5 b).

1862 F. Wilford *Maiden of our own day* 97, I can make this °frock-body while you are making the skirt. **1769** *Public Advertiser* 1 June 3/2 Silk Cloths ..for Gentlemens Dress and °Frock Cloaths. **1854** J. Buchanan in *Harper's Mag.* Jan. (1884) 256/1, I was invited 'in °frock dress' to the dinner. **1886** W. J. Tucker *E. Europe* 183 From beneath his vest there hung..the °frock-like 'gatya' (drawers) of the Magyar peasant. **1657** Reeve *God's Plea for Nineveh* ii. 46 If ye fight for the wall, let not the °frokman take the right hand of you in worth. **1810** Wellington in Gurw. *Desp.* VI. 591 We..shall be highly flattered by your company..whether in full or in °frock uniforms.

Hence **Fro·ckhood,** the state of being dressed in a (short) frock; † **Fro·ckified** *ppl. a.,* clad in a (monk's) frock.

1708 Motteux *Rabelais* iv. xlvi. (1737) 186 A frockify'd Hobgoblin. **1861** Wynter *Soc. Bees* 124 How many Billies and Bobbies, revelling in all the glorious ease of frockhood, have you not reduced to the cruel purgatory of breeches.

4. What are some of the possible causes of semantic change?

5. Consult your desk dictionary for these words:

    a. *pejorative*— What is a good synonym? Is there a verb made from *pejorative*? What subjects, other than semantic change, can you use the word *pejorative* in or on?

    b. *thingumabob, gadget, jigger, gimmick:* Where did these come from and how did they develop?

    c. *starve*— When did it cease to mean *die of any cause?* (Consult the *OED*.) How can the lexicographer decide that the change has taken place?

    d. *hussy*— How did it develop its present meaning?

    e. *monstrous*— What has happened to this word's meaning, and why?

    f. *twist,* n.— This dance craze hit the country in full force in 1961. Is it in the dictionaries? Account for the semantic development. What else does *twist* mean as a noun?

Topics for Writing

1. Here is the *OED* entry for *genius*. Compare it with other dictionary discussions of the word, and then write an essay in which you discuss all its changes of meaning since it first entered the language. Try to offer explanations for each of these changes.

Genius (dʒīˑniɒs). Pl. genii (dʒīˑni͵əi), geniuses, († genius's). [a. L. *genius*, f. *gen- root of *gi-gn-ĕre* to beget, Gr. γίγνεσθαι to be born, come into being.

In Lat. the word has mainly the sense 1 below (the extended sense 2 occurs post-classically), and a fig. sense approaching 3. As a word of learned origin it is found in the Rom. langs.: F. *génie* (whence Ger. *genie*), It., Sp., Pg. *genio*, which have approximately the same senses as in Eng. To some extent the sense-development in Rom. has been affected by confusion with *ingenium* (see ENGINE): cf. for example F. *génie civil* 'civil engineering'.]

1. With reference to classical pagan belief: The tutelary god or attendant spirit allotted to every person at his birth, to govern his fortunes and determine his character, and finally to conduct him out of the world; also, the tutelary and controlling spirit similarly connected with a place, an institution, etc. (Now only in *sing.*)

In the first two quots. *Genius* is the proper name of an allegorical person who in the *Rom. de la Rose* represents the native moral instincts of mankind as setting bounds to the range of sexual passion.

[1390 GOWER *Conf.* I. 48 O Genius min owne clerke Come forth and here this mannes shrifte. c. 1400 *Rom. Rose* 4768 They..Whom genius cursith, man and wyf, That wrongly werke ageyn nature.] 1513 DOUGLAS *Æneis* IX. iv. 49 Gif that euery mannis schrewit desyre Be as his God and Genyus in that place. 1536 BELLENDEN *Cron. Scot.* (1541) Proheme Cosmogr. xii, Thair is na thing may be so odius To man, as leif in miserie and wo Defraudand god of nature genius. [Cf. Ter. *Phorm.* I. i. 10 and Hor. *Ep.* II. ii. 188.] 1596 DRAYTON *Leg.* iv. 51 The pale Genius of that aged floud. 1605 SHAKS. *Macb.* III. i. 56 Vnder him My Genius is rebuk'd, as it is said Mark Anthonies was by Cæsar. 1612 DRAYTON *Poly-olb.* 1. 10 Thou Genius of the place..Which liued'st long before the All-earth-drowning Flood. c 1630 RISDON *Surv. Devon* § 225 (1810) 237 Genii of the spring. 1647 R. STAPYLTON *Juvenal* 63 Any thing wherein the spirit or soule delighted, was called sacred or peculiar to the genius, especially feasting and marriage. 1663 DRYDEN *To Author* 55 in Charleton *Stone-heng*, Watch'd by the Genius of this Royal place. 1701 ROWE

Amb. Step-Moth. I. i. 51 Let their Guardian Genii still be watchful. **1745** COLLINS *Ode Col. Ross* i, Britannia's Genius bends to earth. *c* **1800** K. WHITE *Childhood* II. 260 Kind genii of my native fields benign. **1831** CARLYLE *Sart. Res.* (1858) 87 It was his guiding Genius (*Dämon*) that inspired him; he must go forth and meet his Destiny. **1843** DICKENS *Christm. Carol* i, It seemed as if the Genius of the Weather sat in mournful meditation on the threshold. **1863** *Scotsman* 12 Aug., We are now able..to thank our stars that the genius of red tape was so strong even in France. **1871** FARRAR *Witn. Hist.* iii. 99 Christians..who would die rather than fling into the altar-flame a pinch of incense to the Genius of the Emperors. **1887** BOWEN *Virg. Æneid* v. 95 His sire's familiar, or genius haunting the shore.

† b. After Lat. use: This spirit viewed as propitiated by festivities; hence, one's appetite. *Obs.*

1605 B. JONSON *Volpone* I. i. B 2 a, What should I do, But cocker vp my Genius, and liue free To all delights, my fortune calls me to? **1693** DRYDEN *Juvenal* iv. 105 To your glad Genius sacrifice this Day; Let common Meats respectfully give way.

c. (*A person's*) *good, evil genius:* the two mutually opposed spirits (in Christian language *angels*) by whom every person was supposed to be attended throughout his life. Hence applied *transf.* to a person who powerfully influences for good or evil the character, conduct, or fortunes of another.

1610 SHAKS *Temp.* IV. i. 27 The strongest suggestion, Our worser Genius can **1613** PURCHAS *Pilgrimage* (1614) 365 A tradition of two Genii, which attend every man, one good, the other evill. **1653** H. MORE *Antid. Ath.* III. xiv. (1712) 130 The Pythagoreans were of opinion that every man has two Genii, a good one, and a bad one. **1660** J. S. *Andromana* III. v. in Hazl. *Dodsley* XIV. 244 My better genius, thou art welcome as A draught of water to a thirsty man. **1702** ROWE *Tamerl.* IV. i. 1689 Thou..art an evil Genius to thyself. **1770** LANGHORNE *Plutarch* (1879) II. 1006/2 Men had their evil genii, who disturbed them with fears, and distressed their virtue. **1868** FREEMAN *Norm. Conq.* (1876) II. vii. 24 It needed the intervention of his better genius in the form of Godwine.

† d. In astrological use the word survived, with some notion of its original sense, passing into a symbolical expression for the combination of sidereal influences represented in a person's horoscope. *Obs.*

1643 MILTON *Divorce* I. x, But what might be the cause, whether each one's allotted Genius or proper star, or [etc.]. **1657** H. PINNELL *Philos. Ref.* 67 The other part therefore of Man, or this sydereall body is called the Genius of man, because it proceedeth from the Firmament; it is called *Penates,* because it is in our power and born with us, the shadow of the visible body, *Lar domesticus,* the good or bad household or private Angell.

e. The quasi-mythologic personification of something immaterial (e.g. of a virtue, a custom, an institution), esp. as portrayed in painting or sculpture. Hence *transf.* a person or thing fit to be taken as an embodied type of (some abstract idea).

1597 SHAKS. *2 Hen. IV,* III. ii. 337 Hee was the very Genius of Famine. **1875** B. HARTE *Tales Argonauts, Baby Sylvester,* A golden lizard, the very genius of desolate stillness, had stopped breathless upon the threshold of one cabin.

2. A demon or spiritual being in general. Now chiefly in pl. *genii* (the *sing.* being usually replaced by GENIE), as a rendering of Arab. جِنّ *jinn,* the collective name of a class of spirits (some good, some evil) supposed to interfere powerfully in human affairs.

c **1590** GREENE *Fr. Bacon* ix. 71 Whereas the pyromantic genii Are mighty, swift, and of far-reaching power. **1646** BUCK *Rich. III* Ded., To the commonrout, they..are another kind of Genius, or *ignis fatuus.* **1653** LD. VAUX *Godeau's St. Paul* 321 The worship of Angels or Geniuses [*printed* Genieuses]. **1655** STANLEY *Hist. Philos.* II. (1701) 83/1 They mock even the Genius of Socrates as a feigned thing. **1681** H. MORE *Exp. Dan.* ii. 25 The activity therefore of the Aerial Genii or Angels may be understood by these Winds. **1688** MRS. BEHN tr. *Van Dale's Hist. Orac.* (1718) 150 Evil Genii, and Spirits condemn'd to eternal punishment. **1756–82** J. WARTON *Ess. Pope* (1782) II. x. 178 It seemed one of those edifices in Fairy Tales, that are raised by Genii in a nights time. **1779** FRANKLIN *Wks.* (1889) VI. 261 Albumazar..was visited nightly by genii and spirits of the first rank. **1832**

W. IRVING *Alhambra* I. 251 Thè genii, who watch over the place, were obedi-
ent to my magic power. **1879** GLADSTONE *Glean.* I. i. 32 The whole narrative
really recalls the most graceful fictions of wise genii and gentle fairies.

3. † a. Of persons: Characteristic disposition; inclination; bent,
turn or temper of mind. *Obs.*

1581 SIDNEY *Apol. Poetrie* (Arb.) 62 A Poet, no industrie can make, if
his owne Genius bee not carried vnto it. **1599** B. JONSON *Ev. Man out of Hum.*
II. i. (1600) D 4 a, I cannot frame me to your harsh vulgar phrase, tis
agaynst my Genius. **1663** GERBIER *Counsel* 36 Those things whereunto their
Genius doth tend. **1686** *Observ. Chinese Char.* in *Misc. Cur.* (1708) III. 215
There have been various ways thought of for Expressing Significancy, according to the several Genii of the Persons that were the Inventors. **1690**
EVELYN *Mem.* (1857) III. 318 Its being suitable to my rural genius, born
as I was at Wotton, among the woods. **1697** tr. *C'tess D'Aunoy's Trav.* (1706)
83 He immediately discovered the Queens Genius, and easily made himself
her Confident. **1713** DERHAM *Phys. Theol.* v. i. 312 There is the same Reason
for the variety of Genii, or Inclinations of Men also. **1761** HUME *Hist. Eng.*
III. lxi. 319 Men of such daring geniuses were not contented with the ancient
and legal forms of civil government. **1780** JOHNSON *Let. to Mrs. Thrale* 10
July, Every man has his genius..my genius is always in extremes. **1781** J.
MOORE *View Soc. It.* (1790) I. xvi. 188 The intriguing genius of Pope Julius.
1804 W. TENNANT *Ind. Recreat.* (ed. 2) II. 162 Operations requiring no
effort..and on that account peculiarly suited to the genius of the indolent
Bengalese.

b. With reference to a nation, age, etc.: Prevalent feeling, opinion, sentiment, or taste; distinctive character, or spirit.

1639 FULLER *Holy War* v. xix. (1640) 260 The warre-genius of the world
is altered now-a-dayes, and supplieth number with policie. *c* **1645** HOWELL
Lett. (1650) II. 74 Before I wean my self from Italy, a word or two touching the genius of the nation. **1665** BOYLE *Occas. Refl.* 189 My Acquainted-
ness with the Genius of the Age had sadly taught me that I was to alter my
Method. **1701** SWIFT *Contests Nobles & Comm.* Wks. 1755 II. 1. 44 The
people of England are of a genius and temper never to admit slavery
among them. ¶ **1711** ADDISON *Spect.* No. 29 ¶ 9 A Composer should fit his
Musick to the Genius of the People. **1754** HUME *Hist. Eng.* (1761) I. ix. 196
The barbarous and violent genius of the age. **1791** BURKE *App. Whigs* Wks.
1842 I. 531 The genius of this faction is easily discerned. **1845** STEPHEN
Comm. Laws Eng. (1874) I. 81 Owing perhaps to some peculiar averseness
in the early genius of the country from change in its legal institutions. **1855**
PRESCOTT *Philip II,* I. 1. i. 2 This flexibility was foreign to the genius of the
Spaniard.

personified. **1871** MORLEY *Voltaire* (1886) 4 The rays from Voltaire's burn-
ing and far-shining spirit..struck upon the genius of the time, seated dark
and dead like the black stone of Memnon's statue.

c. Of a language, law, or institution: Prevailing character or
spirit, general drift, characteristic method or procedure.

1647 N. BACON *Disc. Govt. Eng.* I. xlix. (1739) 85 The right genius of
this Law will also more evidently appear by the practice of those times.
1699 BENTLEY *Phal.* 244 The Genius and Constitution of Tragedy. **1705** ADDI-
SON *Italy* 183 They are chiefly to be ascrib'd to the very Genius of the Roman
Catholick Religion. **1755** JOHNSON *Dict.* Pref., Such [words] as are readily
adopted by the genius of our tongue. **1765** HARRIS *Three Treat.* Advt., Those
Treatises, being written in Dialogue, from their Nature and Genius admit not
of Interruption. **1776** ADAM SMITH *W. N.* I. viii. (1869) I. 77 The genius
of the British Constitution. **1791** BURKE *Th. Fr. Affairs* Wks. VII. 15 They
will examine into the true character and genius of some late events. **1814** T.
BELL *View Coven.* Wks. 270 The Decalogue changed as it were its genius.
a **1850** CALHOUN *Wks.* (1874) III. 219 The genius of our constitution is
opposed to the assumption of power. **1875** JOWETT *Plato* (ed. 2) II. 17 He
expresses the very genius of the old comedy. **1875** STEWART & TAIT *Unseen
Univ.* i. § 36 (1878) 54 The whole genius of Christianity would appear to
point towards a total submission.

d. With reference to a place: The body of associations connected
with, or inspirations that may be derived from it. (Cf. 1 and 7.)

[**1681** DRYDEN *Prol. Univ. Oxf.* 25 By the sacred genius of this place.]
1823 LAMB *Elia.* Ser. II. *Tombs in Abbey,* Is the being shown over a place
the same as silently for ourselves detecting the genius of it? **1844** DISRAELI
Coningsby IV. xv, In Palestine, I met a German student who was accumulat-
ing materials for the History of Christianity, and studying the genius of the
place. **1844** STANLEY *Arnold* I. iii. 101 Whatever peculiarity of character

was impressed on the scholars whom it sent forth, was derived not from the genius of the place, but from the genius of the man.

† **e.** Of material things, diseases, etc.: The natural character, inherent constitution or tendency.

1675 Grew *Anat. Trunks* ii. vi. § 6 Convolvula's do not wind by any peculiar Nature or Genius. **1697** Dryden *Virg. Georg.* i. 80 The Culture suiting to the sev'ral Kinds Of Seeds and Plants; and what will thrive and rise, And what the Genius of the Soil denies. **1725** Pope *Odyss.* ix. 152 Here all products and all plants abound, Sprung from the fruitful genius of the ground. **1728–30** — in Spence *Anecd.* (1858) 9 In laying out a garden, the first thing to be considered is the genius of the place: thus at Riskins..Lord Bathurst should have raised two or three mounts; because his situation is all a plain. **1747** Berkeley *Tar-water in Plague* Wks. III. 483 Fevers..change their genius in different seasons.

4. Natural ability or capacity; quality of mind; the special endowments which fit a man for his peculiar work. (Now only with mixture of sense 5.)

1649 Milton *Eikon.* 241 To unsettle the conscience of any knowing Christian is a thing above the genius of his Cleric elocution. **1662** Evelyn *Chalcogr.* 74 Hugens..so worthily celebrated for his..universal Mathematical Genius. **1725** T. Hearne *Pref. to R. Brunne's Chron.* I. 27 For no Study can be more pleasant to Persons of a genius than that of our National History and Antiquities. **1729** Franklin *Ess.* Wks. 1840 II. 263 Different men have geniuses adapted to a variety of different arts and manufactures. **1759** Robertson *Hist. Scot.* I. i. 68 His genius was of that kind which ripens slowly. **1768** W. Gilpin *Prints* 125 Dorigny seems to have exhausted his genius upon it. **1831** Brewster *Newton* (1855) I. xii. 322 The peculiar genius of Newton has been displayed in his investigation of the law of universal gravitation. **1840** Thirlwall *Greece* VII. 71 A design certainly suited to Alexander's genius. **1853** Lytton *My Novel* ii. x, The Squire, whose active genius was always at some repair or improvement.

b. Natural aptitude, coupled with more or less of inclination † *to*, *for* (something). (Now only with mixture of sense 5.)

1643 Sir T. Browne *Relig. Med.* i. § 6, I have no Genius to disputes in Religion. **1707** J. Archdale *Descr. Carolina* ii, I advise, That such Missionaries be well skill'd in Chymistry, and some natural Genius to seek the Virtues in Herbs, Metts and Minerals. **1727** De Foe *Syst. Magic* i. i. (1840) 7 One having a genius to this, another to that kind of knowledge. **1788** Priestley *Lect. Hist.* v. l. 381 A genius for science by no means depends upon climate. **1798** Ferriar *Illustr. Sterne* ii. 38 He had no great genius for poetry. **1818** Jas. Mill *Brit. India* II. v. viii. 684 He had no genius, any more than Clive, for schemes of policy including large views of the past. **1844** Mrs. Browning *Crowned & Buried* xxvii, He had The genius to be loved. **1871** Smiles *Charac.* vi. (1876) 183 Their genius for borrowing, in the long run, usually proves their ruin. **1878** R. W. Dale *Lect. Preach.* ii. 38 Mr. Gladstone has an extraordinary genius for finance. **1889** Lowell *Latest Lit. Ess., Walton* (1891) 80 Walton had a genius for friendships.

5. (Only in *sing.*) Native intellectual power of an exalted type, such as is attributed to those who are esteemed greatest in any department of art, speculation, or practice; instinctive and extraordinary capacity for imaginative creation, original thought, invention, or discovery. Often contrasted with *talent*.

This sense, which belongs also to F. *génie*, Ger. *genie*, appears to have been developed in the 18th c. (It is not recognized in Johnson's Dictionary.) In sense 4 the word had come to be applied with especial frequency to the kind of intellectual power manifested by poets and artists; and when in this application 'genius', as native endowment, came to be contrasted with the aptitudes that can be acquired by study, the approach to the modern sense was often very close. The further development of meaning was prob. influenced by association with senses 1 and 2, which suggested that the word had an especial fitness to denote that particular kind of intellectual power which has the appearance of proceeding from a supernatural inspiration or possession, and which seems to arrive at its results in an inexplicable and miraculous manner. This use, which app. originated in England, came into great prominence in Germany, and gave the designation of *Genieperiode* to the epoch in German literature otherwise known as the 'Sturm und Drang' period. Owing to the influence of Ger. literature in the present century, this is now the most familiar sense of the Eng. word, and usually colours the other senses. It was by the Ger. writers of the 18th c. that the distinction between 'genius' and 'talent', which had some foundation in Fr. usage, was sharpened into the strong antithesis which is now universally current, so that the one term is hardly ever defined without reference to the other. The difference between *genius* and *talent* has been formulated very variously by different writers, but there is general agreement in regarding the former as the higher of the two, as 'creative' and 'original', and as achieving its results by instinctive perception and spontaneous activity, rather than by processes which admit of being distinctly analyzed.

1749 FIELDING *Tom Jones* XIV. i, By the wonderful force of genius only, without the least assistance of learning. **1755** W. SHARPE (*title*), Dissertation on Genius. **1756–82** J. WHARTON *Ess. Pope* (1782) II. viii. 21 It were to be wished that no youth of genius were suffered to look into Statius. **1783** BLAIR *Rhet.* iii. I. 41 Genius always imports something inventive or creative. **1801** FUSELI in *Lect. Paint.* i. (1848) 348 By Genius I mean that power which enlarges the circle of human knowledge; which discovers new materials of Nature, or combines the known with novelty. **1849** MACAULAY *Hist. Eng.* ii. I. 259 The genius of Halifax bore down all opposition. **1853** DE QUINCEY *Autobiog. Sk.* Wks. L. 198 *note*, Talent and genius. .are not merely different, they are in polar opposition to each other. Talent is intellectual power of every kind, which acts and manifests itself. .through the will and the active forces. Genius. .is that much rarer species of intellectual power which is derived from the genial nature—from the spirit of suffering and enjoying—from the spirit of pleasure and pain. .It is a function of the passive nature. **1858** CARLYLE *Fredk. Gt.* IV. iii. I. 407 Genius. .means transcendant capacity of taking trouble, first of all. **1866** R. W. DALE *Disc. Spec. Occ.* vii. 241 The word hardly knew what music was, till the genius of Handel did homage to the Messiah. **1883** FROUDE *Short Stud.* IV. II. iii. 195 A man of genius. .is a spring in which there is always more behind than flows from it.

6. Applied to a person. † **a.** With qualifying adj.: One who has *great, little*, etc. 'genius' (sense 4) or natural ability. Also, one who has a 'genius' (sense 3) or disposition of a specified kind. *Obs.*

[**1647–1697:** see 6 b.] **1731** A. HILL *Adv. Poets* 18 Vulgar Genii, sowr'd by sharp Disdain. **1768** W. GILPIN *Prints* 237 With a little genius nothing sways like a great name. *Ibid.* 240 A trifling genius may be found, who will give ten guineas for Hollar's shells.

b. A person endowed with 'genius' (in sense 5). (Now only *geniuses* in pl.)

The earlier examples, in which the word is accompanied by a laudatory adj., probably belongs strictly to 6 a.

1647 W. BROWNE tr. *Gomberville's Polexander* IV. IV. 294 Those great Genius's, on whom most Kings disburthen themselves of the government of their Estates. **1697** DRYDEN *Virg., Past.* Pref. (1721) I. 91 Extraordinary Genius's have a sort of Prerogative, which may dispense them from Laws. **1711** ADDISON *Spect.* No. 160 ¶ 1 There is no Character more frequently given to a Writer, than that of being a Genius. I have heard many a little Sonneteer called a *fine Genius*. **1755** AMORY *Mem.* (1769) I. 91 Such admirable genii as Burnet and Butler. **1762–71** H. WALPOLE *Vertue's Anecd. Paint.* (1786) II. 90 Under the direction of that genius [Inigo Jones] the King erected the house at Greenwich. **1793** BEDDOES *Math. Evid.* 61 Why are not geniuses for arts or sciences born among savages? **1800** LAMB *Lett.* (1888) I. 141 All poems are good poems to George; all men are fine geniuses. **1806** H. SIDDONS *Maid, Wife, & Widow* I. 173 Isaac was a good-dispositioned, industrious boy, but no genius. **1873** H. ROGERS *Orig. Bible* ix. (1875) 382 Certain transcendent geniuses—the Bacons, the Newtons, the Shakespeares, the Miltons.

7. *phr.* ‖ genius loci [L. = 'genius of the place'], the presiding deity or spirit (see sense 1); but often used in the sense of 3 d.

1771 SMOLLETT *Humph. Cl., To Dr. Lewis* 8 Aug., The pleasure-grounds are, in my opinion, not so well laid out according to the *genius loci.* **1835** W. IRVING *Crayon Misc., Newstead Abbey* (1863) 286 A white marble bust of the *genius loci*, the noble poet, shone conspicuously from its pedestal. **1878** L. W. M. LOCKHART *Mine is Thine* xix. II. 50 The *genius loci* may be solemn and pensive, but we laugh at him.

8. *attrib.* and *Comb.*, as *genius school; genius-gifted, genii-haunted* adjs.; *genius-born a.*, born of genius; † *genius-chamber*, bridal chamber (see GENIAL *a.*[1]).

1894 MILN *Strolling Players in East* xxi. 194, I represented. .the sweet meek maiden who was the *genius-born daughter of Shakespeare's pen. **1513** DOUGLAS *Æneis* IV. i. 36 War nocht also to me is displesant *Genyus chalmer or matrimone to hant. *a* **1851** Mrs. Sherwood *Life* i. (1854) 17 My °genius-gifted and benevolent father. **1817** Mrs. Hemans *Mod. Greece* Poems (1875) 29 Or Tigris rolls his °genii-haunted wave. **1882** Seeley *Nat. Relig.* (1883) 166 The point of close resemblance between the °genius school in art, and the anti-legal school in morals.

Hence (*nonce-wds.*) **Ge·niused** *a.* [-ED²], endowed with genius; **Ge·niusess** [-ESS], a female genius; **Ge·niuskin** [-KIN], a little genius.

1772 Nugent tr. *Hist. Friar Gerund* I. 145 She was not a common woman, but a geniusess and an elegant writrix. **1880** S. Lanier *Poems* (1884) 108 Led by the soaring-genius'd Sylvester. **1882** H. C. Merivale *Faucit of B.* II. i. xvii. 21 He failed..to catch a single idea out of those words with which my geniuskin of song had inspired me.

2. Choose a word—perhaps a current slang word—and, using all the dictionaries available to you, write an essay in which you describe its development in English.

Wilson: English Grammars and the Grammar of English

Aids to Study

1. When someone apologizes for his grammar, or when you tell someone that he's being "ungrammatical," what kind of grammar is at issue (see Wilson, p. 102)?

2. Make up your own definitions of *noun, adjective, adverb, verb, preposition, conjunction,* and *pronoun.* (Some of your definitions will very likely be paraphrases of school definitions.) Now try to decide whether each definition is based on *form, function,* or *meaning,* or on some combination of these. Compare your definitions with the dictionary definitions you can find, and with Wilson's structural definitions. Why should it concern us if the definitions of different parts of speech seem to have different bases?

3. Wilson's discussion of structural grammars suggests that it is helpful to distinguish between "total meaning" and "grammatical meaning." This is obviously a laboratory kind of exercise, since in use our language comes at us with all kinds of meanings braided together. Of what use is this sort of laboratory separation? What sorts of things can be uncovered by this means that might not be apparent when we work with language as a whole?

Topics for Writing

1. Charles C. Fries had a favorite ambiguous sentence: *The dog looked longer than the cat.* Write an essay in which you analyze this sentence from the point of view of structural grammar, and try to explain what grammatical features cause the ambiguity. What is peculiar about the verb? Test the sentence pattern by trying other words in the various slots. Does a dictionary offer any help?

2. If, as nearly every linguist agrees, we learn our language almost instinctively, without consciously mastering its system, how sound is Wilson's final paragraph? How much effect will objective knowledge of one or more descriptions of the grammar of his language have on the way a man speaks or writes? Can it help at all? How? Discuss this question in an essay, in which you consider other possible advantages in knowing objectively about your native language.

OHMANN: GRAMMAR AND MEANING

Aids to Study

1. Ohmann's essay is the last in the section of this book called "Change." In what ways would the grammatical scheme he describes be better able to deal with a language whose very grammar is constantly changing than either the traditional or structural schemes Wilson describes in the preceding essay?

2. Ohmann's example of look-alike sentences which are actually different in meaning and structure poses an interesting problem:

    The cow was found by a stream.

    The cow was found by a farmer. (p. 129)

    Try using Wilson's structural grammatical scheme to account for the difference between the two sentences. Then try to evolve a transformational generative explanation of the difference. Ohmann works out a transformation to account for the farmer (p. 132); how would you account for the stream?

3. In an earlier essay, Wilson (pp. 49–50) comments on the failure of eighteenth-century "universal" grammar. Now Ohmann (pp. 135–136) suggests that there is after all a set of universal features underlying all natural language. What seems to be the difference between these two ideas of universality in grammar? At what sorts of things is Ohmann looking and how do they differ from the things Dr. Johnson was considering as universals?

Topics for Writing

1. Analyze the ambiguous sentence in Topics for Writing number 1, p. 151, using Ohmann's transformational generative approach. What is the deep structure of each of the two ambiguous meanings? Can you account for the grammatical differences? Do your conclusions here agree with those you reached by structural means? Report your methods and findings.

2. Both the Wilson and Ohmann essays on grammar appeared first as part

of the front matter of desk dictionaries. Why should the editors of dictionaries have thought it useful to put essays of this sort in their books? What
have discussions of grammar to do with the kinds of information stored
in a dictionary? Explore this question in an essay.

3. Ohmann says (p. 126) that "the same conflicts in purpose that have troubled
dictionary editors and their publics beset grammarians as well." What are
some of these conflicts? What is there about language and our attitudes
toward it which would account for these conflicts? Illustrate your essay
with examples from your own experience.

Standards

Language changes, but we wish it wouldn't. Uncertainty, fear, one-upmanship—a whole range of unsteadying behavior results from the fact that language changes, and we don't want it to. As Wilson points out in an earlier essay, the dictionary editor has a difficult time satisfying his audience: the specialists of language want to see all the details, all the variety, all the moot cases wherein our practices differ; but the layman wants to know what's right.

Whitehall tells us how the dictionary as we know it today began. Then the editors of the *New York Times* and MacDonald and Evans argue the case of Webster's Third, whose editors ran afoul of the conflicting needs of the two audiences, laymen and specialists. We get a sense of the high emotions involved when people think somebody is tinkering with the language.

But the varieties, the various kinds of change, the different patterns of use are there always. McDavid shows us the range of these kinds of variation, and Mencken and Perrin show us how values attached to our words make us behave, and cause us to change our language. The picture is often pretty silly, a fine demonstration of human folly.

Standards of another sort—in spelling and punctuation—are the subjects of the next few essays. Jespersen shows us how our spelling got that way, and Hall reminds us of the curiously mixed set of spelling systems we have adopted, a set which now we defend as though it were Mosaic law. Whitehall then gives a succinct analysis of how we punctuate and what our standards of punctuation are.

Finally, Whitehall shows us how hard it is to move from the ease of talk to the struggle of writing. And Veblen reminds us that standards are things we can enforce on each other, and that language is one of the easiest ways we have of holding power over others.

155

In short, Section III shows us the agonies of our desiring an impossible order and a cessation of change, reminds us again that we cannot stop change, yet need order, and pictures for us the endless mixture of folly and pragmatism that sees us through.

HAROLD WHITEHALL

The Development of
the English Dictionary

The evolution of the English dictionary is rooted in the general evolution of the English language. In this development the chief pressures
were exerted by the steady increase in the word stock of English from the
50,000–60,000 words of Anglo-Saxon through the 100,000–125,000 words
of the Middle-English vocabulary to the huge total of some 650,000 words
which could theoretically be recorded in an exhaustive dictionary of
contemporary English. Such an overall increase as this made the dictionary *necessary*. The pressure of vocabulary, however, has always been influenced and reinforced by the intellectual climate of each successive
period of the language. A dictionary is not exactly a work of art, yet it
bears as strongly as an artistic production the impress of the age that bore
it. For that reason, the history of the dictionary is a fascinating chapter
in the history of ideas.

The beginnings of dictionary history are neither national nor concerned with any of the national languages. They are concerned with the
international language of medieval European civilization: Latin. Our first
word books are lists of relatively difficult Latin terms, usually those of a
Scriptural nature, accompanied by glosses in easier or more familiar Latin.
Very early in the Anglo-Saxon period, however, we find glosses containing
native English (i.e., Anglo-Saxon) equivalents for the hard Latin terms,
and it may be that two of these—the *Leiden* and *Erfurt Glosses*—represent the earliest written English we possess. Such glosses, whether Latin-

From the Introduction to the first edition of *Webster's New World Dictionary of the
American Language*. College Edition. © 1958 by The World Publishing Company. Reprinted by permission of the publisher.

Latin or Latin-English, continued to be compiled during the entire Anglo-Saxon and most of the Middle-English period.

The next stage of development, attained in England around 1400, was the collection of the isolated glosses into what is called a *glossarium*, a kind of very early Latin-English dictionary. As it chances, our first example of the glossarium, the so-called *Medulla Grammatica* written in East Anglia around 1400, has never been printed; but two later redactions were among our earliest printed books, and one of these, the *Promptorium Parvulorum sive Clericorum*, issued by Wynkyn de Worde in 1499, was the first work of a dictionary nature ever to be printed on English soil. Significantly enough, this version of the *Medulla* places the English term first and its Latin equivalent second.

The first onset of the Renaissance worked against rather than in favor of the native English dictionary. The breakdown of Latin as an international language and the rapid development of international trade led to an immediate demand for foreign-language dictionaries. The first of such works, Palsgrave's *Lesclaircissement de la Langue Francoyse* (1523), was rapidly followed by Salesbury's Welsh-English dictionary (1547), Percival's English-Spanish dictionary (1591), and finally, by the best known of all such works, Florio's Italian-English dictionary (1599). Meanwhile, the first great classical dictionary, Cooper's *Thesaurus* (1565), had already appeared. The history of dictionaries is larded with strange occurrences: we are not surprised, therefore, that the publication of Cooper's work was delayed five years because his wife, fearing that too much lexicography would kill her husband, burned the first manuscript of his magnum opus. It should be noted, in passing, that none of these various word books of the 16th century actually used the title *dictionary* or *dictionarium*. They were called by various kinds of fanciful or half-fanciful names, of which *hortus* "garden," and *thesaurus* "hoard" were particularly popular.

During the late 16th century, the full tide of the Renaissance had been sweeping a curious flotsam and jetsam into English literary harbors. Constant reading of Greek and Latin bred a race of Holofernes pedants who preferred the Latin or Greek term to the English term. Their principle in writing was to use Latino-Greek polysyllabics in a Latino-English syntax. Their strange vocabulary—studded with what some critics call "inkhorn" terms—eventually affected English so powerfully that no non-Latinate Englishman could ever hope to read many works in his own language unless he was provided with explanations of elements unfamiliar to him. The "Dictionary of Hard Words," the real predecessor of the modern dictionary, was developed to provide precisely such explanations. It is significant that the first English word book to use the name *diction-*

ary, Cokeram's *The English Dictionary* (1623), is subtitled "An Interpreter of Hard Words." Among those explained on its first few pages are *Abequitate, Bulbulcitate,* and *Sullevation.* In point of time, the first "dictionary of hard words" was Robert Cawdrey's *Table Alphabeticall of Hard Words* (1604). Of the various works of the same class appearing after this date may be mentioned John Bullokar's *English Expositor* (1616) and Edward Phillip's *New World of Words* (1658), both of which reveal a strong interest in the reform of spelling, Blount's *Glossographia* (1656) containing the first etymologies ever to appear in a printed English dictionary, and Thomas Kersey's *Dictionarium Anglo-Brittanicum* (1708), which also includes legal terms, provincialisms, and archaisms. If the 16th was the century of the foreign-language dictionary, the 17th was the century of the dictionary of hard words.

Between 1708 and 1721, hard-word dictionaries began to be replaced by word books giving ever-increasing attention to literary usage. The Latino-Greek borrowings of the earlier century had been either absorbed into the language or sloughed away. The French influence, from 1660 onwards, had replaced Renaissance stylistic ideas with notions of a simple elegance in syntax and a quiet effectiveness in vocabulary. These stylistic virtues were actually achieved in the works of Swift, Addison, Steele, and lesser writers. The literary mind of the early 18th century, therefore, was convinced that English had finally attained a standard of purity such as it had never previously known; it was also convinced that the brash outgrowth of mercantile expansionism, later to be reinforced by the infant Industrial Revolution, might very well destroy this hard-won standard of literary refinement. What more natural than that the standard should be enshrined in a dictionary for the admiration and guidance of posterity?

The first word book to embody the ideals of the age was Nathaniel Bailey's *Universal Etymological Dictionary of the English Language,* originally published in 1721, and then, in a beautiful folio volume with illustrations by Flaxman, in 1731. This, one of the most revolutionary dictionaries ever to appear, was the first to pay proper attention to current usage, the first to feature etymology, the first to give aid in syllabification, the first to give illustrative quotations (chiefly from proverbs), the first to include illustrations, and the first to indicate pronunciation. An interleaved copy of the 1731 folio edition was the basis of Samuel Johnson's *Dictionary* of 1755; through Johnson, it influenced all subsequent lexicographical practice. The position of dictionary pioneer, commonly granted to Johnson or to Noah Webster, belongs in reality to one of the few geniuses lexicography ever produced: Nathaniel Bailey.

Johnson's *Dictionary* (1755) enormously extends the techniques developed by Bailey. Johnson was able to revise Bailey's crude etymologies on the basis of Francis Junius' *Etymologicon Anglicanum* (first published in 1743), to make a systematic use of illustrative quotations, to fix the spelling of many disputed words, to develop a really discriminating system of definition, and to exhibit the vocabulary of English much more fully than had ever been attempted before. In his two-volume work, the age and following ages found their ideal word book. Indeed, a good deal of the importance of the book lies in its later influence. It dominated English letters for a full century after its appearance and, after various revisions, continued in common use until 1900. As late as the '90's, most Englishmen used the word *dictionary* as a mere synonym for Johnson's *Dictionary;* in 1880 a Bill was actually thrown out of Parliament because a word in it was not in "the Dictionary."

One of the tasks taken upon himself by Johnson was to remove "improprieties and absurdities" from the language. In short, he became a linguistic legislator attempting to perform for English those offices performed for French by the French Academy. From this facet of his activities we get the notion, still held by many dictionary users, and fostered by many dictionary publishers, that the dictionary is a "supreme authority" by which to arbitrate questions of "correctness" and "incorrectness." The dictionaries of the second half of the 18th century extended this notion particularly to the field of pronunciation. By 1750, the increasing wealth of the middle classes was making itself felt in the social and political worlds. Those who possessed it, speakers, for the most part, of a middle-class dialect, earnestly desired a key to the pronunciations accepted in polite society. To provide for their needs, various pronunciation experts—usually of Scottish or Irish extraction—edited a series of pronunciation dictionaries. Of these, the most important are James Buchanan's *New English Dictionary* (1769), William Kenrick's *New Dictionary of the English Language* (1773), Thomas Sheridan's *General Dictionary of the English Language* (1780), and, above all, John Walker's *Critical Pronouncing Dictionary and Expositor of the English Language* (1791). In such works, pronunciation was indicated by small superscript numbers referring to the "powers" of the various vowel sounds. Despite the legislative function exercised by the authors of almost all of these works, we must admit that they did indicate contemporary pronunciation with great accuracy, and when Walker's pronunciations were combined with Johnson's definitions the result was a dictionary which dominated the word-book field, both in England and the United States, until well after 1850.

If the chief contributions of the 18th century to dictionary making were (1) authoritative recording of literary vocabulary and (2) accurate recording of pronunciation, those of the 19th were unmistakably (1) the recording of word history through dated quotations and (2) the development of encyclopedic word books. Already in 1755, Samuel Johnson had hinted in his preface that the sense of a word "may easily be collected entire from the examples." During the first twenty-five years of the century, the researches of R. K. Rask, J. L. C. Grimm, and F. Bopp clearly defined the historical principle in linguistics. It was only a question of time, therefore, before someone combined Johnson's perception with the findings of the new science of historical linguistics. That person was Charles Richardson, who, in his *New Dictionary of the English Language* (1836), produced a dictionary completely lacking definitions but one in which both the senses and the historical evolution of the senses were accurately indicated by dated defining quotations. Richardson's work leads directly to the great *New English Dictionary on Historical Principles,* first organized in 1858, begun under Sir James Murray in 1888, and completed under Sir William Craigie in 1928. With its supplement (1933), the *New English Dictionary* or *Oxford English Dictionary* (N.E.D. or O.E.D.) covers the vocabulary of English with a completeness of historical evidence and a discrimination of senses unparalleled in linguistic history. No other language has ever been recorded on anything approaching this scale, and no dictionary of English since the *New English Dictionary* was completed has failed to reveal a profound debt to this monumental work. As compared with the effort represented by the N.E.D., the attempt to record the technological vocabularies of the language as first seen in John W. Ogilvie's *Universal Dictionary of the English Language* (1850) seems to be of minor importance, although it has had great practical effect on subsequent American dictionaries.

Since the publication of the O.E.D., the only important British dictionary has been Henry Cecil Wyld's *Universal Dictionary of the English Language* (1932), a work of somewhat restricted vocabulary coverage but one which may well point the way to the dictionary of the future. Wyld has discarded the older logical definitions for definitions of a more functional nature; his examples delve deeply into idiom; his etymologies are of a completeness and modernity unparalleled until this present dictionary in any medium-sized word book. The failure of Wyld's book to achieve much popularity on this side of the Atlantic underlines the fact that the typical American dictionary of the English language is a work *differing in kind* from any of those so far mentioned. It differs because the conditions of American life and culture differ from those of English life and culture.

The modern American dictionary is typically a single compact volume published at a relatively modest price containing: (1) definitive American spellings, (2) pronunciations indicated by diacritical markings,

(3) strictly limited etymologies, (4) numbered senses, (5) some illustrations, (6) selective treatment of synonyms and antonyms, (7) encyclopedic inclusion of scientific, technological, geographical, and biographical items. It owes its development, within the general framework of the evolution sketched above, to the presence of a large immigrant population in this country, to the elaborate American system of popular education, and to the vast commercial opportunities implicit in both of these.

The first American dictionaries were unpretentious little schoolbooks based chiefly on Johnson's *Dictionary* of 1755 by way of various English abridgments of that work. The earliest of these were Samuel Johnson Junior's *School Dictionary* (1798), Johnson and Elliott's *Selected Pronouncing and Accented Dictionary* (1800), and Caleb Alexander's *Columbian Dictionary* (1800). The most famous work of this class, Noah Webster's *Compendious Dictionary of the English Language* (1806), was an enlargement of Entick's *Spelling Dictionary* (London, 1764), distinguished from its predecessors chiefly by a few encyclopedic supplements and emphasis upon its (supposed) Americanism. The book was never popular and contributed little either to Webster's own reputation or to the development of the American dictionary in general.

The first important date in American lexicography is 1828. The work that makes it important is Noah Webster's *An American Dictionary of the English Language* in two volumes. Webster's book has many deficiencies—etymologies quite untouched by the linguistic science of the time, a rudimentary pronunciation system actually inferior to that used by Walker in 1791, etc.—but in its insistence upon American spellings, in definitions keyed to the American scene, and in its illustrative quotations from the Founding Fathers of the Republic, it provided the country with the first *native* dictionary comparable in scope with that of Dr. Johnson. It was not, as is often claimed, the real parent of the modern American dictionary; it was merely the foster-parent. Because of its two-volume format and its relatively high price it never achieved any great degree of popular acceptance in Webster's own lifetime. Probably its greatest contribution to succeeding American dictionaries was the style of definition writing—writing of a clarity and pithiness never approached before its day.

The first American lexicographer to hit upon the particular pattern that distinguishes the American dictionary was Webster's lifelong rival, Joseph E. Worcester. His *Comprehensive Pronouncing, and Explanatory Dictionary of the English Language* (1830), actually a thoroughly revised abridgment of Webster's two-volume work of 1828, was characterized by the additions of new words, a more conservative spelling, brief, well-phrased definitions, full indication of pronunciation by means of diacritics, use of stress marks to divide syllables, and lists of synonyms. Be-cause it was compact and low priced, it immediately became popular—far more popular, in fact, than any of Webster's own dictionaries in his own lifetime. As George P. Krapp, in his *The English Language in America*, says: "If one balances the faults of the Webster of 1828 against the faults of the Worcester of 1830, the totals are greatly in the favor of Worcester." One might feel the same about its merits as compared with those of Webster's own revision of his *American Dictionary* (1841), which featured the inclusion of scientific terms compiled by Professor W. Tully. The first Webster dictionary to embody the typical American dictionary pattern was that of 1847, edited by Noah Webster's son-in-law, Chaun-cey A. Goodrich, and published by the Merriams.

Temperamentally the flamboyant Noah Webster and the cautious Joseph Worcester were natural rivals. Their rivalry, however, was as nothing compared with that which developed between the rival pub-lishers of the Webster and Worcester dictionaries. By 1845, the great flood of immigration and the vast extension of the school system had suddenly lifted dictionary making into the realm of big business. In a "war of the dictionaries" that reflects the rudimentary business ethics of the period, the rival publishers used every device of advertisement and every strat-agem of high-powered salesmanship to drive each other off the market. Unsavory as this war appears in retrospect, it certainly helped to force rapid improvement of the dictionaries that these publishers controlled. Worcester's initial advantages were surpassed in the Merriam-Webster of 1847; the innovations in Worcester's edition of 1860 were more than paralleled in the Merriam-Webster of 1864, one of the best dictionaries ever to appear, but one from which almost everything really characteristic of Noah Webster himself was deleted. The battle was finally decided in favor of the Webster dictionaries, chiefly because the popularity of Webster's "Little Blue Black Speller" had put their name in every house-hold, partly because of the death of Joseph Worcester, and partly because of the merit of the Merriam product from 1864 onwards.

Since about 1870, the climate of American dictionary making has been much more peaceful. In the field of unabridged dictionaries, the most important accretion is the *Century Dictionary* (1889), edited by the great American linguist, William Dwight Whitney, and issued in six volumes. Unfortunately, this magnificent work, considered by many au-thorities to be basically the finest ever issued by a commercial publisher, has lost much of its popularity because of inadequate subsequent revision. The fact that it was not in a one-volume format undoubtedly also worked against its popular success. The only other new unabridged dictionaries that have appeared in the period are Webster's *Imperial Dictionary of the*

English Language (1904), and Funk and Wagnalls' *New Standard Dictionary* (1893). The first of these, the only unabridged dictionary ever published west of the Appalachians, was issued in Chicago by George W. Ogilvie, a publisher who carried on his own private guerrilla "war of the dictionaries" against the Merriam Company between 1904 and circa 1917. At the moment, the most important advances in lexicography are taking place in the field of the abridged collegiate-type dictionaries.

Meanwhile the scholarly dictionary has not been neglected. Once the *New English Dictionary* was published, scholarly opinion realized the need to supplement it in the various periods of English and particularly in American English. The first of the proposed supplements, edited by Sir William Craigie and Professor J. R. Hulbert, is the *Dictionary of American English on Historical Principles,* completed in 1944. This was followed by a *Dictionary of Americanisms,* edited by Mitford M. Mathews and published in 1951. A *Middle English Dictionary,* a *Dictionary of the Older Scottish Tongue,* and a *Dictionary of Later Scottish* are in preparation, and work on the *American Dialect Dictionary* of the American Dialect Society is now finally under way.

Webster's New Word Book

A passel of double-domes at the G. & C. Merriam Company joint in Springfield, Mass., have been confabbing and yakking for twenty-seven years—which is not intended to infer that they have not been doing plenty work—and now they have finalized Webster's Third New International Dictionary, Unabridged, a new edition of that swell and esteemed word book.

Those who regard the foregoing paragraph as acceptable English prose will find that the new Webster's is just the dictionary for them. The words in that paragraph all are listed in the new work with no suggestion that they are anything but standard.

Webster's has, it is apparent, surrendered to the permissive school that has been busily extending its beachhead on English instruction in the schools. This development is disastrous because, intentionally or unintentionally, it serves to reinforce the notion that good English is whatever is popular. At a time when complaints are heard in many quarters that youths entering colleges and graduate schools are unequipped to use their mother tongue and that the art of clear communication has been impaired, the publication of a say-as-you-go dictionary can only accelerate the deterioration. Its appearance is bound to cause dismay among the sounder teachers, among publishers, among editors, among foreigners striving to learn our language—among all those who seek more in a dictionary than a mere mechanical registering of how Polly Adler, Art Linkletter and even bona fide writers use the language.

On the credit side, the editors have coped admirably with the lexical explosion that has showered us with so many new words in recent years; they have included 100,000 new words or new definitions. These are improvements, but they cannot outweigh the fundamental fault.

From *The New York Times*, 12 October 1961. © 1961, 1969 by The New York Times Company. Reprinted by permission.

Webster's is more than just a publishing venture: for generations it has been so widely regarded as a peerless authority on American English as to become almost a public institution. Its editors therefore have to some degree a public responsibility. In issuing the Third New International they have not lived up to it. We suggest to the Webster editors that they not throw out the printing plates of the Second Edition. There is likely to be a continuing demand for it; and perhaps that edition can be made the platform for a new start—admittedly long, arduous and costly. But a new start is needed.

DWIGHT MACDONALD

The String Untuned

The third edition of Webster's New International Dictionary (Unabridged), which was published last fall by the G. & C. Merriam Co.,
of Springfield, Massachusetts, tells us a good deal about the changes in
our cultural climate since the second edition appeared, in 1934. The
most important difference between Webster's Second (hereafter called 2)
and Webster's Third (or 3) is that 3 has accepted as standard English
a great many words and expressions to which 2 attached warning labels:
slang, colloquial, erroneous, incorrect, illiterate. My impression is that
most of the words so labelled in the 1934 edition are accepted in the 1961
edition as perfectly normal, honest, respectable citizens. Between these
dates in this country a revolution has taken place in the study of English
grammar and usage, a revolution that probably represents an advance in
scientific method but that certainly has had an unfortunate effect on such
nonscientific activities as the teaching of English and the making of dictionaries—at least on the making of this particular dictionary. This scientific revolution has meshed gears with a trend toward permissiveness, in
the name of democracy, that is debasing our language by rendering it
less precise and thus less effective as literature and less efficient as communication. It is felt that it is snobbish to insist on making discriminations—the very word has acquired a Jim Crow flavor—about usage. And
it is assumed that true democracy means that the majority is right. This
feeling seems to me sentimental and this assumption unfounded.

There have been other recent dictionaries calling themselves "unabridged," but they are to Webster's 3 as a welterweight is to a heavy-
weight. 3 is a massive folio volume (thirteen inches by nine and a half
by four) that weighs thirteen and a half pounds, contains four hundred
and fifty thousand entries—an "entry" is a word plus its definition—in

From *The New Yorker*, 10 March 1962. © 1962 by The New Yorker Magazine, Inc. Reprinted by permission of the publisher.

2,662 pages, cost three and a half million dollars to produce, and sells for $47.50 up, according to binding. The least comparable dictionary now in print is the New Webster's Vest Pocket Dictionary, which bears on its title page the charmingly frank notation, "This dictionary is not published by the original publishers of Webster's Dictionary or by their successors." It measures five and a half inches by two and a half by a half, weighs two and a quarter ounces, has two hundred and thirty-nine pages, and costs thirty-nine cents. The only English dictionary now in print that *is* comparable to 3 is the Great Oxford English Dictionary, a unique masterpiece of historical research that is as important in the study of the language as the King James Bible has been in the use of the language. The O.E.D. is much bigger than 3, containing sixteen thousand four hundred pages in thirteen folio volumes. It is bigger because its purpose is historical as well as definitive; it traces the evolution of each word through the centuries, illustrating the changes in meaning with dated quotations. The latest revision of the O.E.D. appeared in 1933, a year before Webster's 2 appeared. For the language as it has developed in the last quarter of a century, there is no dictionary comparable in scope to 3.

The editor of 2, Dr. William A. Neilson, president of Smith College, followed lexical practice that had obtained since Dr. Johnson's day and assumed there was such a thing as correct English and that it was his job to decide what it was. When he felt he had to include a sub-standard word because of its common use, he put it in, but with a warning label: *Slang, Dial.,* or even bluntly *Illit.* His approach was normative and his dictionary was an authority that pronounced on which words were standard English and which were not. Bets were decided by "looking it up in the dictionary." It would be hard to decide bets by appealing to 3, whose editor of fifteen years' standing, Dr. Philip Gove, while as dedicated a scholar as Dr. Neilson, has a quite different approach. A dictionary, he writes, "should have no traffic with . . . artificial notions of correctness or superiority. It must be descriptive and not prescriptive." Dr. Gove and the other makers of 3 are sympathetic to the school of language study that has become dominant since 1934. It is sometimes called Structural Linguistics and sometimes, rather magnificently, just Modern Linguistic Science. Dr. Gove gives its basic concepts as:

1. Language changes constantly.
2. Change is normal.
3. Spoken language is the language.
4. Correctness rests upon usage.
5. All usage is relative.

While one must sympathize with the counterattack the Structural Linguists have led against the tyranny of the schoolmarms and the purists, who have caused unnecessary suffering to generations of school-children over such matters as *shall* v. *will* and the *who-whom* syndrome —someone has observed that the chief result of the long crusade against "It's me" is that most Americans now say "Between you and I"—it is remarkable what strange effects have been produced in 3 by following Dr. Gove's five little precepts, reasonable as each seems taken separately. Dr. Gove conceives of his dictionary as a recording instrument rather than as an authority; in fact, the whole idea of authority or correctness is repulsive to him as a lexical scientist. The question is, however, whether a purely scientific approach to dictionary-making may not result in greater evils than those it seeks to cure.

When one compares 2 and 3, the first difference that strikes one is that 2 is a work of traditional scholarship and hence oriented toward the past, while 3—though in many ways more scholarly, or at least more academic, than 2—exhales the breezy air of the present. This is hardly surprising, since the new school of linguistics is non-historical, if not anti-historical. Henry Luce's *Time* rather than Joseph Addison's *Spectator* was the hunting ground for 3's illustrative quotations. There is a four-and-a-half page list of consultants. Its sheer bulk is impressive—until one begins to investigate. One can see why James W. Perry had to be consulted on Non-numerical Computer Applications and Margaret Fulford on Mosses and Liverworts, but it seems overdoing it to have *two* consultants on both Hardware and Salvation Army, and some people might even question the one apiece on Soft Drinks, Boy Scouts, Camp Fire Girls, and Girl Guiding, as well as the enrolling of Mr. Arthur B. LaFar, formerly president of the Angostura-Wuppermann bitters company, as consultant on Cocktails. Such padding is all the more odd, considering that the editors of 3 have forgotten to appoint anybody in Philosophy, Political Theory, or Theatre. The old-fashioned 2 had six consultants on Catholic Church and Protestant Churches. 3 has only one, on Catholic Church. But it also has one on Christian Science, a more up-to-date religion.

The G. & C. Merriam Co. has been publishing Webster's dictionaries since 1847, fours years after Noah Webster died. Work on 3 began the day 2 went to press, but it gathered real momentum only fifteen years ago, when Dr. Gove began building up his staff of lexicographers. The first step was to sort out the words of 2 into a hundred and nine categories, so that specialized-definition writers could deal with them. It took five women two and a half years to do this. (" 'If seven maids with seven mops swept it for half a year, Do you suppose,' the Walrus said, 'that they could get it clear?' "—*Lewis Carroll*.) After that, all that had to be done was to write new definitions for most of the three hundred and fifty thousand entries that were taken over from 2, to select and write a hundred thousand new entries, to collect four and a half million quotations illustrating word usage, and to distribute them among the definition writers. The scope of the operation may be suggested by the fact that in chemistry alone the lexicographers gathered two hundred and fifty thousand quotations and took six and a half years to write the definitions. After that, it was up to the Lakeside Press, of Chicago, to set type from a manuscript that was as bristling with revisions and interlineations, mostly in longhand, as a Proust manuscript. At first they gave the printers clean, retyped copy, but they soon found that the extra step produced an extra crop of errors. The printing was done by the Riverside Press, of Cambridge, Massachusetts, a long-established firm, like Merriam, whose dictionaries it has been printing for almost a century. But antiquity is relative. There is no one at Riverside like the compositor at Oxford's Clarendon Press who began setting type for the O.E.D. in 1884 and was still at it when the last volume came off the presses in 1928.

In seeking out and including all the commonly used words, especially slang ones, the compilers of 3 have been admirably diligent. Their definitions, in the case of meanings that have arisen since 1900 or so, are usually superior (though, because of the tiny amount of a dictionary it is possible to read before vertigo sets in, all generalizations must be understood to be strictly impressionistic). They have also provided many more quotations (this is connected with the linguistic revolution), perhaps, indeed, too many more. It is quite true, as the promotional material for 3 claims, that this edition goes far beyond what is generally understood by the term "revision" and may honestly be termed a new dictionary. But I should advise the possessors of the 1934 edition to think carefully before they turn it in for the new model. Although the publishers have not yet destroyed the plates of 2, they do not plan to keep it in print, which is a pity. There are reasons, which will presently appear, that buyers should be given a choice between 2 and 3, and that, in the case of libraries and schools, 3 should be regarded as an up-to-date supplement to 2 rather than a replacement of it.

Quantitative comparison between 2 and 3 must be approached cautiously. On the surface, it is considerably in 2's favor: 3,194 pages v. 2,662. But although 2 has six hundred thousand entries to 3's four hundred and fifty thousand, its entries are shorter; and because 3's typography is more compact and its type page larger, it gets in almost as much text as 2. The actual number of entries dropped since 2 is not a hundred and fifty thousand but two hundred and fifty thousand, since a hundred thousand new ones have been added. This incredible massacre—almost half the words in the English language seem to have disappeared between 1934 and 1961—is in fact incredible. For the most part, the dropped entries fall into very special categories that have less to do with the language than with methods of lexicography. They are: variants; "nonce words," like *Shakespearolatry* ("excessive reverence or devotion to Shakespeare"), which seemed a good idea at the time, or for the nonce, but haven't caught on; a vast number of proper names, including nearly every one in both the King James and the Douay Bibles; foreign terms; and obsolete or archaic words. This last category is a large one, since 2 includes "all the literary and most of the technical and scientific words and meanings in the period of Modern English beginning with the year 1500," plus all the words in Chaucer, while 3, in line with its modernization program, has advanced the cut-off date to 1755. A great many, perhaps most, of the entries dropped from 2 were in a section of small type at the foot of each page, a sort of linguistic ghetto, in which the editors simply listed "fringe words"—the definitions being limited to a synonym or often merely a symbol—which they thought not important enough to put into the main text. 3 has either promoted them to the text or, more frequently, junked them.

Some examples of the kinds of word that are in 2 but not in 3 are: *arrousement, aswowe* (in a swoon), *dethronize, devoration* (act of devouring), *disagreeance, mummianize* (mummify), *noyous* (annoying), *punquetto* (strumpet), *ridiculize,* and *subsign* (subscribe). Two foreign words that one might expect to find in 3 were left out because of insufficient "backing"; i.e., the compilers didn't find enough usages to justify inclusion. They were *Achtung* and *niet;* the researchers must have skipped spy movies and Molotovian diplomacy. *Pot holder* was left out, after considerable tergiversating, because (a) for some reason the compilers found little backing for it, and (b) it was held to be self-explanatory (though considering some of the words they put in . . .). If it had been considered to be a single word, it would have been admitted, since one rule they followed was: No word written solid is self-explanatory.

The hundred thousand new entries in 3 are partly scientific or technical terms, partly words that have come into general use since 1934. The sheer quantity of the latter is impressive. English is clearly a living, growing language, and in this portion of their task the compilers of 3 have done an excellent job. Merriam-Webster has compiled some interesting lists of words in 3 that are not in 2.

Some of the political ones are:

character assassination	loyalty oath
desegregation	McCarthyism
freedom of speech	segregated
globalize	red-baiting
hatemonger	shoo-in
integrationist	sit-in
welfare capitalism	subsistence economy

Among the new entries in the cocktail-party area are:

club soda	name-dropping
elbow bending	pub crawler
gate-crasher	quick one
glad-hander	rumpot
good-time Charlie	silent treatment
Irish coffee	table-hop
jungle juice	yakety-yak

The most important new aspect of 3, the rock on which it has been erected, is the hundred thousand illustrative quotations—known professionally as "citations" or "cites"—drawn from fourteen thousand writers and publications. (Another hundred thousand "usage examples" were made up by the compilers.) Most of the cites are from living writers or speakers, ranging from Winston Churchill, Edith Sitwell, Jacques Maritain, J. Robert Oppenheimer, and Albert Schweitzer to Billy Rose, Ethel Merman, James Cagney, Burl Ives, and Ted Williams. Many are from publications, extending from the Dictionary of American Biography down to college catalogues, fashion magazines, and the annual report of the J. C. Penney Company. The hundred thousand cites were chosen from a collection of over six million, of which a million and a half were already in the Merriam-Webster files; four and a half million were garnered by Dr. Gove and his staff. (The O.E.D. had about the same number of cites in its files—drawn mostly from English literary classics—but used a much larger proportion of them, almost two million, which is why it is five or six times as long as 3.) For years everybody in the office did up to three hours of reading a day—the most, it was found, that was possible without attention lag. Dr. Gove presently discovered a curious defect in this method: the readers tended to overlook the main meanings of a word and concentrate on the peripheral ones; thus a hundred and fifty cite slips were turned in for *bump* as in burlesque stripping but not one for *bump* as in a road. To compensate for this, he created a humbler task force, whose job it was to go through the gutted carcasses of books and magazines after the first group had finished with them and arbitrarily enter on a slip one word—plus its context—in the first sentence in the fourth line from the top of each surviving page. The percentage of useful slips culled by this method approximated the percentage of useful slips made out by the readers who had used their brains. Unsettling.

The cites in 2 are almost all from standard authors. Its cite on *jocund* is from Shakespeare; 3's is from Elinor Wylie. Under *ghastly* 2 has cites from Gray (two), Milton (three), Poe, Wordsworth, Shakespeare, Shelley, Hawthorne, and—as a slight concession to modernity—Maurice Hewlett. 3 illustrates *ghastly* with cites from Louis Bromfield, Macaulay, Thackeray, Thomas Herbert, Aldous Huxley, H. J. Laski, D. B. Chidsey, and J. C. Powys. For *debonair,* 2 has Milton's "buxom, blithe and debonair," while 3 has H. M. Reynolds' "gay, brisk and debonair." One may think, as I do, that 3 has dropped far too many of the old writers, that it has overemphasized its duty of recording the current state of the language and skimped its duty of recording the past that is still alive (Mr. Reynolds would hardly have arrived at his threesome had not Mr. Milton been there before). A decent compromise would have been to include both, but the editors of 3 don't go in for compromises. They seem imperfectly aware of the fact that the past of a language is part of its present, that tradition is as much a fact as the violation of tradition.

The editors of 3 have labored heroically on pronunciation, since one of the basic principles of the new linguistic doctrine is that Language is Speech. Too heroically, indeed. For here, as in other aspects of their labors, the editors have displayed more valor than discretion. Sometimes they appear to be lacking in common sense. The editors of 2 found it necessary to give only two pronunciations for *berserk* and two for *lingerie,* but 3 seems to give twenty-five for the first and twenty-six for the second. (This is a rough estimate; the system of notation is very complex. Dr. Gove's pronunciation editor thinks there are approximately that number but says that he is unable to take the time to be entirely certain.) Granted that 2 may have shirked its duty, one may still find something compulsive in the amplitude with which 3 has fulfilled its obligations. Does anybody except a Structural Linguist need to know that much? And what use is such plethora to a reader who wants to know how to pronounce a word? The new list of pronunciation symbols in 3 is slightly shorter than the one in 2 but also—perhaps for that reason—harder to understand. 2 uses only those nice old familiar letters of the alphabet, with signs over them to indicate long and short and so on. (It also repeats its pronunciation guide at the foot of each page, which is handy; 3 does not, to save space and dollars, so one has to flop over as much as thirteen and a half pounds of printed matter to refer back to the one place the guide appears.) 3 also uses the alphabet, but there is one catastrophic exception. This is an upside-down "e," known in the trade as a "schwa," which stands for a faint, indistinct sound, like the "e" in *quiet,* that is unnervingly common and that can be either "a," "e," "i," "o," or "u," according to circumstance. Things get quite lively when you trip over a schwa. *Bird* is given straight as *bûrd,* in 2, but in 3 it is *bərd, bɔ̄d,* and *beid.* This last may be *boid,* but I'm not sure. Schwa trouble. ("Double, double schwa and trouble."—*Shakespeare.*)

Almost all 3's pictures are new or have been redrawn in a style that is superior to 2's—clearer and more diagrammatic. The new cut of "goose," with no less than twenty-four parts clearly marked, is a special triumph. The other animal illustrations, from *aardvark* to *zebu,* are less picturesque but more informative than those in 2. The illustrations are—rightly—chosen for utility rather than ornament. On facing pages we have pictures of *coracles, corbel,* and *corbiesteps,* all definitely needed, though, on another, *pail* might have been left to the imagination. One of the few illustrations repeated from 2 is *digestive organs,* and a fine bit of uncompromising realism it is, too.

I notice no important omissions in 3. *Namby-pamby* is in. However, it was coined—to describe the eighteenth-century Ambrose Philips' insipid verses—not "by some satirists of his time" but by just one of them, Henry Carey, whose celebrated parody of Philips is entitled "Namby-Pamby." *Bromide* is in ("a conventional and commonplace or tiresome person"), but not the fact that Gelett Burgess invented it. Still, he gets credit for *blurb* and *goop. Abstract expressionism* is in, but *Tachism* and *action painting* are not. The entries on Marxist and Freudian terms are skimpy. *Id* is in, but without citations and with too brief a definition. *Ego* is defined as Fichte, Kant, and Hume used it but not as Freud did. The distinction between *unconscious* and *subconscious* is muffed; the first is adequately defined and the reader is referred to the latter; looking that up, he finds "The mental activities just below the threshold of consciousness; also: the aspect of the mind concerned with such activities that is an entity or a part of the mental apparatus overlapping, equivalent to, or distinct from the unconscious." I can't grasp the nature of something that is overlapping, equivalent to, *or* distinct from something else. While *dialectical materialism* and *charisma* (which 2 treats only as a theological term, although Max Weber had made the word common sociological currency long before 1934) are in, there is no *mass culture,* and the full entry for the noun *masses* is "pl. of mass." There is no reference to Marx or even to Hegel under *reify,* and under *alienation* the closest 3 comes to this important concept of Marxist theory is "the state of being alienated or diverted from normal function," which is illustrated by "alienation of muscle." Marx is not mentioned in the very brief definition of *class struggle.*

The definitions seem admirably objective. I detected only one major lapse:

> McCarthyism—a political attitude of the mid-twentieth century closely allied to know-nothingism and characterized chiefly by opposition to elements held to be subversive and by the use of tactics involving personal attacks on individuals by means of widely publicized indiscriminate allegations esp. on the basis of unsubstantiated charges.

I fancy the formulator of this permitted himself a small, dry smile as he leaned back from his typewriter before trudging on to *McClellan saddle* and *McCoy* (the real). I'm not complaining, but I can't help remembering that the eponymous hero of *McCarthyism* wrote a little book with that title in which he gave a rather different definition. The tendentious treatment of *McCarthyism* contrasts with the objectivity of the definition of *Stalinism,* which some of us consider an even more reprehensible *ism:* "The political, economic and social principles and policies associated with Stalin; *esp:* the theory and practice of communism developed by Stalin from Marxism-Leninism." The first part seems to me inadequate and the second absurd, since Stalin never had a theory in his life. The definitions of *democratic* and *republican* seem fair: "policies of broad social reform and internationalism in foreign affairs" v. "usu. associated with business, financial, and some agricultural interests and with favoring a restricted governmental role in social and economic life." Though I wonder what the Republican National Committee thinks.

One of the most painful decisions unabridgers face is what to do about those obscene words that used to be wholly confined to informal discourse but that of late, after a series of favorable court decisions, have been cropping up in respectable print. The editors of 2, being gentlemen and scholars, simply omitted them. The editors of 3, being scientists, were more conscientious. All the chief four- and five-letter words are here, with the exception of perhaps the most important one. They defend this omission not on lexical grounds but on the practical and, I think, reasonable ground that its inclusion would have stimulated denunciations and boycotts. There are, after all, almost half a million other words in their dictionary—not to mention an investment of three and a half million dollars—and they reluctantly decided not to imperil the whole enterprise by insisting on that word.

Two useful features of 2 were omitted from 3: the gazetteer of place names and the biographical dictionary. They were left out partly to save money—they took up a hundred and seventy-six pages, and the biographical dictionary had to be brought up to date with each new printing—and partly because Dr. Gove and his colleagues, more severe than the easygoing editors of 2, considered such items "encyclopedic material" and so not pertinent to a dictionary. The force of this second excuse is weakened because although they did omit such encyclopedic features of 2 as the two pages on *grasses,* they put in a page-and-a-half table of currencies under *money* and three and a half pages of *dyes.* It is also worth noting that Merriam-Webster added a new item to its line in 1943—the Webster's Biographical Dictionary. While I quite understand the publishers' reluctance to give away what their customers would other-wise have to buy separately, I do think the biographical dictionary should have been included—from the consumer's point of view, at any rate.

However, the editors have sneaked in many proper names by the back door; that is, by entering their adjectival forms. *Walpolian* means "1: of, relating to, or having the characteristics of Horace Walpole or his writings," and "2: of, relating to, or having the characteristics of Robert Walpole or his political policies," and we get the death dates of both men (but not the birth dates), plus the information that Horace was "Eng. man of letters" and Robert "Eng. statesman" (though it is not noted that Horace was Robert's son). This method of introducing proper names produces odd results. Raphael is in (*Raphaelesque, Raphaelism, Raphaelite*), as are Veronese (*Veronese green*) and Giotto and Giorgione and Michaelangelo, but not Tintoretto and Piero della Francesca, be-cause they had the wrong kind of names. Caravaggio had the right kind, but the editors missed him, though *Caravaggesque* is as frequently used in art criticism as *Giottesque.* All the great modern painters, from Cézanne on, are omitted, since none have appropriate adjectives. Yeats is in (*Yeatsian*) but not Eliot, Pound, or Frost (why not *Frosty?*). Some-times one senses a certain desperation, as when *Smithian* is used to wedge in Adam Smith. *Menckenian* and *Menckenese* get an inch each, but there is no *Hawthornean,* no *Melvillesque,* no *Twainite.* All the twentieth-century presidents are in—Eisenhower by the skin of *Eisenhower jacket* —except Taft and Truman and Kennedy. Hoover has the most entries, all dispiriting: *Hoover apron* and *Hooverize,* because he was food administrator in the First World War; *Hooverville,* for the depression shanty towns; *Hoovercrat,* for a Southern Democrat who voted for him in 1928; and *Hooverism.*

This brings up the matter of capitalization. 2 capitalized proper names; 3 does not, with one exception. There may have been some esoteric reason of typographical consistency. Whatever their reasons, the result is they must cumbersomely and forever add *usu. cap.* (Why *usu.* when it is *alw?*) The exception is *God,* which even these cautious linguisticians couldn't quite bring themselves to label *usu. cap. Jesus* is out because of adjectival deficiency, except for *Jesus bug,* a splendid slang term, new to me, for the waterbug ("fr. the allusion to his walking on water," the "his" being firmly lower case). He does get in via His second name, which, luckily, has given us a rather important adjective, *usu. cap.*

At first glance, 3's typography is cleaner and more harmonious. Dr. Gove estimates that the editors eliminated two million commas and periods (as after adj., n., and v.), or eighty pages' worth. A second glance shows a major and, from a utilitarian point of view, very nearly a fatal defect. Words that have more than one meaning—and many have dozens —are much easier to follow in 2, which gives a new paragraph to each meaning, than in 3, which runs the whole entry as one superparagraph. ("What! Will the line stretch out to the crack of doom?"—*Shakespeare.*) Thus 2 not only starts each new meaning of *cut* with a paragraph but also puts in an italicized heading: *Games & Sports, Bookbinding, Card Playing, Motion Pictures.* In 3 one has to look through a solid paragraph of nine inches, and there are no headings. The most extreme example I found was 3's entry on the transitive verb *take,* which runs on for a single paragraph two feet eight inches long, in which the twenty-one main meanings are divided only by boldfaced numerals; there follow, still in the same paragraph, four inches of the intransitive *take,* the only sign of this gear-shifting being a tiny printer's squiggle. *Take* is, admittedly, quite a verb. The Oxford English Dictionary gives sixty-three meanings in nine feet, but they are spaced out in separate paragraphs, as is the mere foot and a half that 2 devotes to *take.*

A second glance also suggests second thoughts about the richness of citations in 3. Often it seems *plethoric,* even *otiose* ("lacking use or effect"). The chief reason 3's entries on multiple-meaning words are so much longer than 2's is that it has so many more citations. Many are justified and do indeed enrich our sense of words, but a good thing can be overdone. The promotional material for 3 mentions the treatment of *freeze* as an improvement, but does anybody really need such illustrative richness as:

> 6a: to make (as the face) expressionless [with instructions to recognize no one; and in fact he did *freeze* his face up when an old acquaintance hailed him—Fletcher Pratt] [a look of incredulity *froze* his face . . . and his eyes went blank with surprise—Hamilton Basso] b. to preserve rigidly a particular expression on [he still sat, his face *frozen* in shame and misery—Agnes S. Turnbull]

The question is rhetorical.

One of the problems of an unabridger is where completeness ends and madness begins. The compilers of 2 had a weakness for such fabrications as *philomuse, philomythia* ("devotion to legends . . . sometimes, loquaciousness"), *philonoist* ("a seeker of knowledge"), *philophilosophos* ("partial to philosophers"), *philopolemic, philopornist* ("a lover of harlots"), and *philosopheress* (which means not only a woman philosopher, like Hannah Arendt, but a philosopher's wife, like Xantippe). These are omitted by the compilers of 3, though they could not resist *philosophastering* ("philosophizing in a shallow or pretentious manner"). But why do we need *nooky* ("full of nooks") or *namecaller* ("one that habitually engages in name-calling") or all those "night" words, from *night clothes*—"garments worn in bed," with a citation from Jane Welsh Carlyle, of all people—through *nightdress, nightgear, nightgown, nightrobe, nightshirt,* and *nightwear?* What need of *sea boat* ("a boat adapted to the open sea" or *sea captain* or *swimming pool* ("a pool suitable for swimming," lest we imagine it is a pool that swims) or *sunbath* ("exposure to sunlight"—"or to a sun lamp," they add cautiously) or *sunbather* ("one that takes sun baths")? Why *kittenless* ("having no kitten")? Why need we be told that *white-faced* is "having the face white in whole or in part"? Or that *whitehanded* is "having white hands"? (They missed *whitelipped.*)

Then there are those terrible negative prefixes, which the unwary unabridger gets started on and slides down with sickening momentum. 3 has left out many of 2's absurdities: *nonborrower, nonnervous, non-Mohammedan, non-Welsh, non-walking.* But it adds some of its own: *non-scientist, nonphilatelic, non-inbred, nondrying* (why no *nonwetting?*), *nonbank* ("not being or done by a bank"), and many other non-useful and nonsensical entries. It has thirty-four pages of words beginning with *un-,* and while it may seem carping to object to this abundance, since the O.E.D. has three hundred and eighty such pages, I think, given the difference in purpose, that many may be challenged. A reasonably bright child of ten will not have to run to Daddy's Unabridged to find the meaning of *unreelable* ("incapable of being wound on a reel"), *un-*

lustrous ("lacking luster"), or *unpowdered* ("not powdered"). And if it's for unreasonably dumb children, why omit *unspinnable, unshining,* and *unsanded?*

For a minor example of gnostimania, or scholar's knee, see the treatment of numbers. Every number from *one* to *ninety-nine* is entered and defined, also every numerical adjective. Thus when the reader hits *sixty* he goes into a skid fifteen inches long. *Sixty* ("being one more than 59 in number") is followed by the pronoun ("60 countable persons or things not specified but under consideration and being enumerated") and the noun ("six tens: twice 30: 12 fives," etc.). Then comes *sixty-eight* ("being one more than 67 in number") and *sixty-eighth* ("being number 68 in a countable series"), followed by *sixty-fifth, sixty-first,* and so on. The compilers of 2 dealt with the *sixty* problem in a mere two entries totalling an inch and a half. But the art of lexicography has mutated into a "science" since then. (*"Quotation mark* . . . sometimes used to enclose . . . words . . . in an . . . ironical . . . sense . . . or words for which a writer offers a slight apology.") In reading 3 one sometimes feels like a subscriber who gets two hundred and thirty-eight copies of the May issue because the addressing machine got stuck, and it doesn't make it any better to know that the operators jammed it on purpose.

My complaint is not that 3 is all-inclusive—that is, unabridged—but that *pedantry* is not a synonym of *scholarship.* I have no objection to the inclusion of such pomposities, mostly direct translations from the Latin, as *viridity* (greenness), *presbyopic* (farsighted because of old age), *vellication* (twitching), *pudency* (modesty), and *vulnerary* (wound-healing). These are necessary if only so that one can read James Gould Cozzens' "By Love Possessed," in which they all occur, along with many siblings. And in my rambles through these 2,662 pages I have come across many a splendid word that has not enjoyed the popularity it deserves. I think my favorites are *pilpul,* from the Hebrew *to search,* which means "critical analysis and hairsplitting; casuistic argumentation"; *dysphemism,* which is the antonym of *euphemism* (as, *axle grease* for *butter* or *old man* for *father*), *subfusc,* from the Latin *subfuscus,* meaning brownish, which is illustrated with a beautiful citation from Osbert Sitwell ("the moment when the word Austerity was to take to itself a new subfusc and squalid twist of meaning")—cf. the more familiar *subacid,* also well illustrated with "a little subacid kind of . . . impatience," from Laurence Sterne; *nanism,* which is the antonym *of gigantism; mesocracy,* which is the form of government we increasingly have in this country; and *lib-lab,* which means a Liberal who sympathizes with Labor—I wish the lexicographers had not restored the hyphen I deleted when I imported it from England twenty years ago. One might say, and in fact I will say, that H. L. Mencken, whose prose was dysphemistic but never subfusc, eschewed pilpul in expressing his nanitic esteem for lib-lab mesocracy. Unfortunately, 3 omits 2's *thob* ("to think according to one's wishes"), which someone made up from *think-opinion-believe,* or else I could also have noted Mencken's distaste for thobbery.

Dr. Gove met the problem of *ain't* head on in the best traditions of Structural Linguistics, labelling it—reluctantly, one imagines—*substandard* for *have not* and *has not,* but giving it, unlabelled, as a contraction of *am not, are not,* and *is not,* adding "though disapproved by many and more common in less educated speech, used orally in most parts of the U.S. by many cultivated speakers esp. in the phrase *ain't I."* This was courageous indeed; when Dr. C. C. Fries, the dean of Structural Linguists today, said, at a meeting of the Modern Language Association several years ago, that *ain't* was not wholly disreputable, a teapot tempest boiled up in the press. When Dr. Gove included a reference to the entry on *ain't* in the press announcement of 3, the newspapers seethed again, from the Houston *Press* ("It Ain't Uncouth To Say Ain't Now") to the San Francisco *Examiner* ("Ain't Bad at All—In Newest Revised Dictionary") and the *World-Telegram* ("It Just Ain't True That Ain't Ain't in the Dictionary"). But moral courage is not the only quality a good lexicographer needs. Once the matter of education and culture is raised, we are right back at the nonscientific business of deciding what is correct—*standard* is the modern euphemism—and this is more a matter of a feeling for language (what the trade calls *Sprachgefühl*) than of the statistics on which Dr. Gove and his colleagues seem to have chiefly relied. For what Geiger counter will decide who is in fact educated or cultivated? And what adding machine will discriminate between *ain't* used because the speaker thinks it is standard English and *ain't* used because he wants to get a special effect? "Survival must have quality, or it ain't worth a bean," Thornton Wilder recently observed. It doesn't take much *Sprachgefühl* to recognize that Mr. Wilder is here being a mite folksy and that his effect would be lost if *ain't* were indeed "used orally in most parts of the U.S. by many cultivated speakers." Though I regret that the nineteenth-century schoolteachers without justification deprived us of *ain't* for *am not,* the deed was done, and I think the *Dial. or Illit.* with which 2 labels all uses of the word comes closer to linguistic fact today.

The pejorative labels in 2 are forthright: *colloquial, erroneous incorrect, illiterate.* 3 replaces these self-explanatory terms with two that are both fuzzier and more scientific-sounding: *substandard* and *nonstandard.* The first "indicates status conforming to a pattern of linguistic usage that exists throughout the American language community but differs in choice of word or form from that of the prestige group in that community," which is academese for "Not used by educated people." *Hisself* and *drownded* are labelled *substand.*, which sounds better than *erron.*—more democratic. *Nonstandard* "is used for a very small number of words that can hardly stand without some status label but are too widely current in reputable context to be labelled *substand.*" *Irregardless* is given as an example, which for me again raises doubts about the compilers' notion of a reputable context. I think 2's label for the word, *erron.* or *humorous,* more accurate.

The argument has now shifted from whether a dictionary should be an authority as against a reporter (in Dr. Gove's terms, prescriptive v. descriptive) to the validity of the prescriptive guidance that 3 does in fact give. For Dr. Gove and his colleagues have not ventured to omit all qualitative discriminations; they have cut them down drastically from 2, but they have felt obliged to include many. Perhaps by 1988, if the Structural Linguists remain dominant, there will be a fourth edition, which will simply record, without labels or warnings, all words and nonwords that are used widely in "the American language community," including such favorites of a former President as *nucular* (warfare), *individuous,* and *mischievious.* But it is still 1962, and 3 often does discriminate. The trouble is that its willingness to do so has been weakened by its scientific conscience, so that it palters and equivocates; this is often more misleading than would be the omission of all discriminations.

One drawback to the permissive approach of the Structural Linguists is that it impoverishes the language by not objecting to errors if they are common enough. ("And how should I presume?"—*T. S. Eliot.*) There is a natural tendency among human beings, who are *by def.* fallible, to confuse similar-sounding words. "One look at him would turn you nauseous," Phil Silvers said on television one night, as better stylists have written before. Up to now, dictionaries have distinguished *nauseous* (causing nausea) from *nauseated* (experiencing nausea); 2 labels *nauseous* in the sense of experiencing nausea *obs.*, but it is no longer *obs.* It is simply *erron.*, a fact you will not learn from 3, which gives as its first definition, without label, "affected with or inclining to nausea." So the language is *balled up* and *nauseous* is telescoped into *nauseated* and nobody knows who means which exactly. The magisterial Fowler—magisterial, that is, until the Structural Linguists got to work—has an entry on Pairs & Snares that makes sad reading now. He calls *deprecate* and *depreciate* "one of the altogether false pairs," but 3 gives the latter as a synonym of the first. It similarly blurs the distinction between Fowler's *forcible* ("effected by force") and *forceful* ("full of force"), *unexceptional* ("constituting no exception to the general rule") and *unexceptionable* ("not open or liable to objection," which is quite a different thing). A Pair & Snare Fowler doesn't give is *disinterested* (impartial) and *uninterested* (not interested); 2 lists the *uninterested* sense of *disinterested* but adds, *"now rare"; even such permissive lexicographers as Bergen and Cornelia Evans, in their "Dictionary of Contemporary American Usage," state firmly, "Though *disinterested* was formerly a synonym for *uninterested,* it is not now so used." But 3 gives *disinterested* as a synonym of *uninterested.*

Each such confusion makes the language less efficient, and it is a dictionary's job to *define* words, which means, literally, to set limits to them. 3 still distinguishes *capital* from *capitol* and *principle* from *principal,* but how many more language-community members must join the present sizable band that habitually confuses these words before they go down the drain with the others? Perhaps nothing much is lost if almost everybody calls Frankenstein the monster rather than the man who made the monster, even though Mrs. Shelley wrote it the other way, but how is one to deal with the *bimonthly* problem? 2 defines it as "once in two months," which is correct. 3 gives this as the first meaning and then adds, gritting its teeth, *"sometimes:* twice a month." (It defines *biweekly* as "every two weeks" and adds "2: twice a week.") It does seem a little awkward to have a word that can mean every two weeks *or* every eight weeks, and it would have been convenient if 3 had compromised with scientific integrity enough to replace its perfectly accurate *sometimes* with a firm *erroneous.* But this would have implied authority, and authority is the last thing 3's modest recorders want. ("Let this cup pass from me."—*New Testament.*)

The objection is not to recording the facts of actual usage. It is to failing to give the information that would enable the reader to decide which usage he wants to adopt. If he prefers to use *deprecate* and *depreciate* interchangeably, no dictionary can prevent him, but at least he should be warned. Thus 3 has under *transpire*—"4: to come to pass; happen, occur." 2 has the same entry, but it is followed by a monitory pointing hand: *"transpire* in this sense has been disapproved by most authorities on usage, although the meaning occurs in the writings of many authors of good standing." Fair enough. I also prefer 2's handling of the common misuse of *infer* to mean *imply*—"5: loosely and erroneously, to imply." 3 sounds no warning, and twice under *infer* it advises "compare imply." Similarly, 2 labels the conjunctive *like* "illiterate" and "incorrect," which it is, adding that "in the works of careful writers [it] is replaced by *as.*" 3 accepts it as standard, giving such unprepossessing citations as "impromptu programs where they ask questions much like I do on the air—Art Linkletter" and "wore his clothes like he was . . . afraid of getting dirt on them—*St. Petersburg (Fla.) Independent*." *Enthuse* is labelled *colloq.* in 2 but not in 3. It still sounds *colloq.* if not *godawf.* to me, nor am I impressed by 3's citations, from writers named L. G. Pine and Lawrence Constable and from a trade paper called *Fashion Accessories*. Or consider the common misuse of *too* when *very* is meant, as "I was not too interested in the lecture." 2 gives this use but labels it *colloq.* 3 gives it straight and cites Irving Kolodin: "an episodic work without too consistent a texture"; Mr. Kolodin probably means "without a very consistent texture," but how does one know he doesn't mean "without an excessively consistent [or monotonous] texture"? In music criticism such ambiguities are not too helpful.

In dealing with words that might be considered slang, 2 uses the label wherever there is doubt, while 3 leans the other way. The first procedure seems to me more sensible, since no great harm is done if a word is left waiting in the antechamber until its pretensions to being standard have been thoroughly tested (as long as it is admitted into the dictionary), while damage may be done if it is prematurely admitted. Thus both 2 and 3 list such women's-magazine locutions as *galore, scads, scrumptious,* and *too-too,* but only 2 labels them slang. (Fowler's note on *galore* applies to them all: "Chiefly resorted to by those who are reduced to relieving the dullness of matter by oddity of expression.") Thus *rummy, spang* (in the middle of), and *nobby* are in both, but only 2 calls them slang.

Admittedly, the question is most difficult. Many words begin as slang and then rise in the world. Dean Swift, a great purist, objected to *mob* (from the Latin *mobile vulgus*), *banter, bully,* and *sham;* he also objected to *hyp,* which has disappeared as slang for *hypochondriac,* and *rep,* which persists for *reputation* but is still labelled slang even in 3. Some slang words have survived for centuries without bettering themselves, like the Jukes and the Kallikaks. *Dukes* (fists) and *duds* (clothes) are still slang, although they go back to the eighteenth and the sixteenth century, respectively.

The definition of *slang* in 3 is "characterized primarily by connotations of extreme informality . . . coinages or arbitrarily changed words, clipped or shortened forms, extravagant, forced, or facetious figures of speech or verbal novelties usu. experiencing quick popularity and relatively rapid decline into disuse." A good definition (Dr. Gove has added that slang is "linguistically self-conscious"), but it seems to have been forgotten in making up 3, most of whose discriminations about slang strike me as arbitrary. According to 3, *scram* is not slang, but *vamoose* is. *"Goof* 1" ("to make a mistake or blunder") is not slang, but *"goof* 2" ("to spend time idly or foolishly") is, and the confusion is compounded when one finds that Ethel Merman is cited for the non-slang *goof* and James T. Farrell for the slang *goof*. *"Floozy* 1" ("an attractive young woman of loose morals") is standard, but *"floozy* 2" ("a dissolute and sometimes slovenly woman") is slang. Can even a Structural Linguist make such fine distinctions about such a word? The many synonyms for *drunk* raise the same question. Why are *oiled, pickled,* and *boiled* labelled slang if *soused* and *spiflicated* are not? Perhaps cooking terms for *drunk* are automatically slang, but why?

I don't mean to *imply* (see *infer*) that the compilers of 3 didn't give much thought to the problem. When they came to a doubtful word, they took a staff poll, asking everybody to check it, after reviewing the accumulated cites, as either slang or standard. This resulted in *cornball's* being entered as slang and *corny's* being entered as standard. Such scientific, or quantitative, efforts to separate the goats from the sheep produced the absurdities noted above. Professor Austin C. Dobbins raised this point in *College English* for October, 1956:

> But what of such words as *boondoggle, corny, frisk, liquidate, pinched, bonehead, carpetbagger, pleb, slush fund,* and *snide?* Which of these words ordinarily would be considered appropriate in themes written by cultivated people? According to the editors of the ACD [the American College Dictionary, the 1953 edition, published by Random House] the first five of these words are slang; the second five are established usage. To the editors of WNCD [Webster's New Collegiate Dictionary, published by Merriam-Webster in the same year] the first five of these words represent established usage; the second five are slang. Which authority is the student to follow?

Mr. Dobbins is by no means hostile to Structural Linguistics, and his essay appears in a recent anthology edited by Dr. Harold B. Allen, of the University of Minnesota, an energetic proponent of the new school. "Perhaps the answer," Mr. Dobbins concludes, "is to advise students to study only one handbook, consult one dictionary, listen to one instructor. An alternate suggestion, of course, is for our textbooks more accurately to base their labels upon studies of usage." Assuming the first alternative is ironical, I would say the second is impractical unless the resources of a dozen Ford Foundations are devoted to trying to decide the matter scientifically—that is, statistically.

Short of this Land of Cockaigne, where partridges appear in the fields ready-roasted, I see only two logical alternatives: to label all doubtful words slang, as 2 does, or to drop the label entirely, as I suspect Dr. Gove would have liked to do. Using the label sparingly, if it is not to produce bizarre effects, takes a lot more *Sprachgefühl* than the editors of 3 seem to have possessed. Thus *horse* as a verb ("to engage in horseplay") they accept as standard. The citations are from Norman Mailer ("I never horse around much with the women") and J. D. Salinger ("I horse around quite a lot, just to keep from getting bored"). I doubt whether either Mr. Mailer or Mr. Salinger would use *horse* straight; in these cites, I venture, it is either put in the mouth of a first-person narrator or used deliberately to get a colloquial effect. Slang is concise and vivid—*jalopy* has advantages over *dilapidated automobile*—and a few slang terms salted in a formal paragraph bring out the flavor. But the user must know he *is* using slang, he must be aware of having introduced a slight discord into his harmonics, or else he coarsens and blurs his expression. This information he will not, for the most part, get from 3. I hate to think what monstrosities of prose foreigners and high-school students will produce if they take 3 seriously as a guide to what is and what is not standard English.

Whenever the compilers of 3 come up against a locution that some (me, or I) might consider simply wrong, they do their best, as Modern Linguists and democrats, to be good fellows. The softening-up process begins with substituting the euphemistic *substandard* for 2's blunt *erroneous* and *illiterate*. From there it expands into several forms. *Complected* (for *complexioned*) is *dialect* in 2, *not often in formal use* in 3. *Learn* (for teach) is *now a vulgarism* in 2, *now chiefly substand.* in 3. (*Chiefly* is the thin end of the wedge, implying that users of standard English on occasion exclaim, "I'll learn you to use bad English!") *Knowed* is listed as the past of *know,* though *broke* is labelled substandard for *broken*—another of those odd discriminations. Doubtless they counted noses, or citation slips, and concluded that "Had I but knowed!" is standard while "My heart is broke" is substandard.

(To be entirely fair, perhaps compulsively so: If one reads carefully the five closely printed pages of Explanatory Notes in 3, and especially paragraphs 16.0 through 16.6 (twelve inches of impenetrable lexical jargon), one finds that light-face small capitals mean a cross-reference, and if one looks up KNOW—which is given after *knowed* in light-face small capitals—one does find that *knowed* is dialect. This is not a very practical or sensible dictionary, one concludes after such scholarly labors, and one wonders why Dr. Gove and his editors did not think of labelling *knowed* as substandard right where it occurs, and one suspects that they wanted to slightly conceal the fact or at any rate to put off its exposure as long as decently possible.)

The systematic softening or omitting of pejorative labels in 3 could mean: (1) we have come to use English more loosely, to say the least, than we did in 1934; or (2) usage hasn't changed, but 3 has simply recorded The Facts more accurately; or (3) the notion of what is a relevant Fact has changed between 2 and 3. I suspect it is mostly (3), but in any case I cannot see *complected* as anything but *dialected*.

In 1947 the G. & C. Merriam Co. published a little book entitled "Noah's Ark"—in reference to Noah Webster, who began it all—celebrating its first hundred years as the publisher of Webster dictionaries. Toward the end, the author, Robert Keith Leavitt, rises to heights of eloquence which have a tinny sound now that "Webster" means not 2 but 3:

> This responsibility to the user is no light matter. It has, indeed, grown heavier with every year of increasing acceptance of Webster. Courts, from the United States Supreme Court down, rely on the *New International's* definitions as a sort of common law: many a costly suit has hinged on a Webster definition, and many a citizen has gone behind prison bars or walked out onto the streets a free man, according to the light Webster put upon his doings. The statute law itself is not infrequently phrased by legislators in terms straight out of Webster. Most daily newspapers and magazines, and nearly all the books that come off the press, are edited and printed in accordance with Websterian usage. Colleges and schools make the *New International* their standard, and, for nearly half a century, students have dug their way through pedantic obscurity with the aid of the *Collegiate*. In business offices the secretary corrects her boss out of Webster and the boss holds customers and contractors alike in line by citing how Webster says it shall be done. In thousands upon thousands of homes, youngsters lying sprawled under the table happily absorb from Webster information which teachers have striven in vain to teach them from textbooks. Clear through, indeed, to the everyday American's most trivial and jocose of doings, Webster is the unquestioned authority.

While this picture is a bit idyllic—Clarence Barnhart's American College Dictionary, put out by Random House, is considered by many to be at least as good as the Webster Collegiate—it had some reality up to 1961. But as of today, courts that Look It Up In Webster will often find themselves little the wiser, since 3 claims no authority and merely records, mostly deadpan, what in fact every Tom, Dick, and Harry is now doing—in all innocence—to the language. That freedom or imprisonment should depend on 3 is an alarming idea. The secretary correcting her boss, if he is a magazine publisher, will collide with the unresolved *bimonthly* and *biweekly* problem, and the youngsters sprawled under the table will happily absorb from 3 the information that *jerk* is standard for "a stupid, foolish, naïve, or unconventional person." One imagines the themes: "Dr. Johnson admired Goldsmith's literary talent although he considered him a jerk." The editors of the New Webster's Vest Pocket Dictionary, thirty-nine cents at any cigar store, label *jerk* as *coll.* But then they aren't Structural Linguists.

The reviews of 3 in the lay press have not been enthusiastic. *Life* and the *Times* have both attacked it editorially as a "say-as-you-go" dictionary that reflects "the permissive school" in language study. The usually solemn editorialists of the *Times* were goaded to unprecedented wit:

> A passel of double-domes at the G. & C. Merriam Company joint in Springfield, Mass. [the editorial began], have been confabbing and yakking for twenty-seven years—which is not intended to infer that they have not been doing plenty work—and now they have finalized Webster's Third New International Dictionary, Unabridged, a new edition of that swell and esteemed word book.
>
> Those who regard the foregoing paragraph as acceptable English prose will find that the new Webster's is just the dictionary for them.

But the lay press doesn't always prevail. The irreverent may call 3 "Gove's Goof," but Dr. Gove and his editors are part of the dominant movement in the professional study of language—one that has in the last few years established strong beachheads in the National Council of Teachers of English and the College English Association. One may grant that for the scientific study of language the Structural Linguistic approach is superior to that of the old grammarians, who overestimated the importance of logic and Latin, but one may still object to its transfer directly to the teaching of English and the making of dictionaries. As a scientific discipline, Structural Linguistics can have no truck with values or standards. Its job is to deal only with The Facts. But in matters of usage, the evaluation of The Facts is important, too, and this requires a certain amount of general culture, not to mention common sense—commodities that many scientists have done brilliantly without but that teachers and lexicographers need in their work.

The kind of thinking responsible for 3 is illustrated by Dr. Gove's riposte, last week, to the many unfavorable reviews of his dictionary: "The criticisms involve less than one per cent of the words in the dictionary." This quantitative approach might be useful to novelists who get bad reviews. It is foolproof here; a reviewer who tried to meet Dr. Gove's criterion and deal with a sizable proportion of 3's words—

say, ten per cent—would need forty-five thousand words just to list them, and if his own comments averaged ten words apiece he would have to publish his five-hundred-thousand-word review in two large volumes. Some odd thinking gets done up at the old Merriam-Webster place in Springfield.

Dr. Gove's letter to the *Times* objecting to its editorial was also interesting. "The editors of *Webster's Third New International Dictionary* are not amused by the ingenuity of the first paragraph of your editorial," it began loftily, and continued, "Your paragraph obscures, or attempts to obscure, the fact that there are so many different degrees of standard usage that dictionary definitions cannot hope to distinguish one from another by status labelling." (But the *Times'* point was precisely that the editors did make such distinctions by status labelling, only they were the wrong distinctions; i.e., by omitting pejorative labels they accepted as standard words that, in the opinion of the *Times,* are not standard.) There followed several pages of citations in which Dr. Gove showed that the *Times* itself had often used the very words it objected to 3's including as standard language. "If we are ever inclined to the linguistic pedantry that easily fails to distinguish moribund traditions from genuine living usage [the adjectives here are perhaps more revealing than Dr. Gove intended] we have only to turn to the columns of the *Times,*" Dr. Gove concluded. The *Times* is the best newspaper in the world in the gathering and printing of news, but it has never been noted for stylistic distinction. And even if it were, the exigencies of printing a small book every day might be expected to drive the writers and editors of a newspaper into usages as convenient as they are sloppy—usages that people with more time on their hands, such as the editors of an unabridged dictionary, might distinguish from standard English.

There are several reasons that it is important to maintain standards in the use of a language. English, like other languages, is beautiful when properly used, and beauty can be achieved only by attention to form, which means setting limits, or de-fining, or dis-criminating. Language expresses the special, dis-tinctive quality of a people, and a people, like an individual, is to a large extent defined by its past—its traditions— whether it is conscious of this or not. If the language is allowed to shift too rapidly, without challenge from teachers and lexicographers, then the special character of the American people is blurred, since it tends to lose its past. In the same way a city loses it character if too much of it is torn down and rebuilt too quickly. "Languages are the pedigrees of nations," said Dr. Johnson.

The effect on the individual is also unfortunate. The kind of permissiveness that permeates 3 (the kind that a decade or two ago was more common in progressive schools than it is now) results, oddly, in less rather than more individuality, since the only way an individual can "express himself" is in relation to a social norm—in the case of language, to standard usage. James Joyce's creative distortions of words were possible only because he had a perfect ear for orthodox English. But if the very idea of form, or standards, is lacking, then how can one violate it? It's no fun to use *knowed* for *known* if everybody thinks you're just trying to be standard.

Counting cite slips is simply not the way to go about the delicate business of deciding these matters. If nine-tenths of the citizens of the United States, including a recent President, were to use *inviduous,* the one-tenth who clung to *invidious* would still be right, and they would be doing a favor to the majority if they continued to maintain the point. It is perhaps not democratic, according to some recent users, or abusers, of the word, to insist on this, and the question comes up of who is to decide at what point change—for language does indeed change, as the Structural Linguists insist—has evolved from *slang, dial., erron.,* or *substand.* to *standard.* The decision, I think, must be left to the teachers, the professional writers, and the lexicographers, and they might look up Ulysses' famous defense of conservatism in Shakespeare's "Troilus and Cressida":

> The heavens themselves, the planets and this centre
> Observe degree, priority and place,
> Insisture, course, proportion, season, form,
> Office and custom in all line of order. . . .
> Take but degree away, untune that string,
> And, hark, what discord follows! Each thing meets
> In mere oppugnancy. The bounded waters
> Should lift their bosoms higher than the shores
> And make a sop of all this solid globe.
> Strength should be lord of imbecility
> And the rude son should strike his father dead.
> Force should be right, or rather right and wrong
> (Between whose endless jar justice resides)
> Should lose their names, and so should justice too.
> Then every thing includes itself in power,
> Power into will, will into appetite
> And appetite, a universal wolf,
> So doubly seconded with will and power,
> Must make perforce a universal prey
> And, last, eat up himself. . . .

Dr. Johnson, a dictionary-maker of the old school, defined *lexicographer* as "a harmless drudge." Things have changed. Lexicographers may still be drudges, but they are certainly not harmless. They have untuned the string, made a sop of the solid structure of English, and encouraged the language to eat up himself.

BERGEN EVANS

But What's a Dictionary For?

The storm of abuse in the popular press that greeted the appearance of *Webster's Third New International Dictionary* is a curious phenomenon. Never has a scholarly work of this stature been attacked with such unbridled fury and contempt. An article in the *Atlantic* viewed it as a "disappointment," a "shock," a "calamity," "a scandal and a disaster." The New York *Times,* in a special editorial, felt that the work would "accelerate the deterioration" of the language and sternly accused the editors of betraying a public trust. The *Journal* of the American Bar Association saw the publication as "deplorable," "a flagrant example of lexicographic irresponsibility," "a serious blow to the cause of good English." *Life* called it "a non-word deluge," "monstrous," "abominable," and "a cause for dismay." They doubted that "Lincoln could have modelled his Gettysburg Address" on it—a concept of how things get written that throws very little light on Lincoln but a great deal on *Life.*

What underlies all this sound and fury? Is the claim of the G. & C. Merriam Company, probably the world's greatest dictionary maker, that the preparation of the work cost $3.5 million, that it required the efforts of three hundred scholars over a period of twenty-seven years, working on the largest collection of citations ever assembled in any language—is all this a fraud, a hoax?

So monstrous a discrepancy in evaluation requires us to examine basic principles. Just what's a dictionary for? What does it propose to do? What does the common reader go to a dictionary to find? What has the purchaser of a dictionary a right to expect for his money?

Before we look at basic principles, it is necessary to interpose two brief statements. The first of these is that a dictionary is concerned with words. Some dictionaries give various kinds of other useful information. Some have tables of weights and measures on the flyleaves. Some list historical events, and some, home remedies. And there's nothing wrong with their so doing. But the great increase in our vocabulary in the past three decades compels all dictionaries to make more efficient use of their space. And if something must be eliminated, it is sensible to throw out these extraneous things and stick to words.

Yet wild wails arose. The *Saturday Review* lamented that one can no longer find the goddess Astarte under a separate heading—though they point out that a genus of mollusks named after the goddess is included! They seemed to feel that out of sheer perversity the editors of the dictionary stooped to mollusks while ignoring goddesses and that, in some way, this typifies modern lexicography. Mr. Wilson Follett, folletizing (his mental processes demand some special designation) in the *Atlantic,* cried out in horror that one is not even able to learn from the Third International "that the Virgin was Mary the mother of Jesus"!

The second brief statement is that there has been even more progress in the making of dictionaries in the past thirty years than there has been in the making of automobiles. The difference, for example, between the much-touted Second International (1934) and the much-clouted Third International (1961) is not like the difference between yearly models but like the difference between the horse and buggy and the automobile. Between the appearance of these two editions a whole new science related to the making of dictionaries, the science of descriptive linguistics, has come into being.

Modern linguistics gets it charter from Leonard Bloomfield's *Language* (1933). Bloomfield, for thirteen years professor of Germanic philology at the University of Chicago and for nine years professor of linguistics at Yale, was one of those inseminating scholars who can't be relegated to any department and don't dream of accepting established categories and procedures just because they're established. He was as much an anthropologist as a linguist, and his concepts of language were shaped not by Strunk's *Elements of Style* but by his knowledge of Cree Indian dialects.

The broad general findings of the new science are:

1. All languages are systems of human conventions, not systems of natural laws. The first—and essential—step in the study of any language is observing and setting down precisely what happens when native speakers speak it.

2. Each language is unique in its pronunciation, grammar, and vocabulary. It cannot be described in terms of logic or of some theoretical,

ideal language. It cannot be described in terms of any other language, or even in terms of its own past.

3. All languages are dynamic rather than static, and hence a "rule" in any language can only be a statement of contemporary practice. Change is constant—and normal.

4. "Correctness" can rest only upon usage, for the simple reason that there is nothing else for it to rest on. And all usage is relative.

From these propositions it follows that a dictionary is good only insofar as it is a comprehensive and accurate description of current usage. And to be comprehensive it must include some indication of social and regional associations.

New dictionaries are needed because English has changed more in the past two generations than at any other time in its history. It has had to adapt to extraordinary cultural and technological changes, two world wars, unparalleled changes in transportation and communication, and unprecedented movements of populations.

More subtly, but pervasively, it has changed under the influence of mass education and the growth of democracy. As written English is used by increasing millions and for more reasons than ever before, the language has become more utilitarian and more informal. Every publication in America today includes pages that would appear, to the purist of forty years ago, unbuttoned gibberish. Not that they are; they simply show that you can't hold the language of one generation up as a model for the next.

It's not that you mustn't. You *can't*. For example, in the issue in which *Life* stated editorially that it would follow the Second International, there were over forty words, constructions, and meanings which are in the Third International but not in the Second. The issue of the New York *Times* which hailed the Second International as the authority to which it would adhere and the Third International as a scandal and a betrayal which it would reject used one hundred and fifty-three separate words, phrases, and constructions which are listed in the Third International but not in the Second and nineteen others which are condemned in the Second. Many of them are used many times, more than three hundred such uses in all. The Washington *Post,* in an editorial captioned "Keep Your Old Webster's," says, in the first sentence, "don't throw it away," and in the second, "hang on to it." But the old Webster's labels *don't* "colloquial" and doesn't include "hang on to," in this sense, at all.

In short, all of these publications are written in the language that the Third International describes, even the very editorials which scorn it. And this is no concidence, because the Third International isn't setting up any new standards at all; it is simply describing what *Life, the Washington Post,* and the New York *Times* are doing. Much of the dictionary's material comes from these very publications, the *Times,* in particular, furnishing more of its illustrative quotations than any other newspaper.

And the papers have no choice. No journal or periodical could sell a single issue today if it restricted itself to the American language of twenty-eight years ago. It couldn't discuss half the things we are interested in, and its style would seem stiff and cumbrous. If the editorials were serious, the public—and the stockholders—have reason to be grateful that the writers on these publications are more literate than the editors.

And so back to our questions: what's a dictionary for, and how, in 1962, can it best do what it ought to do? The demands are simple. The common reader turns to a dictionary for information about the spelling, pronunciation, meaning, and proper use of words. He wants to know what is current and respectable. But he wants—and has a right to—the truth, the full truth. And the full truth about any language, and especially about American English today, is that there are many areas in which certainty is impossible and simplification is misleading.

Even in so settled a matter as spelling, a dictionary cannot always be absolute. *Theater* is correct, but so is *theatre.* And so are *traveled* and *travelled, plow* and *plough, catalog* and *catalogue,* and scores of other variants. The reader may want a single certainty. He may have taken an unyielding position in an argument, he may have wagered in support of his conviction and may demand that the dictionary "settle" the matter. But neither his vanity nor his purse is any concern of the dictionary's; it must record the facts. And the fact here is that there are many words in our language which may be spelled, with equal correctness, in either of two ways.

So with prounciation. A citizen listening to his radio might notice that James B. Conant, Bernard Baruch, and Dwight D. Eisenhower pronounce *economics* as ECKuhnomiks, while A. Whitney Griswold, Adlai Stevenson, and Herbert Hoover pronounce it EEKuhnomiks. He turns to the dictionary to see which of the two pronunciations is "right" and finds that they are both acceptable.

Has he been betrayed? Has the dictionary abdicated its responsibility? Should it say that one *must* speak like the president of Harvard or like the president of Yale, like the thirty-first President of the United

States or like the thirty-fourth? Surely it's none of its business to make a choice. Not because of the distinction of these particular speakers; lexicography, like God, is no respecter of persons. But because so widespread and conspicuous a use of two pronounciations among people of this elevation shows that there *are* two pronounciations. Their speaking establishes the fact which the dictionary must record.

Among the "enormities" with which *Life* taxes the Third International is its listing of "the common mispronunciation" *heighth*. That it is labeled a "dialectal variant" seems, somehow, to compound the felony. But one hears the word so pronounced, and if one professes to give a full account of American English in the 1960s, one has to take some cognizance of it. All people do not possess *Life's* intuitive perception that the word is so "monstrous" that even to list it as a dialect variation is to merit scorn. Among these, by the way, was John Milton, who, in one of the greatest passages in all literature, besought the Holy Spirit to raise him to the "highth" of his great argument. And even the *Oxford English Dictionary* is so benighted as to list it, in full boldface, right alongside of *Height* as a variant that has been in the language since at least 1290.

Now there are still, apparently, millions of Americans who retain, in this as in much else, some of the speech of Milton. This particular pronunciation seems to be receding, but the *American Dialect Dictionary* still records instances of it from almost every state on the Eastern seaboard and notes that it is heard from older people and "occasionally in educated speech," "common with good speakers," "general," widespread."

Under these circumstances, what is a dictionary to do? Since millions speak the word this way, the pronunciation can't be ignored. Since it has been in use as long as we have any record of English and since it has been used by the greatest writers, it can't be described as substandard or slang. But it is heard now only in certain localities. That makes it a dialectical pronunciation, and an honest dictionary will list it as such. What else can it do? Should it do?

The average purchaser of a dictionary uses it most often, probably, to find out what a word "means." As a reader, he wants to know what an author intended to convey. As a speaker or writer, he wants to know what a word will convey to his auditors. And this, too, is complex, subtle, and forever changing.

An illustration is furnished by an editorial in the Washington *Post* (January 17, 1962). After a ringing appeal to those who "love truth and accuracy" and the usual bombinations about "abdication of authority" and "barbarism," the editorial charges the Third International with "pretentious and obscure verbosity" and specifically instances its definition of "so simple an object as a door."

The definition reads:

> a movable piece of firm material or a structure supported usu. along one side and swinging on pivots or hinges, sliding along a groove, rolling up and down, revolving as one of four leaves, or folding like an accordion by means of which an opening may be closed or kept open for passage into or out of a building, room, or other covered enclosure or a car, airplane, elevator, or other vehicle.

Then follows a series of special meanings, each particularly defined and, where necessary, illustrated by a quotation.

Since, aside from roaring and admonishing the "gentlemen from Springfield" that "accuracy and brevity are virtues," the *Post's* editorial fails to explain what is wrong with the definition, we can only infer from "so simple" a thing that the writer takes the plain, downright, man-in-the-street attitude that a door is a door and any damn fool knows that.

But if so, he has walked into one of lexicography's biggest booby traps: the belief that the obvious is easy to define. Whereas the opposite is true. Anyone can give a fair description of the strange, the new, or the unique. It's the commonplace, the habitual, that challenges definition, for its very commonness compels us to define it in uncommon terms. Dr. Johnson was ridiculed on just this score when his dictionary appeared in 1755. For two hundred years his definition of a network as "any thing reticulated or decussated, at equal distances, with interstices between the intersections" has been good for a laugh. But in the merriment one thing is always overlooked: no one has yet come up with a better definition! Subsequent dictionaries defined it as a mesh and then defined a mesh as a network. That's simple, all right.

Anyone who attempts sincerely to state what the word *door* means in the United States of America today can't take refuge in a log cabin. There has been an enormous proliferation of closing and demarking devices and structures in the past twenty years, and anyone who tries to thread his way through the many meanings now included under *door* may have to sacrifice brevity to accuracy and even have to employ words that a limited vocabulary may find obscure.

Is the entrance to a tent a door, for instance? And what of the thing that seals the exit of an airplane? Is this a door? Or what of those sheets and jets of air that are now being used, in place of old-fashioned oak and hinges, to screen entrances and exits? Are they doors? And what of those accordion-like things that set off various sections of many modern apartments? The fine print in the lease takes it for granted that they are doors and that spaces demarked by them are rooms—and the rent is computed on the number of rooms.

Was I gypped by the landlord when he called the folding contraption that shuts off my kitchen a door? I go to the Second International, which the editor of the *Post* urges me to use in preference to the Third International. Here I find that a door is

> The movable frame or barrier of boards, or other material, usually turning on hinges or pivots or sliding, by which an entranceway into a house or apartment is closed and opened; also, a similar part of a piece of furniture, as in a cabinet or bookcase.

This is only forty-six words, but though it includes the cellar door, it excludes the barn door and the accordion-like thing.

So I go on to the Third International. I see at once that the new definition is longer. But I'm looking for accuracy, and if I must sacrifice brevity to get it, then I must. And, sure enough, in the definition which raised the *Post's* blood pressure, I find the words "folding like an accordion." The thing *is* a door, and my landlord is using the word in one of its currently accepted meanings.

We don't turn to a work of reference merely for confirmation. We all have words in our vocabularies which we have misunderstood, and to come on the true meaning of one of these words is quite a shock. All our complacency and self-esteem rise to oppose the discovery. But eventually we must accept the humiliation and laugh it off as best we can.

Some, often those who have set themselves up as authorities, stick to their error and charge the dictionary with being in a conspiracy against them. They are sure that their meaning is the only "right" one. And when the dictionary doesn't bear them out they complain about "permissive" attitudes instead of correcting their mistake.

The New York *Times* and the *Saturday Review* both regarded as contemptibly "permissive" the fact that one meaning of one word was illustrated by a quotation from Polly Adler. But a rudimentary knowledge of the development of any language would have told them that the underworld has been a far more active force in shaping and enriching speech than all the synods that have ever convened. Their attitude is like that of the patriot who canceled his subscription to the *Dictionary of American Biography* when he discovered that the very first volume included Benedict Arnold!

The ultimate of "permissiveness," singled out by almost every critic for special scorn, was the inclusion in the Third International of *finalize*. It was this, more than any other one thing, that was given as the reason for sticking to the good old Second International—that "peerless authority on American English," as the *Times* called it. But if it was such an authority, why didn't they look into it? They would have found *finalize* if they had.

And why shouldn't it be there? It exists. It's been recorded for two generations. Millions employ it every day. Two Presidents of the United States—men of widely differing cultural backgrounds—have used it in formal statements. And so has the Secretary-General of the United Nations, a man of unusual linguistic attainments. It isn't permitting the word but omitting it that would break faith with the reader. Because it is exactly the sort of word we want information about.

To list it as substandard would be to imply that it is used solely by the ignorant and the illiterate. But this would be a misrepresentation: President Kennedy and U Thant are highly educated men, and both are articulate and literate. It isn't even a freak form. On the contrary, it is a classic example of a regular process of development in English, a process which has given us such thoroughly accepted words as *generalize, minimize, formalize,* and *verbalize.* Nor can it be dismissed on logical grounds or on the ground that it is a mere duplication of *complete.* It says something that *complete* doesn't say and says it in a way that is significant in the modern bureaucratic world: one usually *completes* something which he has initiated but *finalizes* the work of others.

One is free to dislike the word. I don't like it. But the editor of a dictionary has to examine the evidence for a word's existence and seek it in context to get, as clearly and closely as he can, the exact meaning that it conveys to those who use it. And if it is widely used by well-educated, literate, reputable people, he must list it as a standard word. He is not compiling a volume of his own prejudices.

An individual's use of his native tongue is the surest index to his position within his community. And those who turn to a dictionary expect from it some statement of the current status of a word or a grammatical construction. And it is with the failure to assume this function that modern lexicography has been most fiercely charged. The charge is based on a naïve assumption that simple labels can be attached in all instances. But they can't. Some words are standard in some constructions and not in others. There may be as many shades of status as of meaning, and modern lexicography instead of abdicating this function has fulfilled it to a degree utterly unknown to earlier dictionaries.

Consider the word *fetch,* meaning to "go get and bring to." Until recently a standard word of full dignity ("Fetch me, I pray thee, a little water in a vessel"—I Kings 17:10), it has become slightly tainted. Perhaps the command latent in it is resented as undemocratic. Or maybe its use in training dogs to retrieve has made some people feel that it is an undignified word to apply to human beings. But, whatever the reason, there is a growing uncertainty about its status, and hence it is the sort of word that conscientious people look up in a dictionary.

Will they find it labeled "good" or "bad"? Neither, of course, because either applied indiscriminately would be untrue. The Third International lists nineteen different meanings of the verb *to fetch.* Of these some are labeled "dialectal," some "chiefly dialectal," some "obsolete," one "chiefly Scottish," and two "not in formal use." The primary meaning—"to go after and bring back"—is not labeled and hence can be accepted as standard, accepted with the more assurance because the many shades of labeling show us that the word's status has been carefully considered.

On grammatical questions the Third International tries to be equally exact and thorough. Sometimes a construction is listed without comment, meaning that in the opinion of the editors it is unquestionably respectable. Sometimes a construction carries the comment "used by speakers and writers on all educational levels though disapproved by some grammarians." Or the comment may be "used in substandard speech and formerly also by reputable writers." Or "less often in standard than in substandard speech." Or simply "dial."

And this very accurate reporting is based on evidence which is presented for our examination. One may feel that the evidence is inadequate or that the evaluation of it is erroneous. But surely, in the face of classification so much more elaborate and careful than any known heretofore, one cannot fly into a rage and insist that the dictionary is "out to destroy . . . every vestige of linguistic punctilio . . . every criterion for distinguishing between better usages and worse."

Words, as we have said, are continually shifting their meanings and connotations and hence their status. A word which has dignity, say, in the vocabulary of an older person may go down in other people's estimation. Like *fetch.* The older speaker is not likely to be aware of this and will probably be inclined to ascribe the snickers of the young at his speech to that degeneration of manners which every generation has deplored in its juniors. But a word which is coming up in the scale—like *jazz,* say, or, more recently, *crap*—will strike his ear at once. We are much more aware of offenses given us than of those we give. And if he turns to a dictionary and finds the offending word listed as standard—or even listed, apparently—his response is likely to be an outburst of indignation.

But the dictionary can neither snicker nor fulminate. It records. It will offend many, no doubt, to find the expression *wise up,* meaning to inform or to become informed, listed in the Third International with no restricting label. To my aging ears it still sounds like slang. But the evidence—quotations from the *Kiplinger Washington Letter* and the *Wall Street Journal*—convinces me that it is I who am out of step, lagging behind. If such publications have taken to using *wise up* in serious contexts, with no punctuational indication of irregularity, then it is obviously respectable. And finding it so listed and supported, I can only say that it's nice to be informed and sigh to realize that I am becoming an old fogy. But, of course, I don't have to use it (and I'll be damned if I will! "Let them smile, as I do now, At the old forsaken bough Where I cling").

In part, the trouble is due to the fact that there is no standard for standard. Ideas of what is proper to use in serious, dignified speech and writing are changing—and with breathtaking rapidity. This is one of the major facts of contemporary American English. But it is no more the dictionary's business to oppose this process than to speed it up.

Even in our standard speech some words are more dignified and some more informal than others, and dictionaries have tried to guide us through these uncertainties by marking certain words and constructions as "colloquial," meaning "inappropriate in a formal situation." But this distinction, in the opinion of most scholars, has done more harm than good. It has created the notion that these particular words are inferior, when actually they might be the best possible words in an informal statement. And so—to the rage of many reviewers—the Third International has dropped this label. Not all labels, as angrily charged, but only this one out of a score. And the doing so may have been an error, but it certainly didn't constitute "betrayal" or "abandoning of all distinctions." It was intended to end a certain confusion.

In all the finer shades of meaning, of which the status of a word is only one, the user is on his own, whether he likes it or not. Despite *Life's* artless assumption about the Gettysburg Address, nothing worth writing is written *from* a dictionary. The dictionary, rather, comes along afterwards and describes what *has been* written.

Words in themselves are not dignified, or silly, or wise, or malicious. But they can be used in dignified, silly, wise, or malicious ways by dignified, silly, wise, or malicious people. *Egghead,* for example, is a perfectly legitimate word, as legitimate as *highbrow* or *long-haired.* But there is something very wrong and very undignified, by civilized standards, in a belligerent dislike for intelligence and education. *Yak* is an amusing word for persistent chatter. Anyone could say, "We were just yakking over a cup of coffee," with no harm to his dignity. But to call a Supreme Court decision *yakking* is to be vulgarly insulting and so, undignified. Again, there's nothing wrong with *confab* when it's appropriate. But when the work of a great research project, employing hundreds of distinguished scholars over several decades and involving the honor of one of the greatest publishing houses in the world, is described as *confabbing* (as the New York *Times* editorially described the preparation of the Third International), the use of this particular word asserts that the lexicographers had merely sat around and talked idly. And the statement becomes undignified—if not, indeed, slanderous.

The lack of dignity in such statements is not in the words, nor in the dictionaries that list them, but in the hostility that deliberately seeks this tone of expression. And in expressing itself the hostility frequently shows that those who are expressing it don't know how to use a dictionary. Most of the reviewers seem unable to read the Third International and unwilling to read the Second.

The *American Bar Association Journal,* for instance, in a typical outburst ("a deplorable abdication of responsibility"), picked out for special scorn the inclusion in the Third International of the word *irregardless.* "As far as the new Webster's is concerned," said the *Journal,* "this meaningless verbal bastard is just as legitimate as any other word in the dictionary." Thirty seconds spent in examining the book they were so roundly condemning would have shown them that in it *irregardless* is labeled "nonstand"—which means "nonstandard," which means "not conforming to the usage generally characteristic of educated native speakers of the language." Is that "just as legitimate as any other word in the dictionary"?

The most disturbing fact of all is that the editors of a dozen of the most influential publications in America today are under the impression that *authoritative* must mean *authoritarian.* Even the "permissive" Third International doesn't recognize this identification—editors' attitudes being not yet, fortunately, those of the American people. But the Fourth International may have to.

The new dictionary may have many faults. Nothing that tries to meet an ever-changing situation over a terrain as vast as contemporary English can hope to be free of them. And much in it is open to honest, and informed, disagreement. There can be linguistic objection to the eradication of proper names. The removal of guides to pronunciation from the foot of every page may not have been worth the valuable space it saved. The new method of defining words of many meanings has disadvantages as well as advantages. And of the half million or more definitions, hundreds, possibly thousands, may seem inadequate or imprecise. To some (of whom I am one) the omission of the label "colloquial" will seem meritorious; to others it will seem a loss.

But one thing is certain: anyone who solemnly announces in the year 1962 that he will be guided in matters of English usage by a dictionary published in 1934 is talking ignorant and pretentious nonsense.

RAVEN I. McDAVID, JR.

Historical, Regional and Social Variation[1]

What James H. Sledd has called the "agonizing deappraisal" of *Webster's Third New International Dictionary,* since its appearance in 1961, has shown that many Americans, in keeping with the national trend to simplistic interpretations, would make a sharp dichotomy between "good language" and "bad language," or between what is "correct" and what is "incorrect." In this same dichotomizing, the villains of the piece are often the linguists, who are accused of advocating "say as you go" attitudes in language practice and of "letting down the bars" where standards are concerned. Though it is perhaps no help to a linguist or lexicographer who has been clawed by an angry journalist or literary critic, the fact is that no responsible linguist has denied the existence of standards or refused to recognize that in any speech community some people are acknowledged as using the language better— that is, in a fashion more worthy of emulation—than others.

There is not in language—or in any other form of human behavior —a simple opposition between good and bad, but a complicated set of interrelated variations; it is necessary for linguists themselves to sort out the many dimensions in which usage may vary and show how these variations are related to each other. This has been done in the past by several scholars; but as a way of introducing this topic it is well to repeat their findings.[2]

Among the scales on which a given detail of usage may be measured, the following have been suggested; others may of course be devised or discovered.

From *Culture, Class, and Language Variety.* Reprinted by permission of the National Council of Teachers of English and the author.

203

1. The dimension of the medium—essentially writing as opposed to speech. There is little chance to use *antidisestablishmentarianism* in conversation, let alone the sesquipedalian terms of organic chemistry. Only in homely fiction (and the authorship of such a distinguished writer as William Faulkner does not refute the homeliness) is there a place for such a term as *fice,* "a small, noisy, generally worthless dog of uncertain ancestry."

2. The dimension of responsibility, as Joos puts it—an understanding of the normal social expectations of the audience in particular or of the community at large. A politician who talks over the heads of his audience may be admired for his cleverness or even brilliance, but will usually be denied the votes he is seeking. Some people—like myself—cannot read Henry James: he is too consciously superior in his style, which begins to seem a set of mannerisms after half a dozen pages. And it has been attested in a variety of situations that a person who is too meticulous in his observation of grammatical shibboleths and in avoiding the speech of his locality may rouse the distrust of his fellows.[3] On the other hand, a complete disregard of these expectations may be equally disastrous. The novelty of the "Beat" writers, free association with a minimum of revision, soon ran its course, except for the most case-hardened cultists: the reading public became impatient.[4]

3. The dimension of maturity—the notion that one should speak as well as act one's chronological age. The sight of a plump Hausfrau in a bikini is no more distressing than the sound of a middle-aged parent trying to keep up with the latest adolescent slang. Even finer distinctions are apparent: college students scorn the kind of language that had delighted them in high school.

4. The scale of vogue. On one hand, this is found in the slang of the year; on another, in certain kinds of jargon and counter-words. Both varieties of vogue language are exceedingly difficult to pin down; most of the time the vogue has passed before the lexicographers have settled down to recording and classifying.

5. The scale of association—the argot or technical language of a group with which one has become identified. Every association group has this—not just teenage gangs and the more formally parasitic subcultures of the underworld. The language of a stamp-collector or a model railroad fan on the one hand, of Anglo-Catholic clergy or Chicago critics on the other, may be just as unintelligible to outsiders not of the true bond as is the lingo of safecrackers or narcotics addicts.

6. The scale of relationship between the speaker or writer and his audience—the "five clocks" of Martin Joos. In the center, as Joos reckons it, is the *consultative* style, of the small committee or social gathering—not more than six people—where free interchange is possible but

background information must be supplied. On the one side are the *formal* style, typified in public address, and the *frozen* style, that of great literature (encompassing principally but not exclusively the "high style" or the "sublime" of traditional criticism)—where the public insists on the text being repeated intact. On the other are the *casual* style, where familiarity of speaker and audience with each other eliminates the need for background information, and the *intimate,* where close association makes possible many syntactic shortcuts. It is noticeable that the frozen and the intimate styles, as opposite poles, share the feature of high allusiveness, created in one by the genius of the author at compressing much into a small space and in the other by the closeness of association.

7. The dimension of history, paralleling, to some extent, the scale of maturity in the individual. Dictionaries have long recognized this dimension: words or senses that have not been observed for some centuries are labeled *obsolete;* those that have appeared only rarely in some centuries, and not at all for a few generations, are marked *archaic.* A more troublesome class is made up of those words and meanings which are still encountered, but only in the usage of the older and less sophisticated—those that I would call *old-fashioned.* So far, there is no traditional label in lexicography, though everybody recognizes the items. Even more troublesome are innovations, which are seldom if ever marked, since by the time they are noticed they have generally become well established. A notorious example is the verb *to finalize,* which did not arouse the ire of the belles-lettristes (because of its vogue in advertising) until a generation after it had been recorded, and much longer after it first appeared.

8. The regional scale. At one end we have pronunciations, words or meanings that are limited to a small part of the English-speaking world; at the other, things that are truly international in that they are shared by several language communities. *Chay!,* a call to summon cattle, is found in the United States (it may still be heard in Northern Ireland) only in a small section of eastern South Carolina; most of the new terms of science and technology, including such everyday words as *telephone,* are found not only in all places where English is spoken but in other languages as well. Within the English-speaking world, there are words, meanings, pronunciations and even grammatical forms characteristic of England proper, Ireland, Scotland, the United States, Canada, Australia, New Zealand, South Africa, and the West Indies—to say nothing of more local subdivisions in each of these. To take a few examples, a *station* in Australia is the same as a *ranch* in Western North America; a *tickle* in Newfoundland is an inlet; and the *telly* in Britain is the television.

9. The social scale. This means, simply, that some varieties of the

language are more esteemed than others. It may be an alien variety of the community language, like British English in parts of the Commonwealth; it may even be an alien language, like French in parts of Africa. In most European countries it is a variety of the language used by the richer and better born and better educated in a focus of national life—economic, cultural, or political—which often turns out to be the area around the capital: Roman-Florentine in Italy, Castilian in Spain, Parisian in France, Muscovite in Russia, London in England (it should be noted that the lower-class speech of the same areas has no prestige; in fact, as we document with traditional London lower class speech, Cockney, it may be the least favored of all lower-class regional varieties). The favored dialect of one century, even one generation, may not be that of the next. In extreme cases, another city may replace the older center of prestige, as London replaced Winchester after the Norman Conquest; in all cases the favored dialect will change as new classes rise in the scale and set new fashions of language behavior.

The American situation, however, is different—both in the United States and in Canada. Partly through geography, partly through the independence of each of the early settlements from each other, partly through a stubborn tradition of individualism and local loyalty, no city has unqualified preeminence of the kind that Paris, London, and Vienna have in their countries. Each of the older cultural centers—Boston, New York, Philadelphia, Richmond, Charleston—had its own élite and boasted its own kind of excellence; as the nation expanded westward, such new cities as Chicago, San Francisco, Atlanta, St. Louis, and Salt Lake City developed their own prestige in their own areas. There is a good deal of ridicule exchanged between cities, most of it good-natured, as to which local pronunciation (for grammar and vocabulary are strikingly uniform among urban educated speakers) is the most outlandish or the most pleasant; but for practical purposes the educated speech of one area is as good as another—and all varieties of uneducated speech are at a disadvantage, especially when the speakers move out of their own areas.

For six of the nine scales of variation, the speaker has some freedom of choice. But for the last three—history, region and society—he is more or less caught up in forces beyond his control. No man can change the generation or place of his birth; his attempts to change the social variety of his speech will be determined by the kind of education he receives and the kind of persons he associates with, and opportunities to make a drastic change are not as common as we would like.

Along all of these scales, for practical purposes, we can expect variation in a number of aspects of human communication. Outside language we have (1) *proxemics*, the phenomena of spatial variation, including the distances at which communication is effective; (2) *haptics,* the phenomena of body contact; (3) *kinesics,* bodily movements in communication, of which gestures are only a small part; (4) *paralanguage,* the non-linguistic but communicatively significant orchestration of the stream of speech, involving such phenomena as abnormally high or low pitch, abnormally fast or slow tempo, abnormal loudness or softness, drawl, clipping, rasp, openness, and the like. These are all in the earliest stages of discussion; linguists and anthropologists recognize their importance but have just begun to develop systems of notation and means of comparison.[5]

Within the domain of language proper, but having a special position, are the *suprasegmentals,* the phenomena that in English include stress, intonation, transitions, and terminals of clauses and utterances. It should be noted that suprasegmentals, like the aspects of communication outside the language system, have so far had no systematic comparative discussion regionally or socially. And all these phenomena are attested only in a limited way historically and in writing have no direct reflection.

Within language proper there is a system of segmental phonemes, of vowels and consonants, capable of variation in the structure of the system, in the articulation of the individual phonemes, and in their incidence in particular environments.[6] The system of morphology likewise varies in its structure, in the shape of particular morphemes (especially of inflections), and in their incidence in particular environments. There is a system of syntax, involving the selection and arrangement of morphemes.[7] And finally there is the body of meaningful forms—the lexicon —with various words possible for the same meaning, and various meanings possible for the same word.

If we look at the history of English, we can see that all kinds of changes have taken place as the result of various forces, borrowing (both from other languages and from one dialect of English to another), phonetic change, and analogy.[8]

In the pronunciation system, we have kept four of the short vowels of Old English: /I, ε, æ, U/; Old English /Y/, however, has unrounded to /I/, so that *fill* and *will* now rhyme. Many of the words which had /U/ in Old English now have /$\wedge$/, and for most American dialects the low-back rounded vowel /ɔ/, as in *God,* has unrounded to /a/. In contrast to these slight changes, all the long vowels and diphthongs of Old English have changed their phonetic shape, and some of them have fallen together; for example, Middle English /sæ:/, "body of water," and /se:/ "to perceive with the eyes" have fallen together as /si/.

The morphological structure of the language has likewise altered.

The noun retains only the general plural and the genitive; the adjective retains comparison (though for many adjectives it is a periphrastic comparison with *more* and *most* instead of the historical inflected comparison with *-er, -est*) but has lost all markers of number, gender, and case. The pronoun system has been drastically simplified: only the neuter *it* retains the old accusative, here undifferentiated from the nominative; in all other pronouns the old dative has assumed all object functions. In the second person the historical dative plural has not only usurped the functions of the accusative but those of the nominative as well, and (with rare exceptions) has become the standard for the singular in object and subject positions. In the third person, *she, they, their* and *them*—borrowings from Northern English dialects—have supplanted the older forms. Throughout the pronominal system there has been a differentiation between the attributive genitive, as *my book,* and the absolute, as *a book of mine.* The article and demonstrative are now distinct from each other; the demonstrative has lost all gender and case distinctions, with the historical neuter nominative-accusatives *this* and *that* in the singular and developing new plurals.

The most spectacular morphological changes have taken place in the verb. It is still a two-tense verb, like all Germanic verbs, but many of the older strong or irregular verbs have become weak or regular, and the survivors have tended to level their principal parts: only *was/were* remains of the historical distinction between preterite singular and preterite plural, and for many verbs preterite and past participle have fallen together. Distinctions of person and number have been lost except for the verb *to be* and for the third singular present indicative. The subjunctive mode has been lost except for the hypothetical *if I (he) were you,* the very formal *if this be treason,* a series of petrified formulas such as *resolved, that this house stand adjourned,* and that-clauses following such verbs as *urge* and *insist.*

Syntactic changes are also numerous. Word order, once flexible and capable of variation, as in classical Latin or contemporary Ojibwa, has now been fixed. New patterns of interrogative and negative structures have developed, with the verb *do* as an auxiliary. And there has been a proliferation of very complicated verb phrases, capable of rendering far more subtle nuances of meaning than could have been rendered in Latin; if some of them rarely occur, as *tomorrow our house will have been redecorated for two months,* they are comprehensible and acceptable when they occur.

Changes in the vocabulary and in meanings are so numerous and familiar that it is almost useless to mention them; a few examples will suffice. *Starve,* originally meaning "to perish" like its German cognate *sterben,* came to signify "to perish of hunger"; as a general verb it has been replaced by *die.* The overworked *nice* originally meant *foolish. Flesh* has lost its meaning of "edible muscular tissue" and has been replaced in this meaning by *meat,* which originally signified anything edible (*sweetmeats* preserves the old meaning); *food* has assumed the general meaning.

To this stage of the presentation we have assumed a more or less linear development, recognizing but disregarding differences within the speech community. Yet we know by experience that no speech community of any size—and the size may be only a few hundred speakers—is without regional and social distinctions. Different communities use the language differently; some speakers are recognized as using it better than others do. The larger the speech community, the more complicated are the relationships between regional and social varieties.

Regional differences may arise in a variety of ways. The classical explanation—which has been used to explain the differences in Modern German, before the new *Wölkerwänderung* after World War II—is that of the original settlement by a group speaking a particular dialect of the same language. The population mixture in all of the early American settlements makes this explanation less cogent here, but such groups have left their traces. We can think of the Ulster Scots in Western Pennsylvania, and less significantly in the Southern uplands and the South Midland derivatives to the west; of the Irish fishermen on Beaver Island in Lake Michigan and in various coves along the Newfoundland coast; of the East Anglian influence, through the early Puritans, on the speech of New England, especially east of the Connecticut River; and in the American Middle West, of the preservation of New England speechways in the Western Reserve around Cleveland and in the Marietta speech-island where the Muskingum flows into the Ohio.

Settlements of speakers of a foreign language also leave their impact on a local dialect. The Palatinate Germans who settled in Eastern Pennsylvania about 1700 have influenced to some degree the English of their area, not only in vocabulary but also in pronunciation, in syntax and in intonation. In similar fashion the Scandinavians in Minneapolis have markedly influenced English intonation; even complete monolinguals cannot escape acquiring the speech tune of the Swedish-Americans they played with as children. So have the Cajans of southwestern Louisiana influenced the intonation of Louisiana English, and—on all but the most educated level—caused a loss of final consonant clusters and most inflectional endings.

Regional dialects also reflect historical patterns of migration and communication. In Germany the Rhine has disseminated the South German speech forms northward, and vice versa; in the United States the Mississippi has done likewise. In the Middle West, settlers from New England followed the shores of Lake Erie westward and did not cross the swamplands of the Maumee and Kankakee, while settlers from the Upland South moved north along the tributaries of the Ohio, taking up holdings in the bottom-lands; today, despite subsequent industrialization, the speech of Ohio, Indiana, and Illinois is split between Yankee and Southern highland. Conversely, even what now seems a trivial geographical barrier could inhibit the spread of settlement and speech: Chesapeake Bay isolated the Delmarva Peninsula from the focal area of the Virginia Tidewater and Piedmont; the Virginia Blue Ridge limited the westward spread of plantation culture, so that the Shenandoah Valley was settled by migration from western Pennsylvania; and in Vermont the crest of the Green Mountains marks the division between Eastern and Western New England speechways.

If a cultural focus exists, its speech forms spread into the surrounding countryside or even leap rural areas to become established in what one could call satellite cities. The prestige of Boston has led to the establishment of its speech as the model for Eastern New England and as a type to imitate in much of the northern United States; Philadelphia dominates Eastern Pennsylvania and Pittsburgh the western half of the state; the cultivated speech of Richmond and other Virginia Piedmont cities has been emulated not merely in the Shenandoah Valley but in cities of eastern North Carolina and as far west as Charleston, West Virginia. New York seems to be an exception: its vocabulary has spread but not its pronunciation, possibly because the city has for so long boasted very large foreign-language concentrations.[9] Where communities have been geographically or culturally isolated, of course, the opposite is true: the speech of the Maine coast, the Southern Appalachians, or northeastern North Carolina does not spread and in fact gives way to outside models as these remote areas become accessible.

Political boundaries, old and new, are reflected in Europe as limits of pronunciations or words; they are so recent in the United States, and so ineffective on the movement of people and goods, that they seldom cause linguistic differences—though with purely political terms, such as the Ontario *reeve*, "township officer," linguistic and political limits may coincide. But in an indirect way, as in the quality of a school system, state boundaries may be significant. Folk pronunciations and folk grammatical forms survived much more strongly in Western Maryland and West Virginia than in Pennsylvania, though the early settlers were the same kinds of people and the easy routes of communications cross the state boundaries; but Pennsylvania had an earlier and deeper commitment to public education than the states further south.

By now it is possible to summarize in some detail the kinds of regional differences that appear in American English. In addition to the usual features of grammar, pronunciation and vocabulary, there are probably regional variations in proxemics, haptics, kinesics, paralanguage, and suprasegmentals, though no systematic statement is possible. The entomologist Henry K. Townes has noted that some hand gestures seem to occur only in the South Carolina Piedmont; Southern speech seems to have a wider range of stress and pitch than the speech of other regions, especially the dialects of the Middle West; the so-called "Southern drawl" does not reflect a slower tempo—for Southerners normally speak more rapidly than Middle Westerners—but rather this heavier stress, combined with prolongation of the heavily stressed syllables and shortening of the weak stressed ones.

Within the pronunciation of American English, there is only one major difference in the system of phonemes: most dialects contrast unrounded /a/ and rounded /ɔ/, as cot and caught, but some do not. Where the contrast does not exist, some dialects—Eastern New England, Western Pennsylvania, the St. Louis area—have a low-back rounded vowel, while others—the Upper Peninsula of Michigan, northern Minnesota, western Canada—have a low-central or low-back unrounded one. Until recently, some dialects in the area of New England settlement had a falling diphthong /iu/ in such words as blue, suit, grew, where most speakers of American English have /u/, and in such words as due, tube, new, student, where some regions have /u/ and others have /ju/; however, the /iu/ is generally considered old fashioned, and it is rapidly disappearing.

Although general structural differences in the pronunciation systems of dialects are rare, conditioned structural differences are more common. As we have indicated, the consonant sequences /tj-, dj-, nj-, stj-/—in such words as tube, due, new, student—simply do not occur in some regions, though all of these consonants are found in all American dialects. Dialects that contrast /a/ and /ɔ/, as in cot and caught, may not have the contrast before /-r/, as in barn and born; this is especially true in the St. Louis area, in parts of the Southwest, and in the Rocky Mountains. All varieties of American English contrast /ɔ/ and /o/, as in law and low, but before /-r/, as in horse and hoarse, the contrast is retained only in parts of the South. Again, only in parts of the South and some Atlantic seaboard Yankee areas—and probably not so common there as it used to be—does one find the contrast between met, *mat,* and *mate* maintained before intervocalic /-r-/, in *merry, marry* and *Mary;* from Cleveland west these three words are generally homonyms. And in the Charleston area there seems to be only one front vowel before postvocalic /-r/ or its derivative /ə/, so that *fear* and *fair, ear* and *air* are homonyms.

The phonemes may differ in phonetic shape; /e/ in *date* is an up-gliding diphthong with a high beginning [eI] in the South Midland, an up-gliding diphthong with a low beginning [ɛ I] in the Delaware Valley and the Pittsburgh area, a monophthong [e ·] in the Pennsylvania German area and an in-gliding diphthong [e . ə] in the South Carolina Low-Country. The /ɔ/ of *law, dog* has a high beginning and an in-glide in much of the Middle Atlantic Seaboard, including old-fashioned New York City speech; in much of the South and South Midland, it has a low beginning with an up-glide and increasing rounding.

More familiar are differences in incidence of phonemes. Upstate New York has /a/ in *fog, hog* and *on;* Pennsylvania has /ɔ/. The fish *crappie* has /a/ in the stressed syllable in Michigan, /æ/ in South Carolina. The North and North Midland prevailingly have /-s-/ in *greasy* and /I/ in *creek;* the South and South Midland have /-z-/ and /i/.

Differences in inflection are less frequent than in pronunciation. Systematic differences are very rare: a few British dialects retain the old second person singular *thou, thy, thine, thee;* some American dialects have developed a new second person plural, *you-all, you-uns, youse, mongste-ye, oona,* though none of these has standing in formal writing and only *you-all* has achieved the dignity of standard informal status; possibly some dialects have lost the distinctiveness of the third singular present indicative *-s* and consistently have either *-s* or zero throughout the present.[10] In the shape of the morpheme there are more differences: standard *drank* as a preterit, versus *drunk* and *drinkt;* standard *climbed* versus *clim, clum, clome, cloom* and the like; and on the standard level, such variations as between *kneeled* and *knelt* or between *dove* /dov/ and *dived.*

It is notorious that the description of English syntax is less adequate than that of its pronunciation or inflections. But even at this point we can recognize some regional patterns. In the South and South Midland such compounded auxiliaries as *might could* and *used to could* are common in educated informal speech; the New England settlement area forms the negative of *ought* by the periphrastic *hadn't ought;* in eastern Kentucky *used to* has become a sentence-initial adverb, as in *used to everybody around here baked their own bread.*

Regional differences in vocabulary still abound, despite the homogenizing effect of twentieth-century urban civilization. Perhaps few of our students today would recognize the Northern *whippletree* or Midland *singletree* by any name, and urban living has probably prospered *dragonfly* and *earthworm* at the expense of such regional designations as Northern *darning needle,* South Midland-Southern *snake doctor* and Southern coastal *mosquito hawk,* or Merrimac Valley *mudworm,* Pennsylvania German *rainworm,* Southern mountain *redworm.* But a drycleaning establishment in Boston is a *cleanser;* the New Orleans *poorboy,* a sandwich on a small loaf of bread, is a *submarine* in Boston, a *grinder* in upstate New York, a *hero* in New York City, a *hoagy* in Philadelphia; the grass strip between sidewalk and street, still unnamed in some regions, is a *boulevard* in Minneapolis, a *tree belt* in Springfield, Massachusetts, a *tree lawn* in Cleveland, and a *devil strip* in Akron. And similar differences in meanings persist. It may be only academic that in the Carolina mountains a *corn dodger* is a small loaf, in the coastal plain a *dumpling,* in Savannah a *pancake,* and in Brunswick, Georgia, a *hush puppy;* but one who customarily uses *brat* to describe a noisy child may run into difficulties in parts of Indiana where it denotes a bastard, and the Middle Westerner used to ice cream in a *milk shake* will be disappointed in Boston, where it contains only milk and syrup.

If the basis of regional dialects is the fact that communities or regions differ in their history, the basis of social dialects is that people of different social standing in a given community will use different forms, and that the status of the linguistic forms will be determined by the standing of their users in the community.

Although this general principle has been recognized for generations, the procedures for discussing the correlation between speech differences and differences in status have been systematically worked out only in recent years and are still being refined. For a long time the difference between what was good and what was bad was more a matter of the observer's prejudices than of his observations. However, with Fries's *American English Grammar* (1940) and the American Linguistic Atlas project (1933–, with the first publication in 1939), it has become customary to identify the social status of informants first, by non-linguistic means, and then to describe, simply, the forms they use. A further refinement has been recently introduced by William Labov, in his dissertation, *The Social Stratification of English in New York City* (Washington, 1966), by limiting himself to a smaller number of variables, by obtaining examples in a variety of contexts—ranging from the reading of potentially minimal pairs to the account of an incident in which the informant thought he was going to be killed—and informants' identifications of the social status of particular variants. Labov has revealed that in pronunciation New Yorkers have a considerable gap between their target and their actual usage; whether or not such a gap exists in other regions—I suspect it is less important in the South than in the urban Northeast—can be determined only by further investigation. But whatever the answer, Labov has already rendered the profession an invaluable service by providing a kind of instrument for answering questions that have long been felt.

Although the situation in any given community is far more complex, a working evaluation of social dialects starts with a threefold classification:

1. Uneducated, or folk speech.
2. Common speech—in the more general sense of everyday usage of the average citizen, not in the Southern pejorative sense.
3. Educated, cultivated, or standard speech.

It is from the last group that speech with national prestige has developed. In the European situation, as we have pointed out, there is often a single prestigious variety of the language—in origin, normally the upper-class speech of the capital or the surrounding area, or of some other important center. In the New World, on the other hand, there are a number of prestigious regional varieties, deriving from regional cultural traditions; one has only to think of the differences in the speech of the last five college-educated Presidents: Calvin Coolidge (western New England), Herbert Hoover (northern Middle Western, modified by travel), Franklin Roosevelt (Hudson Valley), John F. Kennedy (Boston), Lyndon Johnson (southern Texas).

When we have discovered the principal dialect levels in our society, and their regional variants, we must still observe a few cautions. First, the social distance between levels is not the same in all communities. In, say, the older plantation communities, the distance between common and cultivated—the distance between plain, everyday people and the élite—was greater than that between folk and common. On the other hand, in such urban centers as Detroit, Cleveland, and Chicago, the distance between uneducated speech and common speech is greater than that between common and cultivated. In New York City the spacing between the various levels may be fairly wide; in a small Midwestern town without heavy industry it may be narrow.

Second, who is or is not cultivated depends on local standards, and is more or less relative. It is only a slight exaggeration to cite the experience of a graduate student from Georgia who went with his Harvard classmates to a performance of *Tobacco Road*. In their discussion afterward, one of the New Englanders asked if Jeeter Lester and his family were really typical of rural Georgia. "Hell, no;" exclaimed the Georgian. "Back home we'd call people like that the country club set." It is very likely that in terms of absolute education and cultural exposure a store-keeper in a college community like Ann Arbor or Chapel Hill would rank above the local doctor or superintendent of schools in a county seat in southern West Virginia.

Third, local mores differ strikingly in the tolerated differences between formal and informal educated speech. Where social differences are based on tradition and on family status, as among the "county" families of England and their analogues in the older parts of the American South, informal cultivated speech addressed to equals or other intimates may differ remarkably from the norms of formal expository prose. For Middle Western suburbs, one may agree with the melancholy observation of James H. Sledd that "any red-blooded American would prefer incest to *ain't*"; but in a community like Charleston one may encounter *ain't* a hundred times a day in conversation among the proudest families. So the educated Midwesterner often considers the informal speech of the educated Southerner very careless; the educated Southerner, in turn, missing the familiar conversational cues to informality, often considers the conversation of educated Middle Westerners strained and anxious. In short, each suspects the other's cultural credentials. Perhaps it is inevitable in an ostensibly open society that covert class markers become more significant as the overt ones disappear.

Regardless of the degree of difference in a locality, there seem to be two basic situations in which social dialects arise. The most familiar one is that in which different groups within the same community acquire different status, thanks to differences in education and wealth and power, so that the speech of one group is deemed worth emulating and that of other groups is not. This is the situation that has developed over the years in the small towns of much of New England, upstate New York, and the Southern Uplands; it is probably the same kind of situation out of which the manners and speech of the gentry acquired status in rural England.

The other situation, perhaps more common in our industrialized and urbanized society, is that in which groups of original settlers differ in their social status or a large group of new immigrants may acquire a peculiar status in the community. Most of the time this peculiar status is that of social inferiority, though we can all think of the exception, the outsiders who bring social prestige with them—the English civil servant in the colonies; the Swedish pastor in Minnesota; the proper Bostonian in Rochester, New York; the Richmond family in Charleston,

West Virginia. But these are atypical. The social dialect problems created by immigration are of three basic kinds:

1. The speech of those whose native language is something different from that of the community, whether Yiddish, Cajan French, Puerto Rican Spanish, or Hungarian.

2. The speech of groups who use a nonstandard dialect from the same region; a classical example is the speech of the rural Southern Negroes or poor whites who come to cities like Savannah or Birmingham in search of better jobs.

3. The third situation involves the migration into one region of speakers of substandard dialects of another region. Here we have not only the problem of clearly recognizable social differences, but that of regional ethnocentrism: of the tendency to look upon what is regionally different as ipso facto inferior. Detroiters often overtly try to eradicate West Virginia vowels (or what they think are West Virginia vowels); South Carolinians often remark—not so publicly as Detroiters, because they have a tradition of greater politeness, or at least of a wry diffidence in such matters—that to their ears educated Middle Westerners sound like uneducated Southerners, since the strong post-vocalic /-r/ in *barn* and *beard* is in the South traditionally associated with poor white speech. To this category belong the language problems of Appalachian whites and Southern Negroes in such Northern and Western cities as New York, Cleveland, Chicago, and Los Angeles.

It is in this last situation that historical and regional and social differences intersect. For example, in much of Southern England the uninflected third singular present indicative, as *he do,* is found in old-fashioned rural speech. This feature must have been brought to all of the American colonies. However, it is unevenly distributed today, because of differences in the cultural situation. The Southern colonies were more rural than the rest, more dependent on agriculture for a longer time and on money-crop agriculture that required a great deal of low-grade hand labor—cotton and tobacco. The average income in the South is still lower than that in other regions; Southerners travel less; they have, on the average, fewer years of schooling and that of an inferior quality to what is available in other regions. It is therefore not surprising that such forms as *he do* are today more widely distributed in the South and South Midland than in other dialect regions, simply because the conditions there were more favorable to their survival.

But this not all. Within the South itself, a similar cultural differential operated to the disadvantage of the Negro—long enslaved, and discriminated against even after Emancipation. For a long time the Southern Negro population was more rural than the Southern white, more confined to agriculture and to the more menial kinds of agricultural work. The Southern Negro was less given to travel; his income was—and is—lower than that of his white neighbor; schooling is for fewer years and of poorer quality. For this reason, in the South, such forms as *he do* will be heard from a greater proportion of Negroes than of whites. And since, in recent years, the migrants from the South to Northern and Western urban areas are more likely to be Negroes than whites, and Negroes are more likely to be identified as recent migrants, in such areas forms like *he do* are likely to be considered as simply Negro speech forms, though historically they are regional forms widely disseminated in southern England, and regionally in the United States they are characteristically Southern. Though the origins of Negro dialects in the United States are undoubtedly more complicated than nineteenth-century observers suggested—Lorenzo Turner's *Africanisms in the Gullah Dialect* (Chicago, 1949) has been particularly helpful in providing a new perspective—it is clear that, for the most part, Negro usages that differ from middle-class white practice are largely the result of this kind of selective cultural differentiation.[11]

Our knowledge of none of these three dimensions—historical, regional, and social—is so complete that we can close our eyes to the need of adding further data. Yet even now we know enough to provide a richer understanding to all those who are concerned with dimensions of usage—whether they are interested in dictionary labeling, school programs, or simply the phenomena of cultural history and social structure. If our statements are more complicated than some of our friends would wish, the fault is not in our science but in the tangled web of human relationships.

NOTES

1. Statements about American regional dialects are drawn principally from the archives of the Linguistic Atlas of the United States and Canada, by permission of the American Council of Learned Societies. Many details have appeared in previous derivative studies, notably Hans Kurath, *A Word Geography of the Eastern United States* (Ann Arbor, 1949), E. Bagby Atwood, *A Survey of Verb Forms in the Eastern United States* (Ann Arbor, 1953), and Kurath and R. I. McDavid, Jr., *The Pronunciation of English in the Atlantic States* (Ann Arbor, 1961).

2. Notably in John S. Kenyon, "Cultural Levels and Functional Varieties of English," *College English*, 10.31–36 (October 1948); Martin Joos, *The Five Clocks* (Bloomington, Indiana, 1962), Harold B. Allen, *Readings in Applied English Linguistics*, 2d ed. (New York, 1964), pp. 272–6.

3. Examples have been cited by the late J. R. Firth, from British officers in India, by Kenneth L. Pike, from a variety of situations, and from my own experiences in the American South.

4. The expectations extend to other behavior as well. The political backlash of 1966 among white middle-class and working-class voters was intensified by the way these expectations were disregarded by the irresponsible dress and behavior of certain well-advertised liberal groups, such as the Berkeley Left and the Chicago Students Against the Rank—beards, stringy hair, sloppy clothing, noise and general boorishness. The invasion of lower middle-class Chicago suburbs by such groups did nothing to further desegregation of private housing; nor did similar invasions of the South in 1964 and 1965 further the civil liberties cause in that region. It will be noted that participants in the original sit-in movements in the South won a great deal of local respect for their essential cause by carefully observing local conventions in such nonessentials as dress and personal grooming and thus providing a striking contrast with the local poor whites who opposed them.

5. Edward T. Hall, *The Silent Language* (New York, 1967) and *The Hidden Dimension* (New York, 1966); Ray Birdwhistell, *Kinesics* (Louisville, 1956); Henry Lee Smith, Jr., and Robert E. Pittenger, "A Basis for Some Contributions of Linguistics to Psychiatry," *Psychiatry*, 20.61–78 (1957); George L. Trager, "Paralanguage: A First Approximation," *Studies in Linguistics*, 13.1–12 (1958); Robert E. Pittenger, Charles F. Hockett, and John J. Danehy, *The First Five Minutes* (Ithaca, 1960); William M. Austin, "Some Social Aspects of Paralanguage," *Canadian Journal of Linguistics*, 11.31–39 (1965). The last also appears in *Communication Barriers for the Culturally Deprived*, Cooperative Research Project 2107, U.S. Office of Education, 1966.

6. A phoneme is a minimal distinctive unit in the sound system; as any reader knows, there are various competing analyses of the phonemes of English. In this paper the phonemic transcriptions, in slashes, follow the analysis of Kurath and McDavid, *The Pronunciation of English in the Atlantic States;* phonetic transcriptions are in square brackets.

7. A morpheme is a minimum meaningful form; it may be derivational, as for the making of abstract nouns from adjectives, or inflectional, as for the forming of the plural.

8. For detailed discussions see, for example, Leonard Bloomfield, *Language* (New York, 1933); Charles F. Hockett, *A Course in Modern Linguistics* (New York, 1958); Thomas Pyles, *The Growth and Development of the English Language* (New York, 1964).

9. Dialect mixture has been so common in American English from the beginning that consistent leveling in the present is probably rare.

10. *Language,* 40.473 (1964).

11. Of course the same forces would also help to preserve features of ancestral languages. As Turner points out, the relative isolation—geographical and social— of the Gullah Negroes of South Carolina and Georgia has preserved many relics of West African languages, and some of these could reinforce forms derived from nonstandard English dialects. The complex backgrounds of American Negro dialects require intense investigations.

H. L. MENCKEN

Euphemisms

The American, probably more than any other man, is prone to be apologetic about the trade he follows. He seldom believes that it is quite worthy of his virtues and talents; almost always he thinks that he would have adorned something far gaudier. Unfortunately, it is not always possible for him to escape, or even for him to dream plausibly of escaping, so he soothes himself by assuring himself that he belongs to a superior section of his craft, and very often he invents a sonorous name to set himself off from the herd. Here we glimpse the origin of a multitude of characteristic American euphemisms, e.g., *mortician* for *undertaker, realtor* for *real-estate agent, electragist* for *electrical contractor, aisle manager* for *floor-walker, beautician* for *hairdresser, exterminating engineer* for *rat-catcher,* and so on. *Realtor* was devised by a high-toned real-estate agent of Minneapolis, Charles N. Chadbourn by name. He thus describes its genesis:

> It was in November, 1915, on my way to a meeting of the Minneapolis Real Estate Board, that I was annoyed by the strident peddling of a scandal sheet: "All About the Robbery of a Poor Widow by a Real Estate Man." The "real estate man" thus exposed turned out to be an obscure hombre with desk-room in a back office in a rookery, but the incident set me to thinking. "Every member of our board," I thought, "is besmirched by this scandal article. Anyone, however unworthy or disreputable, may call himself a real estate man. Why do not the members of our board deserve a distinctive title? Each member is vouched for by the board, subscribes to its Code of Ethics, and must behave himself or get out." So the idea incubated for three or four weeks, and was then sprung on the local brethren.[1]

219

As to the etymology of the term, Mr. Chadbourn says:

> Real estate originally meant a royal grant. It is so connected with land in the public mind that *realtor* is easily understood, even at a first hearing. The suffix *-or* means a doer, one who performs an act, as in *grantor, executor, sponsor, administrator.*

The Minneapolis brethren were so pleased with their new name that Mr. Chadbourn was moved to dedicate it to the whole profession. In March, 1916, he went to the convention of the National Association of Real Estate Boards at New Orleans, and made a formal offer of it. It was accepted gratefully, and is now defined by the association as follows:

> A person engaged in the real estate business who is an active member of a member board of the National Association of Real Estate Boards, and as such, an affiliated member of the National Association, who is subject to its rules and regulations, who observes its standards of conduct, and is entitled to its benefits.[2]

In 1920 the Minneapolis Real Estate Board and the National Association of Real Estate Boards applied to Judge Joseph W. Molyneaux of Minneapolis for an injunction restraining the Northwestern Telephone Exchange Company from using *realtor* to designate some of its hirelings, and on September 10 the learned judge duly granted this relief. Since then the National Association has obtained similar injunctions in Virginia, Utah and other States. Its general counsel is heard from every time *realtor* is taken in vain, and when, in 1922, Sinclair Lewis applied it to George F. Babbitt, there was an uproar. But when Mr. Chadbourn was appealed to he decided that Babbitt was "fairly well described," for he was "a prominent member of the local board and of the State association," and one could scarcely look for anything better in "a book written in the ironic vein of the author of 'Main Street.'"[3] Mr. Chadbourn believes that *realtor* should be capitalized, "like *Methodist* or *American*,"[4] but so far it has not been generally done. In June, 1925, at a meeting of the National Association of Real Estate Boards in Detroit, the past presidents of the body presented him with a gold watch as a token of their gratitude for his contribution to the uplift of their profession. On May 30, 1934, the following letter from Nathan William MacChesney, general counsel of the National Association, appeared in the *New Republic:*

> [*Realtor*] is not a word, but a trade right, coined and protected by law by the National Association of Real Estate Boards, and the term is a

part of the trade-mark as registered in some forty-four States and Canada. Something over $200,000 has been spent in its protection by the National Association of Real Estate Boards in attempting to confine its use to those real estate men who are members of the National Association of Real Estate Boards, subject to its code for ethics and to its discipline for violation. It has been a factor in making the standards of the business generally during the past twenty years, and the exclusive right of the National Association of Real Estate Boards has been sustained in a series of court decisions, a large number of injunctions having been issued, restraining its improper use.

In 1924 the *Realtor's Bulletin* of Baltimore reported that certain enemies of realtric science were trying to show that *realtor* was derived from the English word *real* and the Spanish word *toro,* a bull, and to argue that it thus meant *real bull.* But this obscenity apparently did not go far; probably a hint from the alert general counsel was enough to stop it. During the same year I was informed by Herbert U. Nelson, executive secretary of the National Association, that "the real-estate men of London, through the Institute of Estate Agents and Auctioneers, after studying our experience in this respect, are planning to coin the word *estator* and to protect it by legal steps." This plan, I believe, came to fruition, but *estator* never caught on, and I can't find it in the Supplement to the Oxford Dictionary. *Realtor,* however, is there—and the first illustrative quotation is from *Babbitt!* In March, 1927, J. Foster Hagan, of Ballston, Va., reported to *American Speech* that he had encountered *realtress* on the window of a real-estate office there, but this charming derivative seems to have died a-bornin'. In 1925 or thereabout certain ambitious insurance solicitors, inflamed by *realtor,* began to call themselves *insurors,* but it, too, failed to make any progress.

Electragist, like *realtor,* seems to be the monopoly of the lofty technicians who affect it: "it is copyrighted by the Association of Electragists International, whose members alone may use it." [5] But *mortician* is in the public domain. It was proposed by a writer in the *Embalmers' Monthly* for February, 1895, but the undertakers, who were then *funeral-directors,* did not rise to it until some years later. On September 16, 1916, some of the more eminent of them met at Columbus O., to form a national association, on the lines of the American College of Surgeons, the American Association of University Professors, and the Society of the Cincinnati, and a year later they decided upon National Selected *Morticians* as its designation.[6] To this day the association remains so exclusive that, of the 24,000 undertakers in the United States, only 200 belong to it. But any one of the remaining 23,800 is free to call himself a *mortician,* and to use all the other lovely words that the advance of human taxidermy has brought in. *Mortician,* of course, was suggested by *physician,* for undertakers naturally admire and like to pal with the resurrection men, and there was a time when some of them called themselves *embalming surgeons.* A *mortician* never handles a *corpse;* he *prepares* a *body* or *patient.* This business is carried on in a *preparation-room* or *operating-room,* and when it is achieved the patient is put into a *casket* [7] and stored in the *reposing-room* or *slumber-room* of a *funeral-home.* On the day of the funeral he is moved to the *chapel* therein for the last exorcism, and then hauled to the cemetery in a *funeral-car* or *casket-coach.*[8] The old-time shroud is now a *négligé* or *slumber-shirt* or *slumber-robe,* the mortician's worktruck is an *ambulance,* and the cemetery is fast becoming a *memorial-park.* In the West cemeteries are being supplanted by public mausoleums, which sometimes go under the names of *cloisters, burial-abbeys,* etc.[9] To be laid away in one runs into money. The vehicle that morticians use for their expectant hauling of the ill is no longer an *ambulance,* but an *invalid-coach. Mortician* has been a favorite butt of the national wits, but they seem to have made no impression on it. In January, 1932, it was barred from the columns of the Chicago *Tribune.* "This decree goes forth," announced the *Tribune,* "not for lack of sympathy with the ambition of undertakers to be well regarded, but because of it. If they haven't the sense to save themselves from their own lexicographers, we shall not be guilty of abetting them in their folly." [10] But *mortician* not only continues to flourish; it also begets progeny, e.g., *beautician, cosmetician, radiotrician* and *bootician.*[11] The barbers, so far, have not devised a name for themselves in *-ician,* but they may be trusted to do so anon. In my youth they were *tonsorial artists,* but in recent years some of them have been calling themselves *chirotonsors.*[12] Practically all American press-agents are now *public relations counsels, contact-managers* or *publicists,* all tree-trimmers are *tree-surgeons,* all milk-wagon and bakery-wagon drivers have become *salesmen,* nearly all janitors are *superintendents,* many gardeners have become *landscape-architects* (in England even the whales of the profession are simple *landscape-gardeners*), cobblers are beginning to call themselves *shoe-rebuilders,*[13] and the corn-doctors, after a generation as *chiropodists,* have burst forth as *podiatrists.* The American fondness for such sonorous appellations arrested the interest of W. L. George, the English novelist, when he visited the United States in 1920. He said:

> Business titles are given in America more readily than in England. I know one *president* whose staff consists of two typists. Many firms have four *vice-presidents.* In the magazines you seldom find merely an *editor;* the others need their share of honor, so they are *associate* (not *assistant*) *editors.* A dentist is called a *doctor.* I wandered into a univer-

sity, knowing nobody, and casually asked for the *dean*. I was asked, "Which *dean?*" In that building there were enough deans to stock all the English cathedrals. The master of a secret society is *royal supreme knight commander*. Perhaps I reached the extreme at a theatre in Boston, when I wanted something, I forgot what, and was told that I must apply to the *chief of the ushers*. He was a mild little man, who had something to do with people getting into their seats, rather a come-down from the pomp and circumstance of his title. Growing interested, I examined my programme, with the following result: It is not a large theatre, but it has a *press-representative*, a *treasurer* (box-office clerk), an *assistant treasurer* (box-office junior clerk), an *advertising-agent*, our old friend the *chief of the ushers*, a *stage-manager*, a *head-electrician*, a *master of properties* (in England called *props*), a *leader of the orchestra* (pity this—why not *president?*), and a *matron* (occupation unknown).[14]

George might have unearthed some even stranger magnificoes in other playhouses. I once knew an ancient bill-sticker, attached to a Baltimore theatre, who boasted the sonorous title of *chief lithographer*. To-day, in all probability, he would be called a *lithographic-engineer*. For a number of years the *Engineering News-Record,* the organ of the legitimate engineers, used to devote a column every week to just such uninvited invaders of the craft, and some of the species it unearthed were so fantastic that it was constrained to reproduce their business cards photographically in order to convince its readers that it was not spoofing. One of its favorite exhibits was a bedding manufacturer who first became a *mattress-engineer* and then promoted himself to the lofty dignity of *sleep-engineer*. No doubt he would have called himself a *morphician* if he had thought of it. Another exhilarating specimen was a tractor-driver who advertised for a job as a *caterpillar-engineer*. A third was a beautician who burst out as an *appearance-engineer*. In an Atlanta department-store the *News-Record* found an *engineer of good taste*—a young woman employed to advise newly-married couples patronizing the furniture department, and elsewhere it unearthed *display-engineers* who had been lowly window-dressers until some visionary among them made the great leap, *demolition-engineers* who were once content to be house-wreckers, and *sanitary-engineers* who had an earlier incarnation as garbage-men. The *wedding-engineer* is a technician employed by florists to dress churches for hymeneal orgies. The *commence-ment-e.* arranges college and high-school commencements; he has lists of clergymen who may be trusted to pray briefly, and some sort of fire-alarm connection, I suppose, with the office of Dr. John H. Finley, the champion commencement orator of this or any other age. The *packing-e.* is a scientist who crates clocks, radios and chinaware for shipment. The *correspondence-e.*

writes selling-letters guaranteed to pull. The *income-e.* is an insurance solicitor in a new false-face. The *dwelling-e.* replaces lost keys, repairs leaky roofs, and plugs up rat-holes in the cellar. The *vision-e.* supplies spectacles at cut rates. The *dehorning-e.* attends to bulls who grow too frisky. The *Engineering News-Record* also discovered a *printing-e.,* a *furniture-e.,* a *photographic-e.,* a *financial-e.* (a stock-market tipster), a *paint-e.,* a *clothing-e.,* a *wrapping-e.* (a dealer in wrapping-paper), a *matrimonial-e.* (a psychoanalyst specializing in advice to the lovelorn), a *box-e.* (the *packing-e.* under another name), an *automotive-painting-e.,* a *blasting-e.,* a *dry-cleaning-e.,* a *container-e.,* a *furnishing-e.,* a *socio-religious-e.* (an uplifter), a *social-e.* (the same), a *feed-plant-e.,* a *milk-e.,* a *surface-protection-e.,* an *analyzation-e.,* a *fiction-e.,* a *psychological-e.* (another kind of psychoanalyst), a *casement-window-e.,* a *shingle-e.,* a *fumigating-e.,* a *laminated-wood-e.,* a *package-e.* (the *packing-e.* again), a *horse-e.,* a *podiatric-e.* (a corn-doctor), an *ice-e.,* a *recreation-e.,* a *tire-e.,* a *paint-maintenance-e.,* a *space-saving-e.,* a *film-e.,* (or *film-gineer*), a *criminal-e.* (a criminologist), a *diet-kitchen-e.,* a *patent-e.,* an *equipment-e.,* a *floor-covering-e.,* a *society-e.,* a *window-cleaning-e.,* a *dust-e.,* a *hospitalization-e.,* a *baking-e.,* a *directory-e.,* an *advertising-e.,* a *golf-e.,* (a designer of golf courses), a *human-e.* (another variety of psychoanalyst), an *amusement-e.,* an *electric-sign-e.,* a *household-e.,* a *pageant-e.,* an *idea-e.,* a *ballistics-e.,* a *lace-e.* and a *sign-e.*[15] Perhaps the prize should go to the *dansant-e.* (an agent supplying dancers and musicians to night-clubs), or to the *hot-dog-e.*[16] The exterminating-engineers have a solemn national association and wear a distinguishing pin; whether or not they have tried to restrain non-member rat-catchers from calling themselves *engineers* I do not know. In 1923 the *Engineering News-Record* printed a final blast against all the pseudo-engineers then extant, and urged its engineer readers to boycott them. But this boycott apparently came to nothing, and soon thereafter it abated its indignation and resorted to laughter.[17] Next to *engineer, expert* seems to be the favorite talisman of Americans eager to augment their estate and dignity in this world. Very often it is hitched to an explanatory prefix, e.g., *housing-, planning-, hog-, erosion-, marketing-, boll-weevil-,* or *sheep-dip-,* but sometimes the simple adjective *trained-* suffices. When the Brain Trust came into power in Washington, the town began to swarm with such quacks, most of them recent graduates of the far-flung colleges of the land. One day a humorous member of Congress printed an immense list of them in the *Congressional Record,* with their salaries and academic dignities. He found at least one whose expertness was acquired in a seminary for chiropractors. During the John Purroy Mitchel "reform" administration in New York City (1914–18) so many bogus *experts* were put upon the pay-roll that special designations for them ran out, and in prodding through the Mitchel records later on Bird S. Coler discovered that a number had been carried on the books as *general experts.*

Euphemisms for things are almost as common in the United States as euphemisms for avocations. Dozens of forlorn little fresh-water colleges are called *universities,* and almost all *pawn-shops* are *loan-offices.* When *movie-cathedral* came in few scoffers snickered, but by the generality of fans it was received gravely. *City,* in England, used to be confined to the seats of bishops, and even today it is applied only to considerable places, but in the United States it is commonly assumed by any town with paved streets, and in the statistical publications of the Federal government it is applied to all places of 8000 or more population. The American use of *store* for *shop,* like that of *help* for servant, is probably the product of an early effort at magnification. Before Prohibition saloons used to be *sample-rooms, buffets, exchanges, cafés* and *restaurants;* now they are *taverns, cocktail-rooms, taprooms, American-bars, stubes* and what not. Not long ago the *Furnished-Room Guide* undertook to substitute *hotellette* for *rooming-house,*[18] and in 1928 President E. L. Robins of the National *Fertilizer* Association proposed that the name of that organization be changed to the National Association of *Plant Food* Manufacturers or the American *Plant Food* Association.[19] In Pasadena the public garbage wagons bear the legend: *Table-Waste Disposal Department.* The word *studio* is heavily overworked; there are *billiard-studios, tonsorial-studios, candy-studios,* and even *shoe-studios.*[20] Nor is this reaching out for sweet and disarming words confined to the lowly. Some time ago, in the *Survey,* the trade journal of the American uplifters, Dr. Thomas Dawes Eliot, associate professor of sociology in Northwestern University, printed a solemn argument in favor of abandoning all such harsh terms as *reformatory, house of refuge, reform school* and *jail.* "Each time a new phrase is developed," he said, "it seems to bring with it, or at least to be accompanied by, some measure of permanent gain, in standards or in viewpoint, even though much of the old may continue to masquerade as the new. The series, *alms, philanthropy, relief, rehabilitation, case work, family welfare,* shows such a progression from cruder to more refined levels of charity." Among the substitutions proposed by the learned professor were *habit-disease* for *vice, psycho-neurosis* for *sin, failure to compensate* for *disease, treatment* for *punishment, delinquent* for *criminal, unmarried mother* for *illegitimate mother, out of wedlock* for *bastard, behavior problem* for *prostitute, colony* for *penitentiary, school* for *reformatory, psychopathic hospital* for *insane asylum,* and *house of detention* for *jail.*[21] Many of these terms (or others like them) have been actually adopted. Practically all American insane asylums are now simple *hospitals,* many reformatories and houses of correction have been converted into *homes* or *schools,* all *almshouses* are now *infirmaries, county-farms* or *county-homes,* and most of the more advanced American penologists now speak of criminals as *psychopathic personalities.* By a law of New York it is provided that "in any local law, ordinance or resolution, or in any public or judicial proceeding, or in any process, notice, order, decree, judgment, record or other public document or paper, the term *bastard* or *illegitimate child* shall not be used, but the term *child born out of wedlock* shall be used in substitution therefor, and with the same force and effect." [22] Meanwhile, such harsh terms as *second-hand* and *ready-made* disappear from the American vocabulary. For the former the automobile dealers, who are ardent euphemists, have substituted *reconditioned, rebuilt, repossessed* and *used,* and for the latter department stores offer *ready-tailored, ready-to-wear* and *ready-to-put-on.* For *shop-worn* two of the current euphemisms are *store-used* and *slightly-second.*

The English euphemism-of-all-work used to be *lady.* Back in the Seventeenth Century the court-poet Edmund Waller thought it quite proper to speak of actresses, then a novelty on the English stage, as *lady-actors,* and even today the English newspapers frequently refer to *lady-secretaries, lady-doctors, lady-inspectors, lady-golfers* and *lady-champions. Women's wear,* in most English shops, is *ladies' wear.* But this excessive use of lady seems to be going out, and I note *women's singles* and *women's ice hockey* on the sports pages of the *London Daily Telegraph.*[23] The *Times* inclines the same way, but I observe that it still uses *Ladies International* to designate a golf tournament, *ladies' round* and *ladies' championship* (golf and fencing).[24] In the United States *lady* is definitely out of favor. The *salesladies* of yesteryear are now all *saleswomen* or *salesgirls,* and the female superintendent of a hospital is not the *lady-superintendent,* but simply the *superintendent.* When women were first elected to Congress, the question as to how they should be referred to in debate engaged the leaders of the House of Representatives. For a while the phrase used was "the *lady* from So-and-so," but soon "the *gentlewoman*" was substituted, and this is now employed almost invariably. Its invention is commonly ascribed to the late Nicholas Longworth; if he actually proposed it, it was probably jocosely, for *gentlewoman* is clumsy, and in some cases, as clearly inaccurate as *lady.* The English get round the difficulty by using *the hon. member* in speaking of women M.P.'s, though sometimes the *hon. lady* is used.[25] A member who happens to be a military or naval officer is always, by the way, *the hon. and gallant member,* and a legal officer, say the Attorney-

General or Solicitor-General, or a lawyer member in active practice, is *the hon. and learned member*. The English use *gentleman* much more carefully than we do, and much more carefully than they themselves use *lady*. *Gentleman-author* or *gentleman-clerk* would make them howl, but they commonly employ *gentleman-rider* and *gentleman-player* in place of our *amateur*, though *amateur* seems to be gaining favor. Here the man referred to is always actually a gentleman by their standards.

Notes

1. Private communication, Sept. 28, 1935.
2. Realtor: Its Meaning and Use; Chicago (National Association of Real Estate Boards), 1925.
3. Letter to W. A. Frisbie, editor of the Minneapolis *Daily News*. This was in 1922. The letter was subscribed "Yours *realtorially*." A copy was sent to Mr. Lewis, who preserves it in his archives.
4. Private communication, Sept. 4, 1935.
5. Electragist, by Corneil Ridderhof, *American Speech*, Aug., 1927, p. 477. It means, according to Mr. Ridderhof, "a combined electrical dealer and contractor."
6. I am indebted here to Mr. W. M. Krieger, executive secretary of the organization, the headquarters of which are in Chicago.
7. *Casket* seems to have come in during the Civil War Period. In 1863 Nathaniel Hawthorne denounced it in Our Old Home as "a vile modern phrase, which compels a person . . . to shrink . . . from the idea of being buried at all." At the start it had a rival in *case*. The latter was used in the Richmond *Examiner's* report of the funeral of Gen. J. E. B. Stuart, May 13, 1864. But the *Examiner*, in the same report, used *corpse* and *hearse*.
8. Mortuary Nomenclature, *Hygeia*, Nov., 1925, p. 651.
9. The *Mortician*, by Elmer Davis, *American Mercury*, May, 1927.
10. *Editor and Publisher*, Jan. 30, 1932.
11. I proposed the use of bootician to designate a high-toned big-city bootlegger in the *American Mercury*, April, 1925, p. 450. The term met a crying need, and had considerable success. In March, 1927, the San José *Mercury-Herald* said: "Our bootleggers are now calling themselves *booticians*. It seems that *bootlegger* has some trace of odium about it, while *bootician* has none." (Reprinted in the Baltimore *Evening Sun*, April 4, 1927.) On July 23, 1931, according to the Associated Press, a man arrested in Chicago, on being asked his profession, answered proudly that he was a *bootician*.
12. In 1924 representatives of 3000 of them met in Chicago, and voted for *chirotonsor*. See the *Commonweal*, Nov. 26, 1924, p. 58.
13. There is a *Shoe Rebuilders'* Association in Baltimore. See the Baltimore *Evening Sun*, Oct. 17, 1935.
14. Hail, Columbia!; New York, 1921, pp. 92–3.
15. Many other varieties of engineers have been unearthed by other fanciers. On Oct. 19, 1935, *The New Yorker* announced the discovery of a *persuasion-e.—*"a man sent somewhere by his company to try and sell somebody an idea that would be of advantage to the company." A few months before this the *Professional En-*

gineer found a *pajama-e.* in *The New Yorker's* advertising columns. For this last I am indebted to Mr. M. E. McIver, secretary of the American Association of Engineers. In *Popular Science,* Aug., 1935, a contributor called himself a *coffee-e.*

16. A curious anticipation of the American misuse of *engineer,* by an Englishman, is to be found in a memorandum submitted to Henry Dundas, first Viscount Melville, by Charles Stuart at the end of 1793. Dundas was Home Secretary from 1791 to 1794, and as such was in charge of the government's relations with the press. "I firmly believe, without any vanity," wrote Stuart, "that I know as much in the engineering of the press as any *press engineer* in Britain." See The History of the *Times;* London, 1925, p. 66. But Stuart's attempt to make the manipulation of the press a branch of engineering was not imitated, and there is no mention of pseudo-engineers in any of the English dictionaries.

17. See the issue for Jan. 15, 1925. Also, Some "Engineers" I Have Known, by a Civil Engineer, *Engineering News-Record,* April 19, 1923, p. 701. The engineers themselves have grossly misused the term designating them. In the Structure of the Engineering Profession, by Theodore J. Hoover, dean of the School of Engineering at Stanford University, *Journal of Engineering Education,* Jan., 1935, appears an exhaustive report upon what the 10,542 listed in "Who's Who in Engineering" call themselves. Mr. Hoover finds 2518 different titles, including such absurdities as *sales-e., sales-promotion-e., promotion-e., application-e., college-e., social-e., technical-publicity-e., bank-management-e.,* and *export-e.* He advocates a complete reform of professional nomenclature, but when I last heard from him he didn't seem to have much hope. On Feb. 21, 1935, the Associated Press reported that the National Society of Professional Engineers was trying to induce the American railroads to call their locomotive-engineers *enginemen.* The New York Central and the Pennsylvania, it was said, were already doing so.

18. See *The New Yorker,* Jan. 9, 1935, p. 74. *The New Yorker* expressed a waggish preference for *furnished-roomateria.*

19. United Press report, Nov. 13, 1928.

20. See *Studio,* by John T. Krumpelmann, *American Speech,* Dec., 1926, p. 158.

21. A Limbo for Cruel Words, *Survey,* June 15, 1922.

22. Laws of 1925, Ch. 515, in force April 9, 1925. I have to thank Mr. Sylvan Baruch of the New York Bar for calling my attention to this statute.

23. March 29, 1935.

24. April 12, 1935, p. 6.

25. I am indebted for the following to Mr. James Bone, London editor of the Manchester *Guardian:* "When a Minister answers a question in the House he says *Yes, sir* or *No, sir,* whether the question is asked by a man or a woman M.P. The reason is that he is supposed to be addressing the Speaker. There was some laughter among young members when a Minister replied *Yes, sir* to a question by Lady Astor, but elderly members wrote to the papers at once, rebuking them and explaining the procedure." Some time ago I heard the trial of a case in one of the London Law Courts, with the Lord Chief Justice of England, Lord Hewart, on the bench. There were two women on the jury, but when they finished their labors he said "Thank you, *gentlemen.*"

NOEL PERRIN, JR.

The Future of Bowdlerism

Comic strips are also a mass medium in print, and it is perhaps there that Victorian delicacy most strikingly survives. Scenes of violence are all right in comic strips, just as the spurt of blood at the beheading was all right in Victorian *Gullivers*. Some visual frankness (*e.g.*, vivid rendering of the female bust) is also all right. But the language is bowdlerized. A random issue of the funnies in the New York *Sunday News* supplies the following chastened examples:

General Hasp, USA, of "Terry and the Pirates" says to a Sicilian archeologist, "Blast you, Palma! You know danged well I don't care about your busted crockery."

An angry Indian in "Little Orphan Annie" exclaims, "Uglyface got ugly tongue, by golly!"

Beetle Bailey's sergeant says to his platoon, "All right, you *#&! jerks!"

A native of Slobbovia says to some Americans—they seem to be Peace Corps workers—who have come to introduce Mother's and Father's Day, "By us is already every *!!# day a holiday."

This phenomenon, too, seems likely to pass. New expurgations will cease, and so will printings of old ones. Libraries will gradually clear their shelves of bowdlerized editions, except those they keep deliberately as part of the history of taste. The age of innocence for children is already extremely compressed, and still shrinking. When witty children again call "whore" and cry "bastard," as some at least did in Ben Jonson's time, there will be small point in expurgated comic strips, or even in protectiveness on the part of *The New York Times*.

What then? Then it may be time for the new cycle to begin. Or a different cycle may by then be in full swing. Delicacy has never died, and never will. (So great is the fear of false predictions in our time that I find myself starting to change that to "and seems unlikely to." But one should sometimes go out on limbs, especially a limb as sturdy as this.) It merely takes new forms. At the moment, as everybody knows, the vocabulary of race relations has become a delicate matter. The result is a new little growth of expurgation, and not merely in nursery rhymes like "Catch a tiger by the toe." Lynch and Evans found a high-school text in which *Huckleberry Finn* was expurgated new-style. "A nigger woman" became "one of the servants"; "a young white gentleman" became simply "a young gentleman," and so on. If the rise of "black" continues, "Negro" itself may become obscene; perhaps it already has. If so, those of us who avoid the word will not seem prudish to ourselves, but sensitive—just as Americans in 1875 who avoided the word "crotch," say, felt perceptive.

Delicacy will never die, because it is an essential part of romanticism. A race of computers (unless programmed to be human) would not be moved to expurgate, because a computer does not have illusions about itself, or want to keep a young computer from knowing too much ugly truth too soon. Men do. We don't even want too much just commonplace truth. No computer is disgusted at learning the precise girth of a 1401, or bothered by the sight of a repairman cleaning dirt out of one, but many a human being would rather not know the bust and thigh measurements of his queen or the wife of his president or perhaps his own mother; many would actually avert their eyes to avoid seeing the family pastor seated on a toilet.

Harriet Bowdler certainly did not express it that way, but her basic aim in 1807 was to preserve for the adolescents of England some of the mystery and opaqueness of human behavior without which we are likely to regard ourselves as either animals or machines. Her method was laughable, and it may even be doubted that the human mystery requires deliberate preservation, but the aim was an honorable one.

OTTO JESPERSEN

Spelling

The traditional way of writing English is far from being so consistent that it is possible, if we know the sounds of a word, to know how it is to be spelled, or inversely, from the spelling to draw any conclusions as to its pronunciation. The following words in their traditional garb and in phonetic transcription may serve as illustration:

though [ðou]—rhyming with *low*
through [þru]   "   *true*
plough [plau]   "   *now*
cough [kɔf]   "   *off*
enough [i'nʌf]   "   *cuff*

However chaotic this may seem, it is possible to a great extent to explain the rise of all these discrepancies between sound and spelling, and thus to give, if not rational, at any rate historical reasons for them. A full account of all these anomalies would, however, require a whole volume; here we must, therefore, content ourselves with a succinct exposition of the chief facts that have determined the present English spelling.

The alphabet used in England as well as in most European countries is the Roman alphabet. Though this is better than many Oriental alphabets, it is far from being perfect as a means of rendering sounds, as it is deficient in signs for many simple sounds (*e.g.* the initial consonants of *this* and *thick,* the final one of *sing*); nor does it possess more than five vowel-letters, where many languages distinguish a far greater number of vowels.

At first people could follow no other guide in their spelling than their own ears: writing thus began as purely phonetical. But soon they began to imitate the spellings of others, whose manuscripts they copied,

From *Essentials of English Grammar*, 1933. Reprinted by permission of George Allen & Unwin, Ltd.

231

their teachers and their elders generally. As the spoken forms of words tend continually to change, this would mean that older, extinct forms of speech would continue to be written long after they had ceased to be heard. Such traditional spelling, which is found in all languages with a literary history, has become particularly powerful since the invention of the art of printing; in many respects, therefore, modern English orthography represents the pronunciation prevalent about that time or even earlier.

An equally important factor was the influence of French—later also of Latin—spelling. Norman scribes introduced several peculiarities of French spelling, not only when writing words taken over from that language, but also when writing native English words. Our present-day spelling cannot, therefore, be fully understood without some knowledge of the history of French.

The letters *ch* were used in Old French to denote the sound-combination [tʃ] as in *chaste, chief, merchant;* in English this spelling was used not only in originally French words, but also in native words like *child, much.* In French the stop [t] was later dropped, the sound [ʃ] only remaining; hence *ch* in some late loan-words comes to stand for [ʃ]; *machine, chaise* (which is the Modern French form of the same word that in the old form was taken over as *chair*), *chauffeur.*

In words from the classical languages *ch* denotes the sound [k]: *echo, chaos, scheme.* Schedule is pronounced with [sk] in America, with [ʃ] in England.

The sound-history of French also serves to explain some striking peculiarities concerning the use of the letter *g* in English spelling. Written French *gu* originally served to denote the combination of [g] with a following [u] or [w]; but this combination was later simplified in various ways. In the northernmost French dialects [g] was dropped, and English from those dialects adopted such words as *ward, reward, warden* and *war.* But in other parts of French it was inversely the [u]-sound that disappeared, and a great many words were adopted into English with this simple sound of [g], such as *gallop, garrison;* in some cases English kept the spelling *gu* though French now writes without the *u: guard, guarantee.* In both languages the spelling *gu* came to be extensively used as an orthographic device to denote the sound [g] before *e* and *i,* because in that position *g* was pronounced [dʒ], thus in *guide, guise;* and in English this spelling was even transferred to a certain number of native words like *guess, guest, guild* (sb.), *guilt, tongue,* though it never obtained in some frequently used words like *get, give, begin, gild* (vb.)

In Old French the letter *g* stood for the sound-combination [dʒ], as Latin *g* [g] had developed in that way before [e] and [i]; hence spellings like *gentle, giant, age, manage,* etc. Sometimes after a short vowel *dg* was written: *judge, lodge;* thus also in native words like *edge, bridge.*

As with the corresponding voiceless combination [tʃ], the stop in [dʒ] was later dropped in French; hence *g* is in later loan-words pronounced [ʒ]: *rouge, mirage, prestige.*

Another Old French way of writing [dʒ] was *i*, later *j;* hence we have English spellings like *joy, join, journey.* In *bijou j* has the later French value [ʒ].

In OE. the letter *c* was exclusively used for the sound [k], even before *e, i* and *y*, exactly as in Latin. But in French this Latin sound had become first [ts] and later [s] before *e* and *i;* and this value of the letter *c* is consequently found in English, not only in French and Latin words, like *cease, centre, center, city, peace, pace*—even sometimes where French has *s: ace*, Fr. *as; juice*, Fr. *jus*—but also in some native English words, e.g. *since, hence. Sc* is pronounced in the same way, e.g. *scene, science;* it is written without any etymological reason in *scent* (from French *sentir*).

C is used for the sound [k] in *can, corn, cup, clean, creep* and many similar words, while *k* is written in *kiss, keep, think*, etc., and *y* before *u: queen*, etc. Instead of *ks, x* is written: *six*, etc., even in *coxcomb* and *coxswain* from *cock.*

French influence is responsible for the use of the digraph *ou* for ME. long [uː] as in *couch, spouse* (later Fr. *épouse*); sometimes also for short [u]: *couple, touch.* This was transferred to native words like *house, loud, out, our*, etc. When the long sound was later diphthongized, the spelling *ou* came to be very appropriate. As this diphthongizing did not take place in Scotch, *ou* is there still found for the sound [uː], as in *Dougall, dour, souter,* "shoemaker."

The simple vowel *u* was used for the short vowel as in *up, us, nut, full*, etc., and for the diphthong [iu] or [ju:], frequent in French words like *duke, use, due, virtue*, but also found in native words, e.g. *Tuesday, hue, Stuart* (the same word as *steward*).

But at a time when angular writing was fashionable, it became usual to avoid the letter *u* in close proximity with the letters *n, m,* and another *u* (*v, w*), where it was liable to cause ambiguity (five strokes might be interpreted *imi, inu, mu, um, uni, uui,* especially at a time when no dot was written over *i*); hence the use of *o* which has been retained in a great many words: *monk, money, honey, come, won, wonder, cover* (written *couer* before *v, o* and *u* were distinguished), *love*, etc.

A merely orthographic distinction is made between *son* and *sun, some* and *sum.*

In ME. vowels were frequently doubled to show length, and many of these spellings have been preserved, e.g. *see, deer, too, brood*, though the sounds have been changed so that they no more correspond to the short vowels of *set, hot.*

But neither *a* nor *u* were doubled in that way; and instead of writing *ii* it became usual to write *y*. This letter, which in Old English served to denote the rounded vowel corresponding to [i] (= Fr. *u* in *bu*, German *ü* in *über*), has become a mere variant of *i* used preferably at the end of words, while *i* is used in the beginning and interior of words; hence such alternations as *cry, cries, cried; happy, happier, happiest, happiness; body, bodiless, bodily*, etc. But *y* is kept before such endings as are felt more or less as independent elements, e.g. *citywards, ladyship, twentyfold, juryman*. After another vowel *y* is generally kept, e.g. *plays, played, boys;* cf., however, *laid, paid, said* (but *lays, pays, says:* too much consistency must not be expected). In some cases homophones are kept apart in the spelling: *die* (with *dies*, but *dying*, because *ii* is avoided)—*dye, flys*, 'light carriages,' but otherwise *flies* (sb. and vb.).

Further, *y* is written in many originally Greek words: *system, nymph*, etc.

Before a vowel, *y* is used as non-syllabic [i], i.e. [j], e.g. *yard, yellow, yield, yole, yule, beyond*.

Doubling of consonants has come to be extensively used to denote shortness of the preceding vowel, especially before a weak syllable, e.g. in *hotter, hottest* from *hot, sobbing* from *sob*. Instead of doubling *k, ch* and ·*g* [= dӡ] the combinations *ck, tch* and *dg* (*e*) are written, e.g. *trafficking* from *traffic, etch, edge*.

On account of the phonetic development, however, a double consonant is now written after some long vowels, e.g. in *roll, all, staff, glass*, which had formerly short vowels.

Though since the introduction of printing a great many minor changes have taken place without any great consistency, such as the leaving out of numerous mute *e*'s, only one important orthographic change must be recorded, namely, the regulating of *i* and *j, u* and *v*, so that now *i* and *u* are used for the vowels, *j* and *v* for the consonant sounds, while, for instance, the old editions of Shakespeare print *ioy, vs, vpon, fiue, fauour* = *joy, us, upon, five, favour*. The old use of *u* for the consonant explains the name of *w: double u*.

Scholars have introduced learned spellings in many words, e.g. *debt, doubt*, on account of Latin *debita, dubito*, formerly written as in French *dette, doute; victuals*, formerly *vittles*. In some cases the pronunciation has been modified according to the spelling; thus [p] has been introduced in *bankrupt*, earlier *bankeroute*, and [k] in *perfect*, earlier *perfit, parfit*. In recent years, with the enormous spread of popular education, combined with ignorance of the history of the language, such spelling-pronunciations have become increasingly numerous.

ROBERT A. HALL, JR.

Our English Spelling System

The real nature of writing in its relation to language is so obvious
on a moment's reflection, that it might seem strange that so much misunderstanding could arise about it. Probably the confusion is due to two
things: the nature of our English spelling system, and the age at which
we start to learn it. People whose languages have a simple, relatively accurate conventional spelling, like Italian, Hungarian, or Finnish, are not
confused as to the relation of writing and speech, and are often surprised
at the misunderstanding that spellers of English show. But our traditional orthography for English is quite far removed from the reality of
speech, and our letters certainly do not stand in a wholly one-to-one relationship with the phonemes of our speech. It takes considerable effort
and many years (as we all well know!) to completely master our English
conventional spelling; and once we have learned it, it represents a considerable investment. Nobody likes to give up the fruits of any investment, and the more costly it is, the less we want to discard it; and so it
is with the spelling of English. Once we have learned it, we have a strong
emotional attachment to it, just because we have had considerable difficulty with it and have been forced to put in so much time and effort on
learning it.

Furthermore, we learn to speak long before we are able to do any
kind of reflective or analytical intellectual work; we learn to speak when
we are small children, by a purely unreflecting process of repeated trial
and error. But when we go to school and learn to write, we do so consciously and reflectingly. If, in our first school contacts with writing, we
were taught a scientifically accurate phonemic spelling, which reflected
all the facts of our speech itself, we would have very little trouble and
would learn to use such a spelling in a year or two, as do Italian or

Hungarian children. But we do not learn an accurate phonemic spelling; we learn our inaccurate, confused traditional English orthography, and we talk about it as we do so. When we were little children learning how to speak, we learned only to speak, not how to analyze our speech. When we are older and learn to spell, we also learn how to talk about spelling and how to analyze it: we are taught to name the letters, to tell how we replace letters by apostrophes or how we drop letters, and so forth. But we still learn nothing whatsoever about how to discuss speech and analyze it in its own terms; the only approach, the only vocabulary we end up with for discussing language is the approach and the vocabulary of spelling. Edith Wharton, in *The Custom of the Country*, says of one of her characters:

> Mrs. Spragg, when she found herself embarked on a wrong sentence, always ballasted it by italicizing the last word.

What Mrs. Wharton meant, of course, was "emphasizing" or "stressing" the last word; but the only term at her disposal was the word *italicizing*, the term that referred to spelling rather than to speech.

This entire situation has given results that are little short of disastrous for the understanding of the true nature of language, throughout the English-speaking world. Very few people have any clear idea of what they actually do when they speak—what organs of their body they use and in what way they use them. Many people find it difficult or downright impossible to conceive of sounds as such, or to hear differences in sound that are not directly related to differences in English spelling. Some even develop emotional blockings on the subject of phonetic analysis, because the strange appearance and use of special symbols in a transcription makes them "feel all funny inside," as one such person put it to me. When it comes to discussing sounds, the only way to identify many sounds in writing for the general reader who knows no phonetics, is to avoid all letters entirely, and to give cumbersome definitions like "the vowel sound of *bit*" or "the initial sound of *thing*"; for, if we were to speak of the *i* of *hit* or the *th* of *thing*, almost everyone would immediately read off those definitions as "the 'eye' (*i*) of *hit*" or "the 'tee aitch' (*th*) of *thing*." Likewise for a discussion of grammar or of syntax, we can recognize grammatical facts which we see reflected in the conventional spelling, like the vowel change in *sing sang sung;* but we find it hard to recognize or discuss those grammatical facts which are not indicated in writing, like the difference between the final consonant sounds of *house* (noun, as in *he has a big house*) and *house* (verb, as in *where can we house them?*), or the change in vowel sound between *you* (stressed, as in *is that you?*) and *you* (unstressed, as in *how do you do?*).

All kinds of misunderstandings and misrepresentations arise as a result of this spelling-induced confusion and ignorance. People often think that spelling a word out is the best way to tell someone how to pronounce it, and think that the names of the letters alone will give a key to the sounds that are involved. I once witnessed a prize example of this confusion when a high-school girl named Carlys (normally pronounced as if spelled *Carleece,* stress on last syllable) was trying to tell my four-year-old boy Philip how to pronounce her name, which he had some difficulty with:

PHILIP: Hey, Craleeth!
CARLYS: No, no. Not Craleeth; Carlys. Say that.
PHILIP: Craleeth.
CARLYS: No, no, no. Carlys. CAR-LYS.
PHILIP: Craleeth.
CARLYS: No! Look; shall I spell it out for you?
PHILIP: (not knowing what "spelling it out" meant): Yes.
CARLYS: See, ay, ahr, ell, wye, ess. Now say it.
PHILIP: Craleeth.
CARLYS: ! ! !

Many times we think that, because a word is spelled with a certain letter, we ought to pronounce some sound to correspond to that letter: we pronounce a *t*-sound in *fasten,* we pronounce three syllables in *Wednesday,* we sometimes even try to pronounce the initial *p* in words like *psychology* or *ptarmigan.* This kind of behavior is known as *spelling-pronunciation;* it almost never occurs where a language has a reasonably accurate system of spelling, but always crops up whenever the spelling ceases to represent the language adequately. Our pronunciation of *author* is a case in point. Older English had a word *autor,* meaning "creator, author," which had been borrowed from the French word *autor* of the same meaning, ultimately taken from Latin *auctor.* In the sixteenth century, people came to realize that many words previously spelled with *t* came from Latin or Greek sources in which they were spelled with *th,* such as *theater, thesis.* It came to be a mark of elegance and learning to write *th* instead of *t;* but some people carried their learning too far and wrote *th* even where it didn't belong, as in *author* for *autor.* Then more and more people, seeing the letters *th* in the elegant spelling of *author,* pronounced the *th* with the sound those letters stand for in *thing;* by now, that spelling-pronunciation has become general and we all pronounce *author* with that sound, not with the *t*-sound it originally had. Needless to say, spelling-pronunciation serves no good purpose, and only introduces confusion and misunderstanding into otherwise clear situations, like those of *autor* or *fasten*. That is, once upon a time *autor* was pronounced with a *t*-sound, and everybody was quite happy about it; now, everybody says it with a *th*-sound and is equally happy about it; but nothing has been gained by the change, and there was no need of the uncertainty that prevailed during the period of transition.

"Correct" spelling, that is, obedience to the rules of English spelling as grammarians and dictionary-makers set them up, has come to be a major shibboleth in our society. If I write *seet* instead of *seat, roat* instead of *wrote,* or *hite* instead of *height,* it makes no difference whatsoever in the English language, i.e. in my speech and that of others around me; yet we are all trained to give highly unfavorable reactions to such spellings, and to be either amused or displeased with people who know no better than to "misspell" in such a way. This shibboleth serves, as does that of "correct" speech, as a means of social discrimination: we can class people among the sheep or the goats according as they measure up to the standards we set in spelling. Spelling which is more nearly in accord with speech, and which we might logically expect to be considered better than the conventional spelling, thus comes to be, not praised, but blamed. Spelling "phonetically" becomes equivalent to spelling incorrectly. I once came across a reference to "phonetic" pronunciation, which at first puzzled me, since pronunciation can by definition never be anything but phonetic; it later turned out that the writer was referring to inaccurate pronunciation of a foreign language, such as French *est-ce que vous avez* "have you?" pronounced in a way which he transcribed *ess-ker-vous-avay*. He had come to use the term "phonetic" as equivalent to "incorrect," through the folk use of the term *phonetic spelling* in the meaning of "incorrect spelling."

When we write down the exact words of people whose speech we consider "incorrect," we often purposely misspell their words to indicate their pronunciation and give the reader an idea of what social level they belong to; the realistic novels of Erskine Caldwell, John Steinbeck and others are full of these spelling devices: for instance, *Elviry done tole me she ain' a-gwineta do no sich thing fer nobuddy*. This shocks purists who are attached to "correct" spelling at all costs; but it is spreading more and more as an element of realism, which of course derives its force from the contrast between normal "correct" spelling and pronunciation, and the "incorrect" speech implied by the "incorrect" spelling. A further development of this device is so-called *eye-dialect,* in which misspellings are used to represent normal pronunciations, merely to burlesque words or their speaker. We all pronounce *women* in the same way; but if we spell it *wimmin,* we imply "The person quoted is one who would use a vulgar pronunciation if there were one." Likewise the spellings *licker* instead of *liquor, vittles* instead of *victuals, sez* instead of *says,* and the host of reduced forms such as *I wanna* for *I want to, ya oughta* for *you ought to, watcher gonna do* for *what are you going to do,* or *I hafta* for *I have to.*

This last group of examples may not, at first, seem accurate, because we are often not aware how much we reduce and telescope such combinations in normal speech; but just try observing yourself and see how many times a day you actually use the full, separate forms of the words in such an expression as *what are you going to do,* or *I have to do it.* In fact, *I have to* with a *v*-sound in *have* would be not only unusual, it would be abnormal. But, because of our conventions of spelling, the more realistic and accurate spellings like *I wanna* or *I hafta* are relegated to the comic strips and are made the objects of prejudice, which can be appealed to in whipping up opposition to phonetic transcription or to the writing of, say, the Italian word for "when" as KWAN-*do* instead of the conventional *quando.*

The situation with respect to spelling is much the same as it is with regard to "correct" speech in our society. In each case, an irrational, meaningless standard is set up as a shibboleth for people to conform to, which in many instances puts a premium on lack of realism and on unnaturalness in speech or its representation. In particular, our society's emphasis on the irregularities of English spelling has brought many of us to a point where we cannot distinguish between speech and writing, and where we cannot even conceive of sounds as existing distinct from and prior to letters. Consequently, anyone who goes through our schooling system has to waste years of his life in acquiring a wasteful and, in the long run, damaging set of spelling habits, thus ultimately unfitting himself to understand the nature of language and its function unless he puts in extra effort to rid himself of all the misconceptions and prejudices that our system has foisted on him.

HAROLD WHITEHALL

The System of Punctuation

The traditional purpose of punctuation is to symbolize by means of visual signs the patterns heard in speech. Grammarians of the eighteenth century, strongly conscious of pause but little observant of tone and juncture, thought that the comma indicated pause for a time count of one, the semicolon for a time count of two, the colon for a time count of three, and the period for a time count of four. Nowadays, we know that pause is simply pause, that pause is often optional, and that when present it combines with preceding junctures to build up what may be regarded as an audible punctuation of words, word-groups, and sentences when we are speaking. To these combinations of speech phenomena, the common punctuation marks of writing (.), (?), (;), (—), (,) bear a correlation which is at best only approximate. Moreover, modern English punctuation has become an intricate system of conventions, some logical, some indicating separations or connections of context, all of crucial practical importance. Its most important purpose is "to make grammar graphic." As a kind of visual configurational feature of grammar, punctuation cannot be properly understood unless the other grammatical features of the language are also understood.

Punctuation is employed in the following functions:

a. To *link* sentences and parts of words.
b. To *separate* sentences and parts of sentences.
c. To *enclose* parts of sentences.
d. To *indicate omissions.*

We can thus speak of *linking, separating, enclosing,* and *omission* punctuation in the full realization that each function contrasts directly with

From *Structural Essentials of English.* Copyright 1954, © 1956 by Harcourt Brace Jovanovich, Inc. Reprinted by permission of Harcourt Brace Jovanovich, Inc., and Longmans, Green & Co., Ltd.

240

all the others. It follows, therefore, that when the same marks of punctuation are used in different functions they are very much like words used in different functions: the grammatical meanings of the marks are *different*. The *separating period* (.) is quite distinct in functional use from the *omission period* (.); the *linking dash* (—) is functionally distinct from the *omission dash* (—); the single *separating comma* (,) is functionally distinct from *enclosing commas* (, . . . ,). In an ideal punctuation system, such differences would be clarified by the use of different marks of punctuation. Yet let us be realistic. Man has been speaking for well over 700,000 years. Man has been practicing alphabetic writing only for about 3450 years. Man has punctuated, in the modern sense, for less than 250 years. He has still not mastered an ideal punctuation. In the system as it stands, the distribution of the marks is as follows:

a. For *linking,* use:
    ; the semicolon
    : the colon
    — the linking dash
    - the linking hyphen

b. For *separating,* use:
    . the period
    ? the question mark
    ! the exclamation point
    , the separating comma

c. For *enclosing,* use:
    , . . . , paired commas
    — . . . — paired dashes
    (. . .) paired parentheses
    [. . .] paired brackets
    " . . . " paired quotation marks

d. For *indicating omissions,* use:
    ' the apostrophe
    . the omission period (or dot)
    — the omission dash
    . . . triple periods (or dots)
    . . . . quadruple periods (or dots)

Linking Punctuation

The semicolon (;), colon (:), and dash (—) are symbolic conjunctions capable of linking subject-predicate constructions without need of conjunctions proper. They differ chiefly in the way they direct emphasis. Semicolons distribute it more or less equally between preceding and following statements; colons throw it forwards towards following statements; dashes throw it backwards towards preceding statements. Since they function as symbolic conjunctions, none of these marks is associated with any distinctive tone pattern of the language. In most cases, indeed, statements preceding any one of them would be read with the final h—l tone-pause pattern characteristic of period punctuation. The hyphen differs from the other linking punctuation marks in that it is used to link parts of the words only. The semicolon, colon, and dash may occur in combination with a final quotation mark, in which case they are always placed *outside* the quotation mark.

The *semicolon* (;) is the symbolic conjunction used to link subject-predicate groups that could otherwise occur as separate sentences, particularly if they are parallel in structure and in emphasis:

> The girl is pretty; you will like her.
> I am out of work; I need financial help.
> I was ill that day; nevertheless, I tried to complete the work.
> He was a close friend of the family; moreover, he had a position open.

It is conventionally used to link word groups containing heavy internal comma punctuation:

> My outfit included a rifle, a shotgun, a water bag, and a bedroll; but I did not forget to include a few good books.
> I liked *The Ordeal of Richard Feverel,* by Meredith; *Oliver Twist,* by Dickens; and Oscar Wilde's fine comedy *The Importance of Being Earnest.*

When the semicolon occurs in conjunction with quotation marks, it is placed *outside* them:

> I was reading Shelley's "Adonais"; I did not wish to be disturbed.

The *colon* (:) is the symbolic conjunction used when emphasis is to be thrown forward upon the word-group or word that follows it:

> It was just as I thought: he had stolen the money.
> My outfit included these necessaries: a rifle, a shotgun, a water bag, and a bedroll.
> I could think of only one word to describe him: cad.

In keeping with its general function of *anticipation,* the colon is conventionally used to introduce the chapter figure of a Bible reference, the page number of a volume reference, the minute figure of a clock reference, and the body of a letter following the salutation:

> Number III; 21 (or 3:21)
> American Speech 12: 46–49
> 10:15 A.M.
> Dear Sir:

Like the semicolon, it is always placed *outside* a final quotation mark:

> I found one leading literary tradition in "Adonais": pastoral tone.

The *dash* (—) is the symbolic conjunction to be used when the word-group or word following it is considered to be subsidiary to, a reinforcement or example of, or an unexpected addition to what precedes it. It directs the reader's attention backward:

A year's work at Harvard—that was what he hoped for.
A rifle, shotgun, ammunition—these were the essentials of my outfit.
He comes to dinner, eats your food, smokes your best cigars—then borrows your money.
He was very crude—crude and utterly crazy.

The dash is conventionally used before the name of the author of a quotation:

Here lies our sovereign lord, the King.
Whose word no man relies on;
Who never spoke a foolish thing,
And never did a wise one.

—Anonymous

The dash should *not* be used as a kind of coverall punctuation mark for all linking and separating functions.

The *hyphen* (-) links parts of words together. It is most characteristically used to indicate that contiguous words form compounds not marked by stress modification.

a well-beloved woman
my *commander-in-chief*
his *better-than-thou* attitude

The conventional uses of the hyphen are these:
   a. To indicate that the beginning of a word on one printed line is linked to the rest of the word on the next.
   b. To link the elements of compound numbers from twenty-one to ninety-nine:

thirty-four horses
sixty-seven dollars

   c. To link the elements of fractions:

He had a *two-thirds* lead in the election.

Today we tend to write either separately or as single units those words which were formerly hyphenated:

my *commander in chief*
a *wellbred* woman

Separating Punctuation

The period separates sentences only. The exclamation mark (!) and the question mark (?), normally used to separate special types of sentences, are also used occasionally to separate parts of sentences. The comma separates *parts* of sentences only. Thus, there is every reason why the period, as sentences separator, should never be confused with the comma, as sentence-part separator, or with the semi-colon, the sentence linker. All the separating punctuation marks are roughly correlated with stress-juncture and tone-pause patterns heard in speech, and it is probable that learning to hear the patterns will direct you towards the appropriate punctuation:

John was coming (.)
John was coming (?)
John was coming (!)
John was coming (,) and I still had to dress.

When they occur in combination with final quotation marks, all the separating punctuation marks are placed *inside* them. In this respect, they contrast directly with the linking punctuation marks which are placed *outside*.

The period (.) has the one function of separating declarative subject-predicate sentences (including mild commands) from following sentences. It symbolizes the fall from high to low pitch (h—l) followed by breathing pause. Its grammatical meaning is "end of declarative utterance":

The mountains enclose a valley.
Please return the books as soon as possible.

The period can occur after statements not in subject-predicate form if they conclude with the h—l tone-pause pattern.

The more, the merrier.
To resume.

It is always inserted *before* end quotation marks:

He said to me, "Mother is coming."

The question mark (?) separates questions and quoted questions from a following context. It symbolizes two quite distinct final tone-pause patterns of actual speech:

a. A fall from high to low tone (h—l) used when a question contains an interrogative word or word order:

h_____l
Why did you go to the theater?

b. A rising high tone, usual when a question does not contain an interrogative word or word order:

l_____h
You went to the theater?

The grammatical meaning of the question mark is "answer needed":

Are you leaving tonight?
Is John coming?
You are in Professor Brown's class?
"Where is the salt?" he demanded.

It is always inserted *before* end quotation marks:

He said, "Is this what's wrong?"

The *exclamation point* (!) separates exclamatory sentences or exclamatory words from a following context. It symbolizes various final tone-pause patterns based upon sharply rising or falling tone or a combination of these, or unexpectedly level tone, used in speech when an utterance is surcharged with emotion:

What a marvelous morning!
Listen! I hear John coming.

It is always inserted *before* end quotation marks that occur *within* a sentence, but it is placed outside quotation marks at the end of a sentence when the whole sentence is exclamatory:

"I am finished!" he yelled.
How horrible was their shout, "We're coming to kill you"!

The *separating comma* (,) originally indicated that a part of a sentence preceding or following it was in some way separated from the remainder. Where it corresponds to anything in speech at all, it generally symbolizes internal grammatical juncture followed by pause in slow-tempo speech. Its use, however, is now highly conventionalized: the comma is often used where speech shows internal juncture unaccompanied by pause but where its omission might lead to misunderstanding. The comma never appears between the main structural elements, the *must* parts, of sentences; i.e., it is never used between the subject and verb, between the verb and a complement, or between two complements, and it is never used before movable modifiers of a sentence if these appear *after* the verb; in short, it is never used to indicate optional internal grammatical junctures. The grammatical meaning of the comma is "dissociation." It is inserted:

a. After each word or word-group in a series terminated by *and, or;* here it may symbolize the high rising tone pattern (h):

I took bread, butter, tea, and salt with me.
His cunning, his devious treachery, or his ruthlessness will be enough to make him fight successfully.

b. Between subject-predicate word-groups linked by the coupling conjunctions *and, but, or, not, yet:*

The book is quite good, and it is relatively inexpensive.
The food and service were good, yet I was hard to please.

c. After any movable modifier thought of as displaced from a normal end-of-sentence position:

Instead of the expected twenty, only ten came to the party.
But: Only ten came to the party instead of the expected twenty.

d. Before any other modifier or modifying word-group thought of as out of its normal sentence position:

We thought of Goldsmith, poor but genial.
Talent, Mr. Micawber has; money, Mr. Micawber has not.

e. After an introductory word, word-group, transitional adverb, or vocative expression:

This done, we left the place immediately.
She didn't like the idea; *nevertheless,* she said she would visit us.
Mother, I have brought my friend to be our guest.

f. After a subject-predicate word-group introducing a direct quotation:

He exclaimed, "I had no idea that you were in the room."

g. Between elements in sentences and word-groups which might cause confusion if thought of as combined:

My words are my own; my actions, my ministers'.
a bright, blue hat contrasted with a *bright blue hat*

h. Between items in dates, addresses, books and author references, etc.:

April 1, 1950
Mary Johnson, Cleveland, Ohio
Oliver Twist, by Charles Dickens

The comma is always inserted *before* end quotation marks:

"I am tired of your incompetence," he roared.

Enclosing Punctuation

Paired commas, paired dashes, and parentheses are used to enclose elements outside the main structure of a sentence. They represent a triple scale of enclosure, in which paired commas enclose elements most closely related to the main thought of the sentence and parentheses those elements least closely related. Brackets are merely a specialized type of parentheses. Quotation marks are used principally to enclose the report of words actually spoken.

Paired commas (, . . . ,) have the following uses:

a. To enclose modifying word-groups of the subject-predicate type which are not regarded as essential to the identification of the word which they modify. Such groups are usually called *non-restrictive.*

NON-RESTRICTIVE This invention, *which our army rejected,* became Germany's surprise weapon.

RESTRICTIVE The invention *which our army rejected* became Germany's surprise weapon.

In the first example, the identification is supplied by *this;* the modifying group *which our army rejected* is thus properly enclosed in paired commas. In the second example, the modifying group is needed to identify *invention*.

b. To enclose interpolated words and word-groups, especially when those are transitional adverbs or groups with the function of transitional adverbs:

> Your ideas, *however,* are scarcely valid.
> Your ideas, *as a matter of fact,* are scarcely valid.
> Your ideas, *I conclude,* are scarcely valid.

Paired dashes (— . . . —) enclose elements less closely related to the main thought of a sentence than those enclosed by paired commas but more closely related than those enclosed by parentheses:

> My friends—at that time mostly workers—took me to task for my social attitudes.

They replace paired commas when the enclosed word-group has heavy comma punctuation of its own:

> The artillery—devastating in its sound, fury, and effect—suddenly opened up on us.

Parentheses enclose material which is obviously outside the main scope of the sentence:

> These words (*we might call them determiners*) are important in English but of little importance in many other languages.

Parentheses are used conventionally to enclose the figures numbering parts of a series, and, in legal contexts, to enclose figures expressing monetary value:

> The aims of this course are: (1) to analyze the structure of American English; (2) to examine the resources of its vocabulary; (3) to sketch the history of American English. The signer agrees to pay the sum of one hundred dollars ($100.00).

Brackets ([. . .]) are a special kind of parentheses with the following uses:

a. To insert interpolations in quotations:

> As Jarrold said, "It [poetry] is an attempt to express the inexpressible."

b. To insert pronunciations written in the symbols of the International Phonetic Association (IPA):

The usual pronunciation of *bait* is [bet].

They also enclose parenthetical matter already in parentheses.
Quotation marks (". . .") enclose direct quotations from speech.

"You may say that," said my father, "but you don't believe it."

They may be used with caution to enclose references to specific words, slang expressions, hackneyed expressions, familiar and well-worn phrases, and terms you do not like:

My life is one "if" after another.
His car had the "teardrop" shape of that period.
While "on campus," Jones was something of a "rod."
The "liberal arts" curriculum becomes increasingly illiberal.

They are also used to enclose the titles of poems, plays, essays, paintings, etc. (but not the titles of complete volumes or of major works, which are indicated by italics):

I read Shelley's "Alastor" with distinct pleasure.
I particularly admired El Greco's "Toledo."
He was much impressed by the story "Clay" in Joyce's *Dubliners*.

Omission Punctuation

Originally, the *apostrophe* (') indicated the omission of a letter no longer pronounced or deliberately suppressed in pronunciation. This is what it still indicates when used with the possessive singular forms of nouns, contracted forms of verb helpers (auxiliaries), and words with an omitted initial letter:

the Lord's Prayer (earlier, the Lordes Prayer)
He's not coming, and he won't come.
a blot on the 'scutcheon

Its conventional uses are as follows:

a. It precedes *s* in the plurals of figures, signs, symbols, and letters:

My 8's are difficult to decipher.

There were three x's in this quotation.
I have difficulty in writing r's.

b. It precedes *s* in plurals of words which have no normal plural form:

There were too many if's and but's about the matter.

c. In a purely symbolic function corresponding to nothing actual in speech, it indicates possessive plurals of nouns:

The generals' orders had to be obeyed.
the college girls' escorts

d. It indicates the possessive singular forms of nouns already ending in *s:*

Dr. Caius' (or Caius's) words
Moses' pronouncements

e. It indicates the possessive singular forms of group names:

Thomas, Manchester, and Scott's *Rhetoric*
Chase and Sanborn's coffee

f. It indicates the omission of initial centuries in dates:

the class of '38

The *omission period* or *dot* (.) indicates the omission of several letters, particularly when words are abbreviated:

Mr. V. S. Johnson
Ph.D.
I enjoy the plays of G.B.S.

It is not used after contractions indicated by the apostrophe, after Roman numerals, after numbered ordinals, after nicknames, or after per cent (for *per centum*); it is now often omitted after the abbreviated names of government agencies, labor organizations, and the like:

He'll go.   a five per cent bonus
XXIV   CIC

5th, 6th, 7th   FTC
Dick, Mick, and Ned

When a sentence ends with an abbreviated word, one period punctuates both the abbreviation and the sentence:

I was talking to Richard Hudson, Ph.D.

Triple periods or *dots* (. . .) indicate a more or less extensive omission of material at the beginning of, or within, a quoted passage; followed by a period (. . . .) they indicate omission at its end:

. . . language is . . . the thought itself, its confused cross currents as well as its clear-cut issues. . . .

Triple periods are often used to indicate omissions deliberately left to the reader's imagination:

He took her slowly in his arms . . . from that moment she was his.

In recent advertising practice, this use is greatly extended in order to create appropriate atmosphere:

Fly to Britain . . . Europe . . . and beyond.
Industries are discovering . . . with a rush . . . that the Genie of "Opportunity" is at their beck and call.

The *dash* (—) as used in omission punctuation indicates the deliberate suppression of letters in a person's name in order to avoid positive statement of identification:

My informant, a certain professor *M*—, vouches for the truth of this report.

In an earlier writing it was often used to indicate omissions in oaths, etc.:

"D—n," he said. "I'll see you hanged yet."

No attempt has been made here to deal with all the minute points of punctuation. Such matters as the use of capitals and italics are treated under the appropriate headings in a dictionary: they are matters of format rather than punctuation although they serve a very real purpose in the transference of spoken to written distinctions. What has been attempted here is to present punctuation proper as a system of symbols each one of which contrasts with all others in function. Ideally, the writer should be able to ignore the grammar book or the dictionary when he is faced with a punctuation problem; what he needs most of all is an understanding of the entire system as it determines the individual application.

HAROLD WHITEHALL

Writing and Speech

All of us have a grammar. The fact that we use and understand English in daily affairs means that we use and understand, for the most part unconsciously, the major grammatical patterns of our language. Yet because of the effects of education, many of us have come to think of a relatively formal written English and its reflection among those who "speak by the book" as the only genuine English, and to consider its grammar as the only acceptable English grammar. That is by no means true. The basic form of present-day American English is the patterned, rhythmed, and segmented code of voice signals called *speech*—speech is used in everyday conversation by highly educated people (*cultivated speech*), by the general run of our population (*common speech*), or by some rural persons in such geographically isolated areas as the Ozark Plateau, the Appalachian Mountains, or the woodland areas of northern New England (*folk speech*). From the code of speech, the language of formal writing is something of an abstraction, differing in details of grammar and vocabulary and lacking clear indication of the bodily gestures and meaningful qualities of the voice which accompany ordinary conversation. Thus, serious written English may be regarded as a rather artificial dialect of our language. To acquire that dialect, the would-be writer needs to know a good deal about its structural details, and particularly about those in which it differs from the less formal varieties of speech.

Even a moment's reflection will show that the spoken American language is backed by expressive features lacking in the written language: the rise or fall of the voice at the ends of phrases and sentences; the application of vocal loudness to this or that word or part of a word; the

From *Structural Essentials of English*. Copyright 1954, © 1956 by Harcourt Brace Jovanovich, Inc. Reprinted by permission of Harcourt Brace Jovanovich, Inc., and Longmans, Green & Co., Ltd.

use of gesture; the meaningful rasp or liquidity, shouting or muting, drawling or clipping, whining or breaking, melody or whispering imparted to the quality of the voice. Written English, lacking clear indication of such features, must be so managed that it compensates for what it lacks. It must be more carefully organized than speech in order to overcome its communicative deficiencies as compared with speech. In speech, we safeguard meaning by the use of intonation, stress, gesture, and voice qualities. In writing, we must deal with our medium in such a way that the meaning cannot possibly be misunderstood. In the absence of an actual hearer capable of interrupting and demanding further explanation, a clear writer is always conscious of "a reader over his shoulder." All this despite the fact that writing, being permanent, as compared with speech, which is evanescent, allows not only reading but also rereading.

Nor is this all. If written English is somewhat abstract, somewhat artificial, it is also generalized—national, not geographically or socially limited in scope. We must realize that comparatively few of us make use in our day-to-day affairs of a generalized spoken American English that is at all comparable with it. Such a language—a Received Standard Spoken English—exists, but not for the most part in this country where the practical need for it is slight. It exists in England, where the practical need for it is great. In England, many people still start their linguistic careers speaking one or another of the regional dialects, dialects so different from each other in vocabulary and grammar, so quilt-crazy in their distribution, that they form real barriers to generalized, national communication. Yet, in a modern, democratic country, general communication is a necessity. For that reason, Englishmen are willing to accept the notion both of a generalized spoken and a generalized written form of expression on a level above the dialects, and are willing to make the effort of learning them in school and elsewhere. We would be equally willing if our everyday speech happened to resemble this specimen from the English county of Lancaster:

> Nay! my heart misgi'es me! There's summat abeawt this neet's wark as is noan jannock. Look thee here! Yon chap's noan t' first sheep theaw's lifted tax-free fro't' mooar, an' aw've niver been one to worrit abeawt it, that aw hav'nt. But toneet, someheaw, it's noan t'same. There's summat beawn't 'appen—aw con feel it i' my booans. This een, an unconny wind wor burrin' i't'ling, an' not a cleawd i't' sky; an' whin aw went deawn to' t'well for watter, t'bats wor flyin' reawn it in a widdershins ring. Mark my words, there's mooar to coom.

In the United States, our language situation is quite different. Ours is probably the only country on earth in which three thousand miles of travel will bring no difficulty of spoken communication. We do have, of course, regional and social differences of language. The speech of Maine does not coincide in all points with that of Texas, nor the speech of Georgia with that of Minnesota. The speech of cultivated people in urban centers is not precisely that of the general mass of our citizens, nor that of rural residents of limited education in geographically secluded areas. Yet, unless we deliberately choose to emphasize disparities for social or other reasons, our regional and social speech differences create no great barriers to the free exchange of opinions and ideas. They consist of flavoring rather than substance.

Precisely for that reason, pressures for the adoption of a generalized national spoken American English comparable in acceptance and prestige with Received Standard Spoken British have proved largely unavailing. In American life, one may use cultivated or common speech Southern, cultivated or common speech Northeastern, or cultivated or common speech North Middle Western without encountering any great practical disadvantage. Our standards of speech are mainly regional standards, and most of us, in actual fact, speak some kind of a patois in which one or another of the cultivated or common speech regional varieties of American English blends quite happily with elements absorbed from reading and the educational process. We are very fortunate in this—fortunate that American historical and sociological conditions have removed difficulties of spoken communication found in most other parts of the world.

In a lesser sense, however, our good fortune is something of a misfortune. Because an American can understand other Americans no matter what regional or social class they come from, he is apt to underestimate the necessity for a generalized and abstract written American English. Because he finds no pressing reason for standardizing his speech, he is likely to misunderstand the necessity for standardizing his writing. He would like to write as he speaks. Moreover, the differences between the various regional and social varieties of American speech, being slight, are often of so subtle a nature that he tends to find difficulty in discriminating them. Slight as they are, when transferred to writing they are sufficient to make a reader pause, to induce a momentary feeling of unfamiliarity, to interrupt his consideration of the *matter* of expression by unwittingly calling attention to the *manner* of expression. Outside frankly literary writing (particularly the writing of poetry), such pauses, such unfamiliarities, such interruptions will hinder rather than help the writer's communicative purpose. If writing must be generalized, it must be generalized with a good reason: to speak with a local accent is not disadvantageous; to write serious prose with a local accent definitely is.

The moral of all this is clear. To gain command of serious written English is to acquire, quite deliberately, an abstract and generalized variety of the language differing by nature and purpose from any social or regional variety whatsoever. It is to sacrifice the local for the general, the spontaneous for the permanent. It is to bring to the study of written American English something of the perspective we normally reserve for the study of foreign languages. It is to master a set of grammatical and vocabulary patterns not because they are "correct" but because experience has proved them efficient in the communicative activity of writing.

The word "correct" is deliberately introduced here. The clear distinctions between spoken and written language mentioned in the paragraphs above have been all too often masked by the pernicious doctrine of "correctness." Perhaps that is to be expected. Without the flexible medium of language, a human society in human terms would be impossible. Without language, there could be no continuous records of experience, no diversification of labor, no great social institutions—the humanity of man could never have been achieved. But social activities breed social rituals and social judgments. Because language is *the* basic social instrument, it has inevitably acquired social attitudes so complex and variegated that they have often been allowed to obscure its primary communicative function. For far too many of us, knowledge of language is confused with knowledge of judgments on language that are socially acceptable. Education in the English language has become, for the most part, education in linguistic niceties—a poor substitute for that real linguistic education which ought to show us the major and minor patterns of our language, the way in which they interlock in function, the ways in which they can be manipulated for effective expression. As a result, the instrument of communication which should be every man's servant has become most men's master. This need not be so. Our self-confidence is immediately bolstered, our attitudes towards the study of writing techniques tremendously improved, once we realize that the difficulties of writing English do not spring from faulty nurture, restricted intelligence, or beyond-the-tracts environment but from the necessary changeover from one kind of English to another—that they are neither unpardonable nor irremediable.

No matter what irrationalities surround the details and the perspectives by which English is normally viewed, the fact that it has so admirably served and is still serving the needs of many fine writers guarantees that it is neither an impossible nor an unworthy instrument of human expression. Let us admit that all languages, spoken or written, are man-made things, that their weaknesses as well as their strengths are implicit in their human origin. Let us admit that the world has never known either a faultless language nor one constructed on what to us seems a strictly logical system. The proper approach to written English is first to understand what the medium is; then to concede its limitations and to use its strengths to the best possible effect. Every communicative medium has a set of resistances that the communicator must overcome. Marble is hard; paint relatively unmanageable; music barely descriptive. No small part of any kind of composition is contributed directly by tensions set up between the craftsman's demands on his medium on the one hand and its inherent resistances on the other. To this, the science, craft, and art of expression in written American English is no exception.

THORSTEIN VEBLEN

The Higher Learning

. . . Lately, since college athletics have won their way into a recognized standing as an accredited field of scholarly accomplishment, this latter branch of learning—if athletics may be freely classed as learning—has become a rival of the classics for the primacy in leisure-class education in American and English schools. Athletics have an obvious advantage over the classics for the purpose of leisure-class learning, since success as an athlete presumes, not only a waste of time, but also a waste of money, as well as the possession of certain highly unindustrial archaic traits of character and temperament. In the German universities the place of athletics and Greek-letter fraternities, as a leisure-class scholarly occupation, has in some measure been supplied by a skilled and graded inebriety and a perfunctory duelling.

The leisure class and its standards of virtue—archaism and waste—can scarcely have been concerned in the introduction of the classics into the scheme of the higher learning; but the tenacious retention of the classics by the higher schools, and the high degree of reputability which still attaches to them, are no doubt due to their conforming so closely to the requirements of archaism and waste.

"Classic" always carries this connotation of wasteful and archaic, whether it is used to denote the dead languages or the obsolete or obsolescent forms of thought and diction in the living language, or to denote other items of scholarly activity or apparatus to which it is applied with less aptness. So the archaic idiom of the English language is spoken of as "classic" English. Its use is imperative in all speaking and writing upon serious topics, and a facile use of it lends dignity to even the most commonplace and trivial string of talk. The newest form of English diction is of course never written; the sense of that leisure-class propriety

From *The Theory of the Leisure Class*. Reprinted by permission of The Viking Press, Inc.

which requires archaism in speech is present even in the most illiterate or sensational writers in sufficient force to prevent such a lapse. On the other hand, the highest and most conventionalised style of archaic diction is—quite characteristically—properly employed only in communications between an anthropomorphic divinity and his subjects. Midway between these extremes lies the everyday speech of leisure-class conversation and literature.

Elegant diction, whether in writing or speaking, is an effective means of reputability. It is of moment to know with some precision what is the degree of archaism conventionally required in speaking on any given topic. Usage differs appreciably from the pulpit to the marketplace; the latter, as might be expected, admits the use of relatively new and effective words and turns of expression, even by fastidious persons. A discriminate avoidance of neologisms is honorific, not only because it argues that time has been wasted in acquiring the obsolescent habit of speech, but also as showing that the speaker has from infancy habitually associated with persons who have been familiar with the obsolescent idiom. It thereby goes to show his leisure-class antecedents. Great purity of speech is presumptive evidence of several successive lives spent in other than vulgarly useful occupations; although its evidence is by no means entirely conclusive to this point.

As felicitous an instance of futile classicism as can well be found, outside of the Far East, is the conventional spelling of the English language. A breach of the proprieties in spelling is extremely annoying and will discredit any writer in the eyes of all persons who are possessed of a developed sense of the true and beautiful. English orthography satisfies all the requirements of the canons of reputability under the law of conspicuous waste. It is archaic, cumbrous, and ineffective; its acquisition consumes much time and effort; failure to acquire it is easy of detection. Therefore it is the first and readiest test of reputability in learning, and conformity to its ritual is indispensable to a blameless scholastic life.

On this head of purity of speech, as at other points where a conventional usage rests on the canons of archaism and waste, the spokesmen for the usage instinctively take an apologetic attitude. It is contended, in substance, that a punctilious use of ancient and accredited locutions will serve to convey thought more adequately and more precisely than would the straightforward use of the latest form of spoken English; whereas it is notorious that the ideas of today are effectively expressed in the slang of today. Classic speech has the honorific virtue of dignity; it commands attention and respect as being the accredited method of communication under the leisure-class scheme of life, because it carries a pointed suggestion of the industrial exemption of the speaker. The advantage of the accredited locutions lies in their reputability; they are reputable because they are cumbrous and out of date, and therefore argue waste of time and exemption from the use and the need of direct and forcible speech.

Aids to Study and Topics for Writing

Aids to Study

1. Consult your desk dictionary for its remarks on the size of the English vocabulary. Count the number of entry words on a few typical pages, multiply the average number of entries per page by the number of pages in the dictionary, and get an estimate of the size of its vocabulary. What factors can you think of which might influence the sizes of the various dictionaries?
2. Just out of curiosity, how large do you imagine your own vocabulary is? By sampling pages in your dictionary, figure out what percentage of the entry words (a) you *know* and *use*, either in speaking or writing, and (b) you *recognize* when others use them or when you're reading. How accurate do you think such an estimate might be? What are the weaknesses in this way of estimating size of vacabulary?
3. Vocabulary: Consult your dictionary for these words, and then work out the answers.
   a. *gloss,* n.–What is its technical meaning for language? What is its relation to *glossary,* to the verb *to gloss,* and to the phrase *to gloss over?*
   b. *magnum opus*–Why didn't Whitehall put it in italics? Was he right or wrong?
   c. *inkhorn terms*–What were they? How did the meaning develop? And what is *aureate diction?* What is the difference between the two?
   d. *superscript letters*–What are they?
   e. *encyclopedic dictionaries*–What are they? Is this the best way to spell *encyclopedic?* How do you decide?
   f. *lexicography*–What is it? Where did the word come from?

261

4. Dictionaries of "hard words" seem a rather sensible sort of book, since most of the time it's the "hard words" we use the dictionary for. But there are some problems. Make up two lists, one of "hard" words, one of "easy" words. Put three nouns, three verbs, two adjectives, and two adverbs in each list. Now, without consulting a dictionary, write definitions for all twenty words. Which list is easier to handle? Why? Can you see why we need more than dictionaries of "hard words"?

5. On pp. 161–162, Whitehall lists seven characteristics of modern American dictionaries. Check your own desk dictionary against the list. Is anything missing? Does yours have things not in Whitehall's list?

6. Whitehall says very little about one great series of modern American dictionaries. Which dictionaries are these? Why do you suppose they were not treated fully in his essay? (Note the source of his essay.)

7. Most of the great American dictionaries have been commercial successes. What weaknesses would you expect a dictionary aimed at "the market" to show?

Topics for Writing

1. Consult an encyclopedia or a biographical dictionary for information about Joseph Worcester and Noah Webster. Write a factual essay comparing their characters, careers, and accomplishments.

2. Whitehall says that the typical American dictionary differs from British dictionaries "because the conditions of American life and culture differ from those of English life and culture." Write an essay in which you explore similar factors that might make different demands on dictionaries for these two countries.

TIMES: WEBSTER'S NEW WORLD BOOK

Aids to Study

1. Go through that first sentence of the editorial, isolating the various words that the editors evidently consider unacceptable, but which the new *Webster's* lists without label.

2. On just what grounds does the *Times* consider these words unacceptable? What do they mean by unacceptable?

3. On what grounds do the dictionary makers list the words without label?

4. Is there a sense in which both are right? Can you explain the misunderstanding here?

5. In any case, that first sentence is certainly bad prose by anybody's standards. Why is it bad prose? Because it uses certain dubious words? Or because it juxtaposes a whole mess of words from different worlds of discourse?

6. What sort of English teaching does the *Times* mean when it uses the expression "the sounder teachers"? What did Marckwardt mean by a sound teacher? Is there a disagreement here between a distinguished news-paper and a distinguished professor from Princeton? Is it a serious dis-agreement? Is there anything to be done about it?

Topics for Writing

1. Read the introductory materials in *Webster's Third* that state the as-sumptions or ground rules on which the dictionary is based. Then go back to the first four study-aid questions above, and write an organized essay showing how to reconcile these apparently opposed points of view toward language.

2. Write a short paper on the *Times*'s own editorial style, as revealed here. What sort of voice or personality emerges from this language, and where is the most revealing evidence of it?

Macdonald: The String Untuned

Aids to Study

1. Consult your desk dictionary for these terms, often used as "warning labels" in dictionaries: *slang, colloquial, erroneous, incorrect, illiterate.* Find ex-amples of words to which you would attach these labels if you were a lexicographer. Now check your choices against your desk dictionary and against Merriam-Webster-III (MW-III).

2. On p. 172 of Macdonald's essay is a list of new political terms which MW-III defines. How many are in your desk dictionary? Look in the daily newspaper for some even newer political terms which are not in *any* dictionary. How would you define them?

3. What is a *structural linguist?* Are there other kinds of linguists? What is a *polyglot?*

4. Macdonald says that MW-III is the only English dictionary now in print which is comparable to the *Oxford English Dictionary.* But there are im-portant differences between them. List as many of these as you can. Examine the *OED* entry for *deer,* and compare it in detail with the MW-III entry on the following page.

Deer (dīᵉɹ) Forms: 1 díor, déor, 2–3 deor, (2 dær), 2–4 der, (2–3 dor, 3 dier, 3–4 duer, 4 dur, 5 dure, deure), 4–6 dere, (4–7 deere, 5, 7 diere, 5– (Sc.) deir, 6–7 deare), 4- deer, (5 theer). *Pl.* 1–9 normally same as sing.; also 2 deore, deoran, 2–3 -en; 3–4 deores, dueres, 7–9 *occas.* deers. [A Comm. Teut. sb.: OE., *díor, déor* = OS. *dier*, OFris. *diar, dier* (MDu. and Du. and LG. *dier*), OHG. *tior* (MHG. *tier*, Ger. *tier, thier*):–WG. *dior*, ON. **djúr* (Icel. *dýr*, Sw. *djur*, Da. *dyr*); Goth. *dius, diuz*-:–OTeut. *deuzoᵐ*: –pre-Teut. *dheuso•m*.
Generally referred to a root *dhus* to breathe (cf. *animal* from *anima*), and thought by some etymologists to be the neuter of an adj. used subst. Cf. DEAR a.² (Not connected with Gr. θηρ wild beast.)]

†1. A beast: usually a quadruped, as distinguished from birds and fishes; but sometimes, like *beast*, applied to animals of lower orders. *Obs.*

c 950 *Lindisf. Gosp.* Luke xviii. **25** Se camal þæt *micla dear. a* 1000 *Boeth. Metr.* xxvii. **24** Swa swa fuðl oððe dior. *c* 1000 ÆLFRIC *Voc.* in Wr.-Wülcker 118/31 *Fera*, wild deor. *Bellua, reðe dcor . . Unicornis*, anhyrne deor. **1154** *O. E. Chron.* (Laud MS.) an. 1135 Pais he makede men & dær. *c* 1200 ORMIN 1176 Shep iss . . stille der. *Ibid.* 1312 Lamb iss soffte & stille deor. *a* 1250 *Owl & Night.* 1321 Al swo deth mani dor and man. *c* 1250 *Gen. & Ex.* 4025 Also leun is miðful der. **1482** CAXTON *Reynard* (Arb.) **18** The rybaud and the felle diere here I se hym comen.

B. *plural.*

c 1000 ÆLFRIC *Gen.* i. **25** And he við ofer þa deor. *c* 1175 *Lamb. Hom.* 43 Innan þan ilke sea weren un-aneomned deor, summe feðerfotetd, summe al bute fet. *Ibid.* 115 þene bið his erd ihened . . on wilde deoran. *c* 1200 *Trin. Coll. Hom.* 177 Oref, and deor, and fishshes, and fugeles. *Ibid.* 209 Hie habbeð geres after wilde deore. *Ibid.* 224 Of wilde diere. *c* 1350 *Gen. & Ex.* 4020 On ilc brend eft twin der. *Ibid.* 4032 Efte he sacrede deres mor. *a* 1310 in Wright *Lyric P.* xiii. 44 Deores with huere derne rounes. *Ibid.* xiv 45 In dounes with this dueres plawes. *c* 1340 *Gaw. & Gr. Kt.* 1151 Der drof in þe dale . . bot heterly þay were Restayed with þe stablye.

2. The general name of a family (*Cervidæ*) of ruminant quad-rupeds, distinguished by the possession of deciduous branching horns or antlers, and by the presence of spots on the young: the various genera and species being distinguished as *rein-deer, moose-deer, red deer, fallow deer;* the MUSK DEER belong to a different family, *Moschidæ.*
A specific application of the word, which occurs in OE. only contextually, but became distinct in the ME. period, and by its close remained as the usual sense.

[*c* 893 K. ÆLFRED Oros. I. i. (Sw.) 18 He [Ohthere] hæfde þa ʒyt ða he þone cyningc sohte, tamra deora unbebohtra syx hund. þa deor hi hata ð hranas.] *a* 1131 [see *der fald* in 4]. *c* 1205 LAY. 2586 To huntien after deoren [*c* 1275 after deores]. **1297** R. GLOUC. (Rolls) 9047 He let [make] þe parc of Wodestoke, & der þer inne do. *c* 1325 *Song on Passion* 59 (*O. E. Misc.*) He was todrawe so dur islawe in chace. **1375** BARBOUR *Bruce* VII. 497 [He] went. .to purchase venysoun, For than the deir war in sesoun. *c* 1420 *Anturs of Arth.* (Camden) iv, Thay felle to the female dure, feyful thyk fold. **1464** *Mann. & Househ. Exp.* 195 A payr breganderys cueryd wyth whyte deris leder. **1470–85** MALORY *Arthur* x. lxi, He chaced at the reed dere. **1538** STARKEY *England* I. iii. 98 A dere louyth a lene barren. .ground. **1601** SHAKS. *Jul. C.* III. i. 209 Like a Deere, strocken by many Princes. **1611** CORYAT *Crudities* 10 A goodly Parke. .wherein there is Deere. **1774** GOLDSM. *Nat. Hist.* (1776) III. 80 An hog, an ox, a goat, or a deer. **1855** LONGF. *Hiaw.* III. 169 Where the red deer herd together.

b. occasional plural *deers.*

c 1275 [see 1205 in prec.] **1674** N. Cox *Gentl. Recreat.* II. (1677) 58 The reasons why Harts and Deers do lose their Horns yearly. **1769** HOME *Fatal Discov.* III, Stretch'd on the skins of deers. *c* 1817 HOGG *Tales & Sk.* II. 89. The place of rendezvous, to which the deers weer to be driven.

† c. *Deer of ten:* a stag of ten, i. e. one having ten points or tines on his horns; an adult stag of five years at least, and therefore 'warrantable' or fit to be hunted. *Obs.*

1631 MASSINGER *Emp. of East* IV. ii, He will make you royal sport, He is a deer Of ten, at the least.

3. *Small deer:* a phrase originally, and perhaps still by Shakspere, used in sense 1; but now humorously associated with sense **2.**

14. .*Sir Beues* (1885) p. 74/2 (MS.C.) Ratons & myse and soche smale dere, That was hys mete that vii yere. 1605 SHAKS. *Lear* III. iv. 144 But Mice, Rates, and such small Deare, Haue bin Toms food, for seuen long yeare. 1883 G. ALLEN in *Colin Clout's Calender* 14 Live mainly upon worms, slugs, and other hardy small deer.

transf. 1857 H. REED *Lect. Eng. Poets* x. II. 17 The small deer that were herded together by Johnson as the most eminent of English poets.

4. *attrib.* and *Comb.*, as *deer bed, herd, -hide, -keeper, kind, life, -sinew, -snaring,* etc.; *deer-like, deer-loved* adjs. [Several already in OE., as *déor-fald* an enclosure or cage for wild beasts in the amphitheatre, or for beasts of the chase, a deer-park, *déor-edisc* deer-park, *déor-net* net for wild animals, etc.]

1835 W. IRVING *Tous Prairies* xi, The tall grass was pressed down into numerous ° 'deer beds', where those animals had couched. *a* 1000 *Ags. Gloss.* in Wr.-Wülcker 201 *Causea, domus in theatro,* °deorfald. a 1131 *O. E. Chron.* an. 1123 Se king rad in his der fald [æt Wudestoke]. 1860 G. H. K. *Vac. Tour.* 123 Peaks. .where the scattered remnants of the great °deer herds can repose in security. 1814 SCOTT *Ld. of Isles* III. xix, Goat-skins or °deer-hides o'er them cast. 1849 JAMES *Woodman* vii, I have got my °deer-keepers watching. 1875 LYELL *Princ. Geol.* II. III. xxxix. 359 Animals of the °deer kind. 1860 G. H. K. *Vac. Tour.* 122 The shepherds. .see a good deal of °deer life. 1840 MRS. NORTON *Dream* 127 The dark, °deer-like eyes. 1876 GEO. ELIOT *Dan. Der.* IV. liv. 114 Deer-like shyness. 1831 LYTTON *Godolph.* 23 The °deer-loved fern. *c* 1000 ÆLFRIC *Voc.* in Wr.-Wülcker 167 *Cassis,* °deornet. 1856 KANE *Arct. Expl.* II. vii. 79 To walk up Mary River Ravine until we reach the °deer-plains. 1866 KINGSLEY *Herew.* I. vi. 178 Sea-bows of horn and °deer-sinew. 1862 S. ST. JOHN *Forests Far East* II. 34, I have been out °deer-snaring in this neighbourhood.

b. Special comb.: **deer-brush,** an American shrub in Arizona; **deer-cart,** the covered cart in which a tame stag to be hunted is carried to the meet; **deer-dog** = DEER-HOUND; **deer-drive,** a shooting expedition in which the deer are driven past the sportsman; so *deer-driving;* **deer-eyed** *a.,* having eyes like deer, having soft or languid eyes; **deer-fence,** a high railing such as deer cannot leap over; **deer-flesh,** venison; **deer-forest,** a 'forest' or extensive track of unenclosed wild land reserved for deer; † **deer-goat,** an old name for the capriform or caprine antelopes; **deer-grass,** species of Rhexia (N.O. *Melastomaceæ*); **deer-leap,** a lower place in a hedge or fence where deer may leap; **deer-meat** = *deer-flesh;* **deer-neck,** a thin neck (of a horse) resembling a deer's; **deer-park,** a park in which deer are kept; † **deer-reeve,** a township officer in New England in the colonial days, whose duty it was to execute the laws as to deer; **deer-plain,** a plain inhabited by deer; **deer-saddle,** a saddle on which a slain deer is carried away; **deer's-eye** = BUCK-EYE (the tree); **deer's foot** (*grass*), the fine grass *Agrostis setacea;* **deer's hair** = DEER-HAIR; **deer's milk,** a local name of the wood spurge, *Euphorbia amygdaloides;* **deer's tongue, deer-tongue,** a N. American Cichoraceous plant, *Liatris odoratissima;* **deer-tiger,** the puma or cougar; **deer-yard,** an open spot where deer herd, and where the ground is trodden by them.

1883 W. H. BISHOP in *Harper's Mag.* Mar. 502/2 The °'deer brush' resembles horns. 1840 HOOD *Up the Rhine* 186 The hearse, very like a °deer-cart. 1814 SCOTT *Ld. of Isles* v. xxiii, Many a °deer-dog howl'd around. 1882 *Society* 21 Oct. 19/1 Setting out for a °deer-drive. 1860 G. H. K. *Vac. Tour.* 143 Mr. Scrope. .was a great hand at °deer-driving. 1884 Q. VICTORIA *More Leaves* 14 The gate of the °deer-fence. *a* 1300 *Cursor M.* 3603 (Cott.) If þou me °dere flesse [*v. r. venisun*] ani gete. 1854 *Act* 17–8 *Vict.* c. 91 § 42 Where such shootings or °deer forests are actually let. 1892 E. WESTON BELL *Scot. Deerhound* 80 Probably not more than twenty deer forests, recognized as such, were in existence prior to the beginning of the present century. 1607 TOPSELL *Four-f. Beasts* (1658) 93 Of the first kinde Tragelaphvs which may be called a °Deer-goat. 1693 SIR T. P. BLOUNT *Nat. Hist.* 30 The Deer-Goat . .being partly like a deer partly like a Goat. 1866 *Treas. Bot.* 972/2 Low perennial often bristly herbs, commonly called °Deer-grass, or Meadow-beauty, [with] large showy cymose flowers. 1540–2 *Act* 31 *Hen. VIII, c.* 5 To make °dere leapes and breakes in the sayde hedges and fences. 1838 JAMES *Robber* i, In front appeared a °deer-park. 1860 G. H. K. *Vac. Tour.* 172 It is no light business to get our big stag. .on the °deer saddle. 1762 J. CLAYTON *Flora Virginica* 57 *Æsculus floribus octandris* Linn . . . °Dear's Eye, and Bucks Eyes. 1883 *Century Mag.* XXVI. 383 Among the lily-pads, °deer-tongue, and other aquatic plants. 1880 *7th Rep. Surv. Adirondack Reg. N. Y.* 159 We reached an open forest plateau on the mountain, where we were surprised to find a °'deer-yard.' Here the deep snow was tramped down by deer into a broad central level area.

deer \'di(ə)r, 'diə \ *n, pl* **deer** *also* **deers** [ME, deer, animal, fr. OE *dēor* beast; akin to OHG *tior* wild animal, ON *dȳr*, Goth *dius* wild animal, Lith *dvẽsti* to breathe, expire, Skt *dhvaṁsati* he falls to dust, perishes — more at DUST] **1** *obs* **:** ANIMAL; *esp* **:** a quadruped mammal ⟨rats and mice and such small ~ — Shak.⟩ **2 a :** any of numerous ruminant mammals that constitute the family Cervidae, that have two large and two small hoofs on each foot and antlers borne by the males of

fallow deer

nearly all and by the females of a few forms, that are represented by numerous species and individuals in most regions except most of Africa and Australia, and that constitute an important source of food in many places for man and the larger carnivorous animals — see CARIBOU, ELK, MOOSE, MUSK DEER, REINDEER; VENISON **b :** any of the small or medium-sized members of the family as distinguished from certain esp. large forms (as elk, moose, or caribou) **3 :** DEERSKIN **4 :** a grayish yellowish brown that is lighter and slightly yellower than olive wood and lighter than acorn — called also *bobolink, camel's hair*

5. Vocabulary:

   a. What would a *"Jim Crow* flavor" (p. 167) be?

   b. What kind of approach is a *"normative* approach"?

   c. Is *schoolmarm* a word to use without quotation marks or italics? How would you decide?

   d. What is a *nonce* word? Find some examples in your desk dictionary.

   e. What does *tertgiversating* mean?

   f. Is *scholar's knee* (p. 179) a good synonym for *gnostimania?* What is Macdonald's point?

   g. What is the matter with *irregardless* (p. 181)?

   h. What is "the unresolved *bimonthly* and *biweekly* problem" (p. 182), and how do you think it might best be resolved?

6. Macdonald doesn't like the use of the *schwa* (ə) or "upside-down *e.*" Why not? Does your desk dictionary use it? What difficulty would you encounter in using a conventional English letter to represent that sound in recording pronunciations.

7. Consult your desk dictionary for the meanings of the word *masses*. What is Macdonald's objection to MW-III's treatment of it? Is he justified?

8. What is usually meant by "encyclopedic material" in a dictionary? Why does Macdonald object to its omission in MW-III? What are MW-III's reasons for omitting it? Considering the purposes of a dictionary, who do you think has the better argument?

Topics for Writing

1. Write an essay in which you discuss the purposes for which *you* need a dictionary, and describe a kind of dictionary which would be ideal for those purposes. Then dicuss existing dictionaries to see which ones, if any, meet these needs best.

2. Here are MW-II's, MW-III's, *American Heritage*'s, and *OED*'s entries for *disinterested* and *uninterested*. Write an essay in which you explore the history of the current confusion of these words and decide what you think a modern dictionary ought to say about them. Do you believe your own desk dictionary treats them soundly? How will what you have learned affect your own use of these words, if at all?

dis·in′ter·est·ed (-ĕs·tĕd; -ĭs·tĭd; 119; *cf.* INTERESTED), *adj.*
1. Lacking or revealing lack of interest; indifferent; uninterested. *Now Rare.*
2. Not influenced by regard to personal advantage; free from selfish motive; not biased or prejudiced; as, a *disinterested* decision or judge; *disinterested* sacrifices.
Syn. and **Ant.** — See FAIR.

un·in′ter·est·ed (ŭn·ĭn′tĕr·ĕs·tĕd; *see* INTERESTED), *adj.*
Not interested; as: a *Obs.* Impartial; disinterested. **b** Not having an interest, esp. a property interest (in something); not personally concerned. **c** Not having the mind or feelings engaged; inattentive; apathetic; indifferent; — now the usual sense. — **un·in′ter·est·ed·ly,** *adv.* — **-ed·ness,** *n.*

disinterested *adj* **1 :** lacking or revealing lack of interest **:** INDIFFERENT, UNINTERESTED, APATHETIC, UNCONCERNED **2 :** not influenced by regard to personal advantage **:** free from selfish motive **:** not biased or prejudiced ⟨a ~ decision⟩ ⟨~ sacrifices⟩ **syn** see INDIFFERENT

un·interested \"+\ *adj* [¹un- + *interested,* past part. of *interest*] **:** not interested: as **a :** having no interest and esp. no property interest in **:** not personally concerned **b :** not having the mind or feelings engaged **:** INATTENTIVE, APATHETIC **syn** see INDIFFERENT

dis·in·ter·est·ed (dĭs-ĭn′trĭ-stĭd, -ĭn′tə-rĕs′tĭd) *adj.* **1.** Free of bias and self-interest; impartial: *"The pupil is fully worthy of the praises bestowed by the disinterested instructor."* (Thackeray). **2.** *Nonstandard.* Uninterested; indifferent. See Usage note. —See Synonyms at **indifferent.** —**dis·in′ter·est·ed·ly** *adv.* —**dis·in′ter·est·ed·ness** *n.*
Usage: *Disinterested* differs from *uninterested* to the degree that lack of self-interest differs from lack of any interest. *Disinterested* is synonymous with *impartial, unbiased. Uninterested* has the sense of *indifferent, not interested.* According to 93 per cent of the Usage Panel, *disinterested* is not acceptable in the sense of *uninterested,* though it is often thus employed.

un·in·ter·est·ed (ŭn·ĭn′trĭs-tĭd, -ĭn′tə-rĕs′tĭd) *adj.* **1.** Without an interest; especially, not having a financial interest. **2.** Not paying attention; indifferent; unconcerned. See Usage note at **disinterested.**

Disi·nterested, *ppl. a.* [f. prec. vb + -ED [1]; or f. DIS- 10 + IN-TERESTED.]

† **1.** Without interest or concern; not interested, unconcerned. *? Obs.*

a 1612 DONNE βιαθανατος (1644) 99 Cases, wherein the party is dis-interested. **1684** *Contempl. State of Man* I. x. (1699) 113 How dis-interested are they in all Worldly matters, since they fling their Wealth and Riches into the Sea. **1767** *Junius Lett.* iii. 18 A careless disinterested spirit is no part of his character.

2. Not influenced by interest; impartial, unbiased, unprejudiced; now always, Unbiased by personal interest; free from self-seeking. (Of persons, or their dispositions, actions, etc.)

1659 O. WALKER *Oratory* 115 The soul. .sits now as the most disinterested Arbiter, and impartial judge of her own works, that she can be. **1705** STANHOPE *Paraphr.* III. 435 So should the Love to our Neighbour be. .Not mercenary and designing, but disinterested and hearty. **1726** *Adv. Capt. R. Boyle* 273 Any disinterested Person would make the same Judgement; your Passion has blinded yours. **1800** MRS. HERVEY *Mourtray Fam.* II. 82, I fairly own I was not disinterested in wishing you here. **1865** LIVINGSTONE *Zambesi* xxii. 446 His disinterested kindness to us. .can never be forgotten.

Uni·nterested, *ppl. a.* [UN-[1] 8.]

† **1.** Unbiassed, impartial. *Obs.*

a 1646 J. GREGORY *Posthumâ, Episc. Puerorum* (1649) 107 By this uninterested disguis the more to justifie the Celebrations. **1660** R. COKE *Power & Subj.* 49 Nor do I think that any uninterested casuist will deny [etc.].

† **2.** Free from motives of personal interest; disinterested. *Obs.*

1661 (*title*), A Relation of the business. .concerning Bedford Levell,. . by a person uninterested. **1704** N. N. tr. *Boccalini's Advts. fr. Parnass.* III. 191 What think you of uninterested Men, who value the Publick Good beyond their own private Interest? **1767** COWPER *Let.* Wks. 1837 XV. 17 You know me to be an uninterested person.

3. Unconcerned, indifferent.

1771 *Ann. Reg.* II. 253/1 He is no cold, uninterested, and uninteresting advocate for the cause he espouses. **1774** *Trinket* 54 In this amiable society can my heart be uninterested? **1823** BYRON *Juan* x. lxxiii, In the same quaint, Uninterested tone. **1850** THACKERAY *Pendennis* lvii, An almost silent but not uninterested spectator.

Hence **Uni·nterestedly** *adv.,* **-ness.**

1691 T. H[ALE] *Acc. New Invent.* 55 As to that Uninterestedness so pretended to by them. **1891** H. HERMAN *His Angel* 108 He looked upon the. . crowds. .uninterestedly.

3. Write a *précis* (look it up!) of Macdonald's review, stating as clearly as possible his objections to the editorial policies of MW-III, as well as his commendations.

4. Look at a copy of *The American Heritage Dictionary of the English Language* and examine its editorial front matter and a number of its entries to discover its editorial policies. How many of these seem to have been influenced by the kinds of criticism Macdonald levels at MW-III? Discuss your findings in an essay.

EVANS: BUT WHAT'S A DICTIONARY FOR?

Aids to Study

1. Evans says (p. 200), ". . . the trouble is due to the fact that . . ." Is this good standard English usage? What do the dictionaries say on this point?

2. "The broad general findings of the new science" are stated in full on pp. 192–93. Compare them closely with Mcdonald's views of language, stated and implicit.

3. Evans says that all usage is relative. Relative to *what?*

4. "Words in themselves are not dignified, or silly, or wise, or malicious. But they can be used in dignified, silly, wise, or malicious ways by dignified, silly, wise or malicious people" (p. 200). How sensible is this statement? Why?

Topics for Writing

1. If you were about to buy an unabridged dictionary and could buy either MW-II or MW-III, which one would you buy? Write an essay in which you discuss your decision, especially in the light of the reviews you have read.

2. Write an essay in which you distinguish between the ideal qualities of a desk dictionary and those of an unabridged dictionary. Study your desk dictionary carefully to see what compromises the editors have had to make in order to save space. Did they make the right ones?

3. Now, with the new insights and information you have about dictionaries and lexicography, try again to write on Topic number 3, p. 153, dealing with the Ohmann essay.

McDAVID, HISTORICAL, REGIONAL, AND SOCIAL VARIATION

Aids to Study

1. McDavid's essay is about dialect, and he describes several dimensions on which our language may vary and yet still be English. Find new examples from your experience of your own or others' speech for each of these dimensions: *medium, responsibility, maturity, vogue, association, relationship between speaker or writer and audience, history, region,* and *society.* Is the language which you use and encounter daily unguarded with respect to any of those dimensions?

2. What is the prestige regional dialect of the area where you live? Do you speak the prestige dialect of your home area? Of your campus area if there is a difference? Most campuses contain—both among faculty and students —a number of regional varieties of English. Which ones can you document for your own campus?

3. What specific kinds of social variation in language can you discern between the faculty members on your campus and the cooks, janitors, motor-pool employees, housemothers, and groundskeepers on your campus? List specific characteristics.

4. Why don't political boundaries in the United States have much bearing on variation in language?

5. McDavid says ". . . in such urban centers as Detroit, Cleveland and Chicago, the distance between uneducated speech and common speech is greater than that between common and cultivated" (p. 214). Why should this be so? What is there in the development of these cities which would make language varieties different from those in Charleston, South Carolina?

Topics for Writing

1. After reading McDavid's essay, how would you answer the person who observes, "I was always taught that it is wrong to speak a dialect." Or, how would you answer the person who remarks that he is grateful to his parents for rearing him in an atmosphere in which he could learn to speak the language "without dialect"? What do such comments really mean?

2. History, region, and society seem to have particular power over our language. How can the historical, regional, and social variations in his language affect the Southern black man's reception in a Northern city?

3. What are some of the regional differences in vocabulary you personally have noticed, either by meeting strangers in your own region or visiting some other region? How do you account for them? Can your dictionary help you? Illustrate and explain some of these differences in an essay.

4. McDavid lists a threefold classification for beginning "a working evaluation of social dialects" (p. 214). Which of these do you speak? How can you decide? Can you document your conclusion with evidence of morphological forms, vocabulary, pronunciations, and the like? Report your conclusions and your reasoning in an essay.

5. "Perhaps it is inevitable in an ostensibly open society that covert class markers become more significant as the overt ones disappear" (p. 215). Why? Explore this point in an essay.

MENCKEN: EUPHEMISMS

Aids to Study

1. Americans seem always to be embarrassed about toilets. Make lists of some of the euphemisms you've heard for a toilet and for the room in which it stands.

2. Euphemisms about sex often seem more suggestive than do matter-of-fact, explicit, scientific words. Look up this sense of *suggestive* to be sure you understand it, and then try to decide why the statement might be true.

3. What reasons can you find to explain all the various classes of euphemisms Mencken cites?
4. Is a euphemism a bad thing?
5. What process or processes of semantic change seem to be involved in the creation of euphemisms? Cite some examples to illustrate your conclusions.

Topics for Writing

1. Trades seem to want to be considered professions. Pick a trade not mentioned by Mencken and look for euphemisms in its names for itself and its activities. Write an essay in which you describe what you find.
2. *Druggist* and *pharmacist* have had interesting careers in English. Write an essay in which you reconstruct their histories from the *OED* entries below. Has euphemism had any bearing on their use?

> **Druggist** (drʊ·gist). Also 7 drouguist. [a. F. *droguiste* (1549 in Hatz.-Darm.), f. *drogue* drug: see -IST.] One who sells or deals in drugs.
> In Scotland and United States the usual name for a pharmaceutical chemist. *Chemist and druggist:* see CHEMIST 4.
> **1611** COTGR., *Drogueur,* a druggist, or drug-seller. **1639** J. W. tr. *Guibert's Physic.* I. 10 Two pennyworth of Sene..which they may have at the Apothecaries or drouguists. **1652** GAULE *Magastrom.* 360 Two chymists had agreed upon a cheat, that one of them should turn druggist, and sell strange roots and powders. **1709** ADDISON *Tatler* No. 131 ¶ 3 That this new Corporation of Druggists had inflamed the Bills of Mortality and puzzled the College of Physicians with Diseases, for which they neither knew a Name or Cure. **1799** *Med. Jrnl.* II. 123 Mr. Brown, Wholesale Chemist and Druggist. **1802** *Ibid.* VIII. 247 Compounding and vending medicines in the shop of a druggist or an apothecary.

> **Pharmacist** (fā·ɹmăsist). [f. PHARMACY + -IST: cf. *botanist.*] A person skilled or engaged in pharmacy; one who prepares or dispenses medicines; a druggist or pharmaceutical chemist.
> **1834** LYTTON *Pompeii* I. ii, Unskilful pharmacists! pleasure and study are not elements to be thus mixed together. **1875** H. C. WOOD *Therap.* (1879) 437 He used two samples of the alkaloid prepared by different pharmacists. **1898** *Rev. Brit. Pharm.* 29 The Pharmacopœia, generally a stickler in legality, speaks of 'pharmacists', which, strictly speaking, chemists and druggists are not.

3. Mencken himself makes vigorous use of the language: he speaks of "the advance of human taxidermy," and he describes morticians' "expectant hauling of the ill." Reread his discussion of *mortician* and the other euphemisms connected with that trade, and then write an essay in which you show how Mencken manages to make clear his amusement and disgust while appearing merely to present a factual discussion.
4. Advertising is obviously a good place to look for euphemisms. Analyze the ads for cigarettes, patent medicines, detergents, or some other group of products, and write an essay in which you discuss the euphemisms you find and try to explain the reasons for their existence.

PERRIN, THE FUTURE OF BOWDLERISM

Aids to Study

1. What are the arguments for and against the proposition that the aggressive use and advocacy of four-letter words is essentially like the promotion of "correct" English, that both are simply attempts to impose a particular life-style by linguistic means?
2. Our language often seems to be inherently treacherous, may suddenly sound suggestive ("Miss Smith, a well-endowed young woman, performed effectively under me last semester"). This lurking danger is of course exploited in comic writing and off-color jokes. What possible explanations are there for this state of affairs?
3. Right or wrong, the Bowlders of the world try to change things. Their aim is to improve life by limiting the language. What other attitudes toward the relation between language and morality are possible?

Topics for Writing

1. Write a paper on the desirability of "mystery and Opaqueness" in human behavior. Why is this worth preserving? Or *is* it worth preserving? (This might well be a paper on the nature of love and your experience of it.) Do you find that any desirable mystery surrounding love has been threatened by the current fashion of four-letter words and sexual explicitness?
2. This section of this book is called "Standards." Examine your desk dictionary to see how it handles some of the four-letter words. What sort of policy did the editors seem to have? Can you see any sign of the kinds of thing *bowdlerism* stands for? Check the unabridged dictionaries in the library too, and then write an essay on the current state of affairs.

JESPERSEN: SPELLING; HALL: OUR ENGLISH SPELLING SYSTEM

Aids to Study

1. Make a list of one- and two-syllable English words which use the letter *a* as a vowel, and then transcribe the words phonetically. How many different sounds do you find for the English letter *a*?
2. Now make a list of transcriptions of words which all have the stressed vowel /a/. Then spell these words conventionally. How many different spellings are there for the sound /a/?

3. Do the same thing for the sound /iy/. How many different ways does English spell /iy/?

4. Consult your desk dictionary for the origin of the word *ye* in phrases like *Ye Olde Tea Shoppe*. What other spelling curiosities are traceable to writing and printing?

5. George Bernard Shaw is usually credited with inventing this "logical" English spelling of a common word: *ghoti—gh* as in *rough, o* as in *women,* and *ti* as in *motion; ghoti:* a perfectly reasonable spelling of *fish*. See what similar horrors of English spelling you can invent, the sort that a foreigner trying to spell English phonetically might conceivably propose.

6. What reasons can you think of to explain why Americans put so much emphasis on correct spelling?

7. Find in literature some examples of *eye-dialect*. What, actually, does the writer do: vary the spelling to conform to standard English sounds, vary it to conform to substandard or geographical dialect sounds, or both?

8. Jespersen uses some IPA characters which Roberts does not employ in his system for transcribing English phonemes. What are Roberts's transcriptions for Jespersen's [dʒ], [ʃ] and [ʒ]?

9. List all the English alphabetical symbols for consonants—*letters,* not *phonemes*. After each one list all the possible *phonemic* values each can have in English, with an example of each. For example, *e* can be /e/ as in *met*, /iy/ as in *detour*, etc.

10. What are *spelling-pronunciations?* Find some more examples to add to those Jespersen gives.

11. What is a *shibboleth* (p. 238), and where did we get the word?

12. What is a *ptarmigan?* How *do* we pronounce it? Where did we get the spelling?

13. *Foisted* is a curious word. What is its history? Does it carry a usage label? Should it?

Topics for Writing

1. List twenty nouns ending in *y* in the singular. Then try to draw up a generalization which will explain how these words form their plurals.

2. Do the same thing for ten words whose singulars end in *-o*. You may need more than one generalization.

3. What does Professor Hall seem to think we ought to do about our spelling system? If you are a poor speller, are you comforted by his remarks? Write an essay in which you explore the problem.

4. In view of what Jespersen and Hall say about the oddities of English spellings, how do you think spelling should be taught—by rule, general-

ization, memorization of single words, mnemonic devices, or what? Write an essay in which you consider the problem and offer some reasonable solutions.

5. Transcribe the conversation between Philip and Carlys (p. 237) in phonemic symbols. Then write an essay in which you explain the misunderstanding. How do you treat Carlys's last speech in phonemic symbols?

WHITEHALL: THE SYSTEM OF PUNCTUATION

Aids to Study

1. Punctuate these utterances, following the suggestions Professor Whitehall makes:
   a. I've ordered books stationery and a new typewriter ribbon
   b. She turned and asked Do you want me to come with you or would you prefer to go alone
   c. Stop I cried and I was never more angry in my life or I'll
2. Punctuate the following passage:
   If I were you I told him I'd have nothing more to do with them Their remarks their appearance their very names the whole business seems if you'll take my advice too silly to fool with
3. Make a phonemic transcription of the passage in number 2 above, and then mark stress, pitch, and junctures. Now, what relationships do you see between intonation and punctuation?
4. What assistance does your desk dictionary afford you in problems of conventional punctuation?
5. What intonation curves—combinations of pitch, stress, and juncture—seem to fit with each of the groups of punctuation described on p. 241?
6. Whitehall says (p. 241) that dashes function as *symbolic conjunctions*. What does this mean?
7. *Heavy* punctuation means "a lot of it." Where does this meaning of heavy come from? Consult an historical dictionary and trace the development of that sense of the word *heavy*.
8. *Convention* and *conventional* turn up quite often in this essay. Check your dictionary for the several senses of each. What do you suppose has caused the pejorative overtones some senses have?

Topics for Writing

1. Write an essay in which you explain the relationship between intonation and punctuation as they affect the distinction between restrictive and nonrestrictive modifiers.

2. Your instructor will read the following passage to you. Punctuate it as you hear it read; then compare your punctuation with that of your classmates. Try to account for the difference. You all heard the same reading:

> among that large class of young persons whose reading is almost entirely confined to works of imagination the popularity of Byron was unbounded they bought pictures of him they treasured up the smallest relics of him they learned his poems by heart and did their best to write like him and to look like him many of them practised at the glass in the hope of catching the curl of the upper lip and the scowl of the brow which appear in some of his portraits a few discarded their neckcloths in imitation of their great leader for some years the Minerva press sent forth no novel without a mysterious unhappy Lara-like peer the number of hopeful undergraduates and medical students who became things of dark imaginings on whom the freshness of the heart ceased to fall like dew whose passions had consumed themselves to dust and to whom the relief of tears was denied passes all calculation this was not the worst there was created in the minds of many of these enthusiasts a pernicious and absurd association between intellectual power and moral depravity from the poetry of Lord Byron they drew a system of ethics compounded of misanthropy and voluptuousness a system in which the two great commandments were to hate your neighbour and to love your neighbour's wife

You may see how Lord Macaulay punctuated it by consulting his essay on Moore's *Life of Byron.*

WHITEHALL: WRITING AND SPEECH

Aids to Study

1. List some of the chief differences between writing and speech.
2. How does the British linguistic situation differ from the American? Consult your desk dictionary for its remarks on British pronunciation. What *is* Received Standard British English, and who speaks it?
3. What does Whitehall think *correctness* is?
4. "Education in the English language has become, for the most part, education in linguistic niceties. . . ." What are some of these?
5. In what aspects of the language do you discover the greatest difficulties when you change from speech to writing?
6. *Rhythmed* (p. 253) is a curious word. Does your desk dictionary suggest that *rhythm* regularly exhibits functional shift as verb or adjective? What

limitation, if any, would you place on its use in this form and function?

7. Whitehall speaks of "the code of speech" (p. 253). What is the difference between a *code* and a *cipher?*

8. What sense of *medium* is meant on p. 254? What is the plural of the word? Have you ever heard or seen another plural? How would you decide which one to use in a given speech or writing situation?

Topics for Writing

1. What must one do in a course in English composition, according to Professor Whitehall's last paragraph? How has your own school work in English composition tried to meet these needs? Write an essay in which you describe and evaluate your own work in English composition to date.

2. Write an essay in which you discuss and evaluate some of the arguments in favor of a standardized written American English.

3. Write an essay in which you discuss and illustrate some of the strengths and limitations of written English which Whitehall refers to on p. 000.

VEBLEN: THE HIGHER LEARNING

Aids to Study

1. How do "archaism and waste," the leisure class "standards of virtue," reflect themselves in linguistic practice?

2. *Elegant* has been a very modish word in English. What does it mean now, and how would you describe its overtones?

3. What has *honor* to do with *honorific?*

Topic for Writing

1. How do Veblen's views of English spelling fit with Jespersen's and Hall's? Discuss their views in an essay.

Language as Metaphor and Play

Experts have speculated—not very productively perhaps—about the origins of language. How did words get started in the first place? Some writers on the subject believe that language began in erotic experience, as love-murmurs, yelps of pleasure. In any event man's earliest word-sounds seem likely to have been uttered not to communicate some rational "thought," but more for the fun of it. In this section we are going to try to say something about the fun of language, a fun that survives, in our vastly more complicated styles, right alongside those uses of language that seriously order the chaos of life and make possible the business of the day.

" 'Men sang out their feelings long before they were able to speak their thoughts,' Susanne Langer, following Jespersen, says of language. 'Its beginnings are not natural adjustments, ways to means; they are purposeless lalling-instincts, primitive aesthetic reactions, and dream-like associations of ideas.' And if language has an infantile erotic base, it must be basically a playful activity. Observation of children shows that learning to speak is for them in itself play and then serves to enrich their life of play. And the analysis of language, not a particular language but language generally, reveals its essentially playful structure. In the words of Cassirer, 'Language is by its very nature and essence, metaphorical'; and every metaphor is a play upon words. Jespersen also concludes that 'language originated as play.' "

The essays in this part of the book consider language as play, with particular attention to metaphor as a type of "play upon words."

Our first selection considers a familiar metaphor for the act of writing—the metaphor of discovery or exploration which conceives of the writer as a kind of map-maker. Proposing another metaphor (the writer as pot-maker shaping an artifact on a potter's wheel), the author argues generally for a creative spirit of play in our uses of language. He appeals especially for play-acting or role-playing, particularly in the teaching of writing.

We turn then more specifically to metaphor as a form of linguistic play. Our second selection, "Bluspels and Flalansferes" by C. S. Lewis, argues for the fundamental importance of metaphor both in the historic development of language and in our present-day use. "When we create a new metaphor," he says, "our new understanding is bound up with the new metaphor." He reminds us furthermore that our whole language is filled with old metaphors, metaphors we have become unaware of. And so Lewis appeals to us to become conscious of the "fossillized metaphors" in our words, and to use new metaphors that we create for ourselves, to become comfortable and resourceful with fresh imaginative expression. "All our truth . . . is won by metaphor."

Our third selection is a famous and much reprinted essay by George Orwell, "Politics and the English Language." Among its other delights, it is most valuable for its discussion of metaphor. The distinctions Orwell spells out between fresh, dying, and dead metaphors, and the difficulties of making these distinctions in concrete cases, must become part of every serious student's experience of the language.

Our fourth selection, by a professor at the University of Washington, is a chapter from a new and engaging little book addressed to students and teachers, called simply *On Writing*. Mr. Sale's chapter title echoes Orwell's distinctions—"Metaphors: Live, Dead, and Silly"—and what he is trying to do is to say some things about metaphor-making that "might prove to be a positive help to someone struggling with his own style."

The fifth selection, also by a practicing college teacher, considers the game of student theme-writing more broadly. Here we are reminded of a less attractive side of the *play* idea—the notion of playing a game as a ritualized mechanical way of avoiding any personal belief or commitment. Every reader of this book knows the kind of superficial and hypocritical play-acting that goes into most freshman themes. As Mr. Coles puts it: "One more swing around the prickly pear."

But not just theme-writing! We know that many kinds of modern writing (think of advertising for instance) can develop into game-playing, where the writer seems to repudiate any responsibility for what he is saying. Many modern novels, the critic Wayne Booth has argued, are built around what he calls an "unreliable narrator," a fellow telling the

story who may be saying what he means, or he may be kidding the events
he describes, or he may be kidding himself. The way fiction-writing styles
have invaded the news-writing medium is the subject of our next selection, a chapter from a book on modern prose styles.

Obviously, there are problems about the appropriateness of play in
language, the precise way playfulness is expressed, the way it is interpreted by an audience. This last difficulty is described in our seventh
piece, by a social scientist discussing a serious and practical professional
undertaking, an investigation of some urban ethnic groups. The enormous question of "objectivity" in assessing complicated human beings
will never be solved, and any implication on the part of a reporter or
scientific investigator that he has "certainty" about what he is talking
about is misleading, if not downright immoral. The reader should be
reminded here of the comments on "map-making" and "pot-making" in
the first essay in this section. Even for the hard-headed social scientist
at work, all the problems of play and non-play arise. The author ruefully
points out, in what is surely an understatement, that "the day is not yet
here when the 'public' fully appreciates the playfulness of ideas or the
fun and excitement of knowledge."

Playfulness, kidding around with words, toying with "unreliability,"
seem to characterize recent behavior in many areas. Is it possible that by
maintaining a super-suspicion of everybody's language, including our
own, we find ourselves in a position where nobody dares to take anything seriously? That is a possibility described with some alarm in "The
Put-On," our next selection. Using examples from the current American
scene, Mr. Brackman shows that it is the omnipresence of empty and
windy public language in our culture that has helped to produce the
particular self-defeating phenomenon of the playful put-on.

But this is a recurrent linguistic situation. We are not the only civilization to suffer from windiness in high places. Our next writer tells us
about the overblown rhetoric of nineteenth-century Fourth of July oratory—and what humorists of the time did about it. It may be helpful
to consider that the hifalutin orators of the day were playing a kind of
mechanical, inhuman game in repeating the platitudes of patriotic excess, while their spoofers were playing another kind of game in exaggerating that language for ridicule. Yet the "subject" of both the oratory
and the spoofs is one no one argued about—love of country. In our own
day even this sentiment is seriously called into question, so that the word
"patriot" too has become one to be played with, capable of abusive connotation.

Our last essay returns to metaphor, to remind us that the great
poets have always known all these things. In a talk to college students

some forty years ago, Robert Frost suggested how central metaphor and play are to all of education and to thought itself. In his own playful style he shows us how to play with metaphor, how to watch it working and not working, breaking down before our eyes, as all metaphors must eventually.

WALKER GIBSON

Play and the Teaching of Writing

A familiar metaphor we use when speaking of the act of writing is the metaphor of exploration and discovery, the writer as map-maker. In this view the writer "explores" the environment, he charts it, and his success can be measured by his degree of accuracy in reflecting the actual landscape. Our word "exposition" similarly suggests this act of observing and recording: the writer "exposes" to a reader's view the lineaments of the world.

Obviously this way of looking at composing has been useful, both to writers and to teachers of writing. No doubt it is a necessary way of thinking about their work. Feeling its force, one may say to a writer, "The world simply isn't the way you've described it here. You've made a bad map, you're inaccurate." Everything we criticize in the names of "precision," "exactness," and other such virtues, we do in response to an image of the writer as an explorer and mapper of a universe spread out before him for examination.

Like all metaphors, this one breaks down eventually—perhaps it breaks down pretty soon. Still, much writing can be called similar to map-making, and we should not deny the importance of "precision" in many situations. A good map will tell what turn to take to get onto the thruway; it will show the air route to Rome. These things are testable. Much writing provides similar information of a sort one can act upon and then measure the consequences. Without apology we can cite recipes for cooking. If I carry out the indicated operations, a delicious soufflé will be the result—and the test of the recipe, as well as my skill as a reader and cook, will lie in the quality of the end product. Perhaps

Portions of this essay are reprinted with revisions from "The Play of Rhetoric," *CEE Newsletter,* February 1968, and from "Composing the World: The Writer as Map-Maker," *College Composition and Communication,* October 1970, by permission of the National Council of Teachers of English.

281

we give short shrift to how-to-do-it literature. Accurate directions, painstaking descriptions, careful reports of observations—like good maps—are exceedingly useful and necessary genres of writing that require skill and training. They are not all that writing can do, but we ignore them at our peril.

Nevertheless, the metaphor of the map does break down, and I should like to illustrate its difficulties through an analogy with science. Some fifteen years ago, in *Modern Science and Modern Man*, James B. Conant discussed what he regarded as a fundamental misconception on the part of eighteenth- and nineteenth-century scientists. These investigators, Conant says, "imagined themselves as the equivalent of the early explorers and map-makers. . . . The explorers of the fifteenth and sixteenth centuries had opened up new worlds with the aid of imperfect maps. . . . By the seventeenth century, methods of measuring space and time had laid the foundations for an accurate geography. . . . Therefore, by a series of successive approximations, so to speak, maps and descriptions of distant lands were becoming closer and closer to accurate accounts of reality. Why would not the labors of those who worked in laboratories have the same outcome? . . . Given time and patience, it was assumed the truth would be ascertained. By the same token there must be a truth about the nature of heat, light, and matter."

As we all know, whatever the depths of our scientific illiteracy, "the nature of" things like heat, light, and matter has become in our time ambiguous and fluctuating. Conant concludes that "in view of the revolution in physics, anyone who now asserts that science is an exploration of the universe must be prepared to shoulder a heavy burden of proof. To my mind, the analogy between the map-maker and the scientist is false. A scientific theory is not even the first approximation to a map; it is not a creed; it is a policy—an economical and fruitful guide to action by scientific investigators."

Following Conant's hint, we might be alert, in our daily lives with language, to situations in which a map-maker's view of experience is implied, but in which no accurate map is ever delivered. "Let me make one thing crystal clear." When the President says that, any teenage critic can point to his dead metaphor, but its implications concern us here. When you offer to make something "crystal clear," you are suggesting a pretty close relationship between the complexity of experience on the one hand and your expression of that complexity on the other. You imply that your words are truly telling it like it is. When to all this is added Mr. Nixon's air of sincere solemnity, it's no wonder the young are sometimes turned off.

Mr. Nixon's second-in-command has made some good media copy

lately by slashing at the media. The expected cries of censorship and gestapo tactics were raised, and TV network presidents remonstrated by saying, in effect, No, no, we *are* objective! But of course nobody is objective. A half-hour evening news show represents a series of human, personal, fallible decisions about the relative significance of a thousand competing "stories." Mr. Cronkite every night concludes by intoning, "And that's the way it is, on Monday, January 19, 1970," and one can try to see, in his avuncular half-smile as he performs this little ritual, his own amused disbelief in what he says. As if you could put "the way it is" on a TV screen in a half-hour—or a half-century! But a great many people more naïve than Mr. Cronkite must be viewing the evening news as a map of the day.

An issue of *Newsweek* devoted to "fairness" of the media asked in a cover headline, "Does TV Tell It Straight?" The metaphor of straight and slanted news is worth pursuing briefly. When you call a statement "slanted," you suggest that you know what the straight-up-and-down word—or world—is. It might be better if we simply agreed that most information is slanted, certainly including whatever the reader of this article may be taking in at this moment. The problem is to recognize conflicting slants and live as comfortably as possible without maps. We can compare, and we should, the networks' news of the day against the newspapers' and the White House's handouts, but of course no such comparison will ever lead to any certain interpretation of the True Significance of What Really Happened.

It may be that people generally are beginning to realize the inevitable slanting of the information they receive. And they may be ready now for some new language precisely because the old language has rarely been so discredited. Have public voices ever spoken with less effect—have they ever been greeted with such suspicion? This loss of trust, this "credibility gap," is customarily pointed to with alarm, but I am not taking that line. Popular recognition of a credibility gap is a fine and healthy development; too bad it didn't happen centuries ago. What people may be doing when they withhold belief is recognizing that the metaphor of the map is a misleading metaphor. There is no atlas for experience, for the complexity of our time, for the future. Consider the alterations of attitude this recognition requires. It is natural to the human condition to assume, to need to believe, that *somewhere somebody knows,* knows the score, knows the ropes. Observe these metaphors drawn from games and from nautical exploration. What happens when people begin to realize that nobody knows, there are no ropes, there is no score, and that such map-like metaphors are untrue to the way things are? Our first response to that awareness has to be sheer terror. Does that mean that down there in Washington there's nobody who really knows what the situation is and what ought to be done? That possibility must be occurring to more and more people in recent months, as our public figures put their feet in their mouths with such sensational regularity. But my point is not that our public figures are so especially clumsy, or that they are always deliberate liars. The point is that our public figures, in the enormous and growing complexity of their situations, cannot be held accountable as map-makers. Their crime lies in their willingness to be taken as map-makers when they ought to know better. Of course there is a credibility gap. There should have been one centuries ago.

If the metaphor of exploration breaks down, as I conclude it does, what better image for the act of composing might one suggest? Here is one for you to try. It is the famous metaphor of the potter at his wheel, handling with tentative fingers a shapeless glob of clay. Something is going to emerge, but who knows what? The success of the finished pot will not be measured in terms of accuracy—what's an accurate pot? Instead, success has to be related to a larger and changing context in which questions are asked about responses of audiences, usefulness and beauty, effects on people's actions.

Or, in E. M. Forster's famous question, "How do I know what I mean till I see what I say?"

If we try to think of composing as pot-making rather than as map-making, then there are immediate practical consequences for writing and speaking, for reading and listening. Certain qualities of style receive new value, such as modesty and good humor, irony, variety and inventiveness, a concern for immediate and concrete experience, an awareness that the writer-speaker is forming a man-made structure, not copying down the solid shorelines of the universe, and above all a sense of play.

Suppose we consider further the last of these virtues. The writer conscious of making a pot rather than a map is a writer who has some sense of play—he manipulates his medium and takes pleasure in words. To change the metaphor again (a pool-hall image this time): he is ready to *put some English on his English,* so that words bounce around a little in unexpected ways. Furthermore, he is an actor, a play-actor. Among the many meanings of play, of course, is that of language as drama; the play's the thing. That notion is especially useful in the teaching of writing. If it is possible for English teachers to agree on a single concept, whirling through a K-to-graduate-school spiral, my candidate for that ambitious gyre is this simple notion: language as drama, as play-acting. There is nothing new in this; acting it out, role-playing, have been pedagogical tricks for centuries. But we have tended in the past to think of classroom drama almost on a show-and-tell level, confined to the youngest grades. What may be relatively new is our recognition of dramatic play as important to all teaching at any level. When we can recognize that choices of language are dictated not alone by subject matter, and not alone by audience, but involve as well a self-creating act, the taking on of a role with a personality, an attitude, an identity—for some, at any rate, that perception offers a part way out of the woods. Thus a central activity of the composition teacher becomes the encouraging of students to take on various roles in their writing, through exercises that may simply force upon them, however crudely, various rhetorical characters.

Such an emphasis on dramatic play in language received some prestigious support not long ago from the deliberations of the Anglo-American Conference at Dartmouth in the summer of 1966. John Dixon's little book on the conference, *Growth Through English,* makes plain a concentration on drama and play-acting. "By assuming a role—taking on a stance, setting up a model—a child is trying out a version of himself and his possibilities without committing himself permanently, and as in story-telling or poem-making is both choosing and laying the basis for future choices of personality and values." Older pupils "learn to change and reverse roles, to see the situation from many perspectives, and—in the work of writing scripts—to use the many voices of the 'characters' to build within themselves an image of the complexity of the world as they know it." That this stress on the created character in language can apply at the highest levels of education, and to the professional writer himself, is illustrated by a remark made at Dartmouth by Benjamin De Mott: "Your good writer is your wide and various man: a character nicely conscious of the elements of personhood excluded by this or that act of writing and ever in a half-rage to allude to them: to hint at characterological riches even where these can't be spent." Awareness of role-playing thus becomes an attribute of style, at a pretty sophisticated stage; the *stylish* writer, from this point of view, is one who somehow expresses to us his recognition that his choice of role was after all somewhat arbitrary, and that he feels the sensitive man's polite and rueful regret that he can't be more than one person at the same time. I should like to suppose that this is part of the meaning in Thoreau's statement about being "beside ourselves in a sane sense." "However intense my experience, I am conscious of the presence of a part of me, which, as it were, is not a part of me, but a spectator, sharing no experience, but taking note of it, and that is no more I than it is you."

Most of us are not Thoreaus, but I hope we are not reluctant to involve his kind of mind, his kind of playful double talk, when we are engaged with our own seemingly mundane language. My point is that they are not all that remote from one another—that from the second-grader assuming a role and taking a stance to the word play of H. D. Thoreau is a direct line, a line to which we can give the name, dramatic play through language.

The warning not to take our words *too* seriously, especially in the inflexible forms of the written language, is not a new warning. Let us call Socrates briefly to the stand.

> If anyone ever wrote a document and imagines it has in it certainty to a high degree, then it is a disgrace to the writer, whether anybody says it is or not. . . . But take the man who judges that in the written word, no matter what subject, there is necessarily much for play . . . that man, perchance, my Phaedrus, is such a one as you and I would pray we both of us might become.

A more recent sage, Marshall McLuhan, has something to say about play too:

> The cultural strategy that is desperately needed is humor and play. It is play that cools off the hot situations of actual life by miming them.

And Johan Huizinga, in a book about play in contemporary civilization called *Homo Ludens,* quotes Plato in the *Laws* as follows:

> What then is the right way of living? Life must be lived as play, playing certain games, making sacrifices, singing and dancing, and then a man will be able to propitiate the gods, and defend himself against his enemies, and win in the contest.

To all this talk of miming, role-playing, play-acting, there is an objection that should be troubling you. Am I not encouraging insincerity, cynicism, a sophistical approach to communication and to life? Am I not recommending the superficial styles of the mere entertainer, at the expense of Solid Substance? Let me put it this way—aware, as I put it, of the sophistical character of my own argument. Inherent in our very language, in the way we state the case, is an interplay of play-acting with solemn reality. The word *act* carries with it implications of stagecraft along with its references to our most serious behavior in a serious world. We recall that *person, personality* derive from the word for mask. Other familiar words contain the same built-in ambiguity. Our performance with our local theater group is not the same as our performance as writer, citizen, or parent. Yet it cannot be altogether without significance that the same word does for all these actings-out. Susan Sontag has recently written that "the mask is the face"; to that we should add, of course, that the face is a mask. To say this is not to be cynical; on the contrary it suggests that we have control over our identities, and great responsibility for them—in anguish, possibly, but not without choice.

There is nothing cynical in our recognizing that to do our work we must perform it, to be somebody we must act as somebody. Such recognition implies an attention to the techniques of performance and act; it implies we *can* stand "beside ourselves" to criticize or improve our performances. The sociologist Erving Goffman has attempted to explain much of human interaction through metaphors of the theatre; I find his call for self-consciousness of one's performance useful to the writer. There are many people, he says, "who sincerely believe that the definition of the situation they habitually project is the real reality." But such people may be handicapped in the dramatic and shifting interplay that makes up communication, for a "rigid incapacity to depart from one's inward view of reality may at times endanger one's own performance." In talk like that there is a terrible risk—the risk of seeming to say that anything goes, just so it's a convincing performance. But if we are going to be attentive to acts of performance, as surely writers have to be, then this risk has to be taken. What one says to students of writing, then, comes down to something like this: here are some choices of self-expression; adopt one tentatively, always aware that it's an expression and not a self, and recognize your opportunity and your responsibility for choosing and changing in the light of your argument, your audience, your developing definition of your own identity and values.

C. S. LEWIS

Bluspels and Flalansferes

Philologists often tell us that our language is full of dead metaphors. In this sentence, the word "dead" and the word "metaphors" may turn out to be ambiguous; but the fact, or group of facts, referred to, is one about which there is no great disagreement. We all know in a rough and ready way, and all admit, these things which are being called "dead metaphors," and for the moment I do not propose to debate the propriety of the name. But while their existence is not disputed, their nature, and their relation to thought, gives rise to a great deal of controversy. For the benefit of any who happen to have avoided this controversy hitherto, I had better make plain what it is, by a concrete example. Bréal in his *Semantics* often spoke in metaphorical, that is consciously, rhetorically, metaphorical language, of language itself. Messrs. Ogden and Richards in *The Meaning of Meaning* took Bréal to task on the ground that "it is impossible thus to handle a scientific subject in metaphorical terms." Barfield in his *Poetic Diction* retorted that Ogden and Richards were, as a matter of fact, just as metaphorical as Bréal. They had forgotten, he complained, that all language has a figurative origin and that the "scientific" terms on which they piqued themselves—words like *organism, stimulus, reference*—were not miraculously exempt. On the contrary, he maintained, "these authors who professed to eschew figurative expressions were really confining themselves to one very old kind of figure; they were rigid under the spell of those verbal ghosts of the physical sciences which to-day make up practically the whole meaning-system of so many European minds." [1] Whether Ogden and Richards will see fit, or have seen fit, to reply to this, I do not know; but the lines on which any reply would run are already traditional. In fact the whole debate may be represented by a very simple dialogue.

From *Rehabilitations and Other Essays,* London: Oxford University Press, 1939. Copyright 1939 by C. S. Lewis. Reprinted by permission of Curtis, Brown, Ltd.

A. You are being metaphorical.

B. You are just as metaphorical as I am, but you don't know it.

A. No, I'm not. Of course I know all about *attending* once having meant *stretching,* and the rest of it. But that is not what it means now. It may have been a metaphor to Adam—but I am not using it metaphorically. What I *mean* is a pure concept with no metaphor about it at all. The fact that it *was* a metaphor is no more relevant than the fact that my pen is made of wood. You are simply confusing derivation with meaning.

There is clearly a great deal to be said for both sides. On the one hand it seems odd to suppose that what we *mean* is conditioned by a dead metaphor of which we may be quite ignorant. On the other hand, we see from day to day, that when a man uses a current and admitted metaphor without knowing it, he usually gets led into nonsense; and when, we are tempted to ask, does a metaphor become so old that we can ignore it with impunity? It seems harsh to rule that a man must know the whole semantic history of every word he uses—a history usually undiscoverable—or else talk without thinking. And yet, on the other hand, an obstinate suspicion creeps in that we cannot entirely jump off our own shadows, and that we deceive ourselves if we suppose that a new and purely conceptual notion of *attention* has replaced and superseded the old metaphor of stretching. Here, then, is the problem which I want to consider. How far, if at all, is thinking limited by these dead metaphors? Is Anatole France in any sense right when he reduces "The soul possesses God" to "the breath sits on the bright sky"? Or is the other party right when it urges "Derivations are one thing. Meanings are another"? Or is the truth somewhere between them?

The first and easiest case to study is that in which we ourselves invent a new metaphor. This may happen in one of two ways. It may be that when we are trying to express clearly to ourselves or to others a conception which we have never perfectly understood, a new metaphor simply starts forth, under the pressure of composition or argument. When this happens, the result is often as surprising and illuminating to us as to our audience; and I am inclined to think that this is what happens with the great, new metaphors of the poets. And when it does happen, it is plain that our new understanding is bound up with the new metaphor. In fact, the situation is for our purpose indistinguishable from that which arises when we hear a new metaphor from others; and for that reason, it need not be separately discussed. One of the ways, then, in which we invent a new metaphor, is by *finding* it, as unexpectedly as we might find it in the pages of a book; and whatever is true of the new metaphors that we find in books will also be true of those which we reach by a kind of lucky chance, or inspiration. But, of course, there is another way in which we invent new metaphors. When we are trying to explain, to some one younger or less instructed than ourselves, a matter which is already perfectly clear in our own minds, we may deliberately, and even painfully, pitch about for the metaphor that is likely to help him. Now when this happens, it is quite plain that our thought, our power of meaning, is not much helped or hindered by the metaphor that we use. On the contrary, we are often acutely aware of the discrepancy between our meaning and our image. We know that our metaphor is in some respects misleading; and probably, if we have acquired the tutorial shuffle, we warn our audience that it is "not to be pressed." It is apparently possible, in this case at least, to use metaphor and yet to keep our thinking independent of it. But we must observe that it is possible, only because we have other methods of expressing the same idea. We have already our own way of expressing the thing: we could say it, or we suppose that we could say it, literally instead. This clear conception we owe to other sources—to our previous studies. We can adopt the new metaphor as a temporary tool which we dominate and by which we are not dominated ourselves, only because we have other tools in our box.

Let us now take the opposite situation—that in which it is we ourselves who are being instructed. I am no mathematician; and some one is trying to explain to me the theory that space is finite. Stated thus, the new doctrine is, to me, meaningless. But suppose he proceeds as follows.

"You," he may say, "can intuit only three dimensions; you therefore cannot conceive how space should be limited. But I think I can show you how that which must appear infinite in three dimensions, might nevertheless be finite in four. Look at it this way. Imagine a race of people who knew only two dimensions—like the Flatlanders. And suppose they were living on a globe. They would have no conception, of course, that the globe was curved—for it is curved round in that third dimension of which they have no inkling. They will therefore imagine that they are living on a plane; but they will soon find out that it is a plane which nowhere comes to an end; there are no edges to it. Nor would they be able even to imagine an edge. For an edge would mean that, after a certain point, there would be nothing to walk on; nothing below their feet. But that *below* and *above* dimension is just what their minds have not got; they have only backwards and forwards, and left and right. They would thus be forced to assert that their globe, which they could not see as a globe, was infinite. You can see perfectly well that it is finite. And now, can you not conceive that as these Flatlanders are to you, so you might be to a creature that intuited four dimensions? Can you not conceive how that which seems necessarily infinite to your three-dimensional consciousness might none the less be really finite?" The result of such a metaphor on my mind would be—in fact, has been—that something which before was sheerly meaningless acquires at least a faint hint of meaning. And if the particular example does not appeal to every one, yet every one has had experiences of the same sort. For all of us there are things which we cannot fully understand at all, but of which we can get a faint inkling by means of metaphor. And in such cases the relation between the thought and the metaphor is precisely the opposite of the relation which arises when it is we ourselves who understand and then invent the metaphors to help others. We are here entirely at the mercy of the metaphor. If our instructor has chosen it badly, we shall be thinking nonsense. If we have not got the imagery clearly before us, we shall be thinking nonsense. If we have it before us without knowing that it is metaphor—if we forget that our Flatlanders on their globe are a copy of the thing and mistake them for the thing itself—then again we shall be thinking nonsense. What truth we can attain in such a situation depends rigidly on three conditions. First, that the imagery should be originally well chosen; secondly, that we should apprehend the exact imagery; and thirdly that we should know that the metaphor is a metaphor. (That metaphors, misread as statements of fact, are the source of monstrous errors, need hardly be pointed out.)

I have now attempted to show two different kinds of metaphorical situation as they are at their birth. They are the two extremes, and furnish the limits within which our inquiry must work. On the one hand, there is the metaphor which we invent to teach by; on the other, the metaphor from which we learn. They might be called the Master's metaphor, and the Pupil's metaphor. The first is freely chosen; it is one among many possible modes of expression; it does not at all hinder, and only very slightly helps, the thought of its maker. The second is not chosen at all; it is the unique expression of a meaning that we cannot have on any other terms; it dominates completely the thought of the recipient; his truth cannot rise above the truth of the original metaphor. And between the Master's metaphor and the Pupil's there comes, of course, an endless number of types, dotted about in every kind of intermediate position. Indeed, these Pupil-Teachers' metaphors are the ordinary stuff of our conversation. To divide them into a series of classes and sub-classes and to attempt to discuss these separately would be very laborious, and, I trust, unnecessary. If we can find a true doctrine about the two extremes, we shall not be at a loss to give an account of what falls between them. To find the truth about any given metaphorical situation will merely be to plot its position. In so far as it inclines to the "magistral" extreme, so far our thought will be independent of it; in

so far as it has a "pupillary" element, so far it will be the unique expression, and therefore the iron limit of our thinking. To fill in this
framework would be, as Aristotle used to say, "anybody's business."

Our problem, it will be remembered, was the problem of "dead" or
"forgotten" metaphors. We have now gained some light on the relation
between thought and metaphor as it is at the outset, when the metaphor
is first made; and we have seen that this relation varies greatly according to what I have called the "metaphorical situation." There is, in fact,
one relation in the case of the Master's metaphor, and an almost opposite relation in that of the Pupil's metaphor. The next step must clearly
be to see what becomes of these two relations as the metaphors in question progress to the state of death or fossilization.

The question of the Master's Metaphor need not detain us long. I
may attempt to explain the Kantian philosophy to a pupil by the following metaphor. "Kant answered the question 'How do I know that
whatever comes round the corner will be blue?' by the supposition 'I am
wearing blue spectacles.' " In time I may come to use "the blue spectacles" as a kind of shorthand for the whole Kantian machinery of the
categories and forms of perception. And let us suppose, for the sake of
analogy with the real history of language, that I continue to use this expression long after I have forgotten the metaphor which originally gave
rise to it. And perhaps by this time the form of the word will have
changed. Instead of the "blue spectacles" I may now talk of the *bloospel*
or even the *bluspel*. If I live long enough to reach my dotage I may even
enter on a philological period in which I attempt to find the derivation
of this mysterious word. I may suppose that the second element is derived from the word *spell* and look back with interest on the supposed
period when Kant appeared to me to be magical; or else, arguing that
the whole word is clearly formed on the analogy of *gospel,* may indulge
in unhistorical reminiscences of the days when the *Critique* seemed to
me irrefragably true. But how far, if at all, will my thinking about Kant
be affected by all this linguistic process? In practice, no doubt, there will
be some subtle influence; the mere continued use of the word *bluspel*
may have led me to attribute to it a unity and substantiality which I
should have hesitated to attribute to "the whole Kantian machinery of
the categories and forms of perception." But that is a result rather of
the noun-making than of the death of the metaphor. It is an interesting
fact, but hardly relevant to our present inquiry. For the rest, the mere
forgetting of the metaphor does not seem to alter my thinking about
Kant, just as the original mtaphor did not limit my thinking about
Kant; provided always—and this is of the last importance—that it
was, to begin with, a genuine Master's metaphor. I had my conception

of Kant's philosophy before I ever thought of the blue spectacles. If I have continued philosophical studies I have it still. The "blue spectacles" phrase was from the first a temporary dress assumed by my thought for a special purpose, and ready to be laid aside at my pleasure; it did not penetrate the thinking itself, and its subsequent history is irrelevant. To any one who attempts to refute my later views on Kant by telling me that I don't know the real meaning of *bluspel*, I may confidently retort "Derivations aren't meanings." To be sure, if there was any *pupillary* element in its original use, if I received, as well as gave, new understanding when I used it, then the whole situation will be different. And it is fair to admit that in practice very few metaphors can be purely magistral; only that which to some degree enlightens ourselves is likely to enlighten others. It is hardly possible that when I first used the metaphor of the blue spectacles I did not gain some new awareness of the Kantian philosophy; and, so far, it was not purely magistral. But I am deliberately idealizing for the sake of clarity. Purely magistral metaphor may never occur. What is important for us is to grasp that *just in so far* as any metaphor began by being magistral, so far I can continue to use it long after I have forgotten its metaphorical nature, and my thinking will be neither helped nor hindered by the fact that it was originally a metaphor, nor yet by my forgetfulness of that fact. It is a mere accident. Here, derivations are irrelevant to meanings.

Let us now turn to the opposite situation, that of the Pupil's Metaphor. And let us continue to use our old example of the unmathematical man who has had the finitude of space suggested to him (we can hardly say "explained") by the metaphor of the Flatlanders on their sphere. The question here is rather more complicated. In the case of the Master's metaphor, by hypothesis, the master knew, and would continue to know, what he meant, independently of the metaphor. In the present instance, however, the fossilization of the metaphor may take place in two different ways. The pupil may himself become a mathematician, or he may remain as ignorant of mathematics as he was before; and in either case, he may continue to use the metaphor of the Flatlanders while forgetting its real content and its metaphorical nature.

I will take the second possibility first. From the imagery of the Flatlanders' sphere I have got my first inkling of the new meaning. My thought is entirely conditioned by this imagery. I do not apprehend the thing at all, except by seeing "it could be something like this." Let us suppose that in my anxiety to docket this new experience, I label the inkling or vague notion, "the Flatlanders' sphere." When I next hear the fourth dimension spoken of, I shall say, "Ah yes—the Flatlanders' sphere and all that." In a few years (to continue our artificial parallel)

I may be talking glibly of the *Flalansfere* and may even have forgotten the whole of the imagery which this word once represented. And I am still, according to the hypothesis, profoundly ignorant of mathematics. My situation will then surely be most ridiculous. The meaning of *Flalansfere* I never knew except through the imagery. I could get beyond the imagery, to that whereof the imagery was a copy, only by learning mathematics; but this I have neglected to do. Yet I have lost the imagery. Nothing remains, then, but the conclusion that the word *Flalansfere* is now really meaningless. My thinking, which could never get beyond the imagery, at once its boundary and its support, has now lost that support. I mean strictly nothing when I speak of the *Flalansfere*. I am only talking, not thinking, when I use the word. But this fact will be long concealed from me, because *Flalansfere,* being a noun, can be endlessly fitted into various contexts, so as to conform to syntactical usage and to give an appearance of meaning. It will even conform to the logical rules; and I can make many judgements about the *Flalansfere;* such as *it is what it is,* and has *attributes* (for otherwise of course it wouldn't be a thing, and if it wasn't a thing, how could I be talking about it?), and is a *substance* (for it can be the subject of a sentence). And what *affective* overtones the word may have taken on by that time, it is dangerous to predict. It had an air of mystery from the first: before the end I shall probably be building temples to it, and exhorting my countrymen to fight and die for the *Flalansfere*. But the *Flalansfere,* when once we have forgotten the metaphor, is only a noise.

But how if I proceed, after once having grasped the metaphor of the Flatlanders, to become a mathematician? In this case, too, I may well continue to use the metaphor, and may corrupt it in form till it becomes a single noun, the *Flalansfere*. But I shall have advanced, by other means, from the original symbolism; and I shall be able to study the thing symbolized without reference to the metaphor that first introduced me to it. It will then be no harm though I should forget that *Flalansfere* had ever been metaphorical. As the metaphor, even if it survived, would no longer limit my thoughts, so its fossilization cannot confuse them.

The results which emerge may now be summarized as follows. Our thought is independent of the metaphors we employ, in so far as these metaphors are optional: that is, in so far as we are able to have the same idea without them. For that is the real characteristic both of the magistral metaphors and of those which become optional, as the Flatlanders would become, if the pupil learned mathematics. On the other hand, where the metaphor is our only method of reaching a given idea at all, there our thinking is limited by the metaphor so long as we retain the metaphor; and when the metaphor becomes fossilized, our "thinking'" is not thinking at all, but mere sound or mere incipient movements in the larynx. We are now in a position to reply to the statement that "Derivations are not meanings," and to the claim that "we know what we mean by words without knowing the fossilized metaphors they contain." We can see that such a statement, as it stands, is neither wholly true nor wholly false. The truth will vary from word to word, and from speaker to speaker. No rule of thumb is possible, we must take every case on its merits. A word can bear a meaning in the mouth of a speaker who has forgotten its hidden metaphor, and a meaning independent of that metaphor, but only on certain conditions. Either the metaphor must have been optional from the beginning, and have remained optional through all the generations of its use, so that the conception has always used and still uses the imagery as a mere tool; or else, at some period subsequent to its creation, we must have gone on to acquire, independently of the metaphor, such new knowledge of the object indicated by it as enables us now, at least, to dispense with it. To put the same thing in another way, meaning is independent of derivation, only if the metaphor was originally "magistral"; or if, in the case of an originally pupillary metaphor, some quite new kind of apprehension has arisen to replace the metaphorical apprehension which has been lost. The two conditions may be best illustrated by a concrete example. Let us take the word for *soul* as it exists in the Romance language. How far is a man entitled to say that what he means by the word *âme* or *anima* is quite independent of the image of *breathing,* and that he means just the same (and just as much) whether he happens to know that "derivation" or not? We can only answer that it depends on a variety of things. I will enumerate all the formal possibilities for the sake of clearness: one of them, of course, is too grotesque to appear for any other purpose.

1. The metaphor may originally have been magistral. Primitive men, we are to suppose, were clearly aware, on the one hand, of an entity called *soul;* and, on the other, of a process or object called *breath.* And they used the second figuratively to suggest the first—presumably when revealing their wisdom to primitive women and primitive children. And we may suppose, further, that this magistral relation to the metaphor has never been lost: that all generations, from the probably arboreal to the man saying "Blast your soul" in a publ this evening, have kept clearly before them these two separate entities, and used the one metaphorically to denote the other, while at the same time being well able to conceive the soul unmetaphorically, and using the metaphor merely as a colour or trope which adorned but did not influence their thought. Now if all this were true, it would unquestionably follow that

when a man says *anima* his meaning is not affected by the old image of breath; and also, it does not matter in the least whether he knows that the word once suggested that image or not. But of course all this is not true.

2. The metaphor may originally have been pupillary. So far from being a voluntary ornament or paedagogic device, the ideas of *breath* or *something like breath* may have been the only possible inkling that our parents could gain of the soul. But if this was so, how does the modern user of the word stand? Clearly, if he has ceased to be aware of the metaphorical element in *anima,* without replacing the metaphorical apprehension by some new knowledge of the soul, borrowed from other sources, then he will mean nothing by it; we must not, on that account, suppose that he will cease to use it, or even to use it (as we say) intelligibly—i.e. to use it in sentences constructed according to the laws of grammar, and to insert these sentences into those conversational and literary contexts where usage demands their insertion. If, on the other hand, he has some independent knowledge of the entity which our ancestors indicated by their metaphor of breath, then indeed he may mean something.

I take it that it is this last situation in which we commonly suppose ourselves to be. It doesn't matter, we would claim, what the majestic root GNA really stood for: we have learned a great deal about *knowing* since those days, and it is these more recent acquisitions that we use in our thinking. The first name for a thing may easily be determined by some inconsiderable accident. As we learn more, we mean more; the radical meaning of the old syllables does not bind us; what we have learned since has set us free. Assuredly, the accident which led the Romans to call all Hellenes *Graeci* did not continue to limit their power of apprehending Greece. And as long as we are dealing with sensible objects this view is hardly to be disputed. The difficulty begins with objects of thought. It may be stated as follows.

Our claim to independence of the metaphor is, as we have seen, a claim to know the object otherwise than through that metaphor. If we can throw the Flatlanders overboard and still think the fourth dimension, then, and not otherwise, we can forget what *Flalansfere* once meant and still think coherently. That was what happened, you will remember, to the man who went on and learned mathematics. He came to apprehend that of which the Flatlanders' sphere was only the image, and consequently was free to think beyond the metaphor and to forget the metaphor altogether. In our previous account of him, however, we carefully omitted to draw attention to one very remarkable fact: namely, that when he deserted metaphor for mathematics, he did not really pass from symbol to symbolized, but only from one set of symbols to another. The equations and what-nots are as unreal, as metaphorical, if you like, as the Flatlanders' sphere. The mathematical problem I need not pursue further; we see at once that it casts a disquieting light on our linguistic problem. We have hitherto been speaking as if we had two methods of thought open to us: the metaphorical, and the literal. We talked as if the creator of a magistral metaphor had it always in his power to think the same concept *literally* if he chose. We talked as if the present-day user of the word *anima* could prove his right to neglect that word's buried metaphor by turning round and giving us an account of the soul which was not metaphorical at all. That he has power to dispense with the particular metaphor of *breath*, is of course agreed. But we have not yet inquired what he can substitute for it. If we turn to those who are most anxious to tell us about the soul—I mean the psychologists—we shall find that the word *anima* has simply been replaced by complexes, repressions, censors, engrams, and the like. In other words the *breath* has been exchanged for *tyings-up, shovings-back, Roman magistrates,* and *scratchings.* If we inquire what has replaced the metaphorical *bright sky* of primitive theology, we shall only get a *perfect substance,* that is, a *completely made lying-under,* or—which is very much better, but equally metaphorical—a universal Father, or perhaps (in English) a *loaf-carver,* in Latin a *householder,* in Romance *a person older than.* The point need not be laboured. It is abundantly clear that the freedom from a given metaphor which we admittedly enjoy in some cases is often only a freedom to choose between the metaphor and others.

Certain reassurances may, indeed, be held out. In the first place, our distinction between the different kinds of metaphorical situation can stand; though it is hardly so important as we had hoped. To have a choice of metaphors (as we have in some cases) is to know more than we know when we are the slaves of a unique metaphor. And, in the second place, all description or identification, all direction of our own thought or another's, is not so metaphorical as definition. If, when challenged on the word *anima,* we proceed to define, we shall only reshuffle the buried metaphors; but if we simply say (or think) "what I am," or "what is going on in here," we shall have at least something before us which we do not know by metaphor. We shall at least be no worse off than the arboreal psychologists. At the same time, this method will not really carry us far. "What's going on here" is really the content of *haec anima:* for *anima* we want *"The sort of thing* that is going on here," and once we are committed to *sorts* and *kinds* we are adrift among metaphors.

We have already said that when a man claims to think independently of the buried metaphor in one of his words, his claim may some-times be allowed. But it was allowed only in so far as he could really supply the place of that buried metaphor with new and independent ap-prehension of his own. We now see that this new apprehension will usu-ally turn out to be itself metaphorical; or else, what is very much worse, instead of new apprehension we shall have simply words—each word enshrining one more ignored metaphor. For if he does not know the history of *anima,* how should he know the history of the equally meta-phorical words in which he defines it, if challenged? And if he does not know their history and therefore their metaphors, and if he cannot de-fine *them* without yet further metaphors, what can his discourse be but an endless ringing of the changes on such *bluspels* and *Flalansferes* as seem to mean, indeed, but do not mean? In reality, the man has played us a very elementary trick. He claimed that he could think without meta-phor, and in ignorance of the metaphors fossilized in his words. He made good the claim by pointing to the knowledge of his object which he possessed independently of the metaphor; and the proof of this knowledge was the definition or description which he could produce. We did not at first observe that where we were promised a freedom from metaphor we were given only a power of changing the metaphors in rapid succession. The things he speaks of he has never apprehended *literally.* Yet only such genuinely literal apprehension could enable him to forget the metaphors which he was actually using and yet to have a meaning. Either literalness, or else metaphor understood: one or other of these we must have; the third alternative is nonsense. But literalness we cannot have. The man who does not consciously use metaphors talks without meaning. We might even formulate a rule: the meaning in any given composition is in inverse ratio to the author's belief in his own literalness.

If a man has seen ships and the sea, he may abandon the metaphor of a *sea-stallion* and call a boat a boat. But suppose a man who has never seen the sea, or ships, yet who knows of them just as much as he can glean, say from the following list of *Kenningar*—sea-stallions, winged logs, wave riders, ocean trains. If he keeps all these together in his mind, and knows them for the metaphors they are, he will be able to think of ships, very imperfectly indeed, and under strict limits, but not wholly in vain. But if instead of this he pins his faith on the particular *kenning ocean-trains,* because that *kenning,* with its comfortable air of machinery, seems to him somehow more safely prosaic, less flighty and dangerous than its fellows, and if, contracting that to the form *oshtrans,* he pro-ceeds to forget that it was a metaphor, then, while he talks grammati-cally, he has ceased to think of anything. It will not avail him to stamp his feet and swear that he is literal; to say "An *oshtran* is an *oshtran*, and there's an end. I mean what I mean. What I mean is what I say."

The remedy lies, indeed, in the opposite direction. When we pass beyond pointing to individual sensible objects, when we begin to think of causes, relations, of mental states or acts, we become incurably metaphorical. We apprehend none of these things except through metaphor: we know of the ships only what the *Kenningar* will tell us. Our only choice is to use the metaphors and thus to think something, though less than we could wish; or else to be driven by unrecognized metaphors and so think nothing at all. I myself would prefer to embrace the former choice, as far as my ignorance and laziness allow me.

To speak more plainly, he who would increase the meaning and decrease the meaningless verbiage in his own speech and writing, must do two things. He must become conscious of the fossilized metaphors in his words; and he must freely use new metaphors, which he creates for himself. The first depends upon knowledge, and therefore on leisure; the second on a certain degree of imaginative ability. The second is perhaps the more important of the two: we are never less the slaves of metaphor than when we are making metaphor, or hearing it new made. When we are thinking hard of the Flatlanders, and at the same time fully aware that they *are* a metaphor, we are in a situation almost infinitely superior to that of the man who talks of the *Flalansfere* and thinks that he is being literal and straightforward.

If our argument has been sound, it leads us to certain rather remarkable conclusions. In the first place it would seem that we must be content with a very modest quantity of thinking as the core of all our talking. I do not wish to exaggerate our poverty. Not all our words are equally metaphorical, not all our metaphors are equally forgotten. And even where the old metaphor is lost there is often a hope that we may still restore meaning by pointing to some sensible object, some sensation, or some concrete memory. But no man can or will confine his cognitive efforts to this narrow field. At the very humblest we must speak of things in the plural, we must point not only to isolated sensations, but to groups and classes of sensations; and the universal latent in every group and every plural inflection cannot be thought without metaphor. Thus far beyond the security of literal meaning all of us, we may be sure, are going to be driven by our daily needs; indeed, not to go thus far would be to abandon reason itself. In practice we all really intend to go much farther. Why should we not? We have in our hands the key of metaphor, and it would be pusillanimous to abandon its significant use, because we have come to realize that its meaningless use is necessarily prevalent. We must indeed learn to use it more cautiously; and one of the chief benefits to be derived from our inquiry is the new standard of criticism which we must henceforward apply both to our own apparent thought and to that of others. We shall find, too, that real meaning, judged by this standard, does not come always where we have learned to expect. *Flalansferes* and *bluspels* will clearly be most prevalent in certain types of writers. The percentage of mere syntax masquerading as meaning may vary from something like 100 per cent. in political writers, journalists, psychologists, and economists, to something like forty per cent. in the writers of children's stories. Some scientists will fare better than others: the historian, the geographer, and sometimes the biologist will speak significantly more often than their colleagues; the mathematician, who seldom forgets that his symbols are symbolic, may often rise for short stretches to ninety per cent. of meaning and ten of verbiage. The philosophers will differ as widely from one another as any of the other groups differ among themselves: for a good metaphysical library contains at once some of the most verbal, and some of the most significant literature in the world. Those who have prided themselves on being literal, and who have endeavoured to speak plainly, with no mystical tom-foolery, about the highest abstractions, will be found to be among the least significant of writers: I doubt if we shall find more than a beggarly five per cent. of meaning in the pages of some celebrated "tough minded" thinkers, and how the account of Kant or Spinoza stands, none knows but heaven. But open your Plato, and you will find yourself among the great creators of metaphor, and therefore among the masters of meaning. If we turn to Theology—or rather to the literature of religion—the result will be more surprising still; for unless our whole argument is wrong, we shall have to admit that a man who says *heaven* and thinks of the visible sky is pretty sure to mean more than a man who tells us that heaven is a state of mind. It may indeed be otherwise; the second man may be a mystic who is remembering and pointing to an actual and concrete experience of his own. But it is long, long odds. Bunyan and Dante stand where they did; the scale of Bishop Butler, and of better men than he, flies up and kicks the beam.

It will have escaped no one that in such a scale of writers the poets will take the highest place; and among the poets those who have at once the tenderest care for old words and the surest instinct for the creation of new metaphors. But it must not be supposed that I am in any sense putting forward the imagination as the organ of truth. We are not talking of truth, but of meaning: meaning which is the antecedent condition both of truth and falsehood, whose antithesis is not error but nonsense. I am a rationalist. For me, reason is the natural organ of truth; but imagination is the organ of meaning. Imagination, producing new metaphors or revivifying old, is not the cause of truth, but its condition. It is, I confess, undeniable that such a view indirectly implies a kind of truth or rightness in the imagination itself. I said at the outset that the truth we won by metaphor could not be greater than the truth of the metaphor itself; and we have seen since that all our truth, or all but a few fragments, is won by metaphor. And thence, I confess, it does follow that if our thinking is ever true, then the metaphors by which we think must have been good metaphors. It does follow that if those original equations, between good and light, or evil and dark, between breath and soul and all the others, were from the beginning arbitrary and fanciful—if there is not, in fact, a kind of psycho-physical parallelism (or more) in the universe—then all our thinking is nonsensical. But we cannot, without contradiction, believe it to be nonsensical. And so, admittedly, the view I have taken has metaphysical implications. But so has every view.

NOTE

1. A. O. Barfield, *Poetic Diction,* 1928, pp. 139, 140.

GEORGE ORWELL

Politics and the English Language

Most people who bother with the matter at all would admit that the English language is in a bad way, but it is generally assumed that we cannot by conscious action do anything about it. Our civilization is decadent and our language—so the argument runs—must inevitably share in the general collapse. It follows that any struggle against the abuse of language is a sentimental archaism, like preferring candles to electric light or hansom cabs to aeroplanes. Underneath this lies the half-conscious belief that language is a natural growth and not an instrument which we shape for our own purposes.

Now, it is clear that the decline of a language must ultimately have political and economic causes: it is not due simply to the bad influence of this or that individual writer. But an effect can become a cause, reinforcing the original cause and producing the same effect in an intensified form, and so on indefinitely. A man may take to drink because he feels himself to be a failure, and then fail all the more completely because he drinks. It is rather the same thing that is happening to the English language. It becomes ugly and inaccurate because our thoughts are foolish, but the slovenliness of our language makes it easier for us to have foolish thoughts. The point is that the process is reversible. Modern English, especially written English, is full of bad habits which spread by imitation and which can be avoided if one is willing to take the necessary trouble. If one gets rid of these habits one can think more clearly, and to think clearly is a necessary first step toward political regeneration: so that the fight against bad English is not frivolous and is not the exclusive concern of professional writers. I will come back to this presently, and I hope that by that time the meaning of what I have said here will have become clearer. Meanwhile, here are five specimens of the English language as it is now habitually written.

These five passages have not been picked out because they are especially bad—I could have quoted far worse if I had chosen—but because they illustrate various of the mental vices from which we now suffer. They are a little below the average, but are fairly representative samples. I number them so that I can refer back to them when necessary:

1. I am not, indeed, sure whether it is not true to say that the Milton who once seemed not unlike a seventeenth-century Shelley had not become, out of an experience ever more bitter in each year, more alien [*sic*] to the founder of that Jesuit sect which nothing could induce him to tolerate.   Professor Harold Laski (Essay in *Freedom of Expression*)

2. Above all, we cannot play ducks and drakes with a native battery of idioms which prescribes such egregious collocations of vocables as the Basic *put up with* for *tolerate* or *put at a loss* for *bewilder*.
                    Professor Lancelot Hogben (*Interglossa*)

3. On the one side we have the free personality: by definition it is not neurotic, for it has neither conflict nor dream. Its desires, such as they are, are transparent, for they are just what institutional approval keeps in the forefront of consciousness; another institutional pattern would alter their number and intensity; there is little in them that is natural, irreducible, or culturally dangerous. But *on the other side,* the social bond itself is nothing but the mutual reflection of these self-secure integrities. Recall the definition of love. Is not this the very picture of a small academic? Where is there a place in this hall of mirrors for either personality or fraternity?   Essay on psychology in *Politics* (New York)

4. All the "best people" from the gentlemen's clubs, and all the frantic fascist captains, united in common hatred of Socialism and bestial horror of the rising tide of the mass revolutionary movement, have turned to acts of provocation, to foul incendiarism, to medieval legends of poisoned wells, to legalize their own destruction of proletarian organizations, and rouse the agitated petty-bourgeoisie to chauvinistic fervor on behalf of the fight against the revolutionary way out of the crisis.   Communist pamphlet

5. If a new spirit *is* to be infused into this old country, there is one thorny and contentious reform which must be tackled, and that is the humanization and galvanization of the B.B.C. Timidity here will bespeak canker and atrophy of the soul. The heart of Britain may be sound and of strong beat, for instance, but the British lion's roar at present is like that of Bottom in Shakespeare's *Midsummer Night's Dream*—as gentle as any sucking dove. A virile new Britain cannot continue indefinitely to be traduced in the eyes or rather ears, of the world by the effete languors of Langham Place, brazenly masquerading as "standard

English." When the Voice of Britain is heard at nine o'clock, better far
and infinitely less ludicrous to hear aitches honestly dropped than the
present priggish, inflated, inhibited, school-ma'amish arch braying of blameless bashful mewing maidens!   Letter in *Tribune*

Each of these passages has faults of its own, but, quite apart from avoidable ugliness, two qualities are common to all of them. The first is stale-
ness of imagery; the other is lack of precision. The writer either has a
meaning and cannot express it, or he inadvertently says something else,
or he is almost indifferent as to whether his words mean anything or not.
This mixture of vagueness and sheer incompetence is the most marked
characteristic of modern English prose, and especially of any kind of
political writing. As soon as certain topics are raised, the concrete melts
into the abstract and no one seems able to think of turns of speech that
are not hackneyed: prose consists less and less of *words* chosen for the
sake of their meaning, and more and more of *phrases* tacked together
like the sections of a prefabricated henhouse. I list below, with notes
and examples, various of the tricks by means of which the work of prose-
construction is habitually dodged:

Dying Metaphors

A newly invented metaphor assists thought by evoking a visual image, while on the other hand a metaphor which is technically "dead"
(e.g. *iron resolution*) has in effect reverted to being an ordinary word
and can generally be used without loss of vividness. But in between these
two classes there is a huge dump of worn-out metaphors which have lost
all evocative power and are merely used because they save people the
trouble of inventing phrases for themselves. Examples are: *Ring the
changes on, take up the cudgels for, toe the line, ride roughshod over,
stand shoulder to shoulder with, play into the hands of, no axe to grind,
grist to the mill, fishing in troubled waters, on the order of the day,
Achilles' heel, swan song, hotbed.* Many of these are used without knowledge of their meaning (what is a "rift," for instance?), and incompatible
metaphors are frequently mixed, a sure sign that the writer is not
interested in what he is saying. Some metaphors now current have been
twisted out of their original meaning without those who use them even
being aware of the fact. For example, *toe the line* is sometimes written
tow the line. Another example is *the hammer and the anvil,* now always
used with the implication that the anvil gets the worst of it. In real life
it is always the anvil that breaks the hammer, never the other way about:
a writer who stopped to think what he was saying would be aware of
this, and would avoid perverting the original phrase.

Operators or Verbal False Limbs

These save the trouble of picking out appropriate verbs and nouns, and at the same time pad each sentence with extra syllables which give it an appearance of symmetry. Characteristic phrases are *render inoperative, militate against, make contact with, be subjected to, give rise to, give grounds for, have the effect of, play a leading part (role) in, make itself felt, take effect, exhibit a tendency to, serve the purpose of, etc., etc.* The keynote is the elimination of simple verbs. Instead of being a single word, such as *break, stop, spoil, mend, kill,* a verb becomes a *phrase,* made up of a noun or adjective tacked on to some general-purpose verb such as *prove, serve, form, play, render.* In addition, the passive voice is wherever possible used in preference to the active, and noun constructions are used instead of gerunds (*by examination of* instead of *by examining*). The range of verbs is further cut down by means of the *-ize* and *de-* formations, and the banal statements are given an appearance of profundity by means of the *not un-* formation. Simple conjunctions and prepositions are replaced by such phrases as *with respect to, having regard to, the fact that, by dint of, in view of, in the interests of, on the hypothesis that;* and the ends of sentences are saved by anticlimax by such resounding commonplaces as *greatly to be desired, cannot be left out of account, a development to be expected in the near future, deserving of serious consideration, brought to a satisfactory conclusion,* and so on and so forth.

Pretentious Diction

Words like *phenomenon, element, individual* (as noun), *objective, categorical, effective, virtual, basic, primary, promote, constitute, exhibit, exploit, utilize, eliminate, liquidate,* are used to dress up simple statement and give an air of scientific impartiality to biased judgments. Adjectives like *epoch-making, epic, historic, unforgettable, triumphant, age-old, inevitable, inexorable, veritable,* are used to dignify the sordid processes of international politics, while writing that aims at glorifying war usually takes on an archaic color, its characteristic words being: *realm, throne, chariot, mailed fist, trident, sword, shield, buckler, banner, jackboot, clarion.* Foreign words and expressions such as *cul de sac, ancien régime, deus ex machina, mutatis mutandis, status quo, gleichschaltung, weltanschauung,* are used to give an air of culture and elegance. Except for the useful abbreviations *i.e., e.g.,* and *etc.,* there is no real need for any of the hundreds of foreign phrases now current in

English. Bad writers, and especially scientific, political, and sociological writers, are nearly always haunted by the notion that Latin or Greek words are grander than Saxon ones, and unnecessary words like *expedite, ameliorate, predict, extraneous, deracinated, clandestine, subaqueous,* and hundreds of others constantly gain ground from their Anglo-Saxon opposite numbers.[1] The jargon peculiar to Marxist writing (*hyena, hangman, cannibal, petty bourgeois, these gentry, lackey, flunkey, mad dog, White Guard,* etc.) consists largely of words and phrases translated from Russian, German, or French; but the normal way of coining a new word is to use a Latin or Greek root with the appropriate affix and, where necessary, the -ize formation. It is often easier to make up words of this kind (*deregionalize, impermissible, extramarital, non-fragmentary* and so forth) than to think up the English words that will cover one's meaning. The result, in general, is an increase in slovenliness and vagueness.

Meaningless Words

In certain kinds of writing, particularly in art criticism and literary criticism, it is normal to come across long passages which are almost completely lacking in meaning.[2] Words like *romantic, plastic, values, human, dead, sentimental, natural, vitality,* as used in art criticism, are strictly meaningless, in the sense that they not only do not point to any discoverable object, but are hardly ever expected to do so by the reader. When one critic writes, "The outstanding feature of Mr. X's work is its living quality," while another writes, "The immediately striking thing about Mr. X's work is its peculiar deadness," the reader accepts this as a simple difference of opinion. If words like *black* and *white* were involved, instead of the jargon words *dead* and *living,* he would see at once that language was being used in an improper way. Many political words are similarly abused. The word *Fascism* has now no meaning except in so far as it signifies "something not desirable." The words *democracy, socialism, freedom, patriotic, realistic, justice,* have each of them several different meanings which cannot be reconciled with one another. In the case of a word like *democracy,* not only is there no agreed definition, but the attempt to make one is resisted from all sides. It is almost universally felt that when we call a country democratic we are praising it: consequently the defenders of every kind of régime claim that it is a democracy, and fear that they might have to stop using the word if it were tied down to any one meaning. Words of this kind are often used in a consciously dishonest way. That is, the person who uses them has his own private definition, but allows his hearer to think he means something quite different. Statements like *Marshal Pétain was a true patriot, The Soviet press is the freest in the world, The Catholic Church is opposed to persecution,* are almost always made with intent to deceive. Other words used in variable meanings, in most cases more or less dishonestly, are: *class, totalitarian, science, progressive, reactionary, bourgeois, equality.*

Now that I have made this catalogue of swindles and perversions, let me give another example of the kind of writing that they lead to. This time it must of its nature be an imaginary one. I am going to translate a passage of good English into modern English of the worst sort. Here is a well-known verse from *Ecclesiastes:*

> I returned and saw under the sun, that the race is not to the swift, nor the battle to the strong, neither yet bread to the wise, nor yet riches to men of understanding, nor yet favour to men of skill; but time and chance happeneth to them all.

Here it is in modern English:

> Objective consideration of contemporary phenomena compels the conclusion that success or failure in competitive activities exhibits no tendency to be commensurate with innate capacity, but that a considerable element of the unpredictable must invariably be taken into account.

This is a parody, but not a very gross one. Exhibit (3), above, for instance, contains several patches of the same kind of English. It will be seen that I have not made a full translation. The beginning and ending of the sentence follow the original meaning fairly closely, but in the middle the concrete illustrations—race, battle, bread—dissolve into the vague phrase "success or failure in competitive activities." This had to be so, because no modern writer of the kind I am discussing—no one capable of using phrases like "objective consideration of contemporary phenomena"—would ever tabulate his thoughts in that precise and detailed way. The whole tendency of modern prose is away from concreteness. Now analyze these two sentences a little more closely. The first contains forty-nine words but only sixty syllables, and all its words are those of everyday life. The second contains thirty-eight words and ninety syllables: eighteen of its words are from Latin roots, and one from Greek. The first sentence contains six vivid images, and only one phrase ("time and chance") that could be called vague. The second contains not a single fresh, arresting phrase, and in spite of its ninety syllables it gives only a shortened version of the meaning contained in the first. Yet without a doubt it is the second kind of sentence that is gaining ground in modern English. I do not want to exaggerate. This kind of writing is not yet universal, and outcrops of simplicity will occur here and there in the worst-written page. Still, if you or I were told to write a few lines on the uncertainty of human fortunes, we should probably come much nearer to my imaginary sentence than to the one from *Ecclesiastes*.

As I have tried to show, modern writing at its worst does not consist in picking out words for the sake of their meaning and inventing images in order to make the meaning clearer. It consists in gumming together long strips of words which have already been set in order by someone else, and making the results presentable by sheer humbug. The attraction of this way of writing is that it is easy. It is easier—even quicker, once you have the habit—to say *In my opinion it is not an unjustifiable assumption that* than to say *I think*. If you use ready-made phrases, you not only don't have to hunt about for words; you also don't have to bother with the rhythms of your sentences, since these phrases are generally so arranged as to be more or less euphonious. When you are composing in a hurry—when you are dictating to a stenographer, for instance, or making a public speech—it is natural to fall into a pretentious, Latinized style. Tags like *a consideration which we should do well to bear in mind* or *a conclusion to which all of us would readily assent* will save many a sentence from coming down with a bump. By using stale metaphors, similes, and idioms, you save much mental effort, at the cost of leaving your meaning vague, not only for your reader but for yourself. This is the significance of mixed metaphors. The sole aim of a metaphor is to call up a visual image. When these images clash—as in *The Fascist octopus has sung its swan song, the jackboot is thrown into the melting pot*—it can be taken as certain that the writer is not seeing a mental image of the objects he is naming; in other words he is not really thinking. Look again at the examples I gave at the beginning of this essay. Professor Laski (1) uses five negatives in fifty-three words. One of these is superfluous, making nonsense of the whole passage, and in addition there is the slip—*alien* for *akin*—making further nonsense, and several avoidable pieces of clumsiness which increase the general vagueness. Professor Hogben (2) plays ducks and drakes with a battery which is able to write prescriptions, and, while disapproving of the everyday phrase *put up with,* is unwilling to look *egregious* up in the dictionary and see what it means; (3), if one takes an uncharitable attitude towards it, is simply meaningless: probably one could work out its intended meaning by reading the whole of the article in which it occurs. In (4), the writer knows more or less what he wants to say, but an accumulation of stale phrases chokes him like tea leaves blocking a sink. In (5), words and meaning have almost parted company. People who write in this manner usually have a general emotional meaning—they dislike one thing and want to express solidarity with another—but they are not interested in the detail of what they are saying. A scrupulous writer, in every sentence that he writes, will ask himself at least four questions, thus: What am I trying to say? What words will express it? What image or idiom will make it clearer? Is this image fresh enough to have an effect? And he will probably ask himself two more: Could I put it more shortly? Have I said anything that is avoidably ugly? But you are not obliged to go to all this trouble. You can shirk it by simply throwing your mind open and letting the ready-made phrases come crowding in. They will construct your sentences for you—even think your thoughts for you, to a certain extent—and at need they will perform the important service of partially concealing your meaning even from yourself. It is at this point that the special connection between politics and the debasement of language becomes clear.

In our time it is broadly true that political writing is bad writing. Where it is not true, it will generally be found that the writer is some kind of rebel, expressing his private opinions and not a "party line." Orthodoxy, of whatever color, seems to demand a lifeless, imitative style. The political dialects to be found in pamphlets, leading articles, manifestoes, White Papers and the speeches of undersecretaries do, of course, vary from party to party, but they are all alike in that one almost never finds in them a fresh, vivid, homemade turn of speech. When one watches some tired hack on the platform mechanically repeating the familiar phrases—*bestial atrocities, iron heel, bloodstained tyranny, free peoples of the world, stand shoulder to shoulder*—one often has a curious feeling that one is not watching a live human being but some kind of dummy: a feeling which suddenly becomes stronger at moments when the light catches the speaker's spectacles and turns them into blank discs which seem to have no eyes behind them. And this is not altogether fanciful. A speaker who uses that kind of phraseology has gone some distance toward turning himself into a machine. The appropriate noises are coming out of his larynx, but his brain is not involved as it would be if he were choosing his words for himself. If the speech he is making is one that he is accustomed to make over and over again, he may be almost unconscious of what he is saying, as one is when one utters the responses in church. And this reduced state of consciousness, if not indispensable, is at any rate favorable to political conformity.

In our time, political speech and writing are largely the defense of the indefensible. Things like the continuance of British rule in India, the Russian purges and deportations, the dropping of the atom bombs on Japan, can indeed be defended, but only by arguments which are too

brutal for most people to face, and which do not square with the professed aims of political parties. Thus political language has to consist
largely of euphemism, question-begging and sheer cloudy vagueness. De-
fenseless villages are bombarded from the air, the inhabitants driven out
into the countryside, the cattle machine-gunned, the huts set on fire with
incendiary bullets: this is called *pacification*. Millions of peasants are
robbed of their farms and sent trudging along the roads with no more
than they can carry: this is called *transfer of population* or *rectification
of frontiers*. People are imprisoned for years without trial, or shot in
the back of the neck or sent to die of scurvy in Arctic lumber camps:
this is called *elimination of unreliable elements*. Such phraseology is
needed if one wants to name things without calling up mental pictures
of them. Consider for instance some comfortable English professor de-
fending Russian totalitarianism. He cannot say outright, "I believe in
killing off your opponents when you can get good results by doing so."
Probably, therefore, he will say something like this:

"While freely conceding that the Soviet régime exhibits certain features which the humanitarian may be inclined to deplore, we must, I
think, agree that a certain curtailment of the right to political opposition is an unavoidable concomitant of transitional periods, and that the
rigors which the Russian people have been called upon to undergo have
been amply justified in the sphere of concrete achievement."

The inflated style is itself a kind of euphemism. A mass of Latin
words falls upon the facts like soft snow, blurring the outlines and covering up all the details. The great enemy of clear language is insincerity. When there is a gap between one's real and one's declared aims, one
turns as it were instinctively to long words and exhausted idioms, like
a cuttlefish squirting out ink. In our age there is no such thing as "keeping out of politics." All issues are political issues, and politics itself is a
mass of lies, evasions, folly, hatred, and schizophrenia. When the general atmosphere is bad, language must suffer. I should expect to find—
this is a guess which I have not sufficient knowledge to verify—that the
German, Russian and Italian languages have all deteriorated in the last
ten or fifteen years, as a result of dictatorship.

But if thought corrupts language, language can also corrupt
thought. A bad usage can spread by tradition and imitation, even among
people who should and do know better. The debased language that I
have been discussing is in some ways very convenient. Phrases like *a not
unjustifiable assumption, leaves much to be desired, would serve no
good purpose, a consideration which we should do well to bear in mind*,
are a continuous temptation, a packet of aspirins always at one's elbow.
Look back through this essay, and for certain you will find that I have

again and again committed the very faults I am protesting against. By this morning's post I have received a pamphlet dealing with conditions in Germany. The author tells me that he "felt impelled" to write it. I open it at random, and here is almost the first sentence that I see: ["The Allies] have an opportunity not only of achieving a radical transformation of Germany's social and political structure in such a way as to avoid a nationalistic reaction in Germany itself, but at the same time of laying the foundations of a cooperative and unified Europe." You see, he "feels impelled" to write—feels, presumably, that he has something new to say —and yet his word, like cavalry horses answering the bugle, group themselves automatically into the familiar dreary pattern. This invasion of one's mind by ready-made phrases (*lay the foundations, achieve a radical transformation*) can only be prevented if one is constantly on guard against them, and every such phrase anaesthetizes a portion of one's brain.

I said earlier that the decadence of our language is probably curable. Those who deny this would argue, if they produced an argument at all, that language merely reflects existing social conditions, and that we cannot influence its development by any direct tinkering with words and constructions. So far as the general tone or spirit of a language goes, this may be true, but it is not true in detail. Silly words and expressions have often disappeared, not through any evolutionary process but owing to the conscious action of a minority. Two recent examples were *explore every avenue* and *leave no stone unturned,* which were killed by the jeers of a few journalists. There is a long list of flyblown metaphors which could similarly be got rid of if enough people would interest themselves in the job; and it should also be possible to laugh the *not un*formation out of existence,[3] to reduce the amount of Latin and Greek in the average sentence, to drive out foreign phrases and strayed scientific words, and, in general, to make pretentiousness unfashionable. But all these are minor points. The defense of the English language implies more than this, and perhaps it is best to start by saying what it does *not* imply.

To begin with it has nothing to do with archaism, with the salvaging of obsolete words and turns of speech, or with the setting up of a "standard English" which must never be departed from. On the contrary, it is especially concerned with the scrapping of every word or idiom which has outworn its usefulness. It has nothing to do with correct grammar and syntax, which are of no importance so long as one makes one's meaning clear, or with the avoidance of Americanisms, or with having what is called a "good prose style." On the other hand it is not concerned with fake simplicity and the attempt to make written

English colloquial. Nor does it even imply in every case preferring the Saxon word to the Latin one, though it does imply using the fewest and shortest words that will cover one's meaning. What is above all needed is to let the meaning choose the word, and not the other way about. In prose, the worst thing one can do with words is to surrender to them. When you think of a concrete object, you think wordlessly, and then, if you want to describe the thing you have been visualizing you probably hunt about till you find the exact words that seem to fit it. When you think of something abstract you are more inclined to use words from the start, and unless you make a conscious effort to prevent it, the existing dialect will come rushing in and do the job for you, at the expense of blurring or even changing your meaning. Probably it is better to put off using words as long as possible and get one's meaning as clear as one can through pictures or sensations. Afterward one can choose—not simply *accept*—the phrases that will best cover the meaning, and then switch round and decide what impression one's words are likely to make on another person. This last effort of the mind cuts out all stale or mixed images, all prefabricated phrases, needless repetitions, and humbug and vagueness generally. But one can often be in doubt about the effect of a word or a phrase, and one needs rules that one can rely on when instinct fails. I think the following rules will cover most cases:

i. Never use a metaphor, simile, or other figure of speech which you are used to seeing in print.
ii. Never use a long word where a short one will do.
iii. If it is possible to cut a word out, always cut it out.
iv. Never use the passive where you can use the active.
v. Never use a foreign phrase, a scientific word, or a jargon word if you can think of an everyday English equivalent.
vi. Break any of these rules sooner than say anything outright barbarous.

These rules sound elementary, and so they are, but they demand a deep change of attitude in anyone who has grown used to writing in the style now fashionable. One could keep all of them and still write bad English, but one could not write the kind of stuff that I quoted in those five specimens at the beginning of this article.

I have not here been considering the literary use of language, but merely language as an instrument for expressing and not for concealing or preventing thought. Stuart Chase and others have come near to claiming that all abstract words are meaningless, and have used this as a pretext for advocating a kind of political quietism. Since you don't know what Fascism is, how can you struggle against Fascism? One need not swallow such absurdities as this, but one ought to recognize that the present political chaos is connected with the decay of language, and that one can probably bring about some improvement by starting at the verbal end. If you simplify your English, you are freed from the worst follies of orthodoxy. You cannot speak any of the necessary dialects, and when you make a stupid remark its stupidity will be obvious, even to yourself. Political language—and with variations this is true of all political parties, from Conservatives to Anarchists—is designed to make lies sound truthful and murder respectable, and to give an appearance of solidity to pure wind. One cannot change this all in a moment, but one can at least change one's own habits, and from time to time one can even, if one jeers loudly enough, send some worn-out and useless phrase —some *jackboot, Achilles' heel, hotbed, melting pot, acid test, veritable inferno,* or other lump of verbal refuse—into the dustbin where it belongs.

Notes

1. An interesting illustration of this is the way in which the English flower names which were in use till very recently are being ousted by Greek ones, *snapdragon* becoming *antirrhinum, forget-me-nots* becoming *myosotis,* etc. It is hard to see any practical reason for this change of fashion: it is probably due to an instinctive turning away from the more homely word and a vague feeling that the Greek word is scientific.

2. Example: "Comfort's catholicity of perception and image, strangely Whitmanesque in range, almost the exact opposite in aesthetic compulsion, continues to evoke that trembling atmospheric accumulative hinting at a cruel, an inexorably serene timelessness. . . . Wrey Gardner scores by aiming at simple bull's-eyes with precision. Only they are not so simple, and through this contented sadness runs more than the surface bittersweet of resignation." (*Poetry Quarterly.*)

3. One can cure oneself of the *not un-*formation by memorizing this sentence: *A not unblack dog was chasing a not unsmall rabbit across a not ungreen field.*

ROGER SALE

Metaphors: Live, Dead, and Silly

In a way, metaphor is the heart of the problem, for any writer with a decent understanding of metaphor is probably going to avoid jargon and clichés as a matter of instinctive survival, and is probably also going to begin to see ways of making his style become what he wants it to be. Up to now in this chapter I have talked about what goes wrong in a style, and a good deal of this discussion is a critique of bad and silly metaphors, but some things can be said about metaphor that might prove to be a positive help to someone struggling with his own style.

I may only be betraying my own ignorance, but the way metaphor usually is taught seems to invite my students to think of it as an ornament to their style, an effect achieved in poetry but not really necessary for any decent, hard-working plain style. As a result, most students seem unaware of the way metaphor pervades even the plainest and most hard-working of styles, and is the dominant feature of almost all our speech. Students seem to feel that metaphor is something they can "use" or not "use" as they wish, and so when they decide to use metaphors, they become wildly self-conscious and liable to cliché. When asked, they speak of metaphor as something different from a simile. "The moon was a ghostly galleon tossed upon stormy seas," they have learned, is a metaphor, and "My love is like a red, red rose" is a simile. Their examples, as I say, come from poems; metaphors are what you learn about in English classes, nowhere else.

The definition of metaphor most students have carried with them from English class to English class, however, can serve a wider purpose than it usually does. A metaphor is a comparison in which one thing is said to *be* another thing, as opposed to a simile, which is a comparison in which one thing is said to be *like* another thing. The distinction may have its purpose, but a moment's reflection will show that when one thing is said to *be* another thing, that does not mean that it in fact *is* that other thing but only that it is *like* that thing; metaphors and similes do exactly the same thing. When I say, in the first sentence of this paragraph, that students "have carried" a definition of metaphor from class to class, I do not mean that this carrying is literally the same carrying one might do if the subject were a ball of twine, but only that what students do with their definition of metaphor is *like* what they might do with a ball of twine. The word "carry" is a metaphor here, then. Look at the words "show" and "do" in the third sentence of this paragraph. These are obviously not felt as metaphors, yet they obviously are not meant to be taken literally; a moment's reflection cannot "show," a metaphor cannot "do" or be "felt" except metaphorically.

You can take almost any passage and treat it like the pictures in which you try to find the hidden animals. How many metaphors can you find in the following:

> Sure, I see Joe Fisher every morning. He comes in after class, scrounges around until he finds someone with a dime, buys his coffee and then he parks himself off in the corner. Within five minutes the son-of-a-bitch is holding court with a bunch of women. It's incredible. He sits back, pounds his spoon on the table, blows smoke down their throat, looks bored, yet somehow he manages it all so as to seem the biggest thing in their world. I've seen girls who wouldn't give me the time of day and to whom I've been princely treat him like some guru. It's as though he digs some language or tunes in on some obscure wave length made just for Joe Fisher and women.

Without stretching the idea of metaphor very much, I count nineteen: scrounges, parks, son-of-a-bitch, holding court, bunch, incredible, pounds, blows smoke down their throat, manages, biggest thing, world, seen, give me the time of day, princely, guru, digs some language, tunes in on some wave length, obscure, made. And that doesn't count those that are like metaphors, even if one doesn't want to call them that: every morning, someone with a dime, within five minutes, all, treat. Within a hundred words Joe Fisher is a rodent, a car, a male offspring of a female dog, a king, a stage director, a wise man, a mystic, a favored child of nature for whom things are "made."

Granted that an unprepared speech in conversation has the highest metaphorical density of any language we use, the game can be played even in conversations where everything is short bursts, with newspapers, with dialogue in movies. Our sense of the world involves us so constantly and completely in metaphors that there is little exaggeration in saying that all our speech and writing approaches metaphor; for example, you can hear many people who don't know what a metaphor is make one out of "literally" when they say, "He literally brought the house down," by which, of course, it is not to be understood that that is what he literally did.

Given the way metaphors pervade our speech, a few statements are perhaps in order. A metaphor is a kind of lie or untruth: something is said to be something that it is not. "He parks himself in the corner" compares Joe to an automobile. Unpacking the metaphor, we can say, "Joe is like an automobile in the way he finds his place of rest," or, simply, "Joe is an automobile," or, "Joe is an automobile in this respect." We cannot, nor do we want to, say, "An automobile is Joe." If a metaphor were not a metaphor, it would be an identity and therefore reversible, as in "Sunrise is the beginning of day" and "The beginning of day is sunrise." There is a kind of magic in our key verb "to be," such that it cannot only make equalities and definitions but can also state or imply likenesses between two things that aren't each other and do not, in most respects, resemble each other, like Joe and an automobile. Likewise, metaphors are not capable of replacing each other; "Joe parks himself in the corner" is okay, and so is "The car parks hard," but "Joe parks hard" won't do. All this is perhaps elementary enough, but it can have consequences that are not always easy to determine, so it is best to get the elementary things straight. One of the basic tasks of intelligent living is to understand the extent to which certain statements which use some form of "to be" are statements of identity: "God is . . . ," "My country is . . . ," "You are . . . ." Most really important statements about the human condition or nature of the universe are of the form "x is y," and if "You are the promised kiss of springtime" is only a rather pretty and confused pile-up of metaphors, what are we to say of "God is the Father Almighty"? In any event, we must see that though many metaphors do not take the grammatical form of "x is y," all metaphors can be transformed into statements of that pattern and often can best be understood and evaluated when this transformation is made. This is especially true when the metaphor lies in a verb—"Joe scrounged," "Joe parked," "Joe held court"—and the fact that the statement is metaphorical is apt to pass unnoticed. It is often possible to examine the implications of one's own statements by taking all the metaphors and turning them into the "x is y" form, and quite often writers gain a much better grip on their writing when they practice doing this. If nothing else, to take a paragraph of one's own writing and to unpack and rephrase all its metaphors is to see what a strange and wonderful instrument the language is and how much control it is possible to exert over one's use of it.

Here, for instance, is a paragraph with some rather interesting metaphors that its author probably was unaware he was using:

> In Sherwood Anderson's "I Want to Know Why," only one of the characters is described in depth. Here we see a boy whose entire life has but one goal, to be a trainer or a jockey. His dreams are the dreams of a young boy, not those of a grown man. Hopping freights, exploring strange places, living only for his moments at the stables and the track—these are described so vividly the reader can feel them. The boy's life centers around the track, and as long as this is so, the boy's world is secure. The races are always there, along with the parade of new colts. The boy depends heavily on the horses for this way of life.

Let's again list the metaphors: in depth, see, entire life, dreams, grown man, hopping freights, exploring strange places, moments, feel, centers around, world, secure, always there, parade, depends heavily, way of life. What I want to look at especially are those which are so much a part of the way we speak that the metaphorical quality of the phrase is not easy to see. First, though, a word about "centered around," which must be the commonest mixed metaphor in the present use of the language. A mixed metaphor is not simply two consecutive metaphors; "That man is a snake, a rat" is simply a change of metaphor. A mixed metaphor is an absurdity that arises when someone is not aware that he is using a metaphor: "We pulverized them into sending up the white flag" is such a mix, because to pulverize something is to leave it in no condition to send up white flags; "The foundation of his position must flounder" is mixed because, of the many wonderful things metaphorical foundations can do, floundering is not one. The term "centered around" is, in this sense, self-contradictory, because to center on something is to be, metaphorically, at the one point incapable of motion—around, through, by, or any other way. What happens, of course, is that people forget that "to center" is a metaphor in itself and so demands a preposition appropriate to the action of centering.

Mixed metaphors, however, are really an interesting sidelight, and most writers learn early to avoid them. More important are the metaphors in this paragraph that silently construct this writer's "world": in depth, world, secure. The questions raised by metaphors of depth and shallowness really ask us who we think we are and how we see others. The writer here says that only the boy in this story "is described in depth." One way of stating the curiosity of the problem is to point out that almost certainly this writer means that the boy is the only character described "at length." Surely, "in depth" and "at length" should not mean the same thing, but the fact that they do tells us something. Most studies that are carried on in depth are carried on longer than other studies, but whatever else is implied by "in depth" is seldom made clear. Presumably, to be deep is not to be shallow, and a study in depth would explore the deeps, the profundities, the complexities, of a person or a problem. Presumably, also, one could carry on at great length, that is, for a long time, about a problem and never explore its depths. The difficulty is that no one will ever confess this, because if an analysis that takes five minutes is not deep, no one expected it could be, but an analysis that takes far longer ought to be far deeper. So it is that we presume, or let others presume for us, that length makes depth. It is possible, though in our world it is not allowed to be possible, that someone can be deep about someone else in a single sentence, and it is not only possible but likely that most people can go on at length about a problem without ever being deep. As long as length and depth are allowed to measure the same things, however, no one is apt to find this out, and the confusion of metaphorical reality can only be a really long and deep confusion.

Now, "world," that most fashionable of metaphors. "The boy's world is secure," says the passage; professional football or fashion or Henry Orient or youth or marijuana or almost everything else one can name is said to have its own "world," or "sphere" (it used to be only a "niche"). In James Baldwin's world, in the world of Harlem, in the modern world, in my world, and each time the metaphor is used the implication grows stronger that each item that has a world is isolated from everything else in creation. "This is my Father's world," says the hymn, but that is not the way the term is used now; the metaphor says that it is not all of us, or the physical body known as the earth, but some small segment thereof, that is its world. If someone tells me that I do not live in his world, he implies that the gap between my world and his is so great that I cannot possibly know what his life is like. It is as though there were no common inheritance of humanity, of a Western tradition, of American life, that is shared; each lives in his own world, each peers out onto a universe of strangers, each finds his own world made up of himself and a few other like-minded people. I have, throughout this book, spoken as though the classroom were a separate world, and have constantly deplored the fact that the metaphor may speak truly. It is a common metaphor, and if what it implies is true, then it is hard to know how we are going to get along in "the world."

Finally, "secure" and "security." My dictionary does not really think that the word as it is used in this sentence is metaphorical any longer:

"The boy's world is secure," and "secure" here means "free from or not
exposed to danger." What is interesting here is the way in which the
term so often is used in a context that implies transience, fragility, and
danger. The writer here says: "The boy's life centers around the track,
and as long as this is so, the boy's world is secure." We know, thus, that
the security is temporary. It is a word most often used by or about
people who do not feel in the least safe; or, it may be said, people who
live in their own "world" tend to use the word "secure" but seldom
feel as the word or metaphor implies they do. Here are some common
usages:

> I don't ever feel very secure when called upon to speak. [Here "secure"
> means comfortable or relaxed.]

> She needs more security than he will ever be able to give her. [Here
> "security" means steadiness.]

> If he gets the best job, he will feel secure. [Here "security" almost means
> valuable.]

> The moment he gets outside the security of the classroom, he fumbles
> and feels lost. [Here "security" means protection.]

What we have here is a spectrum of meanings for "secure," no one
clearly literal or metaphorical, no one quite like any of the others, so
that the word has a solidity of tone but no solidity of meaning. Such
a word is harder to use than "in depth" or "world" when what one needs
is a sense that the word *is* a metaphor. The word "security," like the
word "real," can be used well only by someone who is fully aware
of its different shadings and nuances. It is a word that has come to
prominence precisely because what it describes or implies is so seldom
felt, and the word often seems like a cry for help from someone who
knows there is no help. "If he gets that job, he will feel secure"
is a harmless enough sentence, but the "he" it describes is no fun to
contemplate at all, for any "he" that needs this or that job to feel secure
is quite obviously never going to feel secure, no matter what job he gets.
"She needs more security than he will ever be able to give her" means
"She must marry a rock, nothing else will save her." "I don't ever feel
secure when called upon to speak," means, really, "I don't ever feel
secure." As a result, though "secure" and "security" themselves are not,
in the strict sense, metaphors as used most of the time, they can be used
as a means of avoiding a gnawing sense of pathos, loneliness, and insecurity when their potential meanings are clear to both user and
reader or listener.

I have concentrated on the three words discussed above because they were the ones the paragraph offered, and I have done so only to show the kind of awareness about metaphor that any concentrated thought about writing can provoke. Three other words would call for a quite different discussion but not for a different awareness. Metaphor is how we live because it is the way we relate what we see to what we know: this is like that. The only sentences we can construct that are really without metaphors are those we construct just to prove we can do it. Care in the use of metaphor is tantamount to careful writing; sloppiness in the use of metaphor is the same thing as sloppy writing. The best and only way I know to become aware of this is to perform exercises like those I've been doing in the last few pages. Take something you have written that you are rather proud of, or maybe just something that seems all right but from which you don't see how to go on. List its metaphors, unpack a few of the obvious ones, then a few of the hidden ones that may or may not seem like metaphors to you. All of a sudden, instead of being a great writer or a drudge, you are aware of yourself for what, most importantly, you are—a user of words.

I would like to close this section on a somewhat lighter note, by considering a few of the lovely usages that come to use from advertising. Ads themselves will be with us always, but the particular ads come and go so fast that I have no hope that those I mention will still be in use a year or two from now. Certain phrases keep coming up, though, and the new ads of the future will probably only be variations on them. One class of phrases has to do with the inflated noun: "science knows," "doctors say," "tests prove," "experiments show." An ordinary third-grader knows there is something phony about these phrases, but the fun is in ferreting out what it is. The word "science" in the phrase "science knows" is a metaphor, obviously, but for what? Let us say that "Science knows acid indigestion is caused by gas bubbles," just to take a homely example. Who knows this? Science? Obviously, science is not a knower at all, nor, as it is sometimes called upon to be, a speaker ("science says"). "Scientists" is an improvement, but not much of one— what scientists? How do they know it? Most scientists are busy doing whatever it is they do and know nothing about acid indigestion beyond what they hear in advertisements. Presumably, there exists a group of doctors or medical specialists who are "good on" digestion and indigestion, but the difficulty with asking them is that they either will all agree on the assertion that "acid indigestion is caused by gas bubbles" because (I suspect) it is obvious, or else they will quarrel quite violently with the admen and among themselves over the precise definitions of "indigestion," "gas," and "bubbles." Which leads us to this: the word "science" in the assertion "Science knows acid indigestion is caused by gas bubbles" means "people who watch this ad."

One more example. "The coating on this razor blade reduces the pull to a fraction." To what fraction of what? The phrase implies that the pull is reduced so much that you can barely feel it. But what if the pull were reduced to nine-tenths (a fraction) of the pull felt when a sharp stone is scraped along the cheek? The terms of the phrase given in the ad would be fulfilled, but something would happen to our sense of how miraculous the blade is, how much in need we are of a tour of the blade's edge given by a man in a white coat.

WILLIAM E. COLES, JR.

Freshman Composition:
The Circle of Unbelief

In 1891 it was possible for J. F. Genung, a professor of English, to introduce a book on rhetoric with the following remarks on general standards of diction:

> Every author has his peculiar diction, and so has every kind of literature. But beyond these individual and class characteristics there is also a general standard of diction, which every writer must regard. That standard, or ideal, is perhaps best expressed by the word PURITY: the writer must see to it he keeps his mother tongue unsullied, and this by observing, in all his choice of language, the laws of derivation, usage, adaptedness, and taste. Transgressions of the standard are owing to want of culture and tact, either in the general knowledge and use of words, or in the special requirements of the discourse in hand.[1]

That is a statement standing for what its speaker is able to take for granted: the fact of uncommon common decency, the existence of belief and faith as shared values, the moral fusion of writing as an action with the standards by which that action is measured. Purity, culture, tact, and taste: these are not words but the terms of a life style made openly invitational. They call for a community of individuals, for self-transcendence as a means of self-realization. They are terms made by and making the syntax which contains them. Genung knew that his students knew what he knew. And in that end were their beginnings.

So much for what was.

That things have changed is no news to anyone. The appeal for

From *College English*, Vol. 31, No. 2, November 1969. Reprinted by permission of the National Council of Teachers of English and William E. Coles, Jr.

writing now is different, and so (perhaps so, therefore) is the situation in which the students and teachers of it find themselves. The following passage will no doubt sound familiar:

> The aim of this text and of the course using it is to teach effective writing. *Ventures in Composition* thus combines compactly a simple, practical rhetoric with clear-cut writing models. It is arranged so that an inexperienced teacher can start at the beginning and work steadily forward in a systematic manner, and so that a veteran teacher will find a great abundance of materials to use in what way he likes. In making our selections we have sought to bring together interesting, teachable, and challenging essays. [We] have used only complete, current, relatively short, chiefly expository selections and have chosen materials which cover a wide range of subject matter. Such selections as "Under-graduate Kindergarten" and "The Dating Couch" may be directly related to the student's own experience; others, such as "The Negro: Black Peril or Black Pearl?" and "Let's Razz Democracy" are less closely connected but surely will stimulate thought; still others, it is hoped, may provide an occasional shock. Growing out of each essay are exercises that test for the central idea, analyze the organization and the rhetorical principles utilized, improve vocabulary, acquaint the student with some library reference works, provide systematic dictionary study, and suggest subjects for talks and themes. Thus, this material is adaptable for a controlled source paper and also permits the student to go beyond the suggestions included in the essays and to do more independent thinking than is usually possible in projects of this kind.
>
> The first thing a student does in freshman English is attack the problem of theme writing. A major problem for most writers—especially inexperienced ones—is how to transfer thought from mind to paper, how to make the intention and the expression one. Rather than tell the student what not to do, *Ventures in Composition* instructs him in what should be done. We have tried to present teachable principles that apply to student writing rather than to present theoretical rhetorical classifications. Throughout the book generalizations about writing are firmly anchored to detailed consideration of the practice of both professional and student writers. The range of rhetorical approach reflected in the exercises encourages the student to select with discrimination those methods most appropriate to his purpose. The student is addressed directly as one striving to learn principles of clear and vigorous writing of types suitable to his capacities and interests. *Ventures in Composition* is intended essentially to help him face the composition challenge with a measure of ability and confidence.
>
> In hopes of making the task of correcting papers easier for the teacher and more useful for the student, we have provided not only the conventional set of correction symbols, but also a supplementary list of abbreviations which may be used in conjunction with those symbols.

To form the habit of critical reading for rhetorical principles is to begin that lifetime of improvement in reading and writing which a college course on composition should initiate. Learning to think clearly and learning to write correctly, clearly, effectively, appropriately, are worthwile intellectual processes valuable not only in composition class but in all other outreachings of the mind.

In the sense that that preface does not introduce a specific contemporary handbook or text on rhetoric, and in the sense also that its titles are made up, the paragraphs above are a kind of parody, the preface a kind of trick. But with the exceptions of the dubbed titles and a pronoun change, each of the nineteen sentences of the mock preface is reproduced verbatim from a separate introduction to a different textbook, all of them in print and in use at colleges and universities throughout the United States at the present time.[2] So in another sense there is no trick being played here at all.

From the fact that a trick like that of the portmanteau preface is possible, it is of course possible to conclude too much, but it is possible also to conclude more than that different writers of different composition texts sound alike. For the important thing dramatized here is the way the similarity of tone and manner holding the mock preface together creates an interlocked set of assumptions about what it means to write a sentence in English: how the activity of writing is to be taught, how it is to be learned, how it is to be judged and valued. From this perspective, the sentences of the mock preface, no less than the real preface from which they are taken, introduce far more than a text on writing. They also describe a course and the expectation of certain patterns of behavior within that course as well. The sentences are both the beginning and the end of a circular process in which text, attitude, and action are dependent to the point of being indistinguishable: the kind of writing taught and learned implies the text which implies the course which implies the activity which implies the kind of writing taught and learned.

This circle is less an emblem of healthy organic wholeness than of one more swing around the prickly pear, not because any author of any textbook on the subject of writing sets out to teach sterility, but because the desire for a universally realizable standard of writing has resulted in demands which may be interpreted as demands for sterility. To split the activities of thinking and writing ("intention and expression") as do the sentences of the mock preface, to suggest that writing involves no more than the "transfer" of thoughts "from mind to paper," is to invite the substitution of a process for an activity, perhaps a product for a process. At any rate, it is to approach what is finally unteachable as though it were teachable, and so to make non-art stand for art.

I wish to underscore the fact that the issue I am addressing is one of interpretation and not one of intent. I think I know what is intended by sentences such as those making up the mock preface. I also know what I understood to be meant by such sentences when I was a student, and what my students for the past seventeen years have shown me that they understand such sentences to mean. And though the difference has never been, nor is it likely to become, a source of seething discontent, it is probably the largest single reason that most students and most teachers of writing at the college freshman level neither like nor believe very much in what it is they are doing. Belief in a system to which belief has been made irrelevant, however undesignedly, is hard to come by. The writers of the prefaces certainly began with a concern for standards, but the assumptions to be inferred from their sentences will not be Genungian. The process of secularization has emerged in what is more readable as a language of standardization than a language of standards, a language which has the effect of turning the activity of writing and everything associated with it into a kind of computerized skill.

The preface, like the text and the course it introduces, will be read not as a demand for writing, but for something like writing, the reasonable facsimile thereof. It will be read as a demand for that kind of non-writing popularly known as Themewriting. Everyone run through the American school system is yawningly familiar with it. Themewriting is a language, a way of experiencing the world. It is used not for the writing of papers, but of Themes. Invented originally by English teachers for use in English classrooms only, it is as closed a language as the Dewey Decimal System, as calculatedly dissociated from the concerns of its user and the world he lives in as it has been possible to make it. But the selling points of it as a commodity are irresistible. For since the skill of Themewriting is based upon the use of language conceived of entirely in terms of communication, the only standard that need be applied to it is whether it succeeds in creating in the reader—that is, in another Themewriter—the desired response. The writer's character, personality, moral nature, convictions, what Genung calls his "culture and tact," it is taken for granted are in no way engaged in forming sentences out of words and paragraphs out of sentences. Language is a tool, it is said. Or just a tool. If the reader buys the product or the idea, believes something, feels certain emotions, votes a particular ticket, etc., then the writing is good. Then the English is good.

The selling points of this commodity are not only irresistible, they are undeniable; and so is the utility of what is being sold. Writing seen as a trick that can be played, a device that can be put into operation, is also a technique that can be taught and learned—just as one can be taught or learn to run an adding machine, or pour concrete. And once equipped with this skill a writer can write a Theme about anything, and at a moment's notice. It is a valuable technique to know, therefore, because like the American dollar it is negotiable anywhere— and its buying power is unlimited. A college student can use the technique of Themewriting not only to write papers but to plan a career or a marriage, to organize a life even. And if the standards of this imitation writing are those to which the dignity of full commitment is unthinkable; if the orders won by it are more sterile than the chaos from which they are won; if the price paid to teach this kind of writing, and to learn it, may be more than the chance to be Lively or Interesting; there are few to say so. For to make Themewriting or non-writing stand for writing in the way that the traditional Freshman English course does, is to make impossible also the conception of, let alone the demand for, writing as writing inside its circle. . . .

The composition part of the course, in fact, will be confined to seven or eight writing assignments, most of them spun out of the readings, on which the student knows he will be asked to write Themes. "Is the Government of the United States Liberal or Conservative? Discuss, 450-500 words"; "To what extent may Holden Caulfield be considered a tragic hero?" For each of his seven or eight prescribed writing assignments the student will be given such a prescribed topic along with a prescribed word limit. Approximately one week after the assigning of a subject he will turn in his Theme written in a prescribed form, which he knows without being told must be folded lengthwise down the middle (for filing? as a first step in being wadded for disposal?). These Themes will then be marked and graded on a prescribed scale with a prescribed vocabulary, and returned to the student for prescribed revision about a week after he has handed them in.

This process, it is known as Theme revision, the student will believe is to enable him to prove that he is in fact one of those interested in facing "the composition challenge with a measure of ability and confidence." In the margins of his corrected papers there will appear certain "conventional . . . correction symbols" along with certain "abbreviations . . . used in conjunction with those symbols." These notations he will see as serving notice that one or more of the "principles of clear and vigorous writing" has been violated. In order to demonstrate his intention "to think clearly" and to learn "to write correctly, clearly, effectively" etc., he will use the symbols and abbreviations to correct his papers. This is, as the mock preface suggests, a relatively simple matter. On the inside front cover of *Ventures in Composition,* is a table with a title like *Rhetorical Errors* where all of the rhetorical errors that a student can make are capsulated and symbolized in a list. Some texts on composition even go so far as to include a second table called *Grammatical Errors* or *Mechanical Errors.* Both tables are used in very much the same way. A subheading of the table entitled *Rhetorical Errors,* for instance, may include such a term as WORD CHOICE or DICTION which in turn is broken down into a number of separate errors—*awk, viv, vocab,* etc.; or *23-a, b,* and *c.* In either case, the nomenclature enables a student to move easily from the symbol to the section of *Ventures in Composition* which will correct his error. *Viv* next to "I ran" will thus brighten it to "I loped" or " I shambled," or in the case of a notation like *sub,* the student will be informed that "subordination, is needed," a matter that the text explains with something like this:

> A sentence in which the main clause is less important than the subordinate clause exhibits *faulty subordination.* . . .
>
> FAULTY   I finished work at five o'clock, and I went to the movies.
> BETTER   When I finished work at five o'clock, I went to the movies.
> BEST   At five o'clock, when I finished work, I went to the movies.

It is not difficult to see what values the student might attach to the process of Themewriting and Themerevision, particularly when he learns that all of his writing for the course is to be collected at the end of the term and burned. That vague promise of a payoff even more vague (called a "lifetime of improvement in reading and writing") which is claimed to emerge somehow from sportsmanlike obedience to the System, is too easy for him to imagine as just another way in which his course is having its fake and beating it too. Everyone who plays the game according to the rules is promised "a measure of ability and confidence," a share in the collective "outreachings of the mind." But for the student this is likely to mean no more than that everyone can finish work by five o'clock and go to the movies.

The argument here is not that mean or silly assumptions underlie the writing of textbooks on writing, but that such textbooks may be, can be, will be interpreted as meanly assumed no matter what their assumptions—and not because the books are bad ones, but because the books are books. If they do not themselves create a situation of permissive sterility in college Freshman English courses, the situation into which they are introduced creates them as creators of it, no matter what their intentions, no matter how good they may be. Art cannot be taught with the tone and manner of the mock preface and remain art; writing cannot be taught as non-writing and remain writing.

My account of things is hyperbolic, of course, but the argument is not extravagant. Here, for example, is the beginning of an actual preface beginning an actual text on rhetoric:

Preface: to the Student

The aim of this text and of the course using it is to teach effective writing. Only a few students plan careers in creative writing, but every student eventually finds himself deeply involved in problems of expression. Term papers, essay examinations and reports are regular parts of most of the courses you will take while in college. When you enter professional life, your need for writing skill will probably increase. Business correspondence will have to be answered, projects will have to be "written up," brochures and manuals will have to be composed and speeches delivered. Most of these jobs will have to be done on short notice, usually in the midst of other activities. If you write easily they are opportunities; if you write poorly they are at best unpleasant and at worst, episodes that can jeopardize advancement or threaten the success of an important project. For this reason your writing course is of central importance, both to your success as a student and to later success in your career.

Those are arid, but not stupid sentences. They are meant to be helpful, even inspiriting. But when they are fed into the insidious circularity of the traditional college Freshman English course, they develop a context which makes them mean something quite different from what they seem to say. Although it is "effective writing" and not writing which is being presented here, the manner of the sentences creates the illusion that it *is* writing which is being presented, and that what is being said about it is the most that can possibly be said for it. There is no reasonable demand for writing which cannot be articulated, the tone of the paragraph suggests, nothing about writing which cannot be understood. What is offered in the name of ideals, then, becomes an all too realizable actuality. Writing becomes "effective writing" becomes Themewriting.

Thus "effective writing" is differentiated from another kind of writing called "creative writing," something "only a few students plan careers in." Unlike "creative writing," "effective writing" is something one can learn to do "easily" (the alternative is writing "poorly"), and which once learned will enable a student to write "brochures and manuals" and letters in the same way that he has written "term papers" and "essay examinations"; they can all be seen as just "jobs" that he can learn to do "on short notice" and even "in the midst of other activities." In this way, it is asserted, "effective writing" can be used to take advantage of "opportunities," all opportunities, and is thereby, with a slither of logic, said to be "of central importance" in achieving "success" because "poor" writing can "threaten" it.

This does more than suggest that Themewriting will get one by; it suggests that there is no way of getting on without it. "Effective writing" is being offered not just as useful but as indispensable, in that it is the means by which any opportunity to write, for any student from any college, is converted to an occasion demanding another demonstration of his ability to produce "effective writing." And the chimeras of un-realized opportunity, jeopardized advancement, and aborted success which hover on the rim of failure here, are not simply halloweenish horrors for a college student, particularly for a college freshman. There is no mistaking what is meant by "success" in the context of those sentences, and in spite of what Youth is supposed (and supposes itself) to worship, the American Dream is still the American Dream.

Although nothing in the paragraph specifically prohibits the stu-dent from entertaining the question of why he should write to begin with, or for whom, neither is there any gesture made to indicate that these questions might be important or worth asking. It is hard to see how there could be. Such concerns cannot be said to matter because none of what makes possible the use of non-writing to stand for writing would be possible if they were said to matter. No wonder that in both the mock preface and the real one so little is said of the relationship between a writer and what he writes, or between a reader and what he reads. No wonder audience is conceived of as including everyone except the writer who creates it. To suggest that there might be another way of talking about writing, to assume that a student might someday *want* to write a speech or a letter (as opposed to those speeches which "will have to be . . . delivered" and the letters which "will have to be answered"), to attempt to imagine anything like a meaningful relation-ship between the writer, his writing, and his reader would be at variance with an approach to writing which for each party turns out to be founded on the supposed irrelevance of such concerns to the other.

I do not think that tragic is too strong a word for what this mutual misunderstanding can involve: for students' imagining that writing is conceived of by their teachers as mechanical, sterile, meaningless; for teachers' imagining themselves contained inside the proposition that there is no way of teaching what cannot be taught. It is a misunder-standing which results in a pact made without the realization of either party that it is a party, let alone that it has agreed to anything. And so the sealing is made as it is made possible, not in guilt, or in sorrow, or in shame, or in fear, but unconsciously, with each party's assuming that for the other writing as writing simply doesn't matter. What the student is doing, what the teacher is doing, what gets done, these things are important, but none of them matter for themselves. Writing thus becomes no more than a kind of transcription, a known, not a way of knowing, a way of saying something, not something being said.

And the situation is universal. The juxtaposition of the mock preface with a real one makes clear the paradigmic relation of both to an approach to writing entombed in literally hundreds of handbooks and in thousands of college Freshman English programs. Entombed like Madeline Usher. All the books are being used. Year after year the same freshman programs are rerun from the same worn stencil. And so the circle remains unbroken; the emperor continues his naked parade. Teachers of English Composition go on using methods and materials which were obsolete ten years ago, a hundred years ago, ten centuries ago. Balls go on rolling quietly down inclined planes, while students sit quietly by and watch.

The problem is not just one of better books, a tighter syllabus, more carefully worded assignments, a different personnel. It is not just a problem of abstractions either: more dedication, more purpose, more industry. God knows there is enough of this, or at least enough of this kind of talk, already. The problem is one of developing another way of seeing the activity of writing, of establishing the dignity of collective faith necessary to make possible the learning and teaching of writing as art. To eliminate the composition text as a composition text will not of itself create a conception of writing as writing, but it will at least eliminate the most nameable barrier to it.

NOTES

1. J. F. Genung, *The Practical Elements of Rhetoric* (Boston, 1891), p. 28.
2. My sources follow *seriatim:*

    First Paragraph: O. B. Hardison, *Practical Rhetoric* (Appleton-Century-Crofts, 1966). Louise E. Rorabacker, *Assignments in Exposition* (third edition, Harper and Brothers, 1959). Sanders, Jordan, and Magoon, *Unified English Composition* (fourth edition, Appleton-Century-Crofts, 1966). Lee and Moynihan, *Using Prose* (Dodd, Mead and Company, 1961). Martha Cox, *A Reading Approach to College Writing* (Chandler Publishing Company, 1966). Cary Graham, *Freshman English Program* (Scott, Foresman and Company, 1960). Morris, Walker, *et al., College English, The First Year* (fourth edition, Harcourt, Brace and World, Inc., 1964). Irmscher and Hagemann, *The Language of Ideas* (Bobbs-Merrill Company, Inc., 1963).

    Second Paragraph: Buckler and McAvoy, American College Handbook (American Book Company, 1965). Talmadge, Haman, and Bornhauser, *The Rhetoric-Reader* (Scott, Foresman and Company, 1962). Edward P. J. Corbett, *Classical Rhetoric for the Modern Student* (Oxford University Press, 1965). Hulon Willis, *Structure, Style and Usage* (Holt, Rinehart and Winston, 1964). Hans Guth, *A Short New Rhetoric* (Wadsworth Publishing Company, 1964). Richard M. Weaver, *Rhetoric and Composition* (second edition, Holt, Rinehart and Winston, 1967). Harry Shaw, *A Complete Course in Freshman English* (sixth edition, Harper and Row, 1967). J. R. Orgel, *Writing the Composition* (Educators' Publishing Service, 1962).

Third Paragraph: Kane and Peters, *A Practical Rhetoric of Expository Prose* (Oxford University Press, 1966).

Fourth Paragraph: Chittick and Stevick, *Rhetoric for Exposition* (Appleton-Century-Crofts, 1961). Wykoff and Shaw, *The Harper Handbook* (second edition, Harper and Brothers, 1957).

WALKER GIBSON

Dullness and Dishonesty:
The Rhetoric of Newswriting

Must a great newspaper be dull?

We begin with a conventional sample of "straight" reporting, though concerning events that lend themselves to excitable treatment. Here is a reporter for *The New York Times* (Claude Sitton) beginning his lead article on the race riots in Birmingham, Alabama, in the issue for May 8, 1963.

> The police and firemen drove hundreds of rioting Negroes off the streets today with high-pressure hoses and an armored car. The riot broke out after from 2,500 to 3,000 persons rampaged through the business district in two demonstrations and were driven back. The Negroes rained rocks, bottles and brickbats on the law-enforcement officials as they were slowly forced backward by the streams of water. The pressure was so high that the water skinned bark off trees in the parks and along sidewalks. Policemen from surrounding cities and members of the Alabama Highway Patrol rushed to a nine-block area near the business district to help quell the riot. An undetermined number of persons were injured in the demonstrations against segregation. They included the Rev. Fred L. Shuttlesworth, a prominent Negro leader, and two city policemen and a Jefferson County deputy sheriff.
>
> (The National Association for the Advancement of Colored People called for peaceful picketing in 100 cities around the country to protest the actions of the Birmingham officials. In Greenfield Park, N.Y., a group

of Conservative rabbis left for Birmingham in a "testimony on behalf of the human rights and dignity" of Negroes.)

I have called this an example of "straight" reporting, and my quotation marks are intended to suggest, of course, that straightness is as absolutely impossible in writing as it is in higher mathematics. Readers of a semantic turn of mind, looking for loaded language in that introduction, might easily challenge some of it. The Negroes "rampaged" through the business district, and "rained" missiles on the police. The sentence about the velocity of the fire hoses would not have been composed by a Southern reporter. But on the whole it is hard to see how the job could have been done much straighter than it has been done here. A little dull, considering the circumstances? Unfeeling? Perhaps a little Stuffy? Or is the horror the more vivid because of the writer's very restraint? At any rate, taking this account as a base of operations, let us look at some alternative ways of reporting that day's events in Birmingham.

At the time when these events took place, the *New York Herald Tribune* was conducting a publicity campaign directed a little desperately at an obvious front-running competitor. Must a great newspaper be dull?, the billboards were asking, and the answer, in the negative, was presumably to be found in the style of the *Tribune*'s own pages. On the same day when the *Times* piece appeared, the *Tribune*'s story, under the byline of Charles Portis, began as follows:

> Three times during the day, waves of shouting, rock-throwing Negroes had poured into the downtown business district, to be scattered and driven back by battering streams of water from high-pressure hoses and swinging clubs of policemen and highway patrolmen. Now the deserted streets were littered with sodden debris. Here in the shabby streets of the Negro section one of the decisive clashes in the Negro battle against segregation was taking place. Last night a tense quiet settled over the riot-packed city after a day in which both sides altered their battle tactics. The Negro crowds, who for days have hurled themselves against police barriers, divided into small, shifting bands, darted around the police and poured hundreds of separate patrols into the downtown business districts. The police, who had crowded hundreds into the city's jails, abandoned efforts to arrest the demonstrators. They concentrated on herding the mobs toward the 16th Street Baptist Church, headquarters for these unprecedented demonstrations. By day's end, Gov. George Wallace had ordered some 250 state highway patrolmen in to aid beleaguered local police and had warned at an opening session of the Legislature that he would prosecute Negroes for murder if anyone died in the Birmingham riots.

As often, we may begin by asking just where in place and time the two assumed authors are situated. The *Times* man is not, as far as we can tell, anywhere in particular. He is sitting in his hotel room typing out an account of what he has seen or heard during the day just ended. Or he is at a telephone dictating this information to New York. Who knows? Little or no distinction has been made between speaker and assumed author. There is no pretense that the reporter is anywhere else but where, in realistic fact, we assume he *is,* as a working journalist. But the *Tribune* man is far more complex in locating himself. He uses, first, two verb tenses in identifying the time of utterance. During the day waves of Negroes *had poured* (first sentence). When is now? Presumably at the end of the day, at the time of writing. Why, then, *were* littered; why not *are* littered? This particular posture, of using "now" for a time spoken of as already having happened, is common in fiction, where an *imagined* voice can use "now" in that curious and palpably made-up way. The assumed author pretends with one word (now) that he is really there at the moment, while with another word (were) he reminds us that he isn't. Third sentence: *Here* in the shabby streets of the Negro section. Where is here? Where is the speaker? Well, the speaker is apparently in the shabby streets, but the *writer* certainly isn't in the streets. Squatting on the sidewalk with typewriter or telephone? Scarcely. What the writer has done, then, is to invent an imagined speaker, *on the model of the novelist,* who, because he is imaginary, can speak of the situation more authoritatively than any mere hotel-bound reporter. And authoritative this speaker (or, better, narrator) certainly is. It follows, to take a minor example, that he can call the streams from the fire hoses "battering," almost as if he felt them himself. (Compare the *Times* man's sentence about the fire hoses and the bark of trees: evidence he presumably observed personally.) Or, to take a more conspicuous example, it follows that this narrator can label the riot as "one of the decisive clashes in the Negro battle against segregation." How does he know that? He knows it because he is a made-up man, because he is like a teller of a tale, and it is his privilege and his business to know.

Further manifestations of this narrator's free-swinging position can be found in a number of his words and phrases. His willingness to use metaphor (however unoriginally) is characteristic. "Hundreds of rioting Negroes" (*Times*) are "waves" in the *Tribune.* The crowds "hurled themselves" while the police were "herding" the mobs toward the church. Throughout the passage the writer's liberal use of modification is significant . . . we find here a perceptible difference between the two pieces of prose in the number of words used as modifiers—that is, considerably more in the *Tribune* article. And as in Howells, it is the omniscient assumed author who takes the liberty of modifying his nouns with adjectives. Why not? He knows, and can well afford to give us the qualities of things, not just their names. And the difference in genre is of course the whole point: where Howells was writing a clear piece of fiction, the *Tribune* purports to express actual events.

By such language the day's news is transformed into a tale told by a fictitious teller. It may not be dull, but as anyone can see, it can be dangerous. What the *Tribune* writer has done is to impose on a real-life situation an omniscient narrator of the sort familiar to traditional fiction. Must a great newspaper be dull? In this case, at least, the avoidance of "dullness" has been accomplished at the cost of making Birmingham a fictitious place, the kind of place where someone "in charge" (the narrator) can truly know the score. I do not disguise my own moral indignation at this literary make-believe. For Birmingham and its troubles are not fiction; they are serious and complicated matters to be cautiously expressed. Furthermore, insofar as naive readers may not recognize the *Tribune*'s fictitiousness, and may assume that this is a Real Birmingham being described, the damage done in the long run to people's minds may be serious.

There is a problem of *genre* here that has attracted some attention just recently. With the publication of Truman Capote's enormously popular *In Cold Blood* (1965), the issue was explicitly raised. Was this factual journalism, or was it fiction? Mr. Capote has made much of his "invention" of a new style, combining the two. The fictional omniscience of his narrating voice is supposed to be justified by years of research, note-taking, tape-recording, and all the industry of the cautious reporter. Nevertheless he feels free to enter the minds of his protagonists and give us their "thoughts." Where are we? This muddle has upset some of his critics, notably Mr. F. W. Dupee, who has complained that Capote is "exploiting the factual authority of journalism and the atmospheric license of fiction."

But the device of the omniscient narrator in news-writing, as an attempt to avoid dullness, has been with us for quite a while. It has been most conspicuous in *Time,* "the weekly news-magazine." The style of *Time* has irked a great many people, and has inspired parodies of considerable venom. *Time*'s style has also, obviously, impressed many readers favorably, as the magazine's success over the years must demonstrate. It has not generally been understood that both the outrage and the admiration originate in one pervasive device of style: the intrusion into the news of an omniscient narrator, on the model of works of fiction.

Any random sampling of *Time*'s pages will show this omniscient speaker at work. Such a speaker can, for example, know what is going on inside the minds of other people—a privilege open to the fictitious narrator alone.

> The cold war, the President felt, was a stalemate. He sensed a deepening international discouragement. . . .

He can *know* the true significance of the events he describes:

> To eye and ear, the desultory discussion in the Senate seemed like anything but what it actually was: one of the most. . . .

He can be in possession of the most vivid details concerning events no human could possibly know:

> Leaping from his bed one night last January, Dahomey's President Hubert Maga excitedly telephoned military headquarters to report that his residence was being shelled. He soon went back to sleep. At it turned out. . . .

He can temptingly throw out details about a character he is introducing, *as if* the reader already knew whom he was talking about—the suspense-building technique of the story-teller:

> They called him "Tawl Tawm." His flamboyant Senate oratory could down an opponent in sweet molasses or hogtie him in barbed wire. He smoked ten 15¢ cigars a day and wore his white hair so long that it crested in curls at the nape of his neck. He dressed. . . .

This piece is not headlined at all—such as "Senator Connolly Dies." Instead it is *titled*—"Tawl Tawm"—in the slightly mysterious way that stories are conventionally titled.

In fact *Time*'s dependence on models of fiction shows up clearly in its headings, where puns and echoes based on actual titles of fiction are common. "Revolution in the Afternoon," "Sounds in the Night," "The Monkey's Pa," are examples from a single issue. These instances of semi-literary semi-sophistication have their bearing on the tone of the magazine, in which the reader is flattered by being in the know with respect to such little jokes. But tricks of title are only a minor weapon in *Time*'s arsenal for putting the reader (fictitiously) in the know. It is the consistent omniscience of the narrating voice that primarily does the job.

How did *Time* describe the events of May 7, 1963, in Birmingham, Alabama? As follows:

The blaze of bombs, the flash of blades, the eerie glow of fire, the keening cries of hatred, the wild dance of terror at night—all this was Birmingham, Alabama.

Birmingham's Negroes had always seemed a docile lot. Downtown at night, they slouched in gloomy huddles beneath street lamps talking softly or not at all. They knew their place: they were "niggers" in a Jim Crow town, and they bore their degradation in silence.

But last week they smashed that image forever. The scenes in Birmingham were unforgettable. There was the Negro youth, sprawled on his back and spinning across the pavement while firemen battered him with streams of water so powerful that they could strip the bark off trees. There was the Negro woman, pinned to the ground by cops, one of them with his knee dug into her throat. There was the white man who watched hymn-singing Negroes burst from a sweltering church and growled: "We ought to shoot every damned one of them." And there was the little Negro girl, splendid in a newly starched dress, who marched out of a church, looked toward a massed line of pistol-packing cops, and called to a laggard friend: "Hurry up, Lucile. If you stay behind you won't get arrested with our group."

The postures of Knowing taken here are obvious enough and hardly need stressing. "All this was Birmingham." The narrator knows the past, for the Negroes "had always seemed" docile. He has seen them "in gloomy huddles" over a long period of time; this concrete description implies close personal knowledge. They knew their place, he says, echoing ironically the white man's cliché, of which again he seems to have an intimate knowledge. "But last week they smashed that image *forever*": now he knows the future too. Is that the news? Or is it the kind of statement an all-knowing story-teller can make about a place he has invented? (Of course we have to say, for this writer, that subsequent events have justified some of his fictitious wisdom!)

The suspicion is tempting that the *real* author of this piece never left his air-conditioned office in Manhattan's Time-Life Building. What he may have done was to read a lot of other people's accounts of Birmingham, including the *Times* man's observation about fire hoses and tree bark, which he then paraphrased in the manner of the novelist. More accurately, I suppose, this prose is the work of several hands, one or two of whom may actually have been on the scene in Birmingham.

But omniscience is not the only thing to notice about this narrator's use of words. The reader who reacts to that barrage of definite articles in *Time*'s first sentence may be reminded of an old friend.

The blaze of bombs, the flash of blades, the eerie glow of fire, the keening cries of hatred, the wild dance of terror. . . .

Part of the speaker's relation with the reader is that of a shared knowledgeable awareness of just the sort of "blaze" and "flash" and "eerie glow" the speaker is talking about. *You* know what I mean. It is the familiar intimacy of the Tough Talker, who implies that he already knows his reader before the story opens.

Actually, once the first sentence is over with, the writer for *Time* uses somewhat fewer definite articles than the writers of our other two Birmingham passages. But he has additional rhetorical characteristics that, statistically at least, carry him much closer to Frederic Henry than is the case with the other two. Most important is the sheer size of his words. A count of monosyllables in all three passages shows that whereas in the *Times* and *Tribune* a little over half of the words are of one syllable, over three-quarters of *Time*'s diction is monosyllabic. In a count of longer words, those of three syllables or more, the *Times* piece shows 15 per cent, the *Tribune* 12 per cent, and *Time* only 5 per cent. And even these are simple and repetitious; "Birmingham" appears three times. We recall that the Tough Talker is chary with modification. If we list the words in each passage being used to modify nouns (omitting articles and demonstrative and personal pronous), we discover that the *Time* writer, for all his eerie glows and keening cries, has the least modification of the three, while the *Tribune* piece has the most.

A chart of such information may be useful:

	Times	Tribune	Time
Total words in passage	193	201	214
Average sentence length	22	25	19
Monosyllables (% of total words)	55%	57%	78%
Longer words (3 syllables & over)	15%	12%	5%
Modifiers of nouns	15%	19%	11%

Do such figures prove anything? Probably not by themselves, unless we can feel, in the tone of the *Time* passage, that particular intensity and intimacy we noted in the introduction to *Farewell to Arms.* Can we? For all the embarrassing bad writing in the *Time* passage, I hope it is clear that we can. The speaker, surely "a hard man who has been around in a violent world," expects of us intimacy of a special closeness. If we are to become the sympathetic assumed reader of these words (which I personally find most difficult), we share a world defined in tight-lipped simplicity of language. It is a world where policemen are always cops and violence is taken for granted, and where crude pathos (the little Negro girl at the end) is expected to move us deeply right through the toughness. Beneath that harsh voice (as often, even in Hemingway) there beats all too visibly a heart of sugar. In fact the triteness of the piece is such as to give us momentary pause about our whole response so far. Can this very triteness be intended? Those piled-up alliterative clichés at the start—the blaze of bombs, the keening cries —suggest possibly an even further intimacy with the reader that may conceivably run something like this: You and I know this is mostly a verbal game. You recognize as I do the familiar theatrical phrases from who-done-it literature with which I adorn this account, and you recognize that I'm not trying to *tell you* anything about Birmingham. I'm just wittily entertaining you for a few moments after a busy day. After all, you've already read last week's newspapers. This is decorative.

If there is anything to the suspicions I have just uttered (and I am truly doubtful), then Timestyle has to be seen as cynical in the extreme. For if, as seems remotely possible, the sophisticated reader is to see this writer's pose as after all not tough and intense, but mock-tough, then the two of them, reader and writer, are engaged in a most irresponsible game. These are not events to play games with. The real trouble is that I, as a reader, can't tell whether this is a game or not.

And if it is not, then we return to locate again one huge distinction between the Tough Talker we saw in Hemingway and the one we see here. It is true that some of the Tough Talker's rhetoric is here visible: short sentences, simplified diction, relatively low modification. But omniscience has been added! We have an intense, human-sounding, tough-talking narrator *without* any human limitations. He knows. When, in other words, you invent a voice that asserts deep and violent feeling, and close intimacy with the reader, and omniscience, you have a public address system of formidable power. And when you apply that voice to the "reporting" of the *news,* you have committed an act of intellectual dishonesty.

In this comparison of three expressions of the news, the restraint of *The New York Times* has seemed to come off with highest marks. But let not the *Times* relax its vigil. The fact is that the charms of fiction-writing have beguiled the *Times* writers too, though usually without the rhetoric of the Tough Talker. We can see fictitious omniscience especially in the Sunday supplement called "The News of the Week in Review," where, in summarizing the week's news, it is apparently tempting to talk as if one knew what happened.

The Coup
The time was just before 3 A.M. in Washington on Friday. In the "situation room" in the White House basement, a command center which receives diplomatic and intelligence reports from around the world, a message from the U. S. Embassy in Saigon clattered off one of the teletype machines. A watch officer phoned. . . .

Without belaboring the point one can certainly make out in these lines the suspenseful devices of the novelist, from the mysterious title and *in-medias-res* beginning to the teletype machine that clattered off a message. Who heard it clatter? This is a case of the *Times* man having read his *Time* too well and too often rather than the other way around.

One appreciates any effort by journalists to make the reading of the news less of a chore and a bore. Nobody wants to be dull. But if the alternative to dullness is dishonesty, it may be better to be dull. On the other hand there are surely other alternatives. Without trying to tell the newswriter his business, I should suppose that a concrete and sober account of what a reporter *did* during his day's work would be, in many cases, neither dull nor dishonest. Such an account would not, to be sure, leave us with the satisfied feeling of knowing the Real Scoop on Birmingham, or the White House, or the Wide World. But as I have already said too often, this is not a feeling to be encouraged anyway.

THOMAS J. COTTLE

The Politics of Pronouncement:

Notes on Publishing in

the Social Sciences

. . . *The trip to Hannah Brachman's was always interesting. Travelling down Blue Hill Avenue, the most direct route to her house, revealed a panorama of Boston's social history. How many students had come to this area to make their own studies, and then described their impressions of the soul food stores alongside the Kosher butcher shops or the Mogen Davids adorning the cement fronts of record and barber shops. Everyone knows the "story" of blacks moving in, Jews moving out, and the exodus of the young and the affluent to Brookline and Newton.*

Mrs. Brachman was always waiting for me, some food prepared, a neighbor's child reading in the kitchen, eager to make friends with someone from a University. Our discussions usually centered on her feelings about her family, Jewish writers and scholars, events in New York, Jerusalem, and at Brandeis. Always she would have words of praise for the president of Brandeis and more harsh words for blacks occupying buildings and claiming that the University's name should be changed. Mrs. Brachman's loyalties were coming out more strongly. "Who helped us?" she would ask rhetorically. "Who marched down Fifth Avenue or sat in buildings or made revolution for us? They still don't do anything for us."

From *Harvard Educational Review*, Vol. 39, No. 3, Summer 1969. Copyright © 1954 by the President and Fellows of Harvard College.

341

As a favor, Mrs. Brachman read a couple of articles written by social scientists on the activities of Jews in the New Left and the rather significant position of power they seemed to have attained. We both agreed that the pieces were written from sympathetic viewpoints, the authors presumably remaining as objective as possible. The data, I had thought, were well collected, thoughtfully analyzed, and presented without bias. "You can't argue with those numbers. It's hard to fight that. It seems pretty obvious." Soon her eyes moved away from the pages of the reprints, now wrinkled and torn. "You know, not a lot of people know it, but the Jews have done a lot for this country. When you stop to think of all the doctors and lawyers, all the professors, it's really something. It's really some accomplishment. And look at Israel. Is that not something extraordinary? The fears, the wars. What these people have suffered. From one war right into that trouble. What's going to happen? What's going to happen?"

Where in this was the reality our students wish us to discover as they yank us into the world hoping that our observations might be more accurate, our recommendations for change more influential? How are we able to differentiate our research intentions from our policy-making intentions? And how can we separate our desire to make science from a publisher's or reader's desire to make politics?

"What about the article, Mrs. Menter?"

"Oh yes. Well, I don't care what he says here. I know about that Coleman report and this report and that report. You don't need to tell Negroes about that stuff. That's white man's words for white man's ears. When the Negro professors start writing things, you'll see a whole different picture. You go out and bring me some of their work and you'll get a different picture. You'll get a very different picture."

Erlene Menter knew full well the contents of the eight page article I had asked her to read. When all the grammar, paragraphs, and data had been pushed aside, she saw a terrifying message, naked and bleeding. She had read eight pages about black children growing up in ghettos, about absent males, the occurrence of incest and the impact of all this on children and on a race of really not so many people who were struggling to find a pattern that might simultaneously knit them together and then, bounce them all up, upward to where they wouldn't receive such devastating rebukes or, for that matter, such perplexing triumphs. The message she got, was that when this scientist ran his figures and numbers through a computing machine, it came out, as she said, "that the Negroes aren't getting anywhere in particular, too fast."

Debates on the possibility of "value-free" social science are becoming increasingly rare. Some social scientists believe that they can make so-called "value-free" contributions to fact and theory. Others are sure that this freedom from bias can never be achieved, if due only to the more subtle implications of the very act of publishing from a position within a university.

As effortful as each day had become in the eighteen years since Francis Cavanaugh died of a heart attack in the house where she still lives, Kathleen Cavanaugh fulfilled her promise to me by reading twenty rather trying pages on the value and belief systems of working-class Catholic families. I picked the piece especially because we had spoken of such matters before, and because it seemed to me, anyway, that the authors had captured without obvious distortion the lives of people "sociologically similar" to Mrs. Cavanaugh. I had thought she would immediately read of a familiar world, accurately presented. Diligently and methodically she had read the assignment, even taking rather copious notes on the inside of the telephone book in that delicate thin-line handwriting of hers.

"Are they teaching this kind of stuff at your school, because if they are you could sure do a good thing for these students by telling each and every single one just what we do believe. And don't you let them get away with this. I'll bet you those professors never did speak with any of those people they write about. No one talks like that, unless he's composing something, like a story or poem."

Kathleen Cavanaugh was profoundly upset. The article had portrayed something insidious. Undeniably, she had felt betrayed. It was as though her pride had been extinguished, her very soul invaded and found dry and hollow. She had learned more, she would say later on, from television even though it too "favors what the rich people have to say and think. And buy." By what had seemed to me to be an insightful, penetrating glance at a community's social life, Mrs. Cavanaugh had been shot down, right in her steps.

The implications of disseminating the research findings she had read had not been lost on Mrs. Brachman, either.

"Do you know some of the things the students would like to see changed in society?"

"Everyone knows. Even in Washington they know. They don't like this war. Who can like that war? Can you imagine this business with the boat, this Pueblo business? The kids don't like that, do they? They

think it's unfair? I can't blame them. Why are we fighting and spying and killing? Every night on the television that's all you see. Tell me, is it true what I read, Jews are really running these college things? Maybe someone should tell them it doesn't look so good. Do you think it's good for people to read such things, even though they say it's true, you know who I mean? A lot of people read articles like this, don't they?"

It seems almost impossible to publish a report that represents no political bias or implies no political action. Whatever our intention, whatever our assumptions of how "value-free" our research can be, the implications stay with us. Even with our modest intentions to "advance science or knowledge," the popular media and its readers stand ready to greet the applications or the political implications. What, in short, they ask, are the products or profits and the statements of appropriate action to be found in these writings? What can I take and use of this? How can it be reduced to the solid, true laws of human nature that these scholars are, after all, supposed to be discovering?

To these questions, social scientists respond with troubled ambivalence. Pressures from many people have been put on academicians to derive with certainty the state of human nature and programs for the upgrading of everyone. Working against this, naturally, are the "limitations of the art" as well as, perhaps, a primordial reluctance to explain mankind, to explain so much variance that futures become predictable, presents explicable, pasts logical, and certainty guaranteed. There just may be a primitive sense in each of us that will forever prevent a total explanation or perfect experiment. Yet if such a sense exists, it may not be tolerated by audiences demanding exactitude in diagnosis and treatment.

Still, we do little to convey to these audiences the tentativeness and possible inaccuracy of our statements. There are those of us who qualify their televised pronouncements with "we know very little," or "our science is so young," only to proceed to deadly pontification. Others advance the most recently achieved knowledge while ignoring the attendant responsibility of their published words.

Recently, a young social psychologist bemoaned the overnight success of his first book. He had received letters from everywhere, even from soldiers in Viet Nam, asking him whether they could take his tests and undergo his experiments, which somehow were supposed to better their lives. What shocked the author, really, was the way people "could just take over my book and do with it whatever they wanted." No longer was he in control. From even a cursory reading they had come away with political and social strands he himself barely recognized. Where he had used data to reinforce hunches, they had clutched that data as proof of the book's "real" message. They had skipped over the pages where conceptualizations were embellished and had rushed instead to the meaty parts from which they might take something for themselves. Now they begged him to let them be a part of his grand scheme for change and success. There seemed to be nothing in their reactions suggesting an appreciation for any intellectual contribution. "They read that book as though it were a manual on how to ice skate."

His book was taken as a manual because in part the media of popular communication cannot always tolerate messages of what intellectuals think about, work with, or, indeed, play with. Popular media cannot always permit the luxury of theoretical reasoning or development, nor can they spend time dealing with contributions to the history of theory when there are hard, cold facts to be gotten out and publicized. Moreover, there must be a splash, a glimmer, a scintillating explosion in each and every published pronouncement or it won't "catch on." There must be something that one can hold in his hand, a "fistful of reality," as Sartre said.

The conflicting needs of scientists as against those of their publishers, readers and, increasingly, the students, make it progressively more difficult to "get away with" pure and simple contributions to theory and methodology. Despite the many failures and the flood of contradictory books and reports, much of the public remains loyal to the belief that social scientists are experts, suppliers of the right kind of knowledge. In a word, their expertise renders them "solutionists." Their ideas cannot stay as ideas, but must be translated into facts and answers. As speedily as these ideas pass from the page to the eye, they lose their tentativeness and "hunchiness" and become certainty as well as plans for action.

Erlene Menter was laughing again, sitting up straight and pushing the journal back across the table. As it moved, she rotated it slightly, the letters now right side up for her. "Nice colors they use," she said, staring at the cover and fondling its smoothness as though the outline of each letter might stand up just high enough so that she could touch it, then read it with her eyes closed. She let the pages riffle gently along the tips of her fingers, then a few times more. "The paper's nice too. Not like the newspaper."

The article had said as much through its authoritative, bookish appearance as it had through the statements on its pages.

Just as what we study represents a very real system of values, so too do the "products" of our studies perpetrate these values and hold them up as some ideal, however temporary. A popular conception holds that in science, publication implies certainty. Clearly, too much certainty is taken for granted. Among most readers, even editors, scientists simply cannot play with ideas. Tentativeness and unsureness cannot be accepted from them. Maybe that's why correlations too often emerge as causation and why summaries of findings get publicized as incontestible facts.

For Hannah Brachman, a mythic tradition of intellectualism and achievement, spirit and honor along with suffering, welled up within the soul she chooses to share with millions and millions of people. The two studies she had read were bad press; they could not be denied, shoved aside or forgotten. Scientists teach facts, and the facts they had taught her were that Jewish boys and girls were being disruptive, causing problems, getting themselves into serious trouble and going to jail. For her, science is facts, undeniable, incontrovertible facts. "When a man with such education, such erudition speaks, he knows what he's talking about. Maybe I'd like to disagree. To tell you the truth I wish he hadn't written this. Or maybe I wish you hadn't brought it to me. But that's the world. That's the world. It seems a shame."

Some people, naturally, have "adopted" the findings of social sciences and found them valuable for their work and for their lives. But the day is not yet here when the "public" fully appreciates the playfulness of ideas or the fun and excitement of knowledge. Not enough people yet understand the little boy or girl, free from everything and everyone, alone in his room, deeply engrossed in a task only angels dare understand.

Surely there still exists the popular conception of the professor as the man who is "only" playing. This is the notion that speaks to his lack of any tangible product or of "an honest day's work" and concludes that the professor remains as childishly occupied as the children he teaches.

This is hardly the same view as that held by academics about the playfulness of ideas inside the academy. The evolution of intellectualism, just as the development of cognitive abilities in the child, brings cultures to the point where ideas almost stand by themselves, unencumbered by political association with some greater shared reality. Indeed, the highest form of thought permits both the capacity to imagine the impossible or unreal and the capacity to play with ideas, to work with and sculpt them, even if the final product fails to yield anything but joy.

Now, as students argue louder than ever before, only the very elite can still afford the luxury of such playfulness and tentativeness. Only the elite can dare consider "intellectual contributions" sufficient. And yet they must be made. Many students have joined the public in crying for political products and not playfulness. And so, faculty members now fear the end of purely "academic days" as they struggle to defend themselves against what they feel to be an onslaught of anti-intellectualism, anti-rationalism, anti-objectivism and anti-science led by, of all people, their very disciples and apprentices.

"Think of the money spent trying to figure out what's happening in these neighborhoods. That other book you had JoAnne (her daughter) read was all about black folks in Baltimore and Washington. Think of that. They go all the way to Baltimore just to look into their homes when they could come right here. They're all welcome right here. You tell them if they want to make some of their studies, they should come and see me. I'll tell them stories they can write ten books about, fifty books about if their hands don't get tired and those machines of theirs don't die."

"I think maybe those studies were done by people who lived in Baltimore and Washington."

"Maybe so. I thought JoAnne said something about going all the way down there to make their studies. You don't hear anything about this neighborhood, 'cepting that there's trouble with the welfare boards and those . . . Man, they've got a collection of people working for them, you wouldn't believe your eyes. Not too many of your Harvard folks, I'll bet."

Two sorts of familiar political spectrums, really, have emerged: the "horizontal" scale to the left and right of moderate and the "vertical" spectrum about which our students are teaching us. The "vertical" scale extends from elite privilege to disenfranchisement. Coming from a generation of objectivity, students have long advocated total awareness of this spectrum but now demand direct participation in the lives of disenfranchised and oppressed people.

The university model of detachment and non-involvement was seriously shaken by the Civil Rights movement of the 1950's. The initial student involvement in the lives of southern Negroes lead to their emphasis on political intervention and on becoming implicated. Sit-ins quickly turned to voter registration and redistricting campaigns. But the intellectuals remained a step behind, some reporting on the events in the North and South, many banging out research documents investigating the parents, grandparents, school problems, and generalized psychopathologies of student workers. Nevertheless, the result for many scholars was a violent shift from playfulness and sovereign academic goals to a politicization of their research in a way that would, as they say, help mankind. At the very least, this new breed of social scientists was thinking about the concrete products of their enterprises and the implications these products might have in the political arena. For them, academia was a necessary home and tentativeness a necessary constraint, but not a way of distancing themselves from a population for whom they cared, and at times, for whom they grieved. They wanted and needed to be in touch.

JoAnne Menter sat cross-legged on the floor; two friends slouched on the sofa listening to her read sections from a book. As she recited certain passages carefully marked by her earlier, they all screamed with laughter, bouncing up and down from their scattered positions on the floor and furniture. JoAnne would start another passage, and they would cackle and jabber. "You better believe it, baby. This cat sets up right there on the corner. . . ." And they would roar. I couldn't help laugh myself. Erlene, working about as though she weren't paying the four of us any attention, showed by an occasional glance that she would just as soon send all of us maniacs to some institution. But she too understood. . . .

Kathleen Cavanaugh pounded her fist on the open pages: "They're just not going to pin me down that easily." JoAnne Menter, too, had rebuked the characterization of "her people." Her laughter hardly masked the poignancy of the book and her desperate attempts to climb out from under the shackles of categories, divisions of populations, and conceptualizations made by some "smart guy who thinks he knows us just 'cause he's been to school longer than us." As much as in their fight to stay abreast of groups, collectivities, cultures, and hordes of people they could hardly imagine—even after attending a giant rally for black people only—Erlene Menter and her daughter fought hardest of all to maintain a single stretch of their own being and their own singular identities. "Before anything else," JoAnne would say, "I am always me. Somebody told me that God exists in each of us and that we should be proud just to be ourselves. So, I'm going to be me, and if people don't like it. . . ."

Politicized students have managed to convince many academics that even if they shy away from research that has explicit policy implications or from polemical pieces which unequivocally indicate their political persuasion, the very actions of research and writing can be deemed elitist. Our concern for the working class or the blacks is lovely to behold, they argue, but when we offer our ideas as weighted as they are by our proclaimed status they cannot help but be blistered by the dispositions of our enterprises and by the politics of our lives and life styles. Like air bubbles, politics has been pumped into the research of people who have worked diligently to make sure none would be found.

Indeed, the day may never come when students succeed in pushing all scholars into what they call reality. By reality they mean not only that intellectuals should become involved, engaged, politicized, but that they should be aware of the political electricity that illuminates their writing and acts to legitimate their cause and freedom. Students argue that universities cannot remain isolated unless people like Kathleen Cavanaugh or Erlene Menter have a place; and until that time they cannot condone the political elitism of studies and offerings which, in their very prose, protect and distance us from those we study. How often, they ask, would we admit to knowing our "subjects" and "respondents"? How often do we consider the pretense at objectivity which removes us from the world in which we observe and write and think? How often, they ask, do we take seriously the political positions from which our writings unwittingly take shape and from which policy statements ultimately are drawn? And always they throw that word, "elitism," at us, in an effort to extinguish our habits of playfulness and immodest indifference. They want us out of our offices and "into the world." Many of them want our voices to come together in what they call a "new politics."

One of many justifiable statements heard in rejection of assuming political stances or of doing explicitly policy-oriented research is that these actions too easily lead to governmental or societal restraints on research topics and operations. There is much to fear if research is taken over by the constraints imposed by any interest group.

A paradoxical result of current student focus on the politics of their professors is that one utterance can forever—publicly and inaccurately— nail a faculty member to one political position just as he dares to step out of his office and into the realities of a stratified society or into what we call "the field." We have yet to realize fully that the profound political implications of our work do not lie on the left-right political spectrum in which our audience might stereotype us, but in our witting or unwitting participation in that other spectrum which contains poverty, racism, disenfranchisement, and oppression.

The most telling sign of this may be that Mrs. Cavanaugh and Mrs. Menter cannot find themselves in the articles they read. They cannot get the picture moved around so that it includes them. At least this is what they say. For it also may be true that the studies have found them too accurately, too penetratingly and, as sensitive human beings, they must recoil from the unintended stabs and stereotyping of these portraits.

Their reactions, therefore, might be what some call "denial." But if it is denial, it may have something to do with the fact that the studies' portraits bring them nothing more than reading materials from a teacher. Their reactions may well be natural protection against a hope that more might come, that something might happen. For while we in our debates over interpretations of data may take time out for reanalysis, reevaluation, or even for play, they dare not leave the apartments where their children will be raised, nor the houses where their husbands died, for even a moment of truly fresh air.

The self-insulated separation, the lack of sensitivity to the vast and subtle political implications of our publications in part come down to our not hearing the quiet phrases and the ritualized language forms which too often go unnoticed. *When I left Mrs. Brachman for the last time she walked me to the door of the apartment, always so neat and open to guests and family. She looked me squarely in the eyes without shame and without defiance: "When you're done with your work and you have a little time on your hands, you'll go with with your wife and you'll get a haircut, and maybe you'll find some time to come back and we'll talk a little. The three of us. O.K.?"*

JACOB BRACKMAN

The Put-On

Patrons at a Pop gallery chuckle knowingly over a Roy Lichtenstein painting. A bearded young man at a party introduces himself as an undercover agent for the Green Berets. Senator Everett Dirksen recites a deep-throated, eye-rolling, super-rhetorical piece of bombast on God, Country, and Marigolds. Stokely Carmichael answers an interviewer who wants to know what must be done about Harlem: "Burn it to the ground and send one million black men up to invade Scarsdale." Oedipa Maas, wife of disc jockey Mucho Maas and patient of berserk psychiatrist Dr. Hilarius, is at last on the verge of unravelling the prodigious mystery of the Tristero syndicate on page 183 of Thomas Pynchon's much heralded second novel; there is no page 184. Representative Frank Thompson, of New Jersey, before a full session of Congress, proposes the Banana and Other Odd Fruit Disclosure and Reporting Act of 1967 to halt "the sinister spread" of "hallucinogenic" banana-peel smoking. A top-box-office spy film concludes, after a huge explosion wipes out secret agents from five countries (as well as French Legionnaires, United States Cavalrymen, and a Frugging battalion of Indian parachutists), with a mass ascent to Heaven. Students opposed to the war in Vietnam arrive to testify at House Un-American Activities Committee hearings in bizarre costumes: one wears a Revolutionary War uniform, complete with tricorne hat; another identifies himself as James Bond; a third addresses the Chairman, Congressman Joseph Pool, of Texas, as Jo-Jo while under oath. Adam Clayton Powell summons newsmen to his Bimini hideaway for a big scoop; then he plugs his new record, "Keep the Faith, Baby." "What's the big story?" a reporter asks. "You've heard it, baby," Powell replies. The Beatles answer every question at a press conference by saying "Woof, woof." Someone asks if

"Yellow Submarine" is a drug song, and Paul McCartney replies, "You have a dirty mind." In Mont-Saint-Michel, a pretty girl in leotards flourishes a trumpet, elaborately preparing for a street concert. Finally, she begins to blow horrible noises. Obviously, she can't play the trumpet at all. She passes a hat and people give her money. "What Does It Mean? —Who Knows?" asks a *Times* headline above a rave review of "Gorilla Queen," in which a chorus line of apes sings the Chorale from Beethoven's Ninth and both a jungle girl and a blond to-be-sacrificed virgin seem to be men. The playwright's previous works include "Tarzan of the Flicks," "Indira Gandhi's Daring Device," and "The Life of Lady Godiva." Twiggy (31-22-32), the world's No. 1 model and London's "Girl of the Year," has thatched male hair, stands five feet six, weighs ninety-one pounds, wears short pants, sucks her finger, pouts, and answers reporters' questions with "I dunno." She is seventeen years old and earns a hundred and twenty dollars an hour. A famous artist is commissioned to paint the portrait of, say, Mrs. Felice Worthingham. "I'm very busy," he mutters. "Let's see . . ." He writes the words "Portrait of Mrs. Felice Worthington" on a grubby torn-off piece of paper. Then he signs the jotting and hands it over to Mr. Worthingham, who has the "portrait" framed and pays the artist's usual fee—five thousand dollars. Man, you know *some*body's leg is being pulled. Or at least you think *maybe* it is.

By means of a subtle transformation in the ways artists deal with their audiences and people with one another, we suddenly have reason to distrust a good deal of art, fashion, and conversation—to withhold a flat-footed, honest response. More and more often, we suspect we are being tricked. What was once an occasional surprise tactic—called "joshing" around the turn of the century and "kidding" since the twenties— has been refined into the very basis of a new mode of communication. In all its permutations, this phenomenon is known as the "put-on." It occupies a fuzzy territory between simple leg-pulling and elaborate practical joke, between pointed lampoon and free-floating spoof.

Though there are suddenly many more of them, conversational put-ons are related to old-fashioned joshing and kidding, or to the sort of joke that Southerners call "funning" and Englishmen call "taking a mickey out of" someone. Not unlike the put-on, these older cousins depend upon a certain gullibility in the victim. They are like April-fool gags, perpetrated deadpan to get the victim to believe something that isn't so. Miniature hoaxes, their raison d'être is the surprise revelation of truth ("I was only kidding" or "It was just a gag") and laughter at the fall guy's credulity. Naturally, there were, and still are, habitual kidders or practical jokers. But the object of kidding, as of hoaxing, is always manifest: to *pass off* untruth as truth just for the fun of it. Ideally, there's no doubt in anyone's mind. At first, the victim believes the false to be true, whereas the kidder knows the truth. Then, the gulling accomplished, the kidder lets the victim know he's been taken for a ride. This payoff is the kidder's goal. With kidding and other hoax-derived precedents, the perpetrator smooths the rug out, has you stand on it, and then suddenly yanks it out from under you. The put-on is more like one of those irregular moving platforms at an amusement park. The victim must constantly struggle to maintain his balance, constantly awkward, even (perhaps especially) when the floor *stops* moving for an instant; i.e., a "straight" moment, which makes the victim feel he has been paranoid. As he readjusts himself to this vision, the floor, so to speak, starts moving again. If conversation with a kidder is spiced by bosh, conversation with a put-on artist is a process of escalating confusion and distrust. He doesn't deal in isolated little tricks; rather, he has developed a pervasive style of relating to others that perpetually casts what he says into doubt. The put-on is an *open-end* form. That is to say, it is rarely climaxed by having the "truth" set straight—when a truth, indeed, exists. "Straight" discussion, when one of the participants is putting the others on, is soon subverted and eventually sabotaged by uncertainty. His intentions, and his opinions, remain cloudy.

We remember the kidder as a good-natured, teasing sort—that moment when he rendered his victim absurd was quickly dissipated in the general laughter that followed. The put-on artist draws out that derisive moment; the gull has time to reflect (What's he up to? . . . He's trying to make a monkey out of me. . . . How should I respond?), and the joke's latent malice wells close to the surface. As the put-on pursues its course (at times while the subject matter shifts), it becomes clear that the victim is the butt of a generalized ridicule. Occasionally, a victim will try to explain away his confusion by assuming that the put-on artist is "just being ironical"—that he really means precisely the reverse of everything he says. This interpretation is hardly more helpful than taking put-ons at face value. Irony properly suggests the *opposite* of what is explicitly stated, by means of peripheral clues—tone of voice, accompanying gestures, stylistic exaggeration, or previous familiarity with the ironist's real opinions. Thus, for "Brutus is an honorable man" we understand "Brutus is a traitor." Irony is unsuccessful when misunderstood. But the put-on, inherently, *cannot* be understood.

Irony: A known dove delivers an impassioned "kill the gooks" speech.

Put-on: Someone we don't know delivers the same hawk speech. It is wildly hyperbolical, and yet . . . Is he really a dove? Might he be caricaturing his own position? Might he be apolitical and arbitrarily lampooning one extreme? Might he be merely ridiculing the passion of the discussion? Does he know at all how he feels about the Vietnamese war? Does the confusion he produces in his audience mirror his own confusion? Does the put-on, his diversionary artillery, spare him the self-examination required for a "real stand"?

The deliberate ambiguities of conversational put-ons apply as well to put-ons in art, which are often mistaken for parodies or satires. Yet, according to long-established custom, the parody and the satire are rigorous, demanding forms, with the avowed and actual purpose of burlesquing preëxisting situations in art or life. A parody must imitate the original well, effectively exaggerating its peculiarities and weaknesses. In other words, to be good it must be sharp. It may be attacked for inadequate accuracy, pungency, or wit. The spoof (an old and annoying word now back in vogue for the vehicle of the put-on) need not be good to avert attack. It is too dangling, too slippery. It has only the *form* of satire, without the content, without the rules. It attacks, but from no real position of its own. Not holding any real position, it is itself invulnerable to attack.

When audiences "don't know how to take" a piece of work, it may now be the case that a highly ambiguous mode of presentation has rescued the artist from a head-on struggle with his material, from the most crucial dilemmas of art: What am I to make of my experiences? How do I feel about them? What do they teach me of the world? As conversational put-ons may disguise the fact that someone has nothing of interest to say—may, indeed, give precisely the opposite impression—so have put-ons in art come to serve as a refuge for the untalented. This is not to suggest that gifted artists never affect the style of the put-on (the Beatles are excellent examples of artists who do) but, rather, that the style itself clogs critical judgment and scuttles aesthetic standards. The Intellectual Establishment, which once took a dim view of those who believed themselves so above art as to dissemble in its name, now seems eager to play pigeon to the put-on, and accepts—even welcomes—the implied abuse.

Admittedly, confusion or suspicion on the part of the Intellectual Establishment is historically a poor basis for mistrusting the intentions of artists. Almost every experimental or revolutionary artistic movement of the past—Romanticism, Impressionism, Symbolism, Surrealism, a dozen other isms—was in its time accused of being anti-art. Earnest Philistines of our century demanded to know whom Gertrude Stein and Ezra Pound thought they were fooling; they warned E. E. Cummings that he'd never put his nonsense verse over on readers. They exhorted

Picasso that gallery-goers wouldn't be taken in by Cubism, and cried out when Jackson Pollock and Franz Kline tried to pass off random drippings and slashings as paintings. Schoenberg and Webern were believed to have carried sounds past the boundaries of music. Electronic composers were told that people had too much sense to be hoodwinked by "unmusical" cacophony.

Even as contemporary Goths ask, "Who are they trying to kid?," a new avant-garde public rises to testify that future sensibilities will vindicate Claes Oldenburg's proposed hamburger monument in Times Square, or Andy Warhol's eight-hour film of a sleeping man, or La Monte Young's ear-rending, interminable Drone. And perhaps they will. The debatable art of the current scene, as well as already exonerated cases from art history, underscore the crucial question of *intent*. We now believe that heretical movements of the past, doubted and maligned in their own time, were fostered by serious men who cared deeply about art, who struggled to liberate themselves from exhausted conventions in order to revitalize and restore its relevance. Aspects of these revolutions—the extravagances of Artaud-inspired theatre, or the Nihilistic underside of Dada, with its mustached Mona Lisas and empty canvases—we now consider wrong-headed, childish, chaotic, even destructive. But we are at the same time convinced that they were undertaken, whether in anger or fun, in good faith, with a profound commitment to art and its future.

Much "serious" art today—even seemingly outlandish art—is doubtless undertaken with the same commitment. The currency of the put-on, however, has given new meaning to recent Dadist experimentation. Many art consumers, and some critics as well, have come to envisage contemporary art as a giant con game. The game is played in a spirit of desperate suspicion. Its object is twofold: to appreciate what is "good" and "real," and to avoid being taken in by the con jobs. A few modern critics—most notably, Marshall McLuhan—have tried to break up this game by, in effect, redefining art as anything you can put over on anybody. But the world of culture has too much at stake to accept any such permissive redefinition. Art critics, dealers, and curators must protect their identities (and jobs) as people of taste and discrimination. They must continue to insist that they *understand* what art is real and what art is phony, and that their judgment is fit to advise the public.

This staunch orthodoxy in the Cultural Establishment has several peculiar results. A dangerously preëmptive sort of subjectivism has taken over serious criticism. For a critic to call work bad, he must often, in the light of what he's already called good, tell us that it is a fake. In other words, what he likes he deems real art; what he doesn't like he deems "anti-art," or put-on. Since the critic assumes his job is to dope out the con game, disagreement among critics becomes highly explosive. When one considers bad something that others have considered good, he is no longer simply challenging the merits of a specific work; he is telling the public that his colleagues have been taken in by fraud, that they are hoodwinked in their notions of what constitutes art, that none of us really knows for sure anymore what is real and good. A terrible fear is thus generated throughout the Cultural Establishment: in the galleries, the academies, the critical journals. Are we dismissing genius? Are we elevating nonsense? Will someone rock the boat? Will someone suddenly shout that the Emperor is naked? Will someone simply come along and *describe* the objects we have praised, and will those objects then sound stupid?

One upshot of these fears is a wary, "sophisticated" tolerance toward new art—an intellectualized, jargon-full appreciation of it. Much of this art does, indeed, require tolerance, but tolerance of a far more relaxed sort. It is meant to "be experienced," to wash over an audience. Its put-ons are what may be called *set-breaking* put-ons. They afford one an opportunity to observe one's own consciousness reacting to "art" that contradicts all one's expectations of art. When a composer comes onstage in a dinner jacket and seats himself at a grand piano, a familiar set is established. When he continues to sit there without playing a single note—when the audience realizes that his sitting there *is* the concert—the set is broken. There are perhaps three primary responses to a set-breaking aesthetic experience of this sort: (1) you leave; (2) you remain, listening to what other sounds are to be heard in the hall, examining how others in the audience respond to the "concert," and taking an inventory of your *own* responding consciousness; (3) you remain, trying to figure out whether the composer is "serious" or whether you, as a critical intelligence, are being conned. We know that everyone square leaves, or at least very badly wants to leave. Thus, tolerance—at galleries, concerts, Happenings, dance programs, independent cinema—has become a significant aspect of the contemporary aesthetic experience. Being able to bear put-ons has become one of the responsibilites of the modern audience.

The wrong kind of tolerance—suspicious endurance—has, furthermore, opened up the art scene to people who are able to capitalize on unacknowledged critical confusion. This sort of highly marketable wise-guy-ness, as opposed to seriously intended set-breaking, has made the put-on a fundamentally commercial form, finding its purest expression in television, Hollywood cinema, formula radio, fashion, Top Forty sound, advertising, and the most salable of popular art. Whereas artistic rebels of eras past embraced the most extreme risks in prosecuting their aesthetic ideas, popular artists can now *avoid* risk by the suggestion of a put-on. Possibly the bravest gamble a contemporary artist can take is to present himself as unequivocally serious, for he thereby risks making a fool of himself. This risk, along with the risk of appearing naïve, was once an inviolable prerogative of all creative work. Now we have come to believe that an artist who may be fooling cannot be a fool, and, conversely, that one who is in no way making fun of his own efforts is somehow humorless. It's open season on the unabashedly earnest. But as long as the artist's intentions are even slightly in doubt, most critics approach him with some caution.

A put-on may be as short as a phrase or as long as a novel. Still more confounding, the purest put-ons are never altogether pure, never *unmistakable*. The put-on at once elevates the fraudulent and debases the true, rendering the entire proceedings questionable. A remark that *may be* a put-on casts a whole conversation into doubt; a few frames that may be a put-on make us wonder about a whole movie. The pervasive currency of the put-on generates an atmosphere charged with misplaced skepticism. Not even the painfully serious manage to escape incrimination. Is Marshall McLuhan just putting us on? Is John Cage? Is Norman Mailer, in "An American Dream"? Stan Brakhage, in "Dog Star Man"? Does Dwight Macdonald *really* like "MacBird" all that much? Can Frank Stella be laughing up his sleeve at the critical acclaim accorded his paintings? Richard Goldstein can't actually *believe* the Mamas and the Papas are as valid as Bach. Robert Rauschenberg must be kidding with some of those Happenings, right?

Curiously, this sort of misguided suspicion is tendered in a spirit of respect. (When a work is well reviewed nowadays, some critic is almost sure to inform us that the whole thing was a big joke, and so much the better.) If we like the art, jolly good show. If we don't, perhaps the artist is making fun of us. Perhaps we must give him credit for putting something over on us. If a piece of work is stupid, perhaps it's meant to show how stupid *we* are. Such notions are currently so ingrained as to somehow redeem art that is simply and honestly bad. In spite of his obvious ingenuousness, Andy Warhol is widely credited with pulling the wool over the public's eyes. Nothing of the kind. The public has shown itself ready to buy his meagre product, and he places it on the market as fast as his factories can turn it out. The people around Warhol, however—his co-manufacturers, and certain critics who know when to latch on to a good thing—have created an ambiguous, quasi-facetious aura about their work cult. So while Warhol remains true to his profoundly simplistic visions, consumers feel proud to participate in some vast joke on their peers, and on the very concept of beauty.

Time was when artistic hoax meant a talented unknown's offering his work under an opportune name to gain an audience. So Thomas Chatterton "discovered" "ancient" religious manuscripts and poems, Charles Vanderbourg the poetry of "Clotilde," Prosper Mérimée the dramas of "Clara Gazul," Fritz Kreisler "lost compositions" of Vivaldi, Couperin, Porpora, Pugnani, and Padre Martini. The works themselves were fine and deserving. Today, unknowns make names for themselves with hoax works. Even a painting chimpanzee has been employed to play this game. Talk circulates—"Is it for real?"—and the product sells.

Fascination with the possibly fraudulent, while a symptom of a New Sensibility, has powerful precedents in American culture. For a hundred years—from the Crédit Mobilier scandal and the Whiskey Ring fraud to Billie Sol Estes and Bobby Baker—a sizable number of Americans have been amused rather than enraged by the feats of audacity that gulled them. Such a climate enabled P. T. Barnum to become one of the prime architects of the Gilded Age. People took him to their hearts as the Prince of Humbugs; they gave him license to deceive them. In a corrupt era, when the noblest impulses seemed to lead toward contempt and castigation of self and country, audiences implicitly demanded that they themselves be the butt of public jokes. When they laughed and applauded Barnum's unconvincing cozening, they symbolized the amused acquiescence of a republic duped by political sharks. Because his audience would accept bamboozlement as well as genuine spectacle, Barnum was at least partly relieved of responsibility for coming across with the real McCoy. "People like to be fooled," he's supposed to have said. "There's a sucker born every minute." Yet, despite exaggerated claims for his presentations, not *all* of them were frauds—and he drew the line between the sort of hokum that came to be known as Barnum-ism and the out-and-out swindle. (He emptied out his packed freak museum, for example, with a fancy sign that read, "This Way to the Egress." Customers eagerly went through the appointed door and found themselves in an alley.) So even his hip clientele could never be sure of an exhibit's authenticity: perhaps this Negro woman *was* more than a hundred and sixty years old, perhaps she *was* George Washington's nurse. They asked a question much in vogue today: "Is this for real?"

Barnum's "Greatest Show on Earth" anticipated the three classic elements of the put-on: the come-on (buildup), the fake-out (revelation or suspicion that things are not what they seem), and the cop-out (pulling the whole thing off without necessarily delivering the goods).

Let me define my terms. The come-on is like an introduction, only more elaborate. It is the gestaltic self-presentation. The fake-out is like a surprise, only bigger. It is a radical contradiction of one's presuppositions. The fake-out unmasks the come-on. In combination, they yield the put-on—like a hoax, only smaller.

1. You're sucked in.
2. You become confused.
3. You resent (or appreciate) having been tricked.

The cop-out is like a fink-out, only more graceful. It is getting away with a renege. Here is a hypothetical model of the agglomerate phenomenon:

You go to the theatre to see a magician. He *comes on* like a magician, in tails and cape, and announces that for his first trick he will make a pigeon vanish into thin air. He conceals the bird under a kerchief, utters an incantation, and whisks the kerchief away. The pigeon is still there. He looks confused. You *are* confused. He tries again; again the disappearance fails. On the third try, titters run through the audience. On the fourth, the house is in stitches. You've been *faked out*. You have two options:

1. "Hey! What is this? I came to see a magician."
2. "Hey! Terrific! The guy's really a *comedian*. He had me going there for a minute."

The fake-out has transformed his come-on into a put-on.

Now, if this fellow had really been a magician he would have finked out, busted. Instead, he's a success—everybody's laughing. He's *copped out.*

After all, you paid admission to see a trick. Is the put-on a lower order of trick than a real disappearance? Is it easier? Cheaper? Or is it a double trick? If the pigeon had vanished, that would have been a trick *for* you. The revelation that the magician was not a magician has been a trick *on* you—but if you enjoyed being fooled, of course, it's been for you as well. When the "magician" continues his act in the same vein of bungled abracadabra, we are dealing in straightforward comedy. Once the fake-out has been fully realized, the put-on, strictly speaking, is over. The purest put-ons commence credibly, plant their own seeds of doubt, promote growing confusion, and leave their victims foundering. The secret of maintaining a put-on, therefore, is protracting the fake-out. . . .

A distinctive sort of literary or cinematic fake-out hinges on the sudden demolition of a mood, usually high tragedy collapsing into bathos. ("A joke," Nietzsche said, "is the epitaph on an emotion.") Sometimes the fake-out works the other way around—as in the high-spirited scene from "Shoot the Piano Player" when a gun farcically drawn and twirled, Lone Ranger style, shoots the heroine dead—choking a laugh into a sputter of dismay. Such abrupt reversals produce confusion about the entire piece—"Is the whole thing just a joke?"—and condition audiences against allowing themselves to feel deeply about anything on the page or on the screen. . . .

Spoof films train people to keep their cool, as do all put-ons. To put someone on is, almost by definition, to rob him of his cool. For, roughly speaking, loss of cool follows upon involvement of nearly any sort—especially upon involvement in an unworthy object, a hoax. The demands of intricate plotting, allusions to cinematic history, recognizable bits of satire, and other artifices help keep directors at a safe distance from the action of their films. Concomitantly, they never allow audiences to get caught up, either. Both creators and audience manage to avoid "blowing their cool." Their triumph of cool in the face of great excitement (both saw the silliness behind it) is at once paralleled and bolstered by the hero, for whom the retention of cool has become an altogether transcendent value. The hero demonstrates that one may remain uninvolved not only with experience one is depicting or beholding but with experience one is living as well. Whether James Bond is about to be seduced by a beauty queen or bisected by a laser beam, he remains as witty, as self-possessed, as detached—as *cool*—as a cocktail-party raconteur. To be sure, the cool hero descends from a distinguished tradition in American culture, especially in cinema—from Gary Cooper's laconic Westerner to Humphrey Bogart's hard-boiled private eye, who retained their composure at either end of a gun. But the coolness of these old heroes was a tactic rather than an essence; we responded to it not as a mood of detachment that matched our own but as a kind of victory over danger. Because we were involved, because the filmmakers were involved, the climax of our aesthetic pleasure came when the heroes revealed that they were involved, too (revelation of his "humanity" practically became Bogart's trademark), and we learned, finally, that their coolness was only a front. . . .

The put-on is becoming a major communication option in intercourse between artist and critic, or, for that matter, between artist and society at large. . . .

The interview, indeed, offers a prime matrix for the put-on. This may be a perverse rejection of the interview process as a social symbol. (So one enters schools, jobs, the Army, etc.) It is also, surely, a pragmatic response to the difficulty of questions in general. Honest answers are hard, because they can be disadvantageous (How much money are you entitled to deduct from your income tax?), because they are unknown (What do you believe?), or because they are boring (What have you been doing with yourself?). The put-on resolves all difficulties—it breaks up sets, disorients the interviewer, ridicules the interview process, communicates "real" ideas and feelings yet deflates the seriousness of questions and replies. The now classic *Playboy* interview with Bob Dylan, by Nat Hentoff, must represent the apogee of this option. Hentoff deliberately "chose to play straight man in [my] questions, believing that to have done otherwise would have stemmed the freewheeling flow of Dylan's responses." Some excerpts from their dialogue may illustrate the complexity of put-on technique:

PLAYBOY: What about [your old fans'] charge that you vulgarized your natural gifts?

DYLAN: It's like going out to the desert and screaming, and then having little kids throw their sandbox at you. I'm only twenty-four. These people that said this—were they Americans?

PLAYBOY: What made you decide to go the rock-'n'-roll route?

DYLAN: Carelessness. I lost my one true love. I started drinking. The first thing I know, I'm in a card game. Then I'm in a crap game. I wake up in a pool hall. Then this big Mexican lady drags me off the table, takes me to Philadelphia. She leaves me alone in her house, and it burns down. I wind up in Phoenix, I get a job as a Chinaman. . . . Needless to say, he burned the house down and I hit the road. The first guy that picked me up asked me if I wanted to be a star. What could I say?

PLAYBOY: And that's how you became a rock-'n'-roll singer?

DYLAN: No, that's how I got tuberculosis.

PLAYBOY: Let's turn the question around: Why have you stopped composing and singing protest songs?

DYLAN: The word "protest," I think, was made up for people undergoing surgery. It's an amusement-park word. A normal person in his righteous mind would have to have the hiccups to pronounce it honestly. The word "message" strikes me as having a hernia-like sound. It's just like the word "delicious." Also the word "marvellous." You know, the English can say "marvellous" pretty good. They can't say "raunchy" so good, though. Well, we each have our thing.

PLAYBOY: Can't you be a bit more informative?

DYLAN: Nope.

PLAYBOY: How do you get your kicks these days?

DYLAN: I hire people to look into my eyes, and then I have them kick me.

PLAYBOY: And that's the way you get your kicks?

DYLAN: No. Then I *forgive* them; that's where my kicks come in.

PLAYBOY: Did you ever have the standard boyhood dream of growing up to be President?

DYLAN: No. When I was a boy, Harry Truman was President. Who'd want to be Harry Truman?

PLAYBOY: Well, let's suppose that you *were* the President. What would you accomplish during your first thousand days?

DYLAN: Well, just for laughs, so long as you insist, the first thing I'd do is probably move the White House. Instead of being in Texas, it'd be on the East Side in New York. McGeorge Bundy would definitely have to change his name, and General McNamara would be forced to wear a coonskin cap and shades.

. . . Like sentimentality, the put-on offers a lazy man's substitute for feeling as well as for thought. Again, the form contains a built-in escape clause. People are not so much unsure of their feelings as unsure what feeling may be appropriate. Thus, a trite expression of feeling now has the advantage of being equivocal.

"How did you like the play?"

"Very moving."

Perfect, take it how you will. Whether the play was moving, corny, or itself a put-on, the question has been answered—assuming a slightly ambiguous intonation—appropriately.

A related but more calculated and aggressive dodge involves, quite simply, replying in gibberish when no honest response springs to mind.

"How did you like the play?"

"It was over the bush, man."

This sort of remark is seldom challenged. On the rare occasion when a victim asks, "What does 'over the bush' mean?," the perpetrator assumes a vaguely irritated tone and replies, "You know, man, it's like funk, only trippier," or some such nonsense. It takes a hardy victim to press the matter further.

Another subtle, and eventually devastating, ploy might be called the "silent put-on." Its perpetrator sits in rapt attention—nodding vigorously, asking occasional questions—as his victim pontificates. Gradually, the victim begins to suspect, rightly or wrongly, that his silent audience knows a good deal more about the subject at hand than he's letting on ("Here I've been running on about modern art on the basis of catalogue blurbs, and this fellow is obviously an important critic or painter himself"). As the perpetrator begins to reinforce this suspicion with improbable expressions of awe, the victim dimly perceives that, having been given enough rope to hang himself, he has behaved like a pompous, ignorant ass. Typically, he tapers off in embarrassment and excuses himself. . . .

The embarrassment at one's own predicament or identity which produces theatrical tongue-in-cheek (spoof) and conversational tongue-in-cheek (put-on) issues from an intermediate level of awareness—an awareness that reveals the inadequacy of a come-on but fails to suggest any useful alternative. The put-on, then, arises out of a *partial consciousness* of one's own ridiculousness, in the absence of sufficient courage or intellectual perseverance to see that ridiculousness through to its roots and to alter it.

At a large New York advertising agency, communication through hackneyed Madison Avenue-ese has become a source of embarrassment. Certain executives—usually the oldest and highest-ranking—will use a chestnut unselfconsciously; e.g., "Why don't we put it out on the back stoop and see if the cat licks it up?" Others employ such expressions only reluctantly, making it clear that they know a trite saying when they use one: "Why don't we put it out on the back stoop and see if the cat licks it up, as the cliché goes." Yet the phrase "as the cliché goes" has achieved such currency around the agency that a third echelon, of junior executives, has come to recognize *it* as a cliché. Still too lazy or unimaginative to break away into a fresh image, they simply incorporate this further self-consciousness: "Why don't we put it out on the back stoop and see if the cat licks it up, as the cliché goes, as the cliché goes." This last solution is already close to a put-on, for it deals with embarrassment aggressively, ridiculing both the asininity of the top executives and the primitive self-consciousness of the secondary executives. The most "sophisticated" elements of the third group deal in outright put-ons; that is, they utter the unadorned cliché in precisely the same words as the top executives but in a way that suggests a transcendent awareness of its rich meaning or absurdity. Their intonation, gestures, or exaggerated emphases give notice that they are absolutely detached from the actual words, that their real intention is sarcastic, paradoxical, ironic, supportive, or, for that matter, whatever a superior may choose to think it is. (Young men at the agency who habitually express their ideas in this ambiguous mode are considered either especially gifted or subversive and dangerous. Their presence increases the general self-consciousness at conferences, and occasionally forces even some of the older executives into adopting a put-on style.)

A similar breeding pattern for the put-on, as an outgrowth of halfway consciousness, has occurred in advertising proper over the last fifteen years. Parodists, like Harvey Kurtzman's early *Mad* magazine and its imitators, and Jean Shepherd on the radio, helped to promote a growing self-consciousness among purveyors of the hard sell. The precocious soft-sell ads—not the more recent Doyle Dane Bernbach highly polished genre but the initial Bob Elliott and Ray Goulding Piel Bros. Harry-and-Bert campaign (later echoed, for another beer company, by Mike Nichols and Elaine May), or the Chevron campaign ("Chevron Supreme Fits Any Shape Gas Tank!," "With Chevron Supreme Gasoline

Your Car Can Go Forwards and Backwards!," "When Your Car Runs Out of Chevron Supreme Gasoline It Will . . . Stop!")—formed a transitional phase to the reincarnation of hard sell in put-on guise. Humorous soft sell undermined a tradition of advertisement that had a content, a reasonably logical, reasonably structured pitch for a product. Instead, it seemed to indicate that sales might result simply from (1) mention of the product, and (2) a laugh, derived somehow—anyhow—in connection with that mention. (When people began quoting tongue-in-cheek ads, their talk meant more sales as surely as a catchy jingle semi-consciously whistled.) Funny soft sell also seemed to attack the spinal cord of advertising, which is making claims for the product. It made fun of the very idea of making claims, especially exaggerated ones, and, along the way, of most other hard-sell techniques—endorsements, contests, giveaways, coupons.

Before long, hard sell ("coming on strong") tried to incorporate some of the sense of ridiculousness that went into *Mad*-type parodies, and a good deal of the tongue-in-cheek that went into the soft sells of the middle fifties. What resulted was a species of super-hard sell that, figuratively, appends a sophisticated "as the cliché goes" after the cliché. For example, a bathetic fake-out in the final instant of a commercial makes the whole commercial look silly: An announcer seriously praises a brand of pork-and-beans, holding up two cans as he concludes his spiel. He claps the cans together for emphasis and catches his nose between them. Inevitably, some commercials simply use intonation or sheer exaggeration to let *us* know that *they* know better. They become an unspecific but roaring burlesque of themselves and of all advertising, thereby rising, or sinking, to the realm of nearly pure put-on.

The most common tenor for such advertising is super-frenzy or super-ecstasy. Where straight hard sell communicated sincere, if slightly incredible, enthusiasm for the product, put-on hard sell does cartwheels of shrieking exultation. Old TV hard sell for a beauty product might have had a Ted Mack or Arthur Godfrey look earnestly into the camera and say, "Believe me, girls—this stuff really works." A commercial for the same product might now picture a dowdy secretary converted in no time into a man-eating vamp. After a few over-a-bare-shoulder, feline growls, she says, "Buhlieve you *me,* gurrls—*this* stuff *rrrrrrhheeeelly* works." Clearly, a joke is intended; never was a secretary so draggle-tailed nor a temptress so seductive. The transformation seems preposterous—an iteration of Jules Feiffer's "Passionella." Yet the hyperbole cannot have ironic purposes; surely we are expected to come away believing that the beauty product does indeed work. Perhaps not as well as in a dramatization? Then, how well? In a ten-second television spot, a couple find a certain brand of coffee in the supermarket and fall all over each other in hysterical joy. Possibly we are meant to feel that the advertising agency has joined with us in a humorous conspiracy against the sponsor—that we are somehow in on the same joke, and meant to buy the product anyhow, perhaps in gratitude for having been entertained and flattered. (The advertising put-on contains an implicit presumption that straight hard sell insulted our intelligence.)

Just as a person can get away with saying something stupid (cop-out) by effusing peripheral clues that indicate he *knows* what he's saying is stupid (indeed, that imply he might say something smart if he chose to), so can an advertisement now get away with being hard sell and at the same time cop out on hard sell's fundamental responsibility—to explain just how good the product is. The put-on, in the first case, provides a stupid statement with the same apparent value as a smart statement; in the second case, it renders an impossibly vague, impossibly hyperbolic claim as valuable (to the sponsor) as a precise one.

Put-on hyperbole (hyperbole, that is, which is to be taken seriously but not *that* seriously) typically clothes itself in magical or fantastic garb. Thus, among cleansing products potency is represented—not in simile but in metaphor so immediately visual as to seem close to documentary—by armored knights charging on horseback, their whitening lances aimed at small children; by full-scale tornadoes; by meddlesome birds who fly in kitchen windows; by anti-dirt bombs dropped from fighter planes to score direct, highly explosive hits on soiled linen; by transparent shields that jet visitors at six-inch altitudes across scuffproof floors; by washing machines that, seconds after the product is administered, swell to three times their normal height, dwarfing the housewife; by Irish, Mary Poppins-ish maids sailing in from the blue, depositing their wonder-working suds, and soaring off again, singing a jingle; and by a detergent that zooms you out of the kitchen as though your sink were a launching pad. Toward the conclusion of each dramatization, the housewife praises the detergent godsend in a paroxysm of commingled surprise and delight that would seem disproportionate had she just been informed of her husband's election to high office. Had a sample of such frenzied hyperbole been offered fifteen years ago, in the time of earnest hard sell, viewers would have found themselves bewildered at an apparently insane joke. Hyperbole in humor has traditionally served as a device for satire or irony. Advertising, however, uses humorous hyperbole in a new and confusing way—deliberately trafficking in ambiguity to obscure the crucial questions for the consumer: What does the product accomplish, and why is it better than the competition? . . .

It may be that some element of the put-on has always resided at the base of art—what E. M. Forster called "shamming"—but it has taken the contemporary sensibility to discern and articulate these latent elements, to turn facetiousness into a full aesthetic, or even moral, category. It may be that the put-on offers the only remaining possibility for aesthetic or philosophical synthesis in a world that has become staggeringly confused and grotesque. It may be that when reality becomes too complex to master, the best we can do is adopt an attitude toward it. T. S. Eliot wrote that Pope, Dryden, and Swift showed how contempt, resentment, and disgust might be forms for genius. Perhaps our own self-conscious century—with its artists trying to transcend the limits of language, to redefine their media, to find the least uncomfortable view of their own lives—will, in time, produce the Put-On Genius. Unhappily, audiences that can't take any art straight with confidence will have paid a high price in the waiting, and may have a hard time recognizing him when he arrives.

A generation is coming of age in America that doesn't take the news straight, that doesn't take the utterances of public figures straight, that doesn't take social games straight. It suspects not only art but the whole range of modern experience. It sees giant con games everywhere. It sees "the system" itself as a con game. Paradoxically, this generation—so obsessed with the themes of falsehood, phoniness, and hypocrisy—has developed and refined the art of the put-on, as if driven to illustrate that what passes for "truth" and "reality" is often cruelly deceptive. A complex society depends for its survival on some degree of mutual trust among its citizens. But a generation of Americans, having lost all patience with the dishonesties that lubricate social transactions, now appears ready to propagate its own distrust throughout society, to foist upon communication the very cancer it has protested against. The put-on may be a destructive device born out of desperation—a weapon to force people out, through confusion and loss of confidence, toward honesty. Perhaps a hope exists, however dubious, that the debasement of discourse will soon become intolerable—a hope that people, when their legs have been pulled almost to the breaking point, will at last begin to kick.

BARNET BASKERVILLE

19th Century Burlesque of Oratory

It is an odd fact that in a nation in whose early history oratory played so vital a part, a nation which once delighted to honor its orators and to acknowledge their utterances as an important part of the national literature, the terms "orator," "oratorical" and "eloquence" should have become opprobrious epithets. Today in the land of Adams, Otis and Henry, of Clay, Calhoun and Webster, to refer to a public figure as an orator is to brand him a rascal who bears close watching, and to label a speech "oratorical" is to remove it at once from serious consideration. Nor is it any longer necessary to add the qualifier "mere," for "orator" is clearly understood to be a truncation of "mere orator," just as "rhetoric" is automatically read "mere rhetoric." The *Columbia Encyclopedia* notes that "in recent years . . . oratory has become less grandiloquent" (seeming to imply that some measure of grandiloquence is a characteristic of oratory) and adds, "The term *oratory* itself has fallen into disuse, giving way to *public speaking*." But whether one considers oratory to be pompous, bombastic public speaking, or refuses to distinguish between oratory and public speaking and regards all utterance from the public platform as contemptible (a not uncommon attitude), the almost universal practice in our time is not to use the terms "orator" or "oratory" except with humorous or derogatory intent.

Yet in the late 18th and early 19th centuries the orator was a national hero, and eloquence was admired and diligently cultivated as a prime necessity to success in public life. "Eloquence, in its highest flights," proclaimed one writer in 1851 without conscious exaggeration, "is beyond all question the greatest exertion of the human mind. It requires for its conception a combination of the most exalted faculties; for its execution, a union of the most extraordinary powers." [1] Henry

From *American Quarterly*, Vol. XX, No. 4, Winter 1968. Reprinted by permission of the University of Pennsylvania Trustees.

Ward Beecher, who as spokesman for the North during the Civil War had subdued hostile British audiences, asserted that there was not "on God's footstool, anything so crowned and so regal as the sensation of one who faces an audience in a worthy cause, and with amplitude of means, and defies them, fights them, controls them, *conquers* them." [2] A less exuberant, but equally devoted connoisseur of eloquence was Ralph Waldo Emerson, listening with uncommon interest to the speeches of Webster, Everett, Sumner, Phillips, Channing and Father Taylor, and recording his reactions in detail in his journal. As late as 1901 Senator George F. Hoar wrote in *Scribner's Magazine*, "To be a perfect and consummate orator is to possess the highest faculty given to man. He must be a great actor, and more. He must be a master of the great things that interest mankind." [3]

Such sentiments ring strangely in the modern ear. We have difficulty in believing they were expressed seriously. How can this reversal in attitude and usage be accounted for? Why should the designation "orator," once proudly bestowed and gloriously won, be freighted today with connotations of insincerity and pomposity, evoking an image either ludicrous or despicable?

There are undoubtedly several explanations. The mass media have diminished the importance of the orator; he is no longer, as he once was, a principal source of public information, edification and entertainment. And although public speeches continue to be made in large numbers, public taste has changed. A "Bunker Hill Oration" (even if there were a Webster to deliver it) would have little more likelihood of popular acceptance today than would a reissue of the sentimental 19th century ladies' gift books. Yet to what may we attribute this changing taste? Again, certainly, to many factors. But, as this paper will endeavor to demonstrate, a substantial influence was exerted by a small group of 19th century humorists who deserve to be remembered as among the first effective American social critics. With a sharp eye for the pretentious and the phony, and having access to an immense public through newspaper column and public lecture, they succeeded (while seeking ostensibly only to entertain) in modifying public tastes by satire of a variety of institutions and practices. When these men turned their attention to American oratory, it was inevitable that they should concentrate upon the two most vulnerable manifestations of the art—the Fourth of July oration and the "great speech" of Congress or the political campaign.

It is well to remind ourselves that the Fourth of July oration, now almost synonymous with high-sounding patriotic nonsense, was once a highly estimable American institution. John Adams' familiar prediction concerning Independence Day [4] ("I am apt to believe that it will be celebrated by succeeding generations, as the great Aniversary Festival") proved accurate; and though he failed to include it among the appropriate methods of celebration ("pomp, shews, games, sports, guns, bells, bonfires and illuminations"), the oration was incorporated into the festival from the very beginning, and managed to outlive such standard ingredients as the thirteen-gun salute, the thirteen times thirteen toasts, the sermon—and eventually in large cities, thanks to commissions for a Safe and Sane Fourth—even the fireworks.

The oration was the climax of an elaborate birthday celebration of American independence, reviewing early history, eulogizing prominent figures and reaffirming national ideals and values. The purpose of the occasion was clearly stated in 1802 in one of a series of July Fourth orations sponsored by the city of Boston. William Emerson, father of Ralph Waldo, announced his intention "to consider the feelings, manners, and principles which led to the declaration of American Independence, as well as the happy and important effects, whether general or domestic, which have already flowed, or will forever flow, from the auspicious epoch of its date." [5] "It is our great annual national love feast," said Rufus Choate in his Boston oration of 1858, the purpose of which is to light a torch, to engage in reverent exclamation. "Happy, if for us that descending sun shall look out on a more loving, more elevated, more united America!" [6]

Thousands of these orations were delivered, printed and circulated in pamphlet form.[7] Eminent public figures felt honored by invitations to speak, and prepared diligently for the occasion. On July 4, 1778, while the Revolution was in its early stages, Dr. David Ramsay spoke in Charleston, South Carolina on "The Advantages of American Independence," enumerating the blessings accompanying independence and contrasting them with conditions under British tyranny. Daniel Webster delivered his first Fourth of July oration in 1800 when he was an eighteen-year-old Dartmouth College Student, and his last at the laying of the cornerstone of the addition to the national capital in 1851 when he was Secretary of State. Webster's great commemorative speeches—the first and second Bunker Hill Addresses, "The Character of Washington," "Adams and Jefferson," "The First Settlement of New England"— while not strictly speaking Fourth of July orations, nevertheless celebrated the favorite themes of that occasion: the landing of the Pilgrims, the Founding Fathers, Lexington and Concord, Bunker Hill, the Declaration, the Constitution, the federal union.

As would be expected, themes changed, emphases shifted, in response to changing events. The early emphasis upon liberty, patriotism, vigorous abuse of King George and vindictive twisting of the lion's tail,

gave way during the early national period to emphasis upon the Con-
situation and pleas for union. Webster's words were frequently quoted
and paraphrased. John Quincy Adams, to whom the Missouri Compromise controversy in 1820 had seemed "a fire-bell in the night," warned
of the dangers of nullification and state sovereignty and stressed "one
people" and "union forever" in his July Fourth orations at Quincy in
1831 and at Newburyport in 1837. Two years after the enactment of a
more stringent fugitive slave law, Frederick Douglass used the celebration of Independence Day to deliver a withering indictment of the institution of slavery. This is the birthday of *your* national independence,
he told the white people of Rochester on July 5, 1852. The freedom
gained is *yours,* and you may properly celebrate. "*You* may rejoice, *I*
must mourn. To drag a man in fetters into the grand illuminated temple of liberty, and call upon him to join you in joyous anthems, were inhuman mockery and sacrilegious irony." [8] Such dissonant interruptions of
the harmony of the great annual love feast were infrequent, but not
entirely unknown. In 1828 Frances Wright dared to suggest that true
patriotism meant not "mere love of country," but love of human liberty
in general, and the improvement and elevation of all mankind. And in
1845 Charles Sumner shocked a predominantly military audience at a
traditionally military celebration of a war for independence by delivering a courageous, but tactless and intemperate, denunciation of all war,
proposing the thesis that "In our age, there can be no peace that is
not honorable; there can be no war that is not dishonorable."

Further illustrations from early July Fourth oratory are not needed
to demonstrate that it was a focal point of John Adams' "Great anniversary festival," serving to rekindle the American spirit, to reaffirm
American ideals, to instill courage in faint or apathetic hearts by declaring anew devotion to the heroes, the symbols and the sacred myths of
our national history. When dreams of the potentialities of a new nation
conceived in liberty seemed eminently possible of achievement, as well
as when dangers threatened to dissolve the newly formed union, it was
fitting to celebrate a day of recollection, self-congratulation and rededi-
cation. By no means all of these early commemorative orations were
characterized by a florid style, though some indisputably were. But if
the language employed is not the language of our own day, if some orators delighted in multiplying Biblical and classical allusions and in laying figures of speech end to end in glorious profusion, we are not necessarily justified in equating different stylistic preferences with insincerity,
nor in declaring all rhetorical flourishes to be "mere rhetoric."

But before the middle of the 19th century, evidences of a serious
deterioration of this once honored commemorative address were every-

where apparent. The frequency of the occasion, the annual demand for scores of elaborations of familiar themes, the felt obligation to adhere to a pattern prescribed by tradition, brought an inevitable dilution of quality. Not everyone could speak with the same sense of urgency and involvement as David Ramsay on the advantages of independence or Daniel Webster on the blessings of federal union. A host of lesser men managed to copy the form, but not the substance or spirit of their models. This debasement, begun long before the Civil War, continued during the post-war era when the nation's preoccupation with the great themes of liberty and union was diverted—except for the routine incantations on July Fourth—to more practical business matters.

This deterioration did not escape the notice of serious critics. British visitor James Bryce, in his evaluation of 19th century American oratory, observed that the Fourth of July orator felt obliged to talk "his very tallest." In much occasional oratory, Bryce remarked, "the sort of artificial elevation at which the speaker usually feels bound to maintain himself is apt to make him pompous and affected." [9] As early as 1857 a writer in the *North American Review* deplored the sorry state into which the celebration of American holidays had fallen. He denounced the bombast and rhetorical patriotism of the Fourth of July oration, noting the "Pickwickian sentiment, pyrotechnic flashes . . . the disgust of the educated, and the uproar of the multitude." [10] And in 1872 the *Nation,* while expressing hope that the oration might once again be restored to its former glory, observed that it had become "synonymous with blatant nonsense or platitudes in thought, tawdy rhetoric in diction, and crude egoistical chauvinism in spirit." [11]

Despite such expressions of dissatisfaction from the intellectuals, popular enthusiasm for the pyrotechnics (verbal and otherwise) of the Fourth of July was not noticeably diminished. It remained for the satirists to provide more vivid criticism for those who did not read the *Nation* or the *North American Review,* and eventually to extend the "disgust of the educated" even to the uproarious multitude. Both before and after the Civil War, men who wrote under such names as Artemus Ward, John Phoenix, Bill Nye, Petroleum V. Nasby and Orpheus C. Kerr concocted burlesque orations in which they lampooned all the foibles noted by more serious critics.

Examination of serious orations published in the early part of the 19th century reveals that annual repetition over several decades in scores of cities and towns had resulted in a stereotyped formula embracing both form and content. James Fenimore Cooper's familiar observation in *Home as Found* that the Fourth of July oration, like human nature, is the same in all ages and under all circumstances, was made in 1838.

Recognizable characteristics were the initial apology for personal inadequacy; salutes to the local community and to the occasion; historical narrative glorifying early settlers, Revolutionary heroes and makers of the Constitution; embellishment of the themes of liberty and independence, individual opportunity, free education, the union, accomplishments in the arts and sciences, freedom of speech and religion. Though not all orators adopted the grand style, as time went on flowers of rhetoric tended to become ever more lush and colorful. Rhetorical devices most frequently associated with this form of public address were apostrophe, rhetorical question, classical allusion, frequent quotations from poetry introduced to impart a literary flavor, and imagery drawn from Nature—often portraying cataclysmic disturbances such as storms, volcanoes, earthquakes and fire.[12]

Such stereotypes, both of matter and manner, presented irresistible targets for those who delighted in puncturing pretentiousness and exposing excess wherever found. "We are engaged upon a noble work," *Vanity Fair* proclaimed in 1861, "we are simplifying matters—stripping them of their excrescences, and proving that everything is susceptible of being burlesqued. . . ."[13] Coolly taking aim at the Fourth of July oration, soaring like the American eagle through the blue empyrean, the satirists peppered it with ridicule until by the end of the century it was reduced to a maimed and discredited thing.

One of the earliest parodies appeared in July 1855 in *Putnam's Monthly* under the title "Mr. Pepperage's Fourth of July Oration."[14] Mr. Pepperage touched upon most of the standard themes. He begins with a tribute to freedom's natal day ("which has never been surpassed since the primeval day on which the world was created, and will never be equalled till the ultimate day of judgment"), adding a classical allusion in Greek which causes the clergyman to nod approvingly to the schoolmaster, who smiles foolishly in return. He develops the themes of freedom and equality, pausing momentarily to explain away the allegations of "envious and unprincipled foreign tourists" concerning the existence of slavery in the land. He expatiates upon the grandeur of the nation's geography, noting that a country already covering an area of four million square miles could easily be made still bigger if the two oceans were filled in, and suggesting that the Appalachians might be leveled to provide sufficient material for this purpose. He lauds our accomplishments in the useful and fine arts, in jurisprudence and in the arts of warfare. After reaching a crashing climax in his peroration on the union, he is saved from the enthusiasm of an admiring crowd by a group of friends who help him escape through a back window. The audience straightway holds a public meeting and nominates him for President.

Artemus Ward's "Weathersfield Oration," alleged to have been delivered to a large and discriminating audience on July 4, 1859 ("I was 96 minits passin a givin pint"), appeared in *Vanity Fair* in 1861.[15] The oration was accompanied by a picture of the orator standing against a star-studded background, wrapped in the folds of the flag, crowned by an aureole formed by the letters UNION. Ward adds to the themes developed by Pepperage a few others with which contemporary audiences would have been familiar: the personal apology ("When I say that I skurcely feel ekal to the task, I'm sure you will b'lieve me"), the local compliment ("Weathersfield is justly celebrated for her onyins and patritism the world over") and the moral emphasis ("Be virtoous & you'll be happy!"). One of the most elaborate burlesques was John Phoenix's "Fourth of July Oration in Oregon," supposedly delivered at Fort Vancouver in 1856.[16] Printed along with the text of the oration, in humorous imitation of hundreds of serious orations distributed in pamphlet form, is the "Correspondence." This includes the invitation to the orator from a member of the committee, together with his modest (and in this case, verbose and circuitous) acceptance. The decades following the Civil War saw the publication of numerous pieces ridiculing orators and oratory, some of which—notably Bill Nye's "How the Glorious Fourth Was Celebrated at Whalen's Grove" [17]—dealt specifically with the Fourth of July oration.

The arsenal of burlesque contained a variety of deadly weapons. The perennial *Union* theme was some times dealt with by devastating understatement, as when Artemus Ward announces bluntly at Weathersfield: "I'm a Union man. I luv the Union—it is a good thing. . . . I'm for the Union as she air, and whithered be the arm of every ornery cuss who attempts to bust her up. That's me. I hav sed." But more frequently employed was grandiose exaggeration, sometimes suddenly reversed by a catalogue of trivial details, or culminating in a jarring anticlimax which jerks the rug out from under what has gone before. "I shall close," said Mr. Pepperage at Jehosophat, Long Island, "by an allusion to the vital greatness and sempiternal importance of the national Union."

> The Union!—Inspiring theme! How shall I find words to describe its momentous magnificence and its beatific lustre? The Union!—it is the ark of our safety!!—the palladium of our liberties!!!—the safeguard of our happiness!!!!—and the aegis of our virtues!!!!! In the Union we live, and move, and go a-head. It watches over us at our birth—it fans us in our cradles—it accompanies us to the district school—it gives us our victuals in due season—it selects our wives for us from "America's fair daughters," and it does a great many other things; to say nothing of putting us to sleep sometimes, and keeping the flies from our innocent repose.

Artemus Ward, in his oration on "The Crisis," [18] does not rely on such exuberant punctuation, but builds cumulatively through a series of incongruous images and a gorgeous malapropism to a feeble anticlimax:

> Feller Sitterzens, the Union's in danger. The black devil disunion is trooly here, starein us all squarely in the face. We must drive him back. Shall we make a 2nd Mexico of ourselves? Shall we sell our birthrite for a mess of potash? Shall one brother put the knife to the throat of anuther brother? Shall we mix our whiskey with each others' blud? Shall the star spangled Banner be cut up into dishcloths? Standin here in this here Skoolhouse, upon my nativ shore so to speek, I anser—Nary!

In view of the nature of the occasion being celebrated, it is not surprising that the themes of liberty and independence should have received much attention in serious Fourth of July oratory and, as a consequence, in burlesques. Bill Nye has his orator at Whalen's Grove make two beginnings on the traditional encomium to the blessings of liberty, but in each before completing a single sentence he has, by the introduction of a prosaic image or a swift change to a businesslike tone, converted panegyric to travesty. The question "But fellow-citizens, how can we preserve the blessing of freedom and fork it over unimpaired to our children?" presents the incongruous image of freedom's being forked across the table like a pancake or a pork chop. And again,

> We are here today to celebrate the birthday of American freedom, as I understand it, and I am here to say that whatever may be said against our refinement and our pork, our style of freedom is sought for everywhere. It is a freedom that will stand any climate and I hear it very highly spoken of wherever I go.
>
> I am here to state that, as boy and man, I have been a constant user of American freedom for over fifty years, and I can truly say that I feel no desire to turn back; also that there will be a grand, free-for-all scuffle for a greased pig on the vacant lot south of the church at seven o'clock, after which fireworks will be served to those who desire to remain.

The oration ends on this high emotional plane. In another parody Nye develops the freedom theme more fully. The speaker maintains that his party and his country have always championed liberty. He proposes a further extension of the principle—the Emancipation of Rum. The idea of free rum appeals to him.[19]

The most common method of ridiculing the orators' gandiloquent manipulation of the liberty theme is the device of contrasting claims and actualities, of mocking noble words with disconcerting facts—sometimes directly, often ironically. Mr. Pepperage, after paying tribute to the precious heritage of liberty and equality ("We are all free, and we are all equal! The rights, the dignity, the sacredness of man, as man, is the corner-stone of our political faith"), pauses to brand as a libel and an untruth the charge that four million people in America are "nothing more or less than s-l-a-v-e-s." There are, he acknowledges,

> a few of the swarthy children of Africa, who, rescued from the brutalities of their native kings, are held in involuntary servitude under a system inherited from the British two centuries ago,—but they are not half as much slaves as the white serfs of Birmingham and Manchester! Are not their mouths ever full of possum-fat and hominy? Are they not dressed in the best tow-cloth half the year,—while it is too hot to wear anything the other half? . . . The greatest and happiest of mortals are those whose mouths are stuffed with good fat bacon, and whose persons are ornamented with a red bandanna handkerchief!

Besides, the orator adds, it has not yet been proved that Africans are men. "It would be an awful thing to mistake a monkey for a man, and under that terrible delusion, to plunge four millions of inferior animals into all the refinements and delights of civilization!"

Petroleum V. Nasby comments in slightly different fashion upon the disparity between principle and practice. Nasby, represented by his creator to be a southern postmaster, writes a letter from Washington dated June 12, 1862, in which he suggests a plan for the appropriate celebration of the Fourth of July, "the birthday of our Liberties—the day on which Freedum wus perclaimed to all men, exceptin niggers, and them havin a visible admixter uv Aferken blud, et settery." [20] Nasby is impatient with northern Republican domination of the day, and demands a pure *Democratic* celebration for once. He proposes as one of several entries in the parade: "Wagon with a nigger a lyin down, and my esteemed friend Punt a standin onto him—a paregorical illustrashun uv the sooperiority uv the Anglo-Sacksun over the Afrikin races." The festivities would include the singing of the following "Patryotic Song":

Sambo, ketch dat hoe
    And resine dat vane idee:
We've got de power, you kno,
    And you never kin be free.

Bill Nye achieves a similar effect by eschewing indirection and saying precisely what he means, but he puts his comment into the mouth of an Indian warrior:

Warriors! We are met here today to celebrate the white man's Fourth of July. I do not know what the Fourth of July has done for us that we should remember his birthday, but it matters not. . . .

What does the Fourth of July signify to us? It is a hollow mockery! Where the flag of the white man now waves in the breeze, a few years ago the scalp of our foe was hanging in the air. Now my people are seldom. Some are dead and others drunk.

Once we chased the deer and the buffalo across the plains, and lived high. Now we eat the condemned corned beef of the oppressor. . . .

My people once owned this broad land; but the Pilgrim Fathers (where are they?) came and planted the baked bean and the dried apple, and my tribe vamoosed. Once we were a nation. Now we are the tin can tied to the American eagle.

Warriors! This should be a day of jubilee, but how can a man rejoice who has a boil on his nose? How can the chief of a once proud people shoot firecrackers and dance over the graves of his race? . . .

The pale face cannot tickle us with a barley straw on the Fourth of July and make us laugh. You can kill the red man, but you cannot make him hilarious over his own funeral.[21]

The Fourth of July was by common consent a legitimate occasion for boasting about national attributes and accomplishments. Humorists dealt with this aspect of Fourth of July oratory by marshaling a list of absurd specifics to support a grand generalization ("In the arts of peace, and in the deeds of war, you are equally distinguished. It was your happy lot to have produced Singer's sewing machine, the clipper ship Blue Thunder, Blake's fire-proof paint, the aboriginal mint-julep, the improved sherry cobbler, and the trotting horse Fanny Fern"), or by an incongruous catalogue of names ("Ours is a great and glorious land, a land which has developed a Washington, a Franklin, a William M. Tweed, a Longfellow, a Motley, a Jay Gould"). Another favorite device was what might be termed the backhanded boast—a series of vaunted claims which were really criticisms (The Pilgrim Fathers "planted corn and built houses, they killed the Indians, hung the Quakers and Baptists, burned the witches alive, and were very happy and comfortable indeed"). Mark Twain, in a Fourth of July speech he was going to make if the preceding speaker hadn't taken up his time, intended to tell a London audience that "We have a criminal jury system which is superior to any in the world; and its efficiency is only marred by the difficulty of finding twelve men every day who don't know anything and can't read. . . . I think I can say, and say with pride, that we have some legislatures that bring higher prices than any in the world."[22]

In addition to dealing frivolously with the favorite themes of Fourth of July orators, the satirists ridiculed the most egregious characteristics of their literary style. All the stylistic devices noted by more serious critics are cruelly amplified in the burlesques. Artemus Ward mocks the habit of frequent and often gratuitous quotation of classical writers by citing the wise sayings of his Irish friend Mr. McBeth, and by such bows in the direction of antiquity as this peroration: "In the language of Mister Catterline to the Rummins, I go but perhaps I shall cum back agin." Learning is paraded in such sly mis-attributions as "What Virgil refers to in his Childe Harold as . . ." or "as Shakespeel said when Cesar stabbed him in the House of Representatives. . . ." Bill Nye avoids a charge of profanity by a decorous transfer of responsibility to an anonymous poet: "I say let every man rely solely on his own thinker, and damned be he who first cries hold, enough! I am not a profane man, but I quote from a poem in using the above quotation." Nye is adept also in manipulating the mixed metaphor ("I would rather have my right hand cleave to the roof of my mouth than to . . .") and the inappropriate simile (His warrior is "as lonely as the greenback party"; he hasn't enough warriors left to carry one precinct). Nye's imagery, though ludicrous, is often poignant. The once mighty Chief Blackhawk has been reduced to sawing wood for whiskey at the local saloon. "He once rode the war pony into the fray and buried his tomahawk in the phrenology of his foe. Now he straddles the saw-buck and yanks the woodsaw athwart the bosom of the basswood chunk." But though he suffers, he never squeals. "He wraps his royal horse-blanket around his Gothic bones and is silent." The practice of inserting passages of verse in the oration is illustrated by Artemus Ward, who breaks off a eulogy of New England girls with:

Be still, my sole, be still
& you, Hart, stop cuttin up!

One distinguishing feature of Fourth of July oratory was its pre-dominantly generic language, its tendency to eschew the particular for the general and to operate at a consistently high level of abstraction. The detractors of oratory took pleasure in deflating a lofty general-ization by following it with a series of prosaic details or a mixture of the grandiose and the commonplace, or by descending suddenly to an unexpected anti-climax. The orator at Whalen's Grove reminds his auditors that when the Declaration of Independence was signed the spot on which they stand was a howling wilderness. "Where yonder lemon-ade-stand now stands and realizes a clean profit of forty-seven dollars and thirty-five cents on an investment of six dollars and fifty cents, the rank thistle nodded in the wynd, and the wild fox dag his hole unscared."

George Derby's Oregon orator dilates upon equality of opportunity in America. Everyone, he says, has a chance for distinction: "Mrs. Laving Pike's baby, now lying with a cotton-flannel shirt on, in a champagne basket, in Portland, O.T., has just as good a chance of being President of the United States, as the imperial infant of France, now sucking his royal thumbs in his silver cradle at Paris, has of being an emperor." And Mr. Pepperage, contemplating the horrors that would follow a dissolution of the union, cries out:

> The accursed myrmidons of despotism, with gnashing teeth and blood-stained eyes, would rush at large over this planet. They would lap the crimson gore of the most wealthy and respectable citizens. The sobs of females and the screams of children would mingle with the barking of dogs and the crash of falling columns. A universal and horrid night would mantle the skies, and one by one the strong pillars of the universe go crumbling into ruin, amid the gleam of bowie-knives and the lurid glare of exploding steamboats!

Exaggerated rhetoric is burlesqued by still greater exaggeration; sonorous cliché and addled syntax are combined in passages of impenetrable double talk: "How can we enhance the blood-bought right, which is inherent in every human being, of the people, for the people and by the people, where tyrant foot hath never trod nor bigot forged a chain, for to look back from our country's glorious natal day or forward to a glorious, a happy and a prosperous future with regard to purity of the ballot and free speech. I say for one we cannot do otherwise."

No literary form could have withstood such onslaughts. The effectiveness of the attack was due as much to its aptness as to its broad humor. Americans accustomed to an annual diet of Fourth of July oratory could readily recognize the themes and rhetorical devices which satirists carried to their most ridiculous and illogical conclusions, and could gradually learn to laugh at the originals as well. Indeed, some of the originals were as preposterous as the burlesques. Though by no means typical, the oration delivered in 1859 at Rome, Tennessee, by one Edwin H. Tenney, a Nashville attorney, illustrates the ultimate degradation of an honorable institution. Apparently offered with serious inspirational intent, it is a model of unintentional parody:

> Venerable, My Fellow Citizens, on the brilliant calendar of American Independence, is the day we celebrate. Venerable as the revolving epoch in our anniversaries of freedom is this avalanche of time. Venerable as the abacus on the citadel of greatness, thou well-spring of hope. Homestead of Liberty, we venerate thy habitation. Monument of immortality, we adorate

thy worth. Pharos of ages, we hail thy glimmerings 'mid the cataracts of life. Almanac of our country, we would utter thy welcome with reverent awe. Our towers and our battlements, our flags and our heroes, yea, garlanded navies, decorated armies, and unfettered eagles, sleepless at the approach of thy footsteps, have welcomed thee. The clap of thy welcome booms along tessellated lawns, frescoed arbors, and lipping rivulets; while the surges of eloquence join the music of freedom.

Of the impending danger to the union, Tenney has this to say:

The two great problems of our duties and dangers and destiny as a republic, are before us, and its remedy or its corollary are ours. We may choose which we will, but religion and the Union, or irreligion and disunion, are the dilemma. The one, like the banyan tree, blossoms, re-roots and feeds us with figs, the other is as sober as the coffin and blacker than the tassels on the buggy of death. . . .[23]

The closing years of the 19th century brought renewed interest in oratory and a recrudescence (particularly during the imperialism debates) of the old spread-eagle variety. With detached good humor, but with deadly effectiveness, Finley P. Dunne's Martin Dooley deflated the pretentious utterances of political orators by dwelling playfully upon their lyrical qualities: "afther all what is an orator but a kind iv musician or pote?" Dooley, who claimed to have heard speeches that were set to music and played by a silver cornet band, pronounced Beveridge's Senate speech on the Philippines a great speech: "Twas a speech ye cud waltz to." The night he heard Bryan's Cross of Gold speech he went over to Hogan's house and picked out the tune with one finger on the piano; "it was that musical." And many times, he recalled, he had gone home humming to himself bits of a speech on the tariff. Dooley's tour de force was his report of President McKinley's speech at a banquet in his honor. Let it stand here as a crowning illustration of the power of a skilled satirist to assist in laughing "oratory" to death.

"Our duty to civilization commands us to be up an' doin'," he says. "We ar-re bound," he says, "to—to re-elize our destiny, whativer it may be," he says. "We can not tur-rn back," he says, "th' hands iv th' clock that, even as I speak," he says, "is r-rushin' through th' hear-rts iv men," he says, "dashin' its spray against th' star iv liberty an' hope, an' no north, no south, no east, no west, but a steady purpose to do th' best we can, considerin' all th' circumstances iv th' case," he says. "I hope I have made th' matther clear to ye," he says, "an', with these few remarks," he says, "I will tur-rn th' job over to destiny," he says, "which is sure to lead us iver on an' on, back an' forth, a united an' happy people. . . ." [24]

Modern Americans owe a debt of gratitude to these humorist-critics of the preceding century. Their ridicule was richly deserved, and the excesses to which they called derisive attention undoubtedly merited extinction. They had, of course, targets other than oratory; they went to work simultaneously on novels, poems, essays and history. These literary forms survived the attack and were ultimately the better for it. The "sentimental novel," so pitilessly burlesqued, is now a museum piece—but the novel still lives, prospers and undergoes continuous change. Fatuous verse and super-patriotic history, also subject to 19th-century ridicule, are now discredited—but poetry and history continue to be written and admired.

The ridicule of 19th century commemorative and political oratory, however, has been extended by some to a wholesale condemnation and repudiation of all speaking from the public platform. A general impression seems somehow to persist that "oratory is like that" (i.e., like the grotesque image created by the satirists), that this is what oratory *is*. It may be that the term "oratory" is beyond redemption, that it must be permanently relegated to the same limbo as the pompous, inflated discourse it has frequently been used to describe. A more sensible alternative would be to acknowledge that oratory, like poetry or fiction, is of many kinds, and that to expose faults is not completely to discredit the genre. There is no inherent reason why even a Fourth of July oration should be reprehensible; the occasion or date of delivery need not automatically render a speech inane. And surely if the citizens of a democracy come to accept the view that *all* political speaking is "mere rhetoric"—that is to say, that it is to be rejected out of hand as deceitful, untruthful, senseless sound—it would be an incalculable public tragedy. Such indiscriminate condemnation as, for example, Westbrook Pegler's pronouncement that orators (i.e., public speakers) are the worst liars and hypocrites in the world, or H. L. Mencken's confident assertion that the imbeciles, yokels and morons who listen to political speeches do not want ideas but "a loud burble of words, a procession of phrases that roar, a series of whoops," is not only criticism of speakers and their audiences, but an expression of distrust of democratic processes.

We have cited earlier the criticism of E. L. Godkin. Godkin made perfectly clear that his was an attack neither on public speaking in general nor on popular government:

> We may rail at "mere talk" as much we please, but the probability is that the affairs of nations and of men will be more and more regulated by talk. . . . So I shall, in disregard of the great laudation of silence which filled the world in the days of Carlyle, say that one of the functions of an educated man is to talk,—and of course he should try to talk wisely.[25]

It seems a reasonable assumption that most of those who engaged in ridicule of 19th century "oratory" did so not to still all voices from the public platform nor to create mistrust of all public speakers, but in the interest of wiser, more sensible, more responsible talk.

NOTES

1. "Ancient and Modern Eloquence," *Littel's Living Age*, XXIX (May 3, 1851), 193.
2. *Oratory* (Philadelphia, 1893), pp. 46–47.
3. "Oratory," *Scribner's Magazine*, XXIX (June 1901), 756.
4. John Adams to Mrs. Adams, Philadelphia, July 3, 1776. In Hezekiah Niles, *Principles and Acts of the Revolution in America, Centennial Offering* (New York, 1876), p. 106.
5. *Old South Leaflets*, Vol. VI, No. 134 (Boston, n.d.). Emerson is quoting from the resolution establishing this annual public oration, adopted by the citizens of Boston in 1783.
6. "American Nationality," *Addresses and Orations* (Boston, 1891), pp. 481–82.
7. Howard H. Martin, in the preparation of a doctoral dissertation, examined "over 800 of the almost 2500 extant printed orations from 1776–1876." "The Fourth of July Oration," *Quarterly Journal of Speech*, XLIV (Dec. 1958), 393–401.
8. Carter G. Woodson, *Negro Orators and Their Orations* (Washington, D. C., 1925), p. 206.
9. *The American Commonwealth* (New York, 1899), II, 801–4.
10. "Holidays," *North American Review*, LXXXIV (Apr. 1857), 353–54.
11. "Fellow-Citizens, Ladies, and Gentlemen," *Nation*, XV (July 11, 1872), 21–22.
12. For an exhaustive analysis of themes, purposes and distinguishing features, see Howard H. Martin, "Orations on the Anniversary of American Independence, 1776–1876" (Doctoral dissertation, Northwestern University, 1955).
13. "The Burlesque Business," *Vanity Fair*, IV (Nov. 30, 1861), 245.
14. *Putnam's Monthly*, VI (July 1855), 91–98.
15. *Vanity Fair*, IV (July 13, 1861), 15.
16. George H. Derby, *The Squibob Papers* (New York, 1865), pp. 13–42.
17. Edgar Wilson Nye, *Bill Nye's Chestnuts* (Chicago, 1888), pp. 21–29.
18. *Vanity Fair*, III (Jan. 26, 1861), 37.
19. "A Conventional Speech," *Bill Nye's Sparks* (New York, 1901), pp. 136–42.
20. David Ross Locke, *The Struggles of Petroleum V. Nasby* (Boston, 1873), pp. 43–44.
21. "The Warrior's Oration," *Bill Nye's Remarks* (Chicago, 1891), pp. 327–28. There are striking thematic resemblances to Frederick Douglass' oration in 1852, though the tone is vastly different. This, of course, is in no sense a burlesque of the Douglass speech or others like it. Though one man is dead serious and the other at least pretends levity, they seek to make the same point. Nye, through his warrior, is mocking what Douglass is vehemently denouncing—the incompatibility of expansive freedom talk and the cruel exploitation of human beings.
22. Samuel Clemens, *Mark Twain's Sketches* (Hartford, Conn., 1875), pp. 180–81.
23. Edmund Pearson, "Making the Eagle Scream," *Queer Books* (New York, 1928), pp. 30, 37–38. Pearson, a librarian at the New York Public Library, has preserved substantial portions of this remarkable oration in his collection of literary oddities. Of Tenney he says: "He dipped his brush deeper into earthquake and eclipse; he reached higher towards the starry firmament and dragged down more glittering

orbs for his astonished spectators than all the Fourth of July orators who ever
lived and breathed."

24. Finley P. Dunne, "A Speech By President McKinley," *Mr. Dooley in Peace and War* (Boston, 1898), pp. 81–86.

25. "The Duty of Educated Men in a Democracy," *Forum*, XVII (Mar. 1894), 50–51.

ROBERT FROST

Education by Poetry:
A Meditative Monologue

I am going to urge nothing in my talk. I am not an advocate. I am going to consider a matter, and commit a description. And I am going to describe other colleges than Amherst. Or, rather say all that is good can be taken as about Amherst; all that is bad will be about other colleges.

I know whole colleges where all American poetry is barred—whole colleges. I know whole colleges where all contemporary poetry is barred.

I once heard of a minister who turned his daughter—his poetry-writing daughter—out on the street to earn a living, because he said there should be no more books written; God wrote one book, and that was enough. (My friend George Russell, "Æ," has read no literature, he protests, since just before Chaucer.)

That all seems sufficiently safe, and you can say one thing for it. It takes the onus off the poetry of having to be used to teach children anything. It comes pretty hard on poetry, I sometimes think,—what it has to bear in the teaching process.

Then I know whole colleges where, though they let in older poetry, they manage to bar all that is poetical in it by treating it as something other than poetry. It is not so hard to do that. Their reason I have often hunted for. It may be that these people act from a kind of modesty. Who are professors that they should attempt to deal with a thing as high and as fine as poetry? Who are *they?* There is a certain manly modesty in that.

That is the best general way of settling the problem; treat all poetry as if it were something else than poetry, as if it were syntax, language, science. Then you can even come down into the American and into the contemporary without any special risk.

There is another reason they have, and that is that they are, first and foremost in life, markers. They have the marking problem to consider. Now, I stand here a teacher of many years' experience and I have never complained of having had to mark. I had rather mark anyone for anything—for his looks, carriage, his ideas, his correctness, his exactness, anything you please,—I would rather give him a mark in terms of letters, A, B, C, D, than have to use adjectives on him. We are all being marked by each other all the time, classified, ranked, put in our place, and I see no escape from that. I am no sentimentalist. You have got to mark, and you have got to mark, first of all, for accuracy, for correctness. But if I am going to give a mark, that is the least part of my marking. The hard part is the part beyond that, the part where the adventure begins.

One other way to rid the curriculum of the poetry nuisance has been considered. More merciful than the others it would neither abolish nor denature the poetry, but only turn it out to disport itself, with the plays and games—in no wise discredited, though given no credit for. Any one who liked to teach poetically could take his subject, whether English, Latin, Greek or French, out into the nowhere along with the poetry. One side of a sharp line would be left to the rigorous and righteous; the other side would be assigned to the flowery where they would know what could be expected of them. Grade marks were more easily given, of course, in the courses concentrating on correctness and exactness as the only forms of honesty recognized by plain people; a general indefinite mark of X in the courses that scatter brains over taste and opinion. On inquiry I have found no teacher willing to take position on either side of the line, either among the rigors or among the flowers. No one is willing to admit that his discipline is not partly in exactness. No one is willing to admit that his discipline is not partly in taste and enthusiasm.

How shall a man go through college without having been marked for taste and judgment? What will become of him? What will his end be? He will have to take continuation courses for college graduates. He will have to go to night schools. They are having night schools now, you know, for college graduates. Why? Because they have not been educated enough to find their way around in contemporary literature. They don't know what they may safely like in the libraries and galleries. They don't know how to judge an editorial when they see one.

They don't know how to judge a political campaign. They don't know when they are being fooled by a metaphor, an analogy, a parable. And metaphor is, of course, what we are talking about. Education by poetry is education by metaphor.

Suppose we stop short of imagination, initiative, enthusiasm, inspiration and originality—dread words. Suppose we don't mark in such things at all. There are still two minimal things, that we have got to take care of, taste and judgment. Americans are supposed to have more judgment than taste, but taste is there to be dealt with. That is what poetry, the only art in the colleges of arts, is there for. I for my part would not be afraid to go in for enthusiasm. There is the enthusiasm like a blinding light, or the enthusiasm of the deafening shout, the crude enthusiasm that you get uneducated by poetry, outside of poetry. It is exemplified in what I might call "sunset raving." You look westward toward the sunset, or if you get up early enough, eastward toward the sunrise, and you rave. It is oh's and ah's with you and no more.

But the enthusiasm I mean is taken through the prism of the intellect and spread on the screen in a color, all the way from hyperbole at one end—or overstatement, at one end—to understatement at the other end. It is a long strip of dark lines and many colors. Such enthusiasm is one object of all teaching in poetry. I heard wonderful things said about Virgil yesterday, and many of them seemed to me crude enthusiasm, more like a deafening shout, many of them. But one speech had range, something of overstatement, something of statement, and something of understatement. It had all the colors of an enthusiasm passed through an idea.

I would be willing to throw away everything else but that: enthusiasm tamed by metaphor. Let me rest the case there. Enthusiasm tamed to metaphor, tamed to that much of it. I do not think anybody ever knows the discreet use of metaphor, his own and other people's, the discreet handling of metaphor, unless he has been properly educated in poetry.

Poetry begins in trivial metaphors, pretty metaphors, "grace" metaphors, and goes on to the profoundest thinking that we have. Poetry provides the one permissible way of saying one thing and meaning another. People say, "Why don't you say what you mean?" We never do that, do we, being all of us too much poets. We like to talk in parables and in hints and in indirections—whether from diffidence or some other instinct.

I have wanted in late years to go further and further in making metaphor the whole of thinking. I find some one now and then to agree with me that all thinking, except mathematical thinking, is metaphorical, or all thinking except scientific thinking. The mathematical might be difficult for me to bring in, but the scientific is easy enough.

Once on a time all the Greeks were busy telling each other what the All was—or was like unto. All was three elements, air, earth, and water (we once thought it was ninety elements; now we think it is only one). All was substance, said another. All was change, said a third. But best and most fruitful was Pythagoras' comparison of the universe with number. Number of what? Number of feet, pounds, and seconds was the answer, and we had science and all that has followed in science. The metaphor has held and held, breaking down only when it came to the spiritual and psychological or the out of the way places of the physical.

The other day we had a visitor here, a noted scientist, whose latest word to the world has been that the more accurately you know where a thing is, the less accurately you are able to state how fast it is moving. You can see why that would be so, without going back to Zeno's problem of the arrow's flight. In carrying numbers into the realm of space and at the same time into the realm of time you are mixing metaphors, that is all, and you are in trouble. They won't mix. The two don't go together.

Let's take two or three more of the metaphors now in use to live by. I have just spoken of one of the new ones, a charming mixed metaphor right in the realm of higher mathematics and higher physics: that the more accurately you state where a thing is, the less accurately you will be able to tell how fast it is moving. And, of course, everything is moving. Everything is an event now. Another metaphor. A thing, they say, is an event. Do you believe it is? Not quite. I believe it is almost an event. But I like the comparison of a thing with an event.

I notice another from the same quarter. "In the neighborhood of matter space is something like curved." Isn't that a good one! It seems to me that that is simply and utterly charming—to say that space is something like curved in the neighborhood of matter. "Something like."

Another amusing one is from—what is the book?—I can't say it now; but here is the metaphor. Its aim is to restore you to your ideas of free will. It wants to give you back your freedom of will. All right, here it is on a platter. You know that you can't tell by name what persons in a certain class will be dead ten years after graduation, but you can tell actuarially how many will be dead. Now, just so this scientist says of the particles of matter flying at a screen, striking a screen; you can't tell what individual particles will come, but you can say in general that a certain number will strike in a given time. It shows, you see, that the individual particle can come freely. I asked Bohr about that particularly, and he said, "Yes, it is so. It can come when it wills and as it wills; and the action of the individual particle is unpredictable. But it is not so of the action of the mass. There you can predict." He says, "That gives the individual atom its freedom, but the mass its necessity."

Another metaphor that has interested us in our time and has done all our thinking for us is the metaphor of evolution. Never mind going into the Latin word. The metaphor is simply the metaphor of the growing plant or of the growing thing. And somebody very brilliantly, quite a while ago, said that the whole universe, the whole of everything, was like unto a growing thing. That is all. I know the metaphor will break down at some point, but it has not failed everywhere. It is a very brilliant metaphor, I acknowledge, though I myself get too tired of the kind of essay that talks about the evolution of candy, we will say, or the evolution of elevators—the evolution of this, that, and the other. Everything is evolution. I emancipate myself by simply saying that I didn't get up the metaphor and so am not much interested in it.

What I am pointing out is that unless you are at home in the metaphor, unless you have had your proper poetical education in the metaphor, you are not safe anywhere. Because you are not at ease with figurative values: you don't know the metaphor in its strength and its weakness. You don't know how far you may expect to ride it and when it may break down with you. You are not safe in science; you are not safe in history. In history, for instance—to show that is the same in history as elsewhere—I heard somebody say yesterday that Aeneas was to be likened unto (those words, "likened unto"!) George Washington. He was that type of national hero, the middle class man, not thinking of being a hero at all, bent on building the future, bent on his children, his descendants. A good metaphor, as far as it goes, and you must know how far. And then he added that Odysseus should be likened unto Theodore Roosevelt. I don't think that is so good. Someone visiting Gibbon at the point of death, said he was the same Gibbon as of old, still at his parallels.

Take the way we have been led into our present position morally, the world over. It is by a sort of metaphorical gradient. There is a kind of thinking—to speak metaphorically—there is a kind of thinking you might say was endemic in the brothel. It is always there. And every now and then in some mysterious way it becomes epidemic in the world. And how does it do so? By using all the good words that virtue has invented to maintain virtue. It uses honesty, first,—frankness, sincerity—

those words; picks them up, uses them. "In the name of honesty, let us see what we are." You know. And then it picks up the word joy. "Let us in the name of joy, which is the enemy of our ancestors, the Puritans. . . . Let us in the name of joy, which is the enemy of the kill-joy Puritans. . . ." You see. "Let us," and so on. And then, "In the name of health. . . ." Health is another good word. And that is the metaphor Freudianism trades on, mental health. And the first thing we know, it has us all in up to the top knot. I suppose we may blame the artists a good deal, because they are great people to spread by metaphor. The stage too—the stage is always a good intermediary between the two worlds, the under and the upper,—if I may so without personal prejudice to the stage.

In all this I have only been saying that the devil can quote Scripture, which simply means that the good words you have lying around the devil can use for his purposes as well as anybody else. Never mind about my morality. I am not here to urge anything. I don't care whether the world is good or bad—not on any particular day.

Let me ask you to watch a metaphor breaking down here before you.

Somebody said to me a little while ago, "It is easy enough for me to think of the universe as a machine, as a mechanism."

I said, "You mean the universe is like a machine?"

He said, "No. I think it is one. . . . Well, it is like . . ."

"I think you mean the universe is like a machine."

"All right. Let it go at that."

I asked him, "Did you ever see a machine without a pedal for the foot, or a lever for the hand, or a button for the finger?"

He said, "No—no."

I said, "All right. Is the universe like that?"

And he said, "No. I mean it is like a machine, only . . ."

". . . it is different from a machine," I said.

He wanted to go just that far with that metaphor and no further. And so do we all. All metaphor breaks down somewhere. That is the beauty of it. It is touch and go with the metaphor, and until you have lived with it long enough you don't know when it is going. You don't know how much you can get out of it and when it will cease to yield. It is a very living thing. It is as life itself.

I have heard this ever since I can remember, and ever since I have taught: the teacher must teach the pupil to think. I saw a teacher once going around in a great school and snapping pupils' heads with thumb and finger and saying, "Think." That was when thinking was becoming the fashion. The fashion hasn't yet quite gone out.

We still ask boys in college to think, as in the nineties, but we seldom tell them what thinking means; we seldom tell them it is just putting this and that together; it is just saying one thing in terms of another. To tell them is to set their feet on the first rung of a ladder the top of which sticks through the sky.

Greatest of all attempts to say one thing in terms of another is the philosophical attempt to say matter in terms of spirit, or spirit in terms of matter, to make the final unity. That is the greatest attempt that ever failed. We stop just short there. But it is the height of poetry, the height of all thinking, the height of all poetic thinking, that attempt to say matter in terms of spirit and spirit in terms of matter. It is wrong to call anybody a materalist simply because he tries to say spirit in terms of matter, as if that were a sin. Materialism is not the attempt to say all in terms of matter. The only materialist—be he poet, teacher, scientist, politician, or statesman—is the man who gets lost in his material without a gathering metaphor to throw it into shape and order. He is the lost soul.

We ask people to think, and we don't show them what thinking is. Somebody says we don't need to show them how to think; bye and bye they will think. We will give them the forms of sentences and, if they have any ideas, then they will know how to write them. But that is preposterous. All there is to writing is having ideas. To learn to write is to learn to have ideas.

The first little metaphor. . . . Take some of the trivial ones. I would rather have trivial ones of my own to live by than the big ones of other people.

I remember a boy saying, "He is the kind of person that wounds with his shield." That may be a slender one, of course. It goes a good way in character description. It has poetic grace. "He is the kind that wounds with his shield."

The shield reminds me—just to linger a minute—the shield reminds me of the inverted shield spoken of in one of the books of the "Odyssey," the book that tells about the longest swim on record. I forget how long it lasted—several days, was it?—but at last as Odysseus came near the coast of Phoenicia, he saw it on the horizon "like an inverted shield."

There is a better metaphor in the same book. In the end Odysseus comes ashore and crawls up the beach to spend the night under a double olive tree, and it says, as in a lonely farmhouse where it is hard to get fire—I am not quoting exactly—where it is hard to start the fire again if it goes out, they cover the seeds of fire with ashes to preserve it for the night, so Odysseus covered himself with the leaves around him and went to sleep. There you have something that gives you character, something of Odysseus himself. "Seeds of fire." So Odysseus covered the seeds of fire in himself. You get the greatness of his nature.

But these are slighter metaphors than the ones we live by. They have their charm, their passing charm. They are as it were the first steps toward the great thoughts, grave thoughts, thoughts lasting to the end.

The metaphor whose manage we are best taught in poetry—that is all there is of thinking. It may not seem far for the mind to go but it is the mind's furthest. The richest accumulation of the ages is the noble metaphors we have rolled up.

I want to add one thing more that the experience of poetry is to anyone who comes close to poetry. There are two ways of coming close to poetry. One is by writing poetry. And some people think I want people to write poetry, but I don't; that is, I don't necessarily. I only want people to write poetry if they want to write poetry. I have never encouraged anybody to write poetry that did not want to write it, and I have not always encouraged those who did want to write it. That ought to be one's own funeral. It is a hard, hard life, as they say.

(I have just been to a city in the West, a city full of poets, a city they have made safe for poets. The whole city is so lovely that you do not have to write it up to make it poetry; it is ready-made for you. But, I don't know—the poetry written in that city might not seem like poetry if read outside of the city. It would be like the jokes made when you were drunk; you have to get drunk again to appreciate them.)

But as I say, there is another way to come close to poetry, fortunately, and that is in the reading of it, not as linguistics, not as history, not as anything but poetry. It is one of the hard things for a teacher to know how close a man has come in reading poetry. How do I know whether a man has come close to Keats in reading Keats? It is hard for me to know. I have lived with some boys a whole year over some of the poets and I have not felt sure whether they have come near what it was all about. One remark sometimes told me. One remark was their mark for the year; had to be—it was all I got that told me what I wanted to know. And that is enough, if it was the right remark, if it came close enough. I think a man might make twenty fool remarks if he made one good one some time in the year. His mark would depend on that good remark.

The closeness—everything depends on the closeness with which you come, and you ought to be marked for the closeness, for nothing else. And that will have to be estimated by chance remarks, not by question and answer. It is only by accident that you know some day how near a person has come.

The person who gets close enough to poetry, he is going to know more about the word *belief* than anybody else knows, even in religion nowadays. There are two or three places where we know belief outside of religion. One of them is at the age of fifteen to twenty, in our self-belief. A young man knows more about himself than he is able to prove to anyone. He has no knowledge that anybody else will accept as knowledge. In his foreknowledge he has something that is going to believe itself into fulfilment, into acceptance.

There is another belief like that, the belief in someone else, a relationship of two that is going to be believed into fulfilment. That is what we are talking about in our novels, the belief of love. And the disillusionment that the novels are full of is simply the disillusionment from disappointment in that belief. That belief can fail, of course.

Then there is a literary belief. Every time a poem is written, every time a short story is written, it is written not by cunning, but by belief. The beauty, the something, the little charm of the thing to be, is more felt than known. There is a common jest, one that always annoys me, on the writers, that they write the last end first, and then work up to it; that they lay a train toward one sentence that they think is pretty nice and have all fixed up to set like a trap to close with. No, it should not be that way at all. No one who has ever come close to the arts has failed to see the difference between things written that way, with cunning and device, and the kind that are believed into existence, that begin in something more felt than known. This you can realize quite as well— not quite as well, perhaps, but nearly as well—in reading as you can in writing. I would undertake to separate short stories on that principle; stories that have been believed into existence and stories that have been cunningly devised. And I could separate the poems still more easily.

Now I think—I happen to think—that those three beliefs that I speak of, the self-belief, the love-belief, and the art-belief, are all closely related to the God-belief, that the belief in God is a relationship you enter into with Him to bring about the future.

There is a national belief like that, too. One feels it. I have been where I came near getting up and walking out on the people who thought that they had to talk against nations, against nationalism, in order to curry favor with internationalism. Their metaphors are all mixed up. They think that because a Frenchman and an American and an Englishman can all sit down on the same platform and receive honors together, it must be that there is no such thing as nations. That kind of bad thinking springs from a source we all know. I should want to say to anyone like that: "Look! First I want to be a person. And I want you to be a person, and then we can be as interpersonal as you please. We can pull each other's noses—do all sorts of things. But, first of all, you have got to have the personality. First of all, you have got to have the nations and then they can be as international as they please with each other."

I should like to use another metaphor on them. I want my palette, if I am a painter, I want my palette on my thumb or on my chair, all clean, pure, separate colors. Then I will do the mixing on the canvas. The canvas is where the work of art is, where we make the conquest. But we want the nations all separate, pure, distinct, things as separate as we can make them; and then in our thoughts, in our arts, and so on, we can do what we please about it.

But I go back. There are four beliefs that I know more about from having lived with poetry. One is the personal belief, which is a knowledge that you don't want to tell other people about because you cannot prove that you know. You are saying nothing about it till you see. The love belief, just the same, has that same shyness. It knows it cannot tell; only the outcome can tell. And the national belief we enter into socially with each other, all together, party of the first part, party of the second part, we enter into that to bring the future of the country. We cannot tell some people what it is we believe, partly, because they are too stupid to understand and partly because we are too proudly vague to explain. And anyway it has got to be fulfilled, and we are not talking until we know more, until we have something to show. And then the literary one in every work of art, not of cunning and craft, mind you, but of real art; that believing the thing into existence, saying as you go more than you even hoped you were going to be able to say, and coming with surprise to an end that you foreknew only with some sort of emotion. And then finally the relationship we enter into with God to believe the future in—to believe the hereafter in.

Aids to Study and Topics for Writing

GIBSON: PLAY AND THE TEACHING OF WRITING

Aids to Study

1. Think of a scientific "truth" whose lustre has tarnished in the last few decades. (Example: the atom, the smallest possible particle of matter, is indivisible.) How could such a "truth" have been rephrased so as to embody not a creed but a policy, as Conant puts it?
2. What is there in Walter Cronkite's appearance and style that might be called "avuncular"? How might his avuncular manner contribute to a listener's mistaking the evening news for a map of the day?
3. Choose a statement from a public official that seems to you to be encouraging a "credibility gap"—one that you simply cannot take as it's expressed. (Example: The principal problem facing America today is a simple one—law and order.) Revise, rewrite, re-express this statement so as to minimize the gap, so as to make the statement more acceptable to people (especially young people) of sense and sensibility. Is there a loss of force when you do this?
4. Why does the author say there should have been a credibility gap centuries ago? What would such an awareness have accomplished, or avoided? Can you think of some periods in past history when there clearly *was* a credibility gap, though it may have been called something else?
5. Trace the author's pool-hall metaphor—"put some English on your English." What are the likenesses between putting "English" on a pool ball and using language in certain (especially ironic) ways? Give examples from everyday conversation. What are some limitations of the metaphor?

393

6. Why should one be in a "half-rage" to allude to the persons excluded by this or that act of writing (DeMott)? What is the advantage in being a "wide and various man"? Are there any disadvantages?

Topics for Writing

1. Think of an occasion when, as a writer or speaker, you acted as a pot-maker rather than a map-maker. That is, you wrote or said something without quite knowing all you were doing, and, in Forster's phrase, you finally knew what you meant only after you saw what you said. What happened, what exactly did you say or write, and what was accomplished?

   Can you think of another occasion when, as a talker or writer, you "knew exactly what you were doing" and behaved as a map-maker? What were you trying to accomplish; what words did you use; what was their effect?

   Can you make any general distinctions between the first sort of experience and the second?

2. Try some investigation or research on how a typical TV news half-hour is prepared. From how many miles of film available to him does the producer select how many feet? How does he choose; what are his criteria? How much time does he have to arrange things? Is the producer of a news program a map-maker, or a pot-maker?

3. Many people are upset by such remarks as "the mask is the face," feeling that we are *really* more than we reveal, that our personality is more than the masks we present, and our character more than the sum of our performances. If you feel that you are "basically" different from your own expression of your self, try saying in an essay what that difference is.

LEWIS: BLUSPELS AND FLALANSFERES

Aids to Study

1. Lewis asks when does a metaphor become so old that we can ignore it with impunity. Using your dictionary, trace the metaphorical origin of *pen* (mentioned by Lewis) and of *person, personality* (mentioned by Gibson). Each of these is etymologically a dead metaphor. Now that you have this information, can you ignore it with impunity? Equally in each case? Why or why not?

2. Let us imagine a dialogue:
   A: Students today are far more independent than they used to be.
   B: Oh, they are?
   A: Sure. Nowadays they really strike out for themselves.
   B: Oh, you're using metaphor. Is that just a pupillary metaphor, or is it magistral? I mean, can you say what you mean another way?

A: Of course I can. I mean for example that today young people are on top of the political scene. They take part in social movements. They see to it that their voice is heard.

B: Hmm. Sure you're not just trotting out more metaphors?

A: Of course not. When I say that young people today are more independent, more self-reliant, more responsive to the political arena, I mean exactly that.

B: I wonder if you've really said anything at all.

A: Whaddaya mean? I don't see how I could speak plainer.

Now how could we help A to speak plainer? One way is to show him the buried metaphors in his language. (You'll need your dictionary again for this.) After that, it may be that he has two choices. If he *is* aware of his own dead metaphors, then one thing he can do is show in his speech that he is aware, that he knows he is not speaking (perhaps cannot speak) literally. One consequence of this is modesty in tone and style, and a lowering of his indignation level. A second consequence might be that he could *try* for another way of doing it altogether, a way of avoiding the doubletalk of repeated dead metaphors. A possible way of doing this is to cite actual actions, operations, activities, that in his view are to be defined as "independence." This too would have to be argued modestly, of course, because he would be making inductive leaps from admittedly sparse evidence. Still a third choice may lie open to him, as Lewis suggests. Instead of repeating these corny phrases, he might invent new metaphors to create new meanings. This is the way of the great thinkers.

3. What examples of your own can you produce (like Lewis's "space is finite") where you have been introduced to a difficult concept via a Master's Metaphor?

4. Look up *anima* in a good dictionary, and relate some of its history to Lewis's text. Then, continuing to use the dictionary, make sense out of Lewis's sentence on page 297 where he speaks of complexes, repressions, censors, and engrams.

5. Work out Lewis's meaning in his last paragraph by inventing a metaphorical sentence that is neither true nor false, but meaningless, in his sense of those terms.

Topics for Writing

1. Here is a passage from a famous eighteenth-century rhetorician named Hugh Blair. Show in an essay a fundamental distinction between Blair's way of looking at metaphor and Lewis's. Can you find some buried metaphor in Blair's statement?

But I must observe, in the next place, that although this part of style merits attention, and is a very proper object of science and rule; although much of the beauty of composition depends on figurative language; yet we must beware of imagining that it depends solely, or even chiefly, upon such language. It is not so. The great place which the doctrine of tropes and figures has occupied in systems of rhetoric; the over-anxious care which has been shown in giving names to a vast variety of them, and in ranging them under different classes, has often led persons to imagine, that if their composition was well bespangled with a number of these ornaments of speech, it wanted no other beauty: whence has arisen much stiffness and affectation. For it is, in truth, the sentiment or passion, which lies under the figured expression, that gives it any merit. The figure is only the dress; the sentiment is the body and the substance. No figures will render a cold or an empty composition interesting; whereas, if a sentiment be sublime or pathetic, it can support itself perfectly well, without any borrowed assistance. . . . The fact is, that the strong pathetic, and the pure sublime, not only have little dependence on figures of speech, but generally reject them. The proper region of these ornaments is, where a moderate degree of elevation and passion is predominant; and there they contribute to the embellishment of discourse, only when there is a basis of solid thought and natural sentiment; when they are inserted in their proper place; and when they rise, of themselves, from the subject without being sought after.

2. Copy down or tape-record an ordinary conversation between friends and trace some of the buried metaphors in the dialogue.

3. Analyze a political speech or article in an effort to document Lewis's dictum that the meaning in any given composition is in inverse ratio to the author's belief in his own literalness.

4. Here is a list of metaphors often misread as statements of fact or of actual conditions. Show in what way a failure to see these phrases as metaphors can lead to error, confusion, or disaster:

iron curtain
credibility gap
sexual revolution
population explosion
the rat-race of contemporary life

Orwell: Politics and the English Language

Aids to Study

1. Orwell speaks in his first paragraph of "the half-conscious belief that language is a natural growth and not an instrument which we shape for

our own purposes." Is this the issue the linguists were raising? Is this the usage quarrel over again? Would someone like Lloyd agree with Orwell?

2. Speaking of the dead metaphors (page 304), like "iron resolution." Orwell says that it can "generally be used without loss of vividness." Explain why this is so.

3. Lewis of course had much more to say about dead metaphors, without necessarily disagreeing with Orwell. Summarize briefly how he might have qualified Orwell's no-loss-of-vividness remark.

4. Using dictionaries, see how many of Orwell's italicized list of dying metaphors (page 304) you can account for, by explaining the original sense of the expression.

5. Rewrite Laski's sentence (page 303) so that it avoids all the objectionable qualities Orwell discusses.

6. Pick out one of the longer essays in this collection and examine it closely for signs of dying metaphors. What examples can you find, and how would you put life into them?

Topics for Writing

1. Try to rewrite the Communist pamphlet's sentence so that the loaded language disappears. What sorts of genuine ideas are left? Try to state accurately what the writer wanted to get across. Is there a better way? Discuss and illustrate the whole problem in an essay.

2. Almost no one is safe when we start examining prose for signs of pretentious diction. Pick any of these essayists except Veblen and search his essay for big words which could just as well be replaced by smaller, more common ones.

3. Social scientists are said to exhibit a good many symptoms of pretentious diction, particularly in the terminology peculiar to their subject matter. Linguists are social scientists. What signs of this flaw do you find in the linguistic terminology in this book? How much of it could be disposed with? Explore this problem in an essay.

4. "The inflated style itself is a kind of euphemism" (p. 310). Explore this idea in an essay.

Sale: Metaphors: Live, Dead, Silly

Aids to Study

1. After your recent exercises with Lewis, you are in a position to read Sale's second paragraph, for instance, wisely and well. How is it related to the passage quoted from Hugh Blair on pages 395–396?

2. Select a passage you have previously analyzed for metaphor (for example, that tape-recorded dialogue you may have studied, or one of the longer essays in this collection). Try translating some of the metaphors into "x is y" statements, as Sale proposes.

3. Listen for uses of the word *literally*. Thus the sports announcer: Hawkins literally broke the game wide open. What does *literally* mean here (literally)?

4. Can you think of a treatment of something "in depth" that is not also "at length"? What in your own reading and listening experience has been the relation between "depth" and "length"? Are they synonyms?

5. Make sure you understand what Sale is saying about the relation of the classroom and the "outside world" on page 318. What are the consequences if, as he fears, "the metaphor may speak truly." What metaphor?

Topics for Writing

1. Write a paper on the uses of the word "secure," your own uses and that of others. Is Sale right that "the word often seems like a cry for help"? What other paradoxical terms of comfort-amid-danger can you think of? Life insurance? Safety regulations?

2. Lewis, Orwell, and Sale have made many points in common, about metaphor and about writing in general. Make a summary of some of these points. Nevertheless the styles of the three men are markedly different. Show how, by contrasting a few sentences, the three writers "come on" to their readers in different roles, different persons, and imply that t' ey are addressing different audiences. How do these differences in style affect the way you respond to the linguistic points the three writers make? Is one of them more persuasive than the others? Or are they in fact so different in style that what seemed a likeness in content is not so obvious after all? Write a paper exploring these possibilities.

COLES: FRESHMAN ENGLISH: THE CIRCLE OF UNBELIEF

Aids to Study

1. Coles sees in the history of education and culture since Genung's day a "process of secularization." What world does the word "secularization" usually refer to? Coles then is making a kind of metaphor? How does his metaphor affect or reinforce the attitude he takes toward this process?

2. In today's composition texts, then, Coles sees a "language of standardization" rather than "a language of standards." Can you put in your

own words what this distinction amounts to? What, for example, is Coles's objection to separating "intention" from "expression"? (Remember your Forster here!) Why does he apparently think that "transfer" of thoughts "from mind to page" is a poor way of describing the activity of writing? How would he say it better? How would you say it?

3. Here is a list of phrases from Coles's article: reasonable facsimile, computerized skill, selling points of this commodity, buys the product, run an adding machine or pour concrete, the American dollar. What do these phrases have in common? If theme-writing is a reflection of our culture, what do these repeated phrases imply about that culture? And about theme-writing?

4. Take a look at Coles's examples of *Faulty, Better, Best*—the sentences about finishing work and going to the movies. Why does he attack this familiar process of revision and improvement? Does he mean that the *"Best"* sentence is not really best? Why not? (Question: is it more important to finish work or to go to the movies? Answer: that depends. Question: On what?)

5. Find some elegant sentences in this book (there are lots of them) that violate the quoted rule about faulty subordination. What are we clearly invited to conclude about the rule?

Topics for Writing

1. Write an autobiographical paper on your own experience with theme-writing. Be tactful, as Genung suggests, about the course you are now taking.

2. Write a preface for a composition text that might appeal to Coles.

GIBSON: Dullness and Dishonesty: The Rhetoric of Newswriting

Aids to Study

1. This piece makes much of taking the phrase "point of view" almost literally—as a *point* in time and space occupied by the narrator or speaker in a piece of prose. This way of looking at language, especially appropriate to fiction, may be practiced by trying it out on the opening paragraphs in a collection of short stories. Ask the questions: Where is the fellow talking? Whom is he talking to? When?

2. Then the same approach can be tried with the columns of a newspaper. The various items in a single paper will display a wide variety of speakers, occupying different positions in time and space.

3. Just what is Gibson's objection to a newsman occupying a point of view characteristic of a teller of a tale? Is this simply a matter of appropriateness in the two different genres?

4. Gibson notes that relatively "straight" reporting seems to be less free with metaphor. Is this true? Analyze the three passages on the Birmingham riots with attention to dying metaphor. Is there any relation between "postures of knowing" and a generous use of dying metaphors?

5. Since Birmingham in 1963, the news has been fairly full of race riots, student riots, busts, and melees. Find a thorough account of such an event, in a newspaper or newsmagazine, and analyze a passage for position of the narrator, uses of metaphor, and omniscience.

Topics for Writing

1. Coles in his article on Freshman English used the expressions "a trick that can be played" and "the game according to the rules," referring to the standardized patterns of theme-writing. Gibson uses such expressions, about Time-style, as "a verbal game" and "a most irresponsible game." Think of these two styles, theme-writing and time-style, as games. What do they have in common? In an essay, ask the general question whether the good little student who ably produces his themes may be preparing himself for a career with *Time*.

2. This exercise suggests that you try a bit of journalism yourself. Spend a few hours tracking down and writing up a "story"—as if for the student paper. Adopt the position and voice familiar to that paper. Then rewrite this version, as Gibson proposes in his last paragraph, by giving a narrative account of your own activity as a reporter. Do you find any improvement? Is the new version printable, in your newspaper or anywhere else?

COTTLE: THE POLITICS OF PRONOUNCEMENT

Aids to Study

1. This article, which may seem confusing at first, is essentially asking one of the questions posed by the previous writer: is it possible to have an "objective" or, as Cottle puts it, "value-free" point of view, or is all expression inherently biased? Look for passages, usually in roman type, that explicitly raise this issue, asking whether the writing of social science, in particular, must inevitably be political at bottom.

2. It is the structure of the piece that may lead to confusion. Note that the italicized passages describe and comment upon the responses of three ladies to various academic tracts in sociology that the author has asked them to

read. These three ladies, Erlene Menter, Kathleen Cavanaugh, and Hannah Brachman, represent respectively the Negro, Irish Catholic, and Jewish ethnic groups. What attitude do the three have in common toward the academic "pronouncements" about their own groups?

3. The real trouble, Cottle seems to be saying, is that the sociologist's pronouncements appear too positive, too all-embracing, too absolute in pretending to put into neat numbers the complicated quality of human lives. The fault, evidently, lies in two directions. *Authors* adopt too positive and omniscient a stance on matters that nobody can be sure about, like those "postures of Knowing" that Gibson complained of. Second, *readers* fail to see the "play," the tentativeness, that the author actually has tried to place in the language. Find a passage or two where Cottle makes these points, about authors and about readers.

4. "They read that book as though it were a manual on how to ice skate" (page 345). Explain why the young social psychologist was outraged at this response to his book.

5. How is it that printed materials say as much, sometimes, through their "authoritative, bookish appearance" as through their statements? Have you found this phenomenon true to your own experience as a reader? Does it perhaps apply to the book you're now holding in your hand? (How do you think this book looked, before it was printed up nice and pretty?)

6. "The highest form of thought permits both the capacity to imagine the impossible or unreal and the capacity to play with ideas, to work with and sculpt them, even if the final product fails to yield anything but joy" (page 346). Relate this statement to Gibson's first article in this section, on the teaching of writing. Note the buried metaphor of "sculpt" and you should be half way to Gibson's metaphor of the pot-maker.

7. Is there something fundamentally "elitist" about play in language. Is it possible to be playful without being in some sense snobbish?

8. Describe the play in Cottle's final incident with Mrs. Brachman (page 350). Who is being laughed at here? Is Cottle snobbish toward Mrs. Brachman?

Topics for Writing

1. Find if you can an article by a sociologist about your own ethnic group, or your own neighborhood or community. Can you find yourself in those pages, as Cottle's three ladies could not do? Write an essay considering your success or failure in making this identification.

2. The problem for the writer is how to get his sense of play, his hunchiness or tentativeness, *into the writing*. Find a passage from social science that seems to you particularly authoritarian, *un*playful. Rewrite by introducing play, in Cottle's sense. Note the concrete changes you made, what you added

in the interests of a "rhetoric of play." What are the dangers of such rhetoric—how quickly does it become frivolous, cute, too self-conscious?

Brackman: The Put-On

Aids to Study

1. Brackman's first paragraph is a rapid-fire list of situations in which, "Man, you know *some*body's leg is being pulled. Or at least you think *maybe* it is." The best way to get straight the sometimes slippery concept of the put-on is to think up further examples from your own experience—from films you have seen, from pop art, or from conversations or incidents in your daily life. Try to think not simply of incidents in which somebody's leg is being pulled, but, more interestingly for this purpose, of incidents in which you think *maybe* it's being pulled, but you're not sure.

2. It's just this business of not being sure that defines the essence of the put-on. Get clear the difference between the traditional practical joke or spoof ("Ideally, there's no doubt in anyone's mind"), and the more ambiguous form of the put-on. Invent clear-cut examples of each.

3. In art, define the difference between parody or satire on the one hand, and the put-on on the other. Find a print or photograph to illustrate each of these forms.

4. Find some pejorative language in Brackman's treatment of the put-on in art that clearly reveals his own attitude or bias.

5. What is meant by a *set-breaking* put-on? Can this expression be related to the New Math you learned a few years back?

6. Describe a staged put-on, real or invented, like the magician-comedian cited by Brackman. Break down the action into come-on, fake-out, and cop-out.

7. There was once an author of popular books whose readers deluged him with comments, questions, and trivial objections to his statements. Finally he had several hundred postcards printed up with the single reply, "You may have a point at that." These he mailed to all his correspondents. Is this an example of the put-on?

8. Analyze a current TV spot-ad that uses a put-on technique. (Those long cigarettes that always get in the way of the smoker?) How does such an ad leave you feeling about the product? Ready to buy, or not?

Topics for Writing

1. Write a paper on the put-on in popular or rock music, including a concrete analysis of a particular song, its words and the style of its performance. (Example: the Beatles' "When I'm 64" in their *Sergeant Pepper* album.)

2. Write a paper on the put-on in advertising, including a concrete analysis of a particular magazine ad, its language and its lay-out, illustrations, and so on. Speculate on its effectiveness in selling the product.

3. Write a paper about a film in which put-on techniques resulted in your not having much *feeling* about what was happening. (An example might be the famous *Bonnie and Clyde* of a few years ago.) Do you agree with Brackman's generally gloomy view of such entertainment?

4. A very ambitious paper could be written in response to Brackman's final two paragraphs, in which you assess the place of the put-on in our history and culture. Is the put-on simply a misuse of play? Is it a necessary step, to be gotten over with as soon as possible (as Brackman implies)? Is it a respectable and admirable art form, appropriate to our time?

Baskerville: 19th Century Burlesque of Oratory

Aids to Study

1. Is a burlesque a put-on? Make sure you understand clearly the distinction between these two forms.

2. In the nineteenth century, the Fourth of July oration was obviously ripe for parody, and partly as a result of such parody it fell into oblivion. What vestigial forms of oratory can you see in your contemporary culture that seem to be similarly doomed? Commencement addresses, for instance?

3. Analyze in detail one of the parodies quoted—for example, Artemus Ward's "The Crisis" (page 374). What is the effect of the spelling? Explain the "mess of potash" joke. What would Orwell have to say about those metaphors? What does "Nary" mean, and what is its effect here?

4. Mr. Pepperage's remarks on slavery (page 375) will seem offensive to many today, at least on quick reading. But look closely. What stand does the passage finally take toward slavery, and what is the evidence? Note also the following satire by Petroleum Nasby on "the sooperiority uv the Anglo-Sacksun over the Afrikin races."

5. Baskerville concludes with an appeal for us not to condemn all public speaking merely because certain bathetic styles were laughed out of existence in the nineteenth century. Where, if anywhere, in our present culture has some form of public speaking survived with distinction?

Topics for Writing

1. The article on the put-on and the article on burlesque of oratory have many relationships, as we have been suggesting. But their own styles are utterly different. The first, you should observe, was written for *The New Yorker;* the second for *American Quarterly*. Write an essay contrasting the

styles of the two writers, showing how each is characteristic of the periodical for which he is writing.

2. Expressions of patriotism, eloquent or otherwise, have just about disappeared from our society, partly because of these very parodies Baskerville
has discussed. But there are other reasons. Speculate on some of the causes
that have brought the very word "patriot" into such low esteem. Why is it
that most educated people today do not speak of their "love of America"
without embarrassment? Would you say that this means there is less patriotic feeling for America now than in the nineteenth century? How could
one begin to go about collecting evidence to answer such a question?

Frost: Education by Poetry

Aids to Study

1. As you quickly see, this piece is an informal talk given to a group of students at Amherst College in Massachusetts. How did Frost immediately express his own style of playfulness in his opening paragraph?
2. Why is it "hard on poetry," "what it has to bear in the teaching process"?
What are some examples from your own experience?
3. Notice Frost's list of educational objectives on pages 384–385—though he
wouldn't have called them that. Notice that the list culminates in the
problem of "being fooled by metaphor." In the light of what you have read
so far in this book, what do you think is meant by being fooled by metaphor?
4. Frost remarks that he has been coming closer to making "metaphor the
whole of thinking." What other writers in this section of our book have
come close to saying that?
5. What is the difference between saying a thing is an event and that it is
"almost" an event?
6. How does Frost define thinking? Do you find this an adequate definition?
For what purposes?

A Topic for Writing

"Unless you have had your proper poetical education in the metaphor, you
are not safe anywhere. . . . You are not safe in science; you are not safe in
history." Consider carefully two important metaphors you have learned, one
in science and one in history. (Examples: the flow of electrical current, the
decline and fall of Rome.) Show how, with a "proper" education in language and metaphor, you can become "safe," more or less. This essay could
be your culminating response to the message of this book.